C0-COH-618

# The Syntax of Anaphora

OXFORD STUDIES IN COMPARATIVE SYNTAX
Richard Kayne, *General Editor*

*The Higher Functional Field: Evidence from North Italian Dialects*
Cecilia Poletto

*The Syntax of Verb-Initial Languages*
Edited by Andrew Carnie and Eithne Guilfoyle

*Parameters and Universals*
Richard Kayne

*Portuguese Syntax: New Comparative Studies*
Edited by João Costa

*XP-Adjunction in Universal Grammar: Scrambling and Binding in Hindi-Urdu*
Ayesha Kidwai

*Infinitive Constructions: A Syntactic Analysis of the Romance Languages*
Guido Mensching

*Subject Inversion in Romance and the Theory of Universal Grammar*
Edited by Aafke Hulk and Jean-Yves Pollock

*Subjects, Expletives, and the EPP*
Edited by Peter Svenonius

*A Unified Theory of Verbal and Nominal Projections*
Yoshiki Ogawa

*Functional Structures in DP and IP: The Cartography of Syntactic Structures, Volume 1*
Edited by Guglielmo Cinque

*Syntactic Heads and Word Formation*
Marit Julien

*The Syntax of Italian Dialects*
Christina Tortora

*The Morphosyntax of Complement-Head Sequences: Clause Structure and Word Order Patterns in Kwa*
Enoch Oladé Aboh

*The Structure of CP and IP: The Cartography of Syntactic Structures, Volume 2*
Edited by Luigi Rizzi

*The Syntax of Anaphora*
Ken Safir

# The Syntax of Anaphora

*Ken Safir*

OXFORD
UNIVERSITY PRESS

2004

OXFORD
UNIVERSITY PRESS

Oxford New York
Auckland Bangkok Buenos Aires Cape Town Chennai
Dar es Salaam Delhi Hong Kong Istanbul Karachi Kolkata
Kuala Lumpur Madrid Melbourne Mexico City Mumbai Nairobi
São Paulo Shanghai Taipei Tokyo Toronto

Copyright © 2004 by Oxford University Press, Inc.

Published by Oxford University Press, Inc.
198 Madison Avenue, New York, New York 10016

www.oup.com

Oxford is a registered trademark of Oxford University Press

All rights reserved. No part of this publication may be reproduced, stored in a retrieval system, or transmitted, in any form or by any means, electronic, mechanical, photocopying, recording, or otherwise, without the prior permission of Oxford University Press.

Library of Congress Cataloging-in-Publication Data
Safir, Kenneth J.
The syntax of anaphora / Ken Safir.
p. cm. — (Oxford studies in comparative syntax)
Includes bibliographical references and index
ISBN 0-19-516613-2 (cloth); ISBN 0-19-516614-0 (pbk.)
1. Anaphora (Linguistics) 2. Grammar, Comparative and general—Syntax. I. Title.
II. Series.

P299.A5S24 2003
415—dc21 2003042007

9 8 7 6 5 4 3 2 1

Printed in the United States of America
on acid-free paper

*In memoriam:*

*Ken Hale,*
*Osvaldo Jaeggli,*
*and Robert Jeffers*

# PREFACE

When I first began to write the book that this one was to emerge from, I had it in mind to present a comprehensive theory of anaphora that would serve not only as a theoretical monograph supporting new proposals, but also as a handbook for the study of anaphora from an unabashedly theoretical perspective. Since I believe that too much work on anaphora is insufficiently defended over the broad range of anaphoric phenomena, I intended to defend proposals on the nature of dependency relations and weak crossover phenomena, on reconstruction and ellipsis, as well as on the issues surrounding the syntactic and discourse restrictions distribution of anaphoric forms and pronouns. I intended to present case studies of quite a number of languages of different sorts, highlighting not only the successes of my approach across a broad range of data, but also some of the shortcomings so as to pave the way for better theories that would refute mine someday.

This precursor book, which I have taken to calling the *ur-book*, would have been nearly 600 printed pages long, and when I told this to my first publisher, with whom I had a contract for a 200-page book, she abandoned the project sight unseen. A year later, on the advice of some gentle readers and every publisher I spoke to, I had carved up the ur-book into more digestible parts, of which the present volume is one.

This book focuses on the need for a competitive theory of anaphora and on a concrete proposal for a particular competitive theory that has consequences for the architecture of natural language grammars. In creating this focus for the book, I abstracted away, as much as possible, from anaphoric dependencies not ruled by competitive principles, including dependency relations across sentences, reconstruction effects, antireconstruction effects, and any bound variable interpretations that are not immediately relevant to the competitive principles I propose. My theoretical approach to these other phenomena are reserved for Safir (2004), entitled *The Syntax of*

*(In)dependence*, which can be read separately or as a companion volume to this one. For the project before you, I also found it necessary to abstract away from all phenomena, even morphologically marked phenomena, having to do with person, perspective, and discourse role. While I would argue that some of these phenomena are syntactically conditioned (particularly aspects of perspective and logophoricity), others are not necessarily so (particularly coreference relations achieved by person rather than by dependent anaphora). These phenomena will receive a detailed treatment in Safir (in preparation), a manuscript tentatively titled *Person, Perspective and Anaphora*, which is the logical successor work to this one, as it completes my typology of identity-dependent forms.

Since the original ur-book integrated all of three of these books (as well as more discussion of morphology and some more case studies), a great deal of internal reference within the ur-book was ruptured with the dismemberment. While all three manuscripts are designed so they can be read independently, the interconnectivity of the books has resulted in a great many references in each volume to work in the others. In other words, I ask the reader to bear with me as I appear to indulge in an orgy of self-reference, since it is for the purpose of connecting these realms of inquiry for those who choose to read the other books.

There are, of course, additional omissions from this book that have nothing to do with what appears in others. I have very little, scandalously little, to say about language acquisition, where a large and contentious literature has increasingly been informed by theoretical developments in syntactic theories of anaphora and has emerged as a source of evidence for some intriguing ideas. It should not be presumed from my perfunctory treatment of the acquisition literature in this book that I do not regard it seriously, but rather that it would have been the straw that broke this camel's back. Although I will enter into it lightly at a few points, I will also have little to say about language-specific historical developments that may shed light on the emergence of patterns of anaphora in contemporary languages. This is also more a function of fatigue rather than relevance.

I admit a bias in my analysis toward languages that have been examined in detail within generative grammar, and these are most typically those that have been examined by a fairly wide variety of scholars. Well-studied languages permit some of the more subtle issues to be pursued more fruitfully. Moreover, as has often been noted, variation across languages that are both well studied and closely related, such as the Germanic languages, enables us to examine the effects of minimal distinctions of syntactic features or lexical choice as they interact with more general principles. For these reasons, much of my discussion concerns structures encountered in modern European languages (i.e., Romance, Slavic, Germanic, Hungarian, Finnish, and Greek), Japanese and Chinese, and to a lesser extent Hindi and Malayalam, but I occasionally stray from these more familiar realms when a question needs to be explored in a way these languages do not so easily admit (but see Safir, in preparation, for an exploration of other language families and areas). The breadth of crosslinguistic discussion was also curtailed for reasons of space, and so analyses similar to those discussed in a little more detail or analyses too complicated to be dealt with briefly are reduced to footnotes.

Theories change rapidly within generative grammar. That's why many of us find it so interesting. Books that remain useful after their theoretical half-life has expired are those with well-demonstrated empirical generalizations and/or classic argumentation that need not lose its force when adapted to other theoretical architectures. Such insights do not always decide between the competing architectures of the moment, but it would be a mistake to regard as any less interesting the more general architecture that makes these achievements possible. It is my hope that this contribution remains useful whether it catches the next theoretical wave or not.

# ACKNOWLEDGMENTS

However hard one works at it, however appropriate one's talents are to the task, one has to be very lucky to have the resources it takes to write a book like this. Most of that luck involves being in the right place to benefit from the generosity and inspiration that so many others have to provide if one is to have a chance at achieving one's goals. It is a great pleasure for me to acknowledge those who have helped so much.

First, I am pleased to thank those who shaped me as a linguist, particularly Noam Chomsky, Richard Kayne, Morris Halle, Ken Hale, and Jim Higginbotham, all of whom inspired me intellectually and professionally. Although I did not discuss these issues with them in recent years, the continuing influence of Noam and Jim, both in what they taught me and in what they have written, can be traced throughout this manuscript. The range of interests and theoretical issues that have culminated for me in the ideas developed here began as essays on a variety of topics that span a period of more than 15 years (from Safir 1984, through Safir 1999). I cannot recapitulate here the acknowledgments of all those papers, but many of those thanked for their contributions to my understanding in those works deserve further thanks here. This saves quite a lot of space.

In the last years, as a family man, I have not moved around so much, so most of those who I have discussed these matters with are close at hand or else have passed through. Among those who have most influenced me and contributed most directly to the ideas that developed here, I would particularly like to thank Marcel den Dikken, Arild Hestvik, Richard Kayne, Dave Lebeaux, Barry Schein, and Edwin Williams. In my immediate environs at Rutgers, I would like to thank Roger Schwarzschild, Veneeta Dayal, and Mark Baker, who were local sounding boards for these ideas as they developed and who influenced the course these ideas took—not always, perhaps, in ways they would approve of. I would like to thank the participants in two seminars (spring 1999) and (fall 2000) where I presented versions of these ideas and thrashed out what I was trying to say or should have been saying. These include Tom Warner, Szusza Nagy, Graham Horwood, Madeline Holler, Judy Bauer, Olúsèye Adésolá, and Andre Nündel. Visitors Lynn Nichols and Caroline Heycock (in fall 2000) gave invaluable comments on the first drafts of several chapters.

Portions of these ideas were presented at the 14th Comparative Germanic Workshop in Lund, Sweden (January 1999); at the City University of New York (April 1999), at the University of California, Santa Cruz (April 2001); at the University of Utrecht (October 2002); and at the Écoles des Hautes Études in Paris (November 2002). I thank these audiences for their questions and observations.

In addition to all the useful input to the process of producing a draft, I would also like to thank those who read and commented on large portions of later drafts, including Marcel den Dikken, Richard Kayne, and Scot Zola.

Although most of my empirical discussion draws on the reported research of others, I have also relied on a great number of native speaker informants, some sporadically over many years, others with great regularity. Many of these native informants are linguists, and many of these have contributed to my general understanding of the issues in ways that led me to productive new inquiries. Some of these informants polled other native speakers on my behalf. I would like to thank now a small portion of those who helped, some who may not even remember how much: Arild Hestvik, Christer Platzack, Knut Tarald Taraldsen, Sten Vikner, Lars Hellan, and Alma Naess for Mainland Scandinavian; Eric Reuland, Ad Neeleman, Jan-Wouter Zwart, Martin Everaert, and Marcel den Dikken for Dutch; Markus Heller, Suzanne Preuss, Alexandra Zepter, Hubert Truckenbrodt, and Andre Nündel for German; Thiery D'Allant and Viviane Déprez for French; Eric Bakovic for Spanish, Roli Lal and Veneeta Dayal for Hindi; Jóhaness Gisli Jónsson, Sigriðr Sigurjónsdóttir, and Höskuldur Thráinsson for Icelandic; Vieri Samek-Lodovici for Italian; Rachel Yang for Chinese; Olúsèye Adésolá and Akin Akinlabi for Yoruba; Jaklin Kornfilt for Turkish; Yoko Futagi and Masaaki Fuji for Japanese; and Natalia Karaieva for Russian. My English language informants are too numerous to list, including the many different audiences to whom these ideas were presented and anyone who happened to be around, but the first informant outside my head was typically Susan Sidlauskas, my wife, now expert at this task, who brought several theories down to earth, where most of them could not survive.

While I am on the subject, I would like to thank Susan, my fellow academic, for so many years of intellectual and emotional collaboration in the strategies that have kept me writing, surviving, and thriving in academic and family life. As to my children, Miranda and Emma, in whose lives the success of my anaphora theories plays no role at all, I thank them for keeping me in the here and now, in the way that only children can, and I hope they will someday forgive me for the time and presence of mind my obsessive labor has taken from them.

# CONTENTS


1. Introduction 3

2. The Interpretation of Anaphoric Relations from Syntactic Form 23

3. Competition and Complementarity 56

4. Coargument Coconstrual and the Varieties of Dependent Identity 103

5. Anaphors and Domains 146

6. Competitive Narrowing and Morphological Form 182

7. Principles of Anaphora in the Architecture of Syntactic Theory 227

Notes 239

Bibliography 285

Index of Languages 301

Index of Names 303

General Index 307

# The Syntax of Anaphora

1

# Introduction

For the last 40 years, research into the nature of natural language grammars has frequently focused on the distribution of anaphoric interpretations and anaphoric forms. At times, theories and analyses of these distributions have been the driving force in the formulation of central theoretical constructs, while at other times, when new theories held out less promise in this domain, research into the principles regulating anaphora has continued almost as vigorously, just not at center stage. As I write today, it is not always clear where the center of the stage is, but research into the patterns of anaphora appears to have part of it.

The distribution of anaphora in natural language has drawn so much attention because it at once exemplifies a phenomenon where very general patterns reign across the world's languages, and yet there is a bewildering array of language-particular variety that renders some of the central generalizations, however palpable, still obscure. Anglocentric work of the 1970s led to the boldly rigid binding theory (BT) from Chomsky's *Lectures on Government and Binding* (LGB; 1981), but the very system it was couched in, the government–binding approach of the early principles and parameters era, opened the door to a welter of crosslinguistic comparisons that appeared to undermine the empirical generalizations the LGB BT was based on. Nonetheless, the central line of work in generative grammar held to the view that the variety of locality effects for anaphora found across, and internal to, other languages are still ultimately local, still subject to c-command, and thus still syntactically determined by universal principles. Theories of language typology that allow for parametric or lexical variation as they interact with the universal principles (e.g., BT) were taken to account for all major departures from straightforward BT predictions. Although support for BT has frayed over the years and it is largely rejected here, the general approach to the universal and the particular that was established in the 1980s remains at the heart of most current approaches in generative grammar, including this one.

Another reason that the pattern of anaphora has proven such a compelling topic, a reason of particular importance to cognitive science in general, is that the syntactically determined aspects of the anaphoric pattern have consistent consequences for semantic interpretation. It is not hard to imagine that the use of language for communication would lead to strategies of use that might facilitate reference to one or another entity in discourse. Indeed *subsequent reference to an entity already introduced in discourse* could count as a general definition of anaphora, but the sensitivity of certain anaphoric effects to sentence internal phrasal properties does not follow from the communicative function that grammars are pressed to serve. It is the latter distinction that is part of the most compelling justification for the claim that the language faculty does not reduce to a generalized conceptual component of intelligence as it interacts with the pragmatic requirements of communication.[1] Thus the existence of rather specific interpretive effects conditioned by syntax provides one of the foremost arguments for the existence of an innate linguistic capacity independent of other forms of cognitive ability.

For reasons such as these, the syntactically determined pattern of anaphora appears to be a portal into the internal architecture of the human linguistic faculty. Unless we take the principles involved to lack interaction with the rest of grammar, the grammar of anaphora must reflect the deeper properties of *universal grammar* (UG; the term generally employed to refer to the formal characterization of the innate language faculty). Thus we may expect that the formal mechanisms and principles posited to account for anaphora reflect at an even more general level the mechanisms and principles from which UG is constructed.

The approach to anaphora I develop here is modeled on a theoretical mechanism that has become central to the architecture of both the minimalist program and optimality theory; both of these theories are organized around principles that put operations or representations in competition, such that the best operation or representation from among a set of competitors is the winner according to a specified metric (an economy theory in minimalism, a constraint ranking in optimality theory), rendering all the other competitors ungrammatical. My own approach is couched in the minimalist framework, and in the last chapter I will discuss why I made this choice and what would be at stake if I had chosen otherwise, but one of the main theses I hope to establish is that no theory lacking a competitive principle could appropriately account for the patterns of anaphora in natural language.

In what follows, I contend that potentially dependent forms c-commanded by and dependent on their antecedents are in complementary distribution, once the data is controlled for structural and interpretive effects that could be misleading, and furthermore, that a competitive principle of *syntax* derives complementary distributions of potentially dependent forms. The principle in question, the Form to Interpretation Principle, is part of a small conspiracy of principles that derive the distribution of possible dependent identity and coreferential readings (I will use the term *coconstrual* when I want to avoid being specific about what sort of identity relation I have in mind). The conclusions I reach not only help choose between possible theories of syntax, but they also have consequences for any theory of the syntactic representations that serve as the input to semantic interpretation.

## 1.1 A Brief Outline of the Chapters

The consequences of treating the patterns of anaphora as arising from a set of competitions are pervasive and lead to a notion of how the grammar of anaphora should be explained that is rather different than those notions that underlie the leading approach of the 1980s, the LGB BT, and that of the1990s, Reinhart and Reuland's (1993) reflexive predicate and chain theory. While these theories each provided certain advances over what was understood before, certain properties of their shortcomings provide clues about what sort of theory would fare better. Some of these issues are discussed in this chapter, which concludes with some desiderata that serve to motivate a new approach.

Although my discussion in this chapter sets them aside, there is a set of more fundamental questions that any approach to the pattern of anaphora must address: What sorts of identity relations count as coconstruals; how is each specific type of coconstrual represented in syntax, if at all; and how do the restrictions within syntax result in the interpretive effect of blocked or permitted coconstrual? In chapter 2, I argue that dependent identity is crucially represented in syntax and that coreference is not so represented. Any such account must ensure, however, that what the syntax permits or prevents (dependent identity) can make the right contribution to the determination noncoreference, which would appear to be a stronger prohibition than blocked dependent identity. Since only dependency, rather than coreference, is represented in syntax, indices, which represent symmetric coreference, must be eliminated from the grammar, and a representation of asymmetric dependent identity is required. Moreover, a separate principle, not part of the syntax, must then augment failure of dependent identity (as determined by the competitive principle) to expected noncoreference. My position on these questions has pervasive effects on the form of the anaphora theory I propose, and these issues are revisited in chapter 4.

In chapter 3 I introduce the form to interpretation principle (FTIP) as the competitive principle in question, and I consider every aspect of its formulation and of the algorithm that instantiates it. Although competitive principles have been proposed in the past to account for the core BT phenomena, such accounts were largely out of the mainstream until the late 1990s. These earlier competition-based theories, which are critically reviewed in the first part of chapter 3, either situate the effective principle in the pragmatics or else do not spell out any clear relationship between the syntactic prohibition and the expected semantic effects. In the theory I propose, which is embedded in a minimalist syntax, the FTIP is instantiated by a precise algorithm that determines whether a dependent identity reading is possible with respect to some designated antecedent, depending on whether or not the most dependent form available in the syntactic context has been selected from the lexicon to represent the dependent; if a more dependent form than the one employed is available, then it outcompetes the less dependent form to represent the dependent identity reading. Thus complementary distribution is predicted between more and less dependent forms in any context where those forms are in competition.

More concretely, suppose anaphors are more dependent than (potentially independent) pronouns, and pronouns are more dependent than r-expressions (e.g., names, definite descriptions). If we assume that reflexive anaphors are licensed where they have local antecedents (the traditional Principle A of the LGB BT), then pronouns are not possible wherever reflexives are available—complementarity between pronouns and lexical anaphors is assured. Thus coconstrual (marked by italics) for "*John* likes *him*" is excluded because a different lexical choice in this syntactic context, that is, *himself* in place of *him*, is available in the same environment. If the object of *like* is to be identity dependent on the subject of *like*, then only the reflexive form can be used to represent this reading. Similarly, "*He* says Mary likes *John*" is excluded with coconstrual, since a more dependent form than John, namely, him, is available in this context (but not himself). From this perspective, principles B (pronouns cannot be coreferent with local c-commanding antecedents) and C (r-expressions cannot be coreferent with c-commanding antecedents) of the LGB BT are derivable from the competitive algorithm and a reformulation of Principle A.

In many respects, chapter 3 presents the heart of my argument for a competitive approach to anaphora, not only in terms of its theoretical advantages, but also on robust empirical grounds. For example, the competitive approach predicts that perturbations in lexical paradigms, where the more dependent competitor is missing, can mean that a less dependent form is the winning competitor, as some of the earlier approaches I cite have pointed out. For mixed systems such as those in Romance and German, it is predicted that the absence of a first or second person reflexive in those languages entails that the next most dependent form, in these cases, an otherwise independent pronoun, will represent the dependent reading for those persons, even though an anaphor represents third person readings. Moreover, the existence of antisubject-oriented pronouns is predicted as a natural consequence of the distribution of subject-oriented anaphors, and further, it is predicted that the same pronouns are not antisubject oriented just in case they are in positions where no subject-oriented pronoun is possible.

Results such as these and many others show the empirical superiority of the competitive principle I propose over any rigid system that separately regulates pronouns and anaphors (such as the LGB BT, Reinhart and Reuland's, 1993, reflexive predicate and chain theory, or the principles corresponding the binding theory in HPSG—see Pollard and Sag, 1994). It is fair to say, however, that some of the arguments that have been used in the past against theories that predict complementary distribution of pronouns and anaphors have never been addressed by previous competitive theories. I take up this challenge in chapter 3 and show that what needs to be said does not favor any of the rigid approaches (those that assume a Principle B-like principle, for example). Failures of complementary distribution are shown to arise in contexts where independent principles determine that no interpretation is available, or where thematic assignments are not comparable, or where forms that normally compete do not compete for principled reasons (and hence both appear). In short, I argue that the competition theory I propose is not subject to some of the drawbacks that other competition theories can be shown to have.

The key notion embodied in the FTIP is that potentially dependent forms compete to represent a given dependent identity interpretation, but this raises the question of whether or not dependent identity readings are all alike. If they are not, then competition for the dependent identity reading must be relativized to the *kind* of dependent identity reading involved. In chapter 4 I argue that such readings are not all alike, in part because a given form may occupy a different position on the most dependent scale depending on which dependent interpretation it is competing to represent. Codependent covaluation, dependent identity (distributive and nondistributive) and indistinctness readings are all distinguished, in addition to guise and proxy readings, and the position that a form has on the most dependent scale is relativized to the relevant reading (depending on the lexical inventory of the language in question).

Chapter 5 examines issues not intrinsic to the competitive mechanism but still crucial to how forms are ranged in competitions, namely, the class of anaphoric domains. Central to this account is the relationship between movement and anaphoric domain. In the first part of chapter 5, I contend that the connection between the domain of A-chains and the domain of traditional Principle A must be disassociated on conceptual, theory-internal, and empirical grounds. I argue that the reason movement seems to dovetail with certain aspects of anaphoric domains is that movement delivers anaphors into the domain where they can be anteceded by a more local domain requirement. Indeed, the most prominently defended mechanism for explaining the crosslinguistic variety of locality conditions on anaphors has been to posit (covert) movement to the more local domain. The relation of covert movement to subject orientation is explored and syntactic effects are distinguished from discourse role. A sharp line is drawn between anaphors, which are sensitive to a version of Principle A, and UD-forms, another class of dependent forms which, like anaphors, cannot be used deictically, but have a consistent and distinct class of distributional properties that distinguishes them from syntactic anaphors (among them, sensitivity to discourse role).

The distributional generalizations of chapter 5 and the interpretive generalizations in chapter 4 arise essentially from stipulated properties of the forms in question: what meaning competitions they enter, what potential they have to move overtly or covertly to a more local domain, and how they are stipulated to rate on the most dependent scale. These stipulations are in part inherited from previous theories of anaphora that largely take these properties for granted in terms of the properties "is a pronoun/anaphor" or "is a short/medium/long range anaphor," or "is distributive/reciprocal/argumental" and the like. Chapter 6 explores how (much) the class of FTIP competitions that a given form enters into can be predicted from a principled analysis of its internal morphological properties, including its availability with respect to its domain, to its interpretation, and to its position on the most dependent scale.

A fundamental property of the competition theory is that the internal properties of the forms in question only place boundaries on the range of availability that a given form may have, while the full empirical distribution of the form in question, generally a narrower syntactic and interpretive space, depends on the competitions it enters into. Crosslinguistic and intralanguage variation in the distribution and interpretation of anaphora arises as a natural consequence of the interaction between FTIP, which is universal, and the differing range of inputs to the competition. In the last part of chapter 6, these predictions are cashed out in a variety of case studies that produce some fine-grained confirmations as well as some fine-grained questions for further research.

My concluding chapter examines the place of algorithms like the one that instantiates the FTIP within the larger context of the theory of grammar. I outline a view of the relation between syntactic derivation and syntactic interpretation in which competition-based interpretive algorithms may form an important component of natural language grammars. I analyze the relationship of the sorts of competition I propose to notions like economy and optimality, and I defend a more modular approach to competition. Emerging from these considerations is a distinction between a class of interpretive operations that access syntactic derivational mechanisms and the syntactic derivations themselves, while at the same time a sharper line is drawn between the syntactic contribution to the interpretation of coconstrual on the one hand and the contribution of discourse on the other.

## 1.2 The Context for This Study

As I write, the strongest and most widely influential theoretical treatments of the distribution of anaphors and pronouns are the descendants of Chomsky's LGB BT approach and Reinhart and Reuland's (1991, 1993) reflexive predicate and chain theory. In the next two subsections I summarize these theories, their most notable flaws, and their legacies. With the advent of minimalist assumptions in the early and mid 1990s, the anaphora issues were placed in the background in theoretical discussions for a time, though work on the anaphora questions continued unabated largely outside the focus on minimalist reduction. More recently, minimalist-inspired proposals have appeared that are based on radical conceptualizations of movement operations (particularly Kayne, 2001, and Hornstein, 1999, 2001, but I reserve my critique of these more recent developments for Safir, 2003, 2004).

### *1.2.1 The BT*

From the perspective of many generative linguists, including those who do not work within the principles and parameters framework that evolved in the 1980s, the theory of grammar proposed in Chomsky's LGB represents a landmark in the consolidation of the leading ideas of the day into one deductively integrated framework.[2] Many of the ideas adapted (particularly Lasnik 1976; Chomsky 1973; and Chomsky 1980) and newly formulated in LGB and in subsequent LGB-inspired work have become a default descriptive lingua franca, even though many of the organizational principles of that approach have withered away or evolved into rather different principles and relations. Thus any discussion of the anaphora issues requires, as a point of departure, some discussion of the successes and failures of the LGB BT.

One of the central notions of the LGB theory, and perhaps, until the mid-1990s, its most enduring one, is the binding relation, which is a relation between two nodes that is semantically symmetric as notated by indices, but structurally asymmetric (in most cases) in that X only binds Y if X also c-commands Y. The coindexing relation, one represented in syntax by indices, has the semantic force of covaluation; that is to say, if X and Y are coindexed, then the referential value for X is the same as the referential value for Y.[3] The definitions of *binding* and *c-command* are given in (1) and (2) respectively.

1) C-command: X c-commands Y if the first branching node above X also dominates Y.
2) Binding: X binds Y if X and Y are coindexed and X c-commands Y. If Y is not bound, then it is free.

What any theory of syntactically conditioned anaphora must capture is that certain forms require a c-commanding antecedent nearby (for discussion of c-command as a condition on antecedency vs. alternative relations that some have suggested based on thematic hierarchies, see the appendix to chapter 4). This is illustrated in (3).

3a) *The men* praised *themselves*.
b) *The men* expected *themselves* to win.
c) **The men* expected the doctor to praise *themselves*.
d) **The men* expected that *themselves* would win.

Forms requiring an antecedent, like English *himself*, are treated as *syntactic anaphors* and are susceptible to the locality principle, Principle A, while pronouns are required not to be coreferent with any antecedent that binds them in the same local domain since they show complementary distribution with anaphors. As illustrated in (4), pronouns are excluded in just the environments where anaphors are acceptable in (3). Since pronouns do not have to have antecedents, the pronouns in (5) are acceptable if they are not coconstrued with a local antecedent. The construal relation is marked by coindexing in the BT as a crucial part of the binding relation.

4a) *The $\text{men}_i$ praised $\text{them}_i$.
b) *The $\text{men}_i$ expected $\text{them}_i$ to win.
c) The $\text{men}_i$ expected the women to praise $\text{them}_i$.
d) The $\text{men}_i$ expected that $\text{they}_i$ would win.

5a) The $\text{men}_i$ praised $\text{them}_j$.
b) The $\text{men}_i$ expected $\text{them}_j$ to win.

These results are captured by (7) and (8), where Domain D is some structurally local domain.

7) Principle A: An anaphor must be bound in Domain D.
8) Principle B: A pronoun must be free in Domain D.

Setting aside the locality notion characterized by Domain D for the moment, the third principle of BT, adapted from Lasnik's (1976) Noncoreference Condition, is Principle C, which does not permit an r-expression (e.g., a name or a definite description) to be coreferent with any c-commanding antecedent. This is illustrated in (9a), where *he* cannot be coreferent with any of the names it c-commands (Bob, Carl, Ted, and Alex). Compare (9b) where *his* is embedded in the subject, hence does not c-command, and can thus be coreferent with any of the following names.

9a) He says that Bob claims that Carl gave Ted's book to Alex.
 b) His mother says that Bob claims that Karl gave Ted's book to Alex.

Principle C captures this distinction in terms of binding.

10) Principle C: An r-expression must be free.

The BT is taken to be a set of principles that apply at either S-structure, the intermediate level of derived structure that is fed to the phonetic component (PF) or else at the later level, after covert movement, called *LF,* which serves as the formal syntax contribution to semantic interpretation. With the advent of the minimalist program (Chomsky 1995a), both S-structure and D-structure, the initial level of lexical insertion, were argued to be neither conceptually nor empirically necessary and were eliminated. Instead, Chomsky proposes that words selected for use in a derivation (the numeration) are inserted into the tree by a derivational, structure-building process. Morphemes selected as input (the numeration) are either introduced from the numeration into the tree by adjoining them to form a new tree (Merge) or by moving a portion of the tree already built to form a new adjoined node, leaving behind a copy of what is moved. Thus in the minimalist model, there is no single level of lexical insertion, hence no D-structure. Part of the descriptive force of D-structure remains in that the history of movement is preserved by the copy mechanism (as it was by traces ever since they were introduced), but that is all of it that remains. Chomsky argues further that the S-structure level is also unnecessary (and indeed inaccurate as a guide to interpretation). I shall have more to say about how minimalist derivations proceed in chapter 3, but here it is enough to say that I agree that the levels of S-structure and D-structure are unnecessary and should be eliminated (for further arguments against S-structure, see also Safir, 2004). If the only levels the minimalist program posits are PF and LF, and if only LF is an input to semantic interpretation, then the BT must hold at the latter level.

Returning now to Domain D, at least three consequences are considered central to the BT account of how Domain D is determined. One key goal is to unify the relation between a verb and its object and that between certain classes of matrix verbs and the subject of their complement infinitives. With respect to case assignment, the unity of these effects is illustrated with respect to direct objects in (11a) and with respect to infinitival subjects as illustrated in (11b), where in both cases the pronoun has Accusative Case and is excluded by Principle B if it is coconstrued with the subject of the case-assigning verb. The significance of (11b) is that clausal lines are crossed such that the subject of the infinitive is thematically assigned by the infinitive but gets its Accusative Case by virtue of its relation with the matrix verb. Verbs like *expect* are called exceptional Casemarking (ECM) verbs in the literature.

11a) *John* transferred the deed to *himself/*him.*
  b) *John* expects *himself/*him* to win.

Second, Domain D was designed to capture the limits on the distances over which passive and raising structures can be derived by movement, as illustrated in (12a, b) and (12c), respectively.

12a) Peter was praised t.
  b) Peter was considered [t to be intelligent].
  c) Peter seemed [t to be intelligent].

The antecedent/trace relation and the case-assigner/case-assignee relation are unified in the LGB reasoning by the government relation, one definition of which is given in (13) along with a definition for Domain D as in (14) and the restriction on case assignment in (15).

13) Government: A governs B if A is an X° category, and there is no maximal projection (XP) that dominates B and not A.

14) Domain D for X is the minimal IP that contains the governor of X.[4]

15) Case is assigned by a governing X° category.

Since case assignment is assumed to be conditioned by government and since traces must also be governed (properly governed, according to the empty category principle of LGB), both launching sites for movement and Case-assigned positions must be governed. It is always assumed in the LGB-inspired literature of the 1980s that IP does not count as a maximal projection but CP does. This assumption is crucial to unifying the raising and ECM cases, which are both infinitival complements that are stipulated to be IPs, not CPs. If tensed clauses are always CPs, then the contrasts between (11b) and (16a) and between (12c) and (16b) are predicted, since both Case assignment and movement are blocked across CP (at least for movement to a subject position, i.e., A-movement)

16a) **John* thinks [*himself* will win].
  b) *John seems [t is guilty].

A further unification between traces of A-movement and anaphors is achieved by the assumption that A-traces are simply anaphors and thus must have their antecedents as locally as reflexives and reciprocals. This conclusion appeared attractive because posited abstract categories turn out to differ minimally from overt ones only in lacking a phonetic matrix (though I reject the parallel between movement and Domain D in 5.1).

The assumption that Domain D is the same for principles A and B ensures the third important result that the definition is designed to capture, namely, that pronouns and anaphors are in complementary distribution. Wherever an anaphor is local enough to be bound, a pronoun bound in that position would violate Principle B. This would appear to ensure that no form could be both pronominal and anaphoric. In spite of the uniformity of the domain in which they apply, however, principles A and B are stated separately so that they will properly restrict the distribution of PRO, which is presumed to be both pronominal and anaphoric in LGB. Since having a governor for *x* determines that *x* must have a binding domain, PRO must always be ungoverned to ensure that it will always lack a binding domain in which it cannot survive. Thus PRO is predictably found only in ungoverned positions (the PRO theorem), typically in a subset of subject positions of infinitives and of gerunds.

Almost every version of the BT proposed in the 1980s preserved most of the central features of the LGB account that I have just summarized, and these essential assumptions served to focus and invigorate inquiry into the properties of anaphora crosslinguistically well into the 1990s.

### *1.2.2 Challenges Facing the BT*

The BT faced a number of challenges, some of which were important and immediately obvious and others that, though less obvious, grew in importance over the years.

Perhaps first of all it is not clear that what the BT regulates is really coreference. Some standard counterexamples to Principle C are listed in (17).

17a) Everyone hates Oscar. *Even Oscar* hates *Oscar*.
b) *Cicero* turns out to be *Tully*.
c) The Yankees believe that Derek Jeter will be the difference in the series.

Cases like these indicate that noncoreference requires careful formulation if it is to allow for a reading where Oscar hates himself, or for Cicero to be Tully, or for Jeter to be a member of the Yankees (which he is at this writing). The same sort of issues arise for Principle B, where for (18c), once again, Jeter is one of the Yankees.

18a) A: Oscar trusts nobody. B: Not exactly, *Oscar* trusts *HIM*. (emphatic stress)
b) I know Tully, and I'm sure *that guy* is *him/%he*.
c) When *the Yankees* accept the trophy, Jeter will represent *them*.

Moreover, there are cases of enforced anaphora where the coreference relation cannot possibly refer to coextension, as in (19a).

19a) *Ringo* saw *his* likeness in the wax museum. *He* considered *himself* very impressive.
b) The sculptors regarded *Ringo's* finely wrought features to be their greatest triumph. Unfortunately, an earthquake struck, the floor shook, and *Ringo* fell over and crushed *himself*, breaking *his* arm.

In the narrative above (based on some examples originally pointed out by Jackendoff 1992), the reflexive is the likeness, and its antecedent is the person. This asymmetry is striking in the last sentence of (19b), since however it awkward it is to use this sentence to describe the person falling on the statue, it is quite impossible to construe this sentence to describe a situation where the statue falls on the person. Examples like these, as well as many others that will be discussed in chapters 2 and 4, suggest that the coindexation relation that represents binding is too symmetric and thus that the very representation of binding within BT is inappropriate. Alternative representations of coconstrual will be explored in chapters 2 and 4.

A more central concern during the 1980s and 1990s is that Domain D as it applies to Principle A seems too English-specific in light of the range of variation permitted across other languages and even within other languages. Since this variation will be discussed in detail in subsequent chapters, I will merely illustrate the problems for Principle A with some Norwegian examples. In (20), the anaphor *seg* can be bound across an intervening noncoreferent (PRO) subject by a higher subject, but this is only possible if there are no tensed clauses intervening, yet the anaphor *seg selv* can only be bound by a clausemate in such contexts. Moreover, both of these anaphors are subject oriented, which roughly means that their antecedents must be syntactic subjects, while the anaphor *ham selv*, where it is as local as *seg selv*, must not be anteceded by a syntactic subject—it is antisubject oriented (see 3.1.2.2 for more detail).

20) *Jon* fortalte meg om **ham selv/*ham/*seg/seg selv.*
"Jon told me about himself."

If we are not to abandon Principle A, what about it should be allowed to vary, and how much variation is to be permitted? One response to the range of variation is to throw out Principle A and start over, but this would appear to miss the generalization that holds across many of the cases where anaphora varies, which is that c-command is normally required, hence binding (but for challenges to c-command, even for local binding, see the appendix to chapter 4). Another response to these variations is to say that the forms in domains wider than those permitted by Principle A are not syntactic anaphors. This approach distinguishes inherently dependent forms into two classes: those that Principle A applies to and those that it never applies to. While this approach seems defensible for inherently dependent forms, like Chinese *ziji*, which can be bound at any distance across tensed clauses and does not always require a sentence-internal antecedent, forms still subject to syntactic locality requirements and c-command seem better suited to parametric adjustments in the domain of locality, as in the Scandinavian cases. At first, extensions of the parametric domains of anaphors seem entirely driven by empirical concessions, rather than any principled account of the range of domains. Attempts were made to address these questions (see 3.1.1, 5.2, and the introduction to chapter 6) by appeal to more principled accounts of the typology of anaphors and anaphoric domains, but the more general point is that any account assuming a universal Principle A is confronted with the issue of how to deal with locality variations and subject orientation.

More parochially, it was also pointed out that the BT appears to be empirically inadequate even as an account of the facts of English. One extension concerns the distribution of "picture NP [noun phrase] reflexives" for a set of contrasts illustrated in (21) with judgments that were considered standard in the mid-'80s.

21a) *The men* said that pictures of *themselves* would be on sale.
b) *T*he men* said that Mary would want pictures of *themselves.*
c) *T*he men* bought Mary's pictures of *themselves.*
d) *T*he men* said that Mary hated *themselves.*

Chomsky (1981) proposed that the presence of an intervening sentence or NP subject (*Mary/Mary's* in this case) would block anaphora with *the men*, but in (21a), that blocking effect would be neutralized because of an extension of Domain D permitted where the blocking subject contains the anaphor (see the reference cited for discussion of the i-within-i condition). However, since the 1990s, the contrast between (21a, b) has been taken to be minor, perhaps elusive, in comparison to the sharp unacceptability of (21d), about which there is no dispute (issues still remain about the judgment for [21c]). These cases, as well as (22a, b), will be discussed in 3.3.3 and 5.4, but for now it is enough to note that if the mild extension of locality that Chomsky proposed had been adequate and crosslinguistically supported, then the basic locality of the relations involved might have been maintained. However, this does not seem likely for picture NP reflexives, nor for reflexives embedded in contrastive predicates.

22a) *Dewey* doubts that Sharon is sure that physicists like *himself* should be praised.
b) *Maurice* finds it hard to believe that Alice could consider marrying anyone other than *himself.*

For these cases, it appears necessary to say that *himself* is not always subject to Principle A, a position that is dangerous if it is to become so general as to lose the prediction for (21d).

The cases in (21) and (22) are dangerous for another reason, namely, that complementarity between anaphors and pronouns appears to break down, since pronouns inserted in the place of reflexives in (21) and (22) are not excluded, (i.e., pronouns act as though Domain D has not been extended for them). Within BT assumptions, this is only a threat to the PRO theorem, which requires that there be no positions where both anaphors and pronouns are acceptable, but if the PRO theorem is set aside, then it is not even clear, from the BT perspective, that complementarity of pronouns and anaphors is even an empirical desideratum. If it is not, however, then there is no obvious reason to maintain that the domains for principles A and B should ever be similar for any principled reason.

Although the BT faced any number of other challenges (e.g., its level of application,[5] the reliability of c-command [see the appendix to chapter 4], and asymmetries between reflexives and reciprocals [see the appendix to chapter 6], to name a few), the concern expressed in the last paragraph strikes at the heart of the theoretical motivation for the BT: *There is little conceptual rationale for the existence of the principles.* Perhaps the best motivated of the three principles is Principle A, insofar as it is reasonable to suppose that anaphors, which cannot refer independently, are thereby deficient. That deficiency may require an anaphor to establish a relationship with something that has what it needs, and all that Principle A adds is that the relationship in question is conditioned by syntax. But why should a proper name, which picks out the named individual with considerable reliability with every mention, be restricted from doing just that just in case it has a c-commanding antecedent? Unlike the anaphoric form, it is not in the nature of names that they are referentially deficient, so why should this lack of deficiency ever lead to ill-formedness? Similarly, why should an independent pronoun, a form that usually does not require any linguistic antecedent, be forced not to have one in one very restricted domain?

In light of these challenges, there is ample reason to seek a more explanatory BT, or else a more explanatory alternative to the BT.

### *1.2.3 Predicates and Chains—Reinhart and Reuland (1993)*

For many working on the anaphora questions, the Reinhart and Reuland (1993) (R&R) approach holds out the hope that the BT principles A and B are not simply stipulations about domains but are rather "about" something in particular, namely, the reflexivity of predicates. Moreover, their distinctions between coargument effects and other locality effects they attribute to chains drew new attention to some subtle distinctions of form and interpretation that had not been foregrounded before.

The heart of the R&R predication-based approach is embodied in their formulation of the principles that regulate the local distribution of reflexive readings, which are presented in (24), along with the ancillary definitions in (23); these are drawn from Reuland and Reinhart (1995, 247).

23) Definitions
- a) The *syntactic predicate* of (a head) P is P, all its syntactic arguments and an external argument of P (subject). The *syntactic arguments* of P are the projections assigned theta-role or Case by P.
- b) The *semantic predicate* of P is P and all its arguments at the relevant semantic level.
- c) A predicate is *reflexive* iff two of its arguments are coindexed.
- d) A predicate (of P) is reflexive marked iff either P is lexically reflexive or one of P's arguments is a SELF-anaphor.

24) Conditions
- a) A reflexive-marked syntactic predicate is reflexive.
- b) A reflexive semantic predicate is reflexive marked.

These conditions apply as follows: The pronoun in (25a) cannot have a bound interpretation because the predicate *criticize* would not be reflexive marked. Their version of Principle A, namely, (24a), correctly predicts, however, that (25b) is grammatical, since it is reflexive marked. If *himself* has an index other than "i," then (25b) would violate Principle A, since a reflexive-marked predicate must have a reflexive interpretation.

25a) *Max$_i$ criticized him$_i$.
b) Max$_i$ criticized himself$_i$.

The difference between semantic and syntactic representations is illustrated by their treatment of cases like (26).

26) $\text{John}_i$ appears to $\text{himself}_i$ to be a genius.

In (26), *John* is the syntactic subject of *appear*, not its semantic subject, but since (24a) is stated on syntactic representations, not semantic ones, (26) is correctly predicted to be grammatical.[6] The evidence that their Principle B (24b) refers to more semantically complete representations comes from distributively interpreted conjunctions as in (27a, b) as interpreted in (27c, d), respectively.

27a) *The queen* invited Max and *her* (to our party).
  b) *Both *the queen* and I praised *herself/her.*
  c) The queen ($\lambda x$ (($x$ invited Max) & ($x$ invited $x$)))
  d) The queen ($\lambda x$ (($x$ praised $x$) & (I praised $x$)))

Under the interpretation (27c), the bound distributed interpretation for the pronoun is excluded because Principle B applies to it—"$x$ invited $x$" is not reflexive marked. R&R assume that the collective interpretation of (27a) is grammatical (the pronoun is not in a reflexive relation with a coargument subject). Similarly, in (27d), where *both* ensures a distributed reading, a pronoun is not possible as the object of *praise* because the interpretation is not marked reflexive for the first conjunct at the semantic level where some representation with the force of (27d), one of conjoined propositions, is available. A reflexive as the object of *praise* is not possible for (27b) because the syntactic antecedent is *both the queen and I,* and *herself* must agree with its syntactic coargument antecedent, which is plural in this case. (I return to the issues surrounding these examples in 3.3.1 and 4.2.3)

By choosing to state Principle B on semantic representations, however, R&R must then account separately for some cases covered by Principle B of the BT, but not by (24b). For example, if a pronoun replaces the reflexive in (26), as illustrated in (28a), the pronoun is not excluded by (24b), since *John* and *him* are not coarguments, and for the same reason, the pronominal subject of an ECM construction, illustrated in (28b), is not blocked from coreferring with *Elvin.*

28a) *$\text{John}_i$ appears to $\text{him}_i$ to be a genius.
  b) *$\text{Elvin}_i$ believes $\text{him}_i$ to be a genius.

Reuland and Reinhart (1995, 254–255) argue instead that these cases fall under the condition on A-chains that they propose, as stated in (31), assuming Chomsky's (1986a) definition of government in (30) and the chain definition in (29).

29) Generalized Chain Definition: C = ($a_i$, . . . , $a_n$) is a chain iff C is the maximal sequence such that
   i) there is an index $i$ such that for all $j$, 1 < or = $j$ < or = $n$, $a_j$ carries that index, and
   ii) for all $j$, 1 < or = $j$ < $n$, $a_j$ governs $a_{j+1}$.

30) Alpha governs beta iff alpha m-commands beta, and there is no tau, tau a barrier for beta, such that tau excludes alpha.

31) Condition on A-chains: A maximal A-chain ($a_1, \ldots, a_n$) contains exactly one link—$a_1$—which is +R.

The requirement (31) that ensures that the maximal chain of (29) include only one [+R] "referential" element is not to be confused with Principle C, since Principle C does not require c-commanding antecedents to govern names in order to exclude them. Typical Principle C–type cases, such as (32), are instead excluded by Rule I, proposed in Grodzinsky and Reinhart (1993), which is a revision of a proposal in Reinhart (1983). Rule I differentiates r-expressions from pronouns and reflexives, but it does not differentiate the latter two from each other (see 1.3). Thus (31) does not predict (32).

32) *$He_i$ says that Mary loves $Louis_i$.

As R&R point out, the chains conditioned by (31) are not the entities that theta assignment applies to, or else *John loves himself* would be excluded because two theta roles inhabit the same chain. Thus theta-assignment does not motivate (31).

Now let's consider how these definitions achieve their desired effects. In examples like (25a) and (28a, b), no barrier separates *him* and its antecedent, if it is assumed that the higher verb phrases (VPs; headed by *appear* and *believe*), even if they count as barriers, are not effective barriers in relation to the prepositional object or the ECM subject, respectively, in order to permit the matrix subject to count as an antecedent for *himself* in (26) (or *himself* in place of *him* in [28a, b]). Let us allow that a variety of assumptions will permit this antecedence relation without illegitimately crossing a barrier.[7]

One of the main purported advantages of introducing the condition on A-chains in (31) is that the distribution of Germanic SICH-type morphemes as they contrast with personal pronouns and SELF reflexives suddenly appears more tractable. As R&R point out, pronouns cannot be ECM subjects in Dutch as in (33), since they would violate (31), but *zich* can, since *zich* (and *zichzelf*), by hypothesis, is [-R] (translating *zich* and German *sich* as simply "SICH").

33) $Henk_i$ hoorde [zichzelf/zich/*$hem_i$ singen].
$Henk_i$ heard [himself/SICH/$him_i$ sing].
"*Henk* heard *himself* sing."

R&R argue that another advantage of this reformulation is that their Principle B does not exclude SICH or a pronoun in intrinsic reflexive constructions, since these predicates are inherently reflexive marked (in the lexicon). Since neither SICH nor a pronoun is a reflexive marker, they do not doubly mark the predicate *schaamen* (in [34]) as reflexive (though *zichzelf* presumably would, an option excluded under some notion of economy, they suggest).

34a) *Willem$_i$ schaamt hem$_i$.
b) Willem$_i$ schaamt zich$_i$.
Willem shames him.
"Willem is ashamed."

Only (31) excludes (34a), as opposed to (34b), since (31) does not allow a [+R] element (the pronoun *hem*) to be bound within the domain of the first barrier above its governor. In addition to being nonreflexive, SICH is [-R], so (31) does not exclude it.

### *1.2.4 Challenges Facing Reinhart and Reuland's Account*

One particularly suspicious feature of the R&R account is that the condition on A-chains (31), except for regulating the distribution of some pronouns,[8] lacks independent motivation. Moreover, the feature [+/-R], despite their attempt to give it predictive force, is ultimately descriptive (of pronouns).

Even if we are to accept the [+/-R] feature for the sake of argument, it is clear that much of the force of (31) is fully redundant for Principle C–type effects, since anything regulated by Principle C (or whatever achieves the effect of Principle C—see 1.3) cannot be bound at all, as pointed out earlier. Moreover, the condition on A-chains is admitted to be redundant for all cases where semantic Principle B holds sway, and it is unnecessary for SELF anaphors, which are independently regulated by Principle A. In other words, (31) is only crucially motivated by the residue distribution of SICH and pronouns that are not regulated by semantic Principle B.

We have already seen that the definition of chains in (29) is not independently useful outside of its relevance to the entities picked out by (31), since the A-chains relevant for theta assignment, which do not allow two theta roles within a chain, cannot employ the sorts of chains that (31) applies to. If the chain entity that (31) applies to is unmotivated, then we may ask if this condition is, in fact, specific to pronouns. The answer appears to depend on the independent motivation for [+/-R], but at this point we can characterize the force of (31) as in (35a) and compare it with a version of traditional Principle B (following Huang, 1983, I assume for presentational purposes that SUBJECT is not part of the domain for Principle B). If we revise syntactic Principle B to state it in terms of barriers, with the assumption (adopted by R&R) that VP is not a barrier for an accusative assigned object (either a direct object or ECM subject), as in (35c), then the force of Principle B depends entirely on the same sorts of considerations that the condition on A-chains has to consider.

35a) Force of the Condition on A Chains: A [+R] element must be free within the domain of the first barrier that dominates it.
b) Syntactic Principle B: A pronoun must be free within the minimal functional complex containing its governor.
c) Syntactic Principle B—Barriers: A pronoun must be free within the domain of the first barrier that dominates it.

For example, if (36) is considered grammatical, then DP must be a barrier for *him*, in the chain theory or for syntactic Principle B stated in terms of barriers, but not if (36) is considered ungrammatical.

36) %John$_i$ saw a picture of him$_i$.

Thus the force of (31) reduces to (35a), which is minimally different from (35c) in its reference to [+/-R]. In other words, unless [+/-R] refers to a distinction other than [+/-pronoun], then (31) is simply a second syntactic Principle B that complements the semantic one R&R propose.

So let us now consider whether or not the [+/-R] feature is independently motivated and distinct from the [+/-pronoun] distinction. Reuland and Reinhart (1995) consider an element [+R] if it is fully specified for number, Case, and gender. The SICH elements are never specified for gender or Case and often not for number. The supposed intuitive appeal is that if the feature matrix for SICH elements is not completely specified, then they cannot be referential; hence they are [-R].

The intuitive appeal shrivels upon reflection, however. Consider, for example, the proper name *Marion*, which is not specified for Case or gender. One can refer to Maid Marion, a mythical female of the Robin Hood legend, or Marion Morrison, a mythical male (known by his stage name, John Wayne), but it is only through real-world knowledge that one can attach a gender to the name. If so, the name is not independently motivated to be [+R]. But presumably such elements must be [+R] because they can successfully head chains. Without knowing anything about the real world gender value for *Marion,* one can report *Marion left* a grammatical sentence. The same point can be extended to *someone/anyone/everyone,* and so forth, none of which are specified for gender or Case, yet these quantified nominals must head chains as well.

One might try to salvage the force of [+/-R] by stipulating that an element that has more than phi features doesn't need full feature specification to be [+R], but this move does nothing more than reduce the force of (31) to pronouns and SICH elements, especially since SELF elements are independently regulated by Principle A and reciprocals are not discussed. Thus extending [+R] to names and quantifiers is thoroughly ad hoc, if gender and case are criteria. The upshot is that the [+/-R] designation is now effectively stipulated to apply to nothing more than SICH and pronouns, where names and descriptions are simply the elsewhere case.

One claimed benefit of the [+/-R] distinction is that R&R can account for the otherwise problematic Frisian fact illustrated in (37).

37) *Max* hâld him/**himsels*.
Max behaves him.

Frisian lacks a SICH form, and it appears the otherwise independent pronoun *him* in Frisian fills this gap. Now it must be argued that *him* in (37) is not [+R], because if it were, then (37) would be excluded by (31), just as (34a) is. However R&R argue that Frisian *him* is indeed [-R] in this construction (not otherwise), because inherently case-marked elements should count as unspecified for Case, unless, as in German, they participate in Case contrasts (i.e., in German, an oblique selected pronoun has a specific Case selected by the relevant preposition). Thus (31), with this stipulation about inherent Case, accounts for the grammaticality of (37) in Frisian, whereas the BT would be forced to exclude it.

Let us suppose for the sake of argument that inherent Case is indeed the source of the contrast between Frisian and Dutch (but see 3.1.2.2); what relation does inherent case have to any coherent notion of referentiality that [+R] is supposed to capture? The same sort of distinction could easily be tacked on to syntactic Principle B by providing some sort of diacritic (on those elements consisting solely of phi features) as to whether or not syntactic Principle B applies to them. The motivated portion of (31) now reduces to (35c), except that a [+/-pronoun] diacritic replaces [+/-R].

To put it bluntly, R&R's theory surreptitiously proposes two Principle Bs, one semantic and novel, the other syntactic and quite conventional. But just how bad is this? Even if the condition on A-chains (31) does reduce to syntactic Principle B, where is the harm in maintaining (31) as an entity only indirectly related to BT?

Obvious objections arise on the grounds of redundancy as well as the dubious initiative of introducing complex machinery of otherwise unnecessary chains to account for a narrow class of cases. However, what is more troubling, from my point of view, is that positing the two Principle Bs that R&R propose causes their account to miss parallels between the domains regulating pronouns and reflexives that were captured in the traditional BT. In canonical accusative positions, such as direct objects and ECM subjects, pronouns and -SELF forms (in the languages that have them) are always in complementary distribution (including in Frisian). This was so in the traditional BT because government was part of the domain determinations for both principles A and B—even though, as we have seen, that complementarity appears to be compromised in many cases. In the R&R theory, the two domain restrictions on pronouns are not only slightly different from each other, but they also differ from the domain restriction on their Principle A. Their "syntactic predicate" (relevant to Principle A) includes a predicate and its semantic arguments, an external argument (in case it doesn't have one that is a semantic coargument, as in raising contexts), and anything it assigns case to (to include ECM subjects). Described this way, the notion of syntactic predicate merely summarizes the empirical contexts where it must apply to get the right results, and in this respect it is starkly unlike the notion "semantic predicate", which has independently motivated utility (the domain of theta assignment). In short, the claim that the reflexivity of syntactic predicates is only relevant to Principle A introduces an artificial asymmetry, not only with respect to semantic Principle B, but with respect to syntactic Principle B (i.e., [31], when boiled down) that obscures the relationship between the two.[9]

In spite of all of these criticisms, I believe that the R&R theory introduces a number of considerations that lead to a more profound approach. Their emphasis on semantic coargument relations as opposed to noncoargument relations is an important advance, even though I reject the notions of predicate (particularly of syntactic predicate) on which their notions of coargumenthood depend (see 3.3.1 and chapter 4). Although I also reject their contention that Principle B is independently motivated (a position that I have also supported for many years), especially since their Principle B requires a morphological affix to condition abstract semantic representations, the view that Principle B needs motivation and that what enforces it may not be specific to pronouns is an important insight that I shall develop in presenting my own theory.

## 1.3 The Force of Principle C

As mentioned earlier, R&R are assuming an account of Principle C effects that their chain theory, limited by locality, is not adequate to capture. Grodzinsky and Reinhart (1993; G&R), building on a proposal of Reinhart (1983a, 71), assume that coindexation under c-command is necessary for a bound reading. Their account of binding relations, which largely abstracts away from principles A and B (in favor of the R&R account), is essentially embodied in the "translation rule" in (38a, c) along with Rule I stated in (39).

38a) Definition: A node α is *bound* by a node β iff α and β are coindexed, and β c-commands α.
   b) Conditions:
      A. An anaphor is bound in its governing category.
      B. A pronoun is free in its governing category.
   c) An NP is a variable iff either
      i. it is empty and A'-bound, or
      ii. it is A-bound and lacks lexical content.

Other cases of NP coindexation are uninterpretable.

39) Rule I: Intersentential Coreference
   NP A cannot corefer with NP B if replacing A with X, X a variable A-bound by B, yields an indistinguishable interpretation.

Notice that the use of indices is somewhat vestigial in this account[10] since the only indices that "count" are the ones that reside on NPs that have c-commanding antecedents. It is the translation rule, Rule I, conceived of as a pragmatic strategy, that determines noncoreference, as opposed to the failure of a bound variable reading. A potential weakness of this account is that reference to binding (and hence c-command) in (39) means that reference to syntactic structure must be integrated into the account of pragmatic strategies.

To see how this works, consider the examples in (40), drawn from G&R. Examples (40d, e) permit coreference because there is no c-command of the potential coreferent terms; hence neither one could be dependent on the other, and Rule I has nothing to say about them.

40a) **Lucia* adores *her*.
   b) **He* adores *Alfred*.
   c) **He/Alfred* thinks that *Alfred/the guy* is a great cook.
   d) Most of *her* friends can't stand *Lucie*.
   e) A party without *Lucie* annoys *her*.

In the case of (40b, c), a bound variable interpretation is structurally possible because the position in which *Alfred/the guy* resides is c-commanded by the position in which *he* resides. However, neither *Alfred* nor *the guy* is devoid of lexical content; thus neither of these could be variables by clause i. or ii. of (38c). By contrast, (40a) is not distinguished from *Lucia adores herself* by Rule I, since both *herself* and *her* qualify as potential variables. G&R discuss this move explicitly: "[Rule I] differs from the original formulation in Reinhart (1983), which took the relevant factor to be the availability of and alternative bound expression. Here the rule is based on the availability of semantic binding, regardless of the expression used for it" (p. 80, fn. 11). In other words, among the forms that can be variables in the position of the direct object of *adores* in (40a), there is no competition (i.e., between pronouns and reflexives). Thus a pronoun-SELF form cannot obviate a pronoun by virtue of Rule I, and so some form of Principle B is required in this theory, either in the standard LGB formulation, as a local prohibition on the dependence of pronouns in a domain, or in R&R, as a restriction on reflexive interpretation. This disjunction (between the treatment of pronoun/name contrasts vs. the treatment of pronoun/SELF-form contrasts) complicates the G&R theory, and one of the points of this book is that the complication in question is unnecessary.

## 1.4 The Road Ahead

The BT and the reflexive predicate and chain approach have set some standards and goals about what is to be explained and what is to count as an explanation, as does the G&R approach to Principle C effects. I believe that they provide both a foundation and a foil for the theory I propose, in which the elsewhere relation between the purported [-R] and everything else, as well as the existence of Principle B and Principle C effects, follows from a competitive principle, developed in detail in chapter 3, and a version of Principle A. Instead of proceeding directly to the competitive principle, however, I think it prudent to clarify in the next chapter what the syntactic contribution to coconstrual interpretation is. After all, whatever the syntactic portion of the anaphora theory turns out to be, we must be precise about the nature of the effect it purports to explain. In this area, too, much important foundational work has been done, and in chapter 2, I refit that foundation for the competitive approach I intend to build on it.

# 2

# The Interpretation of Anaphoric Relations from Syntactic Form

In many instances, the syntax of anaphora is only revealed through the class of interpretations that are available or unavailable for an otherwise grammatical sentence. As a result, it is inescapable that any aspiring theory of linguistic anaphora must at least supply what a proper theory of interpretation will need in order to interpret anaphora between linguistic expressions. This chapter addresses the latter sense of what a theory of natural language anaphora can contribute to our understanding of these phenomena. More specifically, the main goal of this chapter will be to distinguish *coreference* from *dependency* and develop a proposal concerning just how and just how much these relations should be represented as consequences of formal grammar on the one hand, and in what manner and to what extent they should be treated as consequences of how speakers use grammars in a discourse on the other.

Traditionally, anaphora has been said to mark a relation of *coreference*, a term that was first used without making further distinctions. There is, of course a voluminous philosophical literature on the notions of reference, how reference can succeed or not succeed and how such success is to be understood, how the intentions of speakers may or may not be represented or expressed in what they say or how they choose to say it. In this short discussion of what linguistic coreference is supposed to be, I cannot do justice to the full range of these issues, most of which, moreover, are beyond my competence and/or orthogonal to my concerns. The positions I take will not be defended in a way that critically examines the philosophical literature (or even most of the literature in linguistic semantics), though many of my positions are not at all innocent, neither in terms of their consequences nor in terms of their antecedents.

My emphasis stays close to questions of natural language structure and interpretation as they arise when empirical phenomena are viewed through the narrow lens of formal grammar. From this perspective, how structural conditions affect the linguistic semantic interpretation of anaphora is my core subject matter, though various pragmatic issues about the nature of antecedents in discourse, insofar as they must be distinguished from questions of linguistic form, will frequently play a role in the discussion. Moreover, my discussion is narrowed further in that it is oriented toward supporting the positions I will take in the remainder of the book. A richer view of the literature can be followed in the notes and references and Safir (2004).

## 2.1 Coreference and Dependency—Preliminary Distinctions and a Road Map

There are a variety of ways in which the value of one linguistic expression coincides with another term introduced in discourse, whether that term is linguistically explicit or not. The term I will use for this vague description is *coconstrual*, which I will purposely not define since I will be using the term whenever I wish to refer to some sort of full identity overlap relation between nominals without committing myself to its more specific nature. I will mark coconstrual in most instances by italicizing two or more phrases in example sentences, and occasionally with bolding when there are two such relations to track or I am marking coconstrual in an otherwise italicized sentence. I avoid the use of indices for reasons that will become clear in subsequent discussion. Two forms of coconstrual that have traditionally played a central role in the discussion of anaphora are the relations *coreference* and *dependent identity*.

Informally, dependent reference is when a linguistic expression A can only have its referential value determined as a function of the interpretive content of the linguistic expression B. Dependent identity is when the identity of the antecedent and the identity of the dependent term are understood to be the same, although I will have more to say about what counts as identity in chapter 4. Coreference might be described as covaluation, such that two linguistic expressions are determined to have the same value, where "the same value" typically means that they pick out the same referent in discourse. While it is certainly possible to discuss any sort of entity in these terms, including animate beings, things, abstract ideas, events, activities, times, places, reasons, and so on, our discussion will be limited to nominal phrases, what they most typically describe (beings and things), and relations between them, though this limitation is one of convenience.[1]

One of the typical ways that dependent identity and coreference are empirically distinguished can be illustrated by the contrast in possible entailments for (1) in (1a, b), where (1a) is implied by the "dependent" or "bound" (covariant) reading, the one where the pronoun covaries with the choice of women believers who might antecede it, and (1b) is implied by the independent reading, where the reference of the pronoun remains Mara even if the believer varies.[2]

1) Of all the women, only Mara believes Sean loves her.
   a) None of the other women believe that they are loved by Sean.
   b) None of the other women believe that Sean loves Mara

A similar distinction is also observed in ellipsis contexts, as illustrated in (2), which allows for a "sloppy" reading as in the "filled-in ellipsis" in (2a), which corresponds to the dependent/bound reading, and (2b), which is the filled-in ellipsis that is taken to correspond to the independent/"strict" reading.

2) Mara believes Sean loves her and Sheila does too
 a) *Shiela* believes that Sean loves *her = Shiela.*
 b) Shiela believes that Sean loves Mara

While these distinctions have been known to exist for a long time, the role that such distinctions have been taken to play in the line between structurally conditioned anaphora and discourse conditioned anaphora begins to be regarded as crucial in work of the late 1970s, both in the ellipsis literature (Williams 1977; Sag 1976) and the literature on coreference conditions (Lasnik 1976; Reinhart 1983; Chomsky 1976; Evans 1980).

Developing a line of thought that arose in the late 1970s, I will argue that formal grammar regulates structural conditions on dependency relations, but it only regulates coreference relations indirectly, without direct reference to syntactic structure. Moreover, I contend that c-command is not a licensing condition for dependent identity readings, as many propose, but a restriction on such readings (a restriction that does not apply to independent coreferent readings). I also explore how these different sorts of readings should be represented in syntax, and in so doing I reject indices in favor of an arrow notation like that of Higginbotham (1983). Finally, in the process of exploring the question of whether noncoreference is disjoint reference, I am led to introduce the competitive principle that is the focus of chapter 3, and I place that principle in the context of the interpretive theory I propose. To understand what these statements mean, what is at stake, and how my approach is distinguishable from a number of others, it is necessary to briefly review the history of some of these ideas.

## 2.2 The Emergence of Dependency in the Theory of Anaphora

The distinction between dependent reference and coreference has not always played a role in the discussions of anaphora. The earliest conditions did not distinguish between the two, and some of these accounts (e.g., Lees and Klima 1963; Langacker 1969) saw the work of grammar in stating the conditions, which seemed syntactically conditioned, on the class of cases where coreference, understood as identity of reference (e.g., Chomsky 1965, 146), was possible. Distinctions between bound readings and coreferent ones within generative grammar date at least from Postal (1971), who distinguishes copular identity contexts and stressed pronominals under coreference from coreference between unstressed pronouns; the latter is a bound reference relation (see especially Postal 1971, ch. 19). For example, Postal points out that the copular relation is not one of bound reference, since the *be* has the function of indicating that two independent descriptions have the same referent. Although Postal declines to treat coindexation as more than an illustrative device, he does reject coindexation between *the killer* and *the one wearing the blue hat* for (3a), whereas he would consider coindexation an accurate description of the reading for (3b).

3a) The killer$_i$ is [the one wearing the blue hat]$_{j/*i}$.
b) Charlie$_i$ cut himself$_i$.
c) Charlie$_i$ cut that guy$_i$.

As Postal remarks, "The central fact involved in all occurrences of binding . . . is that entities are provided with only *a single description*" (Postal's emphasis; 1971, 232). We will turn to the question of whether indexation and coindexation should ever be more than descriptive devices as opposed to theoretical entities, but Postal clearly intends for them to be descriptive of covariation. This account is not sufficient, however, since it does not indicate that coreference in (3c) is in any way deviant or at least out of the ordinary if the reference for *Charlie* and the reference for *that guy* arise in different ways.

Examples like (3c) were part of what motivated Lasnik (1976) to resort to a rule of noncoreference, rather than a rule that simply blocks some identity relation or other. A stronger argument for a noncoreference rule was based on the potential for "accidental coreference." Early accounts of coreference replaced names with pronouns or reflexives conditioned by identity, and sometimes versions of what we now call *c-command* further conditioned the change (see, e.g., Lees & Klima 1963; Langacker 1969). After all, pronouns without linguistic antecedents have to be introduced in any case (Postal 1966),[3] and if so, what is to prevent pronouns introduced independently (without overt linguistic antecedent) from being coreferent with those introduced by rule? In other words, proper names and definite descriptions may just happen to have the same referent as other nominals in the sentence "by accident." In (4), for example, what is to prevent *him* from accidentally coreferring with both *John* and *he,* even if *he* is not taken as the antecedent of *John* (i.e., if *John* is not pronominalized by transformational rule to become *he*, as in early accounts)? A noncoreference rule is then still necessary to block accidental coreference between *he* and *John* by transitivity of reference, if both can be coreferent with *him* individually.

4) A person who hates *him* says *he* insulted *John's* mother.

On this view, it is not enough for the theory to fail to permit or fail to require coreference; rather a rule that prohibits coreference is needed (e.g., between *he* and *John* in [4]). For this reason, as well as some split antecedent cases we will return to later, Lasnik introduced the principle that came to be called Principle C of the LGB BT, and he then argued that the c-command-sensitive noncoreference rule of interpretation rendered any rule of transformational pronominalization unnecessary.

On the basis of contrasts like that between (5a) and (5b), Lasnik asserted further that c-command regulates not just a noncoreference effect, but also a disjoint reference relation. The notion of disjoint reference dates back to Chomsky's (1973, 241) rule of interpretation, the ancestor of Principle B. Where disjoint reference is in force, it requires that there be no extensional overlap between the sets denoted by the c-commanded name/definite description and the nominal that c-commands it, according to the standard judgments in (5).

5a) **They* hate the man who forced *Tom* to hit *Harry*.
b) The man who forced *Tom* to hit *Harry* hates *them*.

The empirical motivations for positing disjoint reference as opposed to noncoreference deserve critical scrutiny, but I put off further empirical investigation of this notion until section 2.4.2 and assume for now that disjoint reference is the force of the Principle C effect.

In a very influential essay, however, Evans (1980) discredits the notion that there should be a rule of grammar that establishes noncoreference. Evans points out a variety of contexts where a nominal must be permitted to be understood as coreferent with a nominal that c-commands it (where accent aigue indicates contrastive stress).

6a) I know what John and Bill have in common. Jóhn thinks that Bill is terrific and Bíll thinks that Bill is terrific. (Evans, 1980, 356, ex. 49)
b) Look fathead. If everyone loves Oscar's mother then certainly Oscar must love Oscar's mother. (Evans, 1980, 356, ex. 48)
c) Everyone has finally realized that Oscar is incompetent. Even he has finally realized that Oscar is incompetent. (Evans, 1980, 357, ex. 52)

I will refer to cases like (6a–c) as *instantiation contexts*, in that individuals or sets of individuals are singled out as instantiations, or examples, that serve to support or refute some posited generalization in the common ground. (See Evans 1980, 356–358; Reinhart 1983, 77–78; see also Fiengo and May 1994, 11; and Heim 1993, on *structured meanings,* a term adapted from Cresswell 1985.) These examples have a place in a syllogism, and they induce the listener to come to relevant conclusion only if the disfavored coconstrual is reinstated.

The factor that seems crucial to achieve the coreference effects in (6) is that in each case, part of the property that defines the membership in the salient set under discussion presupposes a referential value for the individual that the property is ascribed to, or else the description can't be interpreted. So for (6a), that set includes those that think that Bill is terrific, for (6b) it includes those who love Oscar, and for (6c) it includes those who realize that Oscar is incompetent. In other words, insofar as the criterion for set membership is already presupposed to be established in the discourse, so is the name contained within that description. Moreover, any person we assert to be in the set is not someone who is already established in discourse by virtue of the set membership (or the statement would be uninformative). Thus *Oscar* must be presupposed to have a value that is established independently of the property asserted to hold of him. So the nature of the assertion involved leads us to expect that neither mention of *Oscar* depends on the other.

If no expectation is created that both terms referring to *Oscar* are necessarily referentially independent, then coreference between a term referring to Oscar and the value for the name *Oscar* that it c-commands is unexpected (as pointed out with respect to Postal's observations, e.g., [3c]). Rather what permits the noncoreference effect to be overcome, or at least suspended, is that (6a–c) are part of a reasoned argument based on the facts in evidence. Notice, by contrast, to say Oscar loves his mother without context does permit a reading where *his* depends on *Oscar*, so no expectation of noncoreference needs to be overcome in such a case (by appeal to the structure of an extrasentential logical argument).

A similar account can be applied to examples of a sort discussed by Higginbotham (1980a, 234–235; 1985, 570).

7) You may not think that that guy is *John*, but *he* put on *John's* coat.

This sentence leaves the listener to draw his or her own conclusion about the man who put on John's coat, but the point is that the individual in question, who we can already identify as salient in discourse whether he is John or not, has met a criterion for being identified as "John," where that criterion is in the common ground for both parties. The statement in (7) once again appeals to an extrasentential logical conclusion based on the facts in evidence. If the listener does not accept the relevant presuppositions, s/he might ask the speaker how one can be certain that the coat in question is John's or why one should be sure that the person who puts on John's coat should be John. Thus the referential values for *he* and for *John* are established separately, and the listener must draw his or her own logical conclusion (see also Fiengo and May 1994, 10) based on whether or not an appropriate criterion has been met (i.e., whoever puts on John's coat must be John). The example would be quite transformed if putting on a coat (any coat) was to be our indication that the secret spy we are meeting is John, in which case one conversant might turn to the other and say, "He put on his coat, so he must be John." This reading, which could be a dependent one for *his*, is avoided by using *John's* in place of *his* in (7).

Evans concludes that a name or definite description can be coreferent with a potential c-commanding antecedent if the c-commanded name does not depend for its reference on what c-commands it. Evans extends this point to identity statements, which should be disjoint under Lasnik's principle insofar as the subject c-commands the object.

8) That man is John.

As Postal posited, there is no dependence between *that man* and *John*; rather the sentence asserts identity of referential value for terms that have independently established values. Thus a crucial property of this account is that dependent identity, unlike coreference, is asymmetric, in that the referential value of the dependent term is a function of its antecedent. Coreference, by contrast, is a relation where neither term is a function of the other. Postal concludes that the coreference is not directly blocked by formal grammar.

Evans also distinguishes antecedents in terms of what relation a dependent term can have to them. In particular, he distinguishes dependency on a quantified antecedent from dependence on a referring expression, since only in the first case is a pronoun necessarily dependent for its reference on its antecedent. Recall the set of distinctions made earlier: We must say that coconstrual in (9a) is formally ambiguous, in that it could be that *he* binds *him* (i.e. that *him* is dependent on *he*), or it could be that *he* and *him* are "accidentally coreferent" in Lasnik's sense, having the same value.

9a) *He* says that Marilyn loves *him*.
b) *Every boy* says that *he* loves Marilyn.

Elements with the same value are in a symmetric relation—except for Casemarking, the pronouns are interchangeable. But this is not true of pronouns anteceded by quantifiers. Quantifiers have no reference, and so there is no accident that can produce in the pronoun a matching referent.[4] In these cases, the pronouns are dependent or else not coconstrued with the quantifier as in (9b).

Now reconsider Principle C from the point of view of the distinction between dependency and coreference. If Principle C is supposed to rule out dependent names, one might object that we have no business supposing that proper names are ever dependents. However, Principle C holds not only for proper names but also for definite descriptions, and it is well known that definite descriptions are anaphoric across a discourse (in contradistinction to indefinite descriptions; see the influential discussion of Heim 1982).

10) *A man* walked in. *He/The man/*A man* sat down.

Yet even when the definite descriptions are understood as epithets that can depend on quantified antecedents (as in [11c]), Lasnik (1976) shows that Principle C still restricts epithets, as in (11b), where c-command is crucial.[5]

11a) **He/Ronnie* claimed that *my cousin/the president* was too smart to get caught.
b) **He/Ronnie/everyone* claimed that *the bastard* was too smart to get caught.
c) *His/Ronnie's/everyone's* mom claims that *the bastard* is too smart to get caught.

If formal grammar only regulates dependency rather than coreference, however, then we face a new problem: Why is it typically the case that noncoreference as well as nondependence is presumed where a name is c-commanded by something on which it might depend? Nothing in the dependency theory explains why independent coreference between two names should require any special context when one c-commands the other. When one does not c-command the other, independent coreference succeeds without any special context, as illustrated in (12) and (11c).

12) *His* mother thinks *Oscar* is incompetent.

Indeed, (12) could very well be used to start a conversation among two people who know Oscar. The difference between cases like (12) as opposed to those in (6) and (7) thus remains unexplained.

This problem was addressed by Reinhart (1983a, 1983b) who follows Evans in that she argues that the only relations regulated by linguistic representations are dependency relations, not coreference relations. However, she suggests a way of connecting the failure of dependency and noncoreference.

Reinhart argues that for the most part a pronoun can have a bound reading in relation to a quantifier only if the quantifier c-commands the pronoun.

13a) *Each man* indicated that *he* would be late.
b) *That the golf cart carried *each man* indicated that *he* would be late.
c) *A report that describes *each man* indicates *he* will be late.
d) ?*A dossier on *each man's* character indicates *he* will be late.

Although there are exceptions to this generalization we will discuss later, the significance of it is that it looks like a positive condition (a relation can exist if *x* holds) that corresponds to the negative relation of Principle C (a relation cannot exist if *x* holds). If the relations involved are similar, a natural scientific strategy is to attempt to derive one condition from the other.

Reinhart then notes that pronouns can also be in a dependency relation with nonquantificational and nonfocused antecedents as in (2), not only with quantificational or focused antecedents, as in (1). Using the lambda abstract notation to describe the bound reading, the term *John* is treated as the value for the *x* of which the property holds that *x* likes *x*'s mother, and the second conjunct is then represented as the same property (an alphabetic variant) where the value for the variable is *Bill*.[6]

14) John likes his mother more than Bill does.
a) Strict reading: "John likes John's mother more than Bill likes John's mother."
b) Bound reading: John ($\lambda x$($x$ likes $x$'s mother)) and Bill ($\lambda y$($y$ likes $y$'s mother)).

Thus referential antecedents, as well as quantified ones, can antecede a dependency relation. The appropriate generalization extending across quantified and nonquantified antecedents is thus (15), which is reminiscent of Evans' view of Lasnik's negative condition, restated as (16) in order to enhance the symmetry with (15).

15) A dependent term must be c-commanded by the term it depends on.

16) A name/definite description cannot be c-commanded by a term it depends on.

Reinhart attempts to exploit the similarity of (15) and (16) by suggesting the assumption in (17) along with the strategies imputed to conversational participants as in (18) from Reinhart (1983a, 76).

17) Dependency (bound anaphora) is used where possible to express coreference.

18a) Speaker's strategy: When a syntactic structure you are using allows bound-anaphora interpretation, then use it if you intend your expressions to corefer, unless you have some reasons to avoid bound anaphora.
b) Hearer's strategy: If the speaker avoids the bound-anaphora options provided by the structure s/he is using, then, unless s/he has reasons to avoid bound anaphora, s/he didn't intend his expressions to corefer.

Reinhart's theory (a predecessor to that of G&R discussed in 1.3) relates (15) and (16) by deriving the latter from the former. Wherever a pronoun is licensed for a bound reading, that is, where it has a c-commanding antecedent, the use of a name in the position of the pronoun signals that bound reference, possible with the pronoun, would have been used if coreference were intended. Where bound reference of a pronoun is not possible, the use of a name in place of a pronoun creates no implication of noncoreference. This is illustrated in (19), where *his* must depend on the quantifier to receive an appropriate interpretation in (19b), but in (19a), where bound reference is not required, *his* and *John* can corefer.

19a) A picture of *his* mother fell on *John.*
b) *A picture of *his* mother fell on *everyone.*

Besides relating the condition on bound-pronoun readings to the noncoreference effect, Reinhart's account also gives us the beginning of an account of why special contexts ("some reason to avoid bound anaphora") are required to achieve coreference where dependent reference is blocked. Although I shall reject Reinhart's attempt to derive (16) from (15), since I think (15) is false, the competitive principle I propose does depend on the idea that the availability of one form renders another obviative. Otherwise, our proposals are quite dissimilar.

One difference between my assumptions and Reinhart's (not the most important one) is that I believe any statement about the speaker's strategy, indeed any statement about the speaker's intentions, and particularly any statement about "intended coreference," is unnecessary and misleading. Consider the following situation. I am sitting behind a rock on the beach, and Albert comes strolling by without seeing me. I suddenly hear him exclaim as follows:

20) That man is hiding behind John's rock!

Now I know that Albert is not talking to any other conversational participant and certainly not to me. In fact, the man and the rock that Albert is exclaiming about may not even be me or the rock I am behind. I do not know, as it turns out later, that Albert has been looking for John, whom he has never met, though John's rock has previously been pointed out to him as the place where John is likely to be found. As he is exclaiming, he is in the act of identifying the individual who is John by virtue of the fact that that individual is hiding behind John's rock. But I know none of this. My expectation is that *that man* does not corefer with the term *John* since I do not have any notion that "hides behind John's rock" is a criterion for identifying John that Albert already has in mind. Nothing mitigates my expectation of noncoreference.

Thus I do not think a speaker's intentions are what is at stake in linguistic theory, at least insofar as anaphora is concerned, and Reinhart (1986, 137) regards them as peripheral. Rather what I take to be at stake is what a hearer in the context of the utterance can take the speaker to have meant without assuming that the speaker is speaking in an extragrammatical code (e.g., "The eagle has landed" means the assassination plan may proceed, or "Is that the sugar next to you?" means "Please pass the sugar" by polite inference). The Albert-on-the-beach scenario is sufficient to show that a listener can produce a grammatically predicted interpretation of what a speaker says even when a speaker has no intent to communicate, and we can't know what the speaker's intended referent was.

The same point can be made with a different sort of example, pointed out by Wettstein (1991, 163). Suppose Ahern, a fictional mad historian, believes he is de Gaulle and in his lecture proclaims, "And then I marched triumphantly into Paris." Ahern may be right about when de Gaulle marched into Paris, and his students, knowing Ahern is mad, may be able to separate Ahern's beliefs about himself from the from the true statements about De Gaulle. His listeners may or may not assume that Ahern is in fact de Gaulle, but the listener must assume that the speaker uttering "I" is referring to the speaker, regardless of whom the speaker intends to be identified as.[7] Once again, the point is that by using certain linguistic devices, the speaker's intentions are irrelevant to the process by which the hearer determines which referents are linguistically possible. In place of (18) I propose a slight revision that assumes a more listener-oriented strategy (which, though inadequate here, I will return to in 2.5).

21) If bound anaphora is not employed where it could be, the listener does not expect coreference unless the listener has a reason to distinguish independent coreference from dependency. The speaker who does not respect the listener's strategy risks being misunderstood.

The problem remains that failure of dependent reference does not logically implicate failure of independent coreference, unless (17), repeated below, can be defended.

17) Dependency (bound anaphora) is used where possible to express coreference.

Reinhart (1983a, 76) asserts, "When syntactically permitted, bound anaphora . . . is the most explicit way available in the language to express coreference, as it involves referential dependency. So, when coreference is desired, this should be the preferred way to express it." However, this particular attempt to bridge the gap between failed dependent identity and failed independent coreference in terms of the supposed explicitness of a dependent interpretation appears misguided.

Consider the fact that examples like (7), repeated below, would not be more explicit if *his* replaced *John's*, since *his* would be ambiguous between a bound interpretation and an independent one;

7) You may not think that that guy is *John*, but *he* put on *John's* coat.

In other words, using the pronoun is the *less explicit* way to achieve the desired form of coreference in this environment. In conversation, the reason one avoids using a term that could be taken to be dependent is to force the listener to assume independent reference, given the speaker's assumptions in common with the listener. Presumably, such concerns are what Reinhart has in mind when she adds the proviso that one uses bound reference for coreference unless one has some reason to avoid bound reference. Something more specific and less attractive needs to be said for cases like (7) where the use of the pronoun *his* could lead the listener to suppose that bound reference was intended. Rather the speaker's strategy, if s/he is to be explicit, must be that one must use bound reference for coreference unless one wants to be sure the listener does not mistake independent coreference for bound reference when one intends to communicate independent coreference. But what this comes down to, in effect, is that if a speaker intends to be explicit, that speaker must respect the listener's strategy—which is to assume that dependent reference is possible unless alerted otherwise (of course, Albert in our scenario does not care if he is understood). When alerted otherwise (by the use of a name in a position where it is c-commanded by its potential antecedent), the listener knows that the dependent interpretation is not possible.

Moreover, it is not always the case that an independent coreference reading requires special contextual cues where a dependent identity reading is otherwise possible, at least under certain assumptions about the provenance of strict readings. For example, consider (22), in which *him* could be coconstrued with *Jens* or not. If *him* is coconstrued with *Jens*, the proposals given so far do not appear to choose a dependent interpretation for *him*, since it is the more explicit coconstrual, rather than an independent coreferent one. Yet, as the two available interpretations for the ellipsis example show, there is no need to use a name in place of *him* to get the strict interpretation.

22a) *Jens* thinks that Martha loves *him*.
   b) *Jens* thinks that Martha loves *him* and Nils thinks so too.

The strict interpretation, where Nils thinks that Martha loves Jens, is not taken to be any more unexpected out of context than the sloppy one, where we understand that Nils thinks that Martha loves Nils. Here it is crucial for Reinhart's account that the use of a pronoun makes dependent reference *possible*, but the use of a pronoun must not exclude the possibility of a strict reading. In other words, Reinhart cannot conclude generally, along the lines of (17), that the availability of a dependent reading always excludes an independent coreferent one in the absence of strong contextual cues, or else the strict reading for cases like (22) would not be available; yet (17) is exactly what she relies on to derive the noncoreference effect for the principle-C-type cases.

Rather it appears that so-called independent coreferent interpretations are generally available where they are not excluded for some reason. In fact, if dependency does not require c-command, then the "independent coreferent" interpretation in question is merely one where the elided pronoun can be dependent on an antecedent in first conjunct (see 2.4). If we persist, however, in the assumption that strict readings are independent coreferent ones, then we would be forced to the messy conclusion that a pronoun c-commanded by its antecedent must permit the possibility of a dependent identity reading (as long as the principle-B effect is respected)—yet it must do so without excluding the possibility of a (neutral context) independent coreferent reading as well.

## 2.3 C-Command and Almost C-Command

In the last section I pointed out how Reinhart exploited the parallelism between Lasnik's principle, which operates on c-command, and the principle that regulates bound readings (15), which requires a quantifier to c-command the dependent pronoun. It is nonetheless well known that there are a significant set of exceptions to the c-command generalization about bound readings that are not matched by exceptions to the c-command generalization for Lasnik's principle (many of them pointed out in Reinhart 1983a, 1983b). Consider the following examples.[8]

23a) *John's* mother loves *him.*
 b) *Everyone's* mother loves *him.*
 c) **Everyone/*John* loves *him.*

24a) *John's* mother thinks *he/the bastard* is crazy.
 b) *Everyone's* mother thinks *he/the bastard* is crazy.
 c) *Everyone/John* thinks *he/*the bastard* is crazy.

25a) Someone in *Johnstown* loves *its* weather.
 b) Someone in *every city* loves *its* weather.
 c) The sound of *each man's* hammer resounded in *his* ears.
 d) The sound of *John Henry's* hammer resounded in *his* ears.

To put it more simply, dependent identity readings are possible in contexts where coreference with a name or definite description is not blocked, which is not predicted if the distribution of linguistically required noncoreference between names and pronouns is predicted solely by the possibility of a dependent reading. If this is true, then the environments where noncoreference is required must be a subset of those where dependency is otherwise possible, namely, the subset that includes only those instances where a quantified nominal as antecedent would c-command its dependent.

The cases in question appear to arise because quantifiers can take scope beyond their surface c-command domain. May (1977) proposes that such interpretations arise because quantifiers can move in covert syntax to positions where they c-command more at LF than they do in the apparent structure assigned to the surface string. The ambiguity of (26) arises, on this view, as a result of a variety of possible covert movements, yielding, for (26c), for example, a representation like (27) (with indices included for illustrative purposes).

26) Two teachers on every school board impressed three parents.
   a) 2*x*, *x* teachers (∀*y*, *y* a school board (3*z*, *z* parents (*x* on *y* impressed *z*)))
   b) ∀*y*, *y* a school board (2*x*, *x* teachers (3*z*, *z* parents (*x* on *y* impressed *z*)))
   c) 3*z*, *z* parents (∀*y*, *y* a school board (2*x*, *x* teachers (*x* on *y* impressed *z*)))

27) [three parents]$_i$ [$_{IP}$ [[every school board]$_j$ [two teachers on t$_j$ ]]$_k$ [$_{IP}$ t$_k$ impressed t $_i$]]

Although one interpretation of (26) permits *two teachers* to have wide scope, the most significant fact for our purposes is that *three parents* can interact scopally with *every school board*, even though *every school board* does not c-command *three parents*. This is evident for the interpretation of (26b), which is true where every school board is such that it has on it at least two teachers that impress at least three parents, as compared to (26c) which is true if there are three parents who, for each school board they meet, are impressed by two teachers on the board.

As Lasnik (1976) was the first to observe,[9] the restrictive conditions on dependent readings for quantifier-bound pronouns mirror the class of nonquantifier-dependent pronouns (sloppy readings) in ellipsis contexts, even with respect to the exceptions to c-command ("almost c-command," as Hornstein, 1995, 108, calls it), as Reinhart (1983a, 68) points out. (28e), for example, is not a possible interpretation of (28c), apparently for the same reason that (28b) does not permit *everyone's* to bind *his*.

28a) I told *Sam* about *his* mother and about *his* sister too.
   b) I told *his* mother about *Sam's/*everyone's* success.
   c) I told *his* mother about *Sam's* success and about Morris' success too
   d) I told *Sam's* mother about *Sam's* success and *Sam's* mother about Morris's success too
   e) I told *Sam's* mother about *Sam's* success and Morris's mother about Morris's success too.

Two rather different properties will have to be distinguished in such cases, namely, whether or not the pronoun can depend upon the position of its antecedent and whether or not the pronoun is in the scope of a quantifier.

If we are to assume, as I will not, that all dependency is based on c-command at LF, then we would be forced to say that LF-movement of the nonquantified elements in (28) is necessary to create a weak crossover environment such that the interpretation in (28e) fails for (28c), while still maintaining that LF-movement of *Sam* is not required for (28b) (in contrast to *everyone*). I am independently assuming that where a quantifier fails to take scope over a pronoun, it cannot bind the pronoun as a variable, even though a pronoun in the same position may be dependent on a nonquantificational antecedent (e.g., "*A man who knows *everyone* hates *him*"). However, contrary to appearances for (28b), what fails for all the unacceptable interpretations in (28c) is not the appropriate quantifier scope (as illustrated by the scopal possibilities in [26]); Rather it seems necessary to argue that coconstrual in (28b) arises from independent coreference, not dependency of the pronoun on *Sam*. The reading for (28c) represented in (28e) requires the dependent reading, not the coreferent one, and it is the dependent reading that fails (for reasons that are discussed in detail Safir 2004).

I also differ from Reinhart (1983a, 63–64, and references cited there) and from Lasnik (1989, 105) in my interpretation of the facts. Lasnik cites the following case, remarking that it "seems to lack a sloppy reading":

29) *Harry's* mother believes *he* is intelligent and Bill's mother does too.

Although these cases may require a little help (and their acceptability decreases with embedding of the name, as in the examples Reinhart cites), there are many cases that sound completely natural with a sloppy reading in the second conjunct copied from a first conjunct where the antecedent does not c-command the pronoun (see also Fiengo and May 1994, 108–109, and fn. 12).

30a) *Bill's* mother loves *him*, though I doubt John's mother does.
b) Al thinks *each boy's* mother will tell on *him*, and you can bet Sam's mother will.
c) *Bill's* mother will tell on *him* too, now that Sam's mother has.
d) *Everyone's* mother loves *him*.
Bill's mother loves him.
Sam's mother does . . . .

As Fiengo and May (F&M) point out, the sloppy reading can even succeed where no quantifier can scope out of a nominal. For example, they point out that the phrase *all of Jane's colleagues* does not permit a quantifier in the position of *Jane's*, yet they accept both strict and sloppy readings for (31) (from F&M, p. 109), as do I.

31) All of *Jane's* colleagues admire *her*, but none of Brenda's colleagues do.

I will assume henceforth that c-command is not crucial to license the dependency relation, although in these parallelism contexts a deeply embedded antecedent may render the dependent reading much less accessible, for reasons that are ill-understood. An extended argument that c-command is not a positive condition for licensing dependency is presented in Safir (2004) where the nature of weak crossover is discussed in detail, although I return to the role of c-command as a negative condition on dependencies in 2.4.

All that is significant for our immediate purposes is that where the domain of dependencies and the domain of surface c-command diverge, the complementary relation between principle-C effects and licensed dependency diverges. It is, of course, possible to add strict c-command into the pragmatic strategy in (21) to recapture the principle-C effects, but besides the fact that it would undercut the explanatory force of the pragmatic account, we must ask if it is ever necessary for the pragmatics to refer to properties of syntactic structure, rather than just to the output of semantic interpretations derived from the formal trees. I return to this question in sections 2.4 and 2.5. However, the relationship between the dependency relation and the noncoreference effect does not have to be abandoned completely. For now we can make just the following, relatively neutral observation: Principle-C effects arise for a name or definite description used in syntactic contexts where dependency relation regulated by strict c-command would have succeeded if we had instead chosen a pronoun—a position strongly reminiscent of the G&R approach described in 1.3.[10]

## 2.4 Representing Anaphoric Relations

Up to this point I have yet to discuss how relations of coconstrual should be notated, except in my discussion of the syntactic consequences of the LGB theory of indexing for binding. Otherwise, I have largely avoided the standard descriptive practice in generative grammar of marking coconstrual relations with indices, choosing instead to mark these relations with italics, except where relations between traces and moved antecedents are involved. I have done so in order to put off discussion until now of exactly how indices should be construed, if indeed they are theoretical entities at all, especially in light of Chomsky's (1995b) proposal to eliminate them from the theory based on his theory of inclusiveness (see 2.4.1).

The use of indices as theoretical entities seems to have emerged as various identity statements were required by early transformational formulations (see Safir, 1985, 14–16, for discussion). The earliest account of the controlled PRO relation, Equi-NP deletion, for example, was formulated as a rule that deletes an identical NP in infinitive contexts. An "identical NP" was not simply to be understood as one identical in phonetic form, but one that referred to the same entity (see, e.g., Chomsky, 1965, 145–146, on reflexivization). The emergence of movement that leaves a trace and controlled PRO relations required the existence of empty categories that are identified by their relation with their overt antecedents, but even at this point, the identity statement did not necessarily require an index to permit the relation to be expressed.

The apparent need for indices arose only when coreference relations between two NPs, A and B, have to be preserved when A and B are related to C. Recall that one of the problems Lasnik's system was designed to overcome is the transitivity problem illustrated in (4), which I illustrate again in (32).

32) *The woman *he* loved told *him* that *John* was a jerk.

The problem here is that it is not enough to say that *him* and *John* fail to be marked as coreferent, since it is always possible that although they are not marked coreferent with each other, they could both be marked coreferent with *he*, and then *him* and *John* would be coreferent by transitivity. Rather it must be the case that *him* and *John* are marked as noncoreferent in a fashion that does not permit mutual identification with a third term. This may be executed by assuming that *him* and *John*, if they are noncoreferent, must be marked with different indices. Then *he* can be coreferent with either *him* or *John*, but not both, since it can only bear the index of one of the two.

Lasnik (1981) assumed that the following three coconstrual relations had to be captured:

33a) coindexed/coreferent and completely overlapping in reference
  b) contraindexed/disjoint in reference
  c) not coindexed/free in reference.

Coindexation was presumed to be necessary to achieve bound readings and reflexive readings, contraindexing is necessary for the effects associated with principles B and C, and noncoindexation, the third relation, is, in effect, the freedom to be coreferent with anything.

The third relation applies to cases like (34).

34) *John's* mother loves *John*.

Where there is no c-command, it is possible that there is no coindexation between the two mentions of *John*, or else there is coindexation and coreference is enforced. If the two mentions of *John* receive different indices, it is always possible that the two *John*s could happen to corefer, since there is nothing that says two different indices could happen to refer to the same individual, other things being equal.

It is the possibility of independent coreference permitted by (33c) that appears to require the existence of (33b), in that accidental coreference has to be controlled if the noncoreference effect is to be upheld. Lasnik (1981) points out that Chomsky's (1980) indexing schema in "On Binding" (OB) is superior to that of LGB in this regard. The OB schema allowed any given nominal to have a referential index unique to it and a set of anaphoric indices that could express noncoreference with however many nominals an element is c-commanded by. The OB schema effectively allows for all three relations, for example, *x* shares that anaphoric index of its potential antecedent, indicating noncoreference with however many c-commanders; *x* fails to include an anaphoric index corresponding to its antecedent, which means elements are free to corefer; and *x* fails to have anaphoric indices altogether but shares the referential index of its antecedent, which is how anaphors and traces are handled. Rules of opacity (the old tensed-S condition and Specified Subject Condition of the Extended Standard Theory) regulate whether or not the antecedent is close enough to share a referential index (anaphors) or far enough away to permit an anaphoric index to be deleted (from the set of anaphoric indices a pronoun must be disjoint from). For our purposes, all that is important is that the output of the system permits the representations in (35).

35a) John/he$_{\{i,0\}}$ says Bill$_{\{j,\{i\}\}}$ loves John$_{\{k,\{i,j\}\}}$
  b) John/he$_{\{i,0\}}$ says Bill$_{\{j,\{i\}\}}$ loves him$_{\{k,\{j\}\}}$
  c) [John's/his$_{\{h,0\}}$ father]$_{\{i,0\}}$ says Bill$_{\{j,\{i\}\}}$ loves John$_{\{k,\{i,j\}\}}$
  d) John/he$_{\{i,0\}}$ loves himself$_{\{i,0\}}$

In (35a), the second *John* has a distinct referential index from the first, but it also has the index of the first *John/he* (and the index of *Bill*) in its set of anaphoric indices, indicating that the second *John* is noncoreferent with both the first *John* and with *Bill*. The opacity conditions permit the pronoun *him* in (35b) to delete all anaphoric indices that are not too close, so *him* is free to refer to *John* or not, but it cannot corefer with *Bill*. Where the potential antecedent does not c-command, its indices are not included in the anaphoric set, as in (35c), where the second *John* is free to corefer with the first *John* or not. Finally, (35d) requires *himself* to be anteceded by *John/he*, since the anaphor is not marked disjoint from anything and does not have an independent referential index (see Lasnik 1989, 133, fn. 4).

In LGB, by contrast, indices for each nominal are unique, which only indicates whether forms are coindexed or not, and the indices are assigned to NPs randomly (except in the case of movement). The outputs are checked at S-structure by the BT, which, where Principle C applies, requires that a name must be free. To be free in the LGB system is merely not to be c-commanded by any NP with the same index, but it does not preclude coreference of NPs with different indices. Thus LGB excludes (36a), but not (36b).

36a) *He/John$_i$ says Mary loves John$_i$
b) He/John$_i$ says Mary loves John$_j$

Lasnik concludes that the LGB system is inferior on this account, in effect arguing that a three-valued indexing system, one that keeps track of noncoreference relations, is necessary to capture the full range of empirically attested relations.

These conclusions concerning a three-valued indexing system have a number of implications for the account of dependency given in 2.1 and 2.2. First, recall that Evans' objection to representing coreference as part of grammar would mean that the coreference relation could not be marked by indices that are any more than descriptive accounts of coconstruals. If this is true, then the binding principles, where they apply, apply to dependencies, however they are represented, and not to coreference. The connection between blocked dependency and noncoreference then needs to be made, in the case of Reinhart's approach, by a pragmatic principle that prefers bound reference to represent coreference where bound reference is possible. Elements not related by bound reference are independent.

Second, the dependency relation, which Evans and Reinhart both would represent in grammar, is asymmetric, whereas indices are symmetric—no property of simplex indices indicates that of two or more coindexed elements, one has primacy over the other in any way. Additional statements have to be made about indices to allow them to represent dependencies.

Since what appears to be crucial, both for determining noncoreference as well as the absence of dependency, is the possibility of whether or not one form may depend on another, it is reasonable to start with the least expressive notation for the dependency relation and then see what else is necessary. Reasoning along these lines, Higginbotham (1983, 1985) introduces arrows that connect dependents with their antecedents. I will meet the orthographic challenge by indicating this relationship as in (37), where the anchor "├" represents the antecedent on which the term marked with the hook "┘" depends.

37) *Everyone* loves *his* mother.

This notation is inherently asymmetric and so seems well suited to the task. One of the advantages of representing dependencies in this way is that it is now possible to represent split antecedency without the complication of "cumulative indices," which appears to be required in index notation. Compare (38a) with (38b).

38a) Every woman$_i$ told [her$_i$ husband]$_j$ that they$_{i+j}$ should flee.
 b) Every woman told [her husband] that they should flee.

Since the value of *they* is dependent on the value of the quantified *every woman*, there is no question of representing just coreference here. However, under the construal where the value for *they* consists of varying sets of woman + husband, the indexing system of LGB could not represent the relation with a single index, since a single index would be neither "i" nor "j" singly, and the index of *they* could not be "k" or else binding would fail altogether.

It is, of course, possible to represent the relevant relations in (38) in the OB indexing system, but for reasons I explore at greater length in Safir (2004), there are a number of reasons to abandon indices in favor of the arrow notation, and even the arrow notation may not be a device crucial to formal syntax (as long as dependency relations can be expressed). From this point, I will simply assume that the arrow notation is sufficient to represent what is crucial for the representation of dependent identity relations, which are the sorts of relations my theory addresses.

I further assume, along with Higginbotham (1983, 402; see also Evans 1980, 355) and Williams (1997), that dependence of a pronoun on an antecedent that does not c-command it is generally possible, as long as the dependent term does not c-command its antecedent:[11]

39) If X c-commands Y, then Y is not an antecedent of X.

This ban, which I will henceforth call the Independence Principle, is defended at length in Safir (2004), which interested readers can consult, but before I assume the Independence Principle, it is perhaps useful to present one advantage of freeing the dependency relation from c-command licensing (as opposed to a c-command restriction like [39]), one which also bears on the representation of coconstrual.

One purported justification for the use of indices is that we need a device to verify in parallelism between conjuncts and so forth, where interpretations are enforced that exclude other possible interpretations, particularly but not exclusively in contexts of ellipsis. In order to limit the scope of our inquiry, let us set aside the structural and semantic conditions (other than those that involve coconstrual) that must be met in order to determine whether parallelism holds in a given context and just assume that we know it when we see it (see F&M for a detailed discussion of structural isomorphism that they argue must hold in such contexts and Merchant, 2001, for arguments that the semantic conditions are paramount). Thus narrowed, the question is simply this: Do we need indices to capture the fact that strict and sloppy readings in (41a, b) are the only ones possible for (40)?

40) John said he was late before Bill did.

41a) *John* said *he* was late before ***Bill*** [said ***he*** was late]
b) *John* said *he* was late before Bill [said *he* was late]
c) **John* said *he* was late before Bill [said he was late]

Some positive requirement must ensure that *he* in the second conjunct must refer to *John* or *Bill* and not to some third party, as in (41c), where there is no coconstrual with *John* or *Bill*.

It is clear that no feature-based account, where a coincidence of features accounts for coconstrual, can compensate for the absence of the third party reading. Consider (42), a variant of a type of example brought into linguistic discussion by Lakoff (1968, 1972; and a variety to which I will return in 4.2.2, but see also Safir in preparation).

42a) Speaker A: If I were you, I would hate myself.
Speaker B: Alas, I do.
b) Speaker A: If I were you, I would hate me.
Speaker B: Alas, I do.

While most informants presume a sloppy interpretation is required for (42a), every speaker requires a strict interpretation for (42b). Although the sloppy interpretation does not preserve the first person reference, it could be argued that it preserves the first person features, which means that the SELF-form must be identified with the speaker of the sentence, speaker B in (42a). However, in (42b) it is the referent, not the form that is preserved in the parallel structure of ellipsis, since the form that would pick out speaker A would presumably be *you*, and incidentally, not a third party. Thus whatever is parallel in parallel structures can include parallelism of reference *in spite* of nonmatching features, and in this case, the strict reading is not just an option but a requirement.

However, given a single assumption about dependency arrows implicit in what has been said already, no indices need to be employed to account for the range of possible coconstrual interpretations in (41). Under the dependency account of coconstrual, the representation for the first conjunct is the same for both interpretations of the second conjunct, but all that differs is whether the elided pronoun depends directly on the corresponding one in the first conjunct, which yields the strict interpretations, as in (43a), or if the dependency arrow as a whole is copied, in which case we get the sloppy reading, as illustrated in (43b).

43a) *Mara* believes Sean loves *her* and Sheila believes Sean loves *her*.

b) *Mara* believes Sean loves *her* and **Sheila** believes Sean loves **her**.

The representation in (43a) is possible in my account because it is not necessary for the dependent form to be c-commanded by its antecedent; hence the elided pronoun can depend directly on a form in the first conjunct. If parallelism requires copying of the dependency or direct dependency on the structurally corresponding antecedent in the first conjunct, then the third-party interpretation cannot arise under the dependency arrow account any more than it could where an index is copied. Thus, neither parallelism nor obviation provides motivation for indices in syntactic representation (but see 4.2.2, 4.3.4 and Safir, 2004, for further discussion).

However, failure of a dependency relation is not necessarily failure of coreference, and for principle-B and principle-C effects, the Independence Principle in (39) is not enough. Higginbotham (1985) points out, "If two positions are marked as obviative, then neither can serve as the antecedent of the other. The general notion of obviativity must, however, be stronger than this . . . " (575). He then proposes (44).

44) If X and Y are obviative, then they cannot be determined by the structure in which they occur to share a value.

This is necessary within the dependency-arrow account to avoid permitting examples like (45a, b) (which are illustrations of Lasnik's transitivity problem), where two elements that must not be coconstrued are neither one dependent on the other, but are both dependent on a third term.

45a) *John* said *he* saw *him.*

b) *John's* mother said *he* saw *him.*

Both (45a, b) are ruled out because *he* and *him* would share a value. The version of Principle B given in (46) (Higginbotham 1985, 572) would determine that *he* and *him* must be obviative, since *him* is not allowed to depend on *he* (where Higginbotham uses the term *linked* to mean connected by the hook end of a dependency arrow).[12]

46a) An anaphor is locally linked.
b) A pronominal is locally obviative.
c) An R-expression is obviative.

Crucially, however, Higginbotham adds, "Obviativity universally applies only with respect to c-commanding potential antecedents," which reintroduces this essential portion of binding, though it replaces indices with dependency arrows.

To reiterate, a key feature of this obviation account that puts it in the same class as that of Evans (1980) and Reinhart (1983) is that its BT is stated on the dependency relation, not on a coreference–covaluation relation, but here the dependency relation is represented by arrows, which are asymmetric, not by indices, which are symmetric. Like the LGB BT, c-command is crucial for antecedency of syntactic anaphors (but unlike Reinhart, 1983, not for dependency generally) and for obviation. A single principle, namely (44), maps obviation arising from both Principle B and Principle C into the noncoreference effect, although Higginbotham continues to treat principles B and C as independent principles.

### *2.4.1 Inclusiveness*

Chomsky (1995b) suggests different grounds for dispensing with indices in syntactic theory. He suggests that the class of possible linguistic representations is limited by his principle of "inclusiveness": "Given the numeration N, $C_{HI}$ [the computational system of human language] computes until it forms a derivation that converges at PF and LF with the pair ($\pi$, $\lambda$), after reducing N to zero (if it does). A 'perfect language' should meet the condition of inclusiveness: any structure formed by the computation (in particular, $\pi$ and $\lambda$) is constituted of elements already present in the lexical items selected for N; no new objects are added in the course of computation apart from rearrangements of lexical properties (in particular, no indices . . . ) . . . " (p.228). To understand the import of this statement, it is necessary to present some minimalist assumptions about the nature of derivations. As mentioned in chapter 1, a key tenet of the minimalist program is that there is no linguistically significant level of S-structure or D-structure where any condition holds. Derivations that build phrase markers are built as follows. A selection operation selects every element that will be used in the derivation from the lexicon. Each form selected comes with an index that indicates the order in which exemplars of that form are selected from the lexicon, so that for a sentence like (47b), there will be two instances of the form *the*, marked, as in the numeration for (47b) in (47a). A rule of combination, merge (variously formulated in the literature), will form a phrase marker by combining two forms or by combining a form with an already formed phrase marker until every element in the numeration is exhausted.

47a) $the_1$, $the_2$, $man_3$, $woman_4$, $see_5$, $past_6$
  b) $The_1$ $man_3$ $see_5$+$past_6$ $the_2$ $woman_4$.

These indices are not referential indices in any sense. They simply keep track of instances of a given form drawn from the lexicon. The example in (48), with its accompanying numeration, shows that the indices of the subject and object do not match, and the indices of the subject are in no way cumulative, yet examples like these are cases where an anaphor is bound in the traditional sense.

48a) $himself_1$, $man_2$, $the_3$, $past_4$, $criticize_5$
  b) $The_3$ $man_2$ $criticize_5$+$past_4$ $himself_1$

Numeration indices are the result of a process of selection from the lexicon; hence they are legitimate by the principle of inclusiveness, unlike referential indices, which represent relations between constituents that require them to have matching values outside of the formal system of phrasemarkers (i.e., to have semantic–referential values)

Let us set aside, for a moment, the question of whether a system conditioned by inclusiveness has sufficient expressive power to capture the range of relationships that indices and arrows have otherwise been employed to capture. Instead we may just consider how this account undercuts one of the justifications that has been marshaled to defend the use of indices as markers of referential value. If indices are a necessary part of movement operations, as they have long been assumed to be, then they are already in the theory and available to represent other sorts of coreference relations. However, in the minimalist program, movement is not an operation that leaves an empty category (or at least not all the time, depending on the theoretical implementation, see Hornstein, 1995; and Safir, 1999, 2004) for some discussion), but rather it leaves a copy of the moved constituent with all of its formatives and, of course, all of the same numeration indices.

49a) $\text{the}_1$, $\text{the}_2$, $\text{of}_3$, $\text{men}_4$, $\text{men}_5$, $\text{speak}_6$, $\text{to}_7$, $\text{will}_8$, $\text{old}_9$, $\text{young}_{10}$, $\text{which}_{11}$
  b) $\text{Which}_{11}$ $\text{of}_3$ $\text{the}_1$ $\text{old}_9$ $\text{men}_4$ $\text{will}_8$ $\text{the}_2$ $\text{young}_{10}$ $\text{men}_5$ $\text{will}_8$ $\text{speak}_6$ $\text{to}_7$ $\text{which}_{11}$ $\text{of}_3$ $\text{the}_1$ $\text{old}_9$ $\text{men}_4$
  c) Which of the old men will the young men speak to?

Principles of PF will determine which of the copies are pronounced, but the point of interest for our discussion is that a trace is now identifiable as the c-commanded member of a pair of constituents such that the constituents dominate identical strings of formatives (with identical structures). If traces can be identified as such without appeal to indices that mark identical semantic–referential value, then indices that mark such relations are not justified by the existence of antecedent–trace relations. This means that indices are not available independently and cannot therefore be employed for coreference relations or dependency relations without cost.[13]

Given that the inclusiveness condition prevents properties that are not lexical from being added to the representation, dependency arrows are excluded from syntactic representations for exactly the same reason that referential indices are. There are two ways to respond to this conclusion.

First, one might conclude that dependency relations are not in syntactic representations, but only in semantic representations. As relations that are functionally necessary for understanding, their existence is a bare output condition, which any computational solution to the relation of form and meaning must permit. The use of arrows, then, is merely descriptive notation, but not part of syntactic representation itself. This view might be consistent with the assumption that the presence of a dependency relation is never necessary to license a syntactic form (see the discussion of c-antecedency for anaphors in 4.1), though syntactic relations can block dependency relations (as in the case of the Independence Principle).

Suppose, however, that it turns out to be necessary to track either dependency relations or blocked dependency relations in the course of a derivation. In that case, a second approach to the challenge of inclusiveness is to weaken it so as to permit arrows, but not symmetric indices. Suppose inclusiveness is considered more as a ban on new properties assigned to unique elements in the derivation rather than a ban on new relations. An index is a property assigned to a head or phrase that could happen to be the same index as that of some other head or phrase, in which case an unwanted (accidental) coincidence of indices could create a commitment to covalued interpretation that is reminiscent of features that happen to match. By contrast, arrows are inherently relational: One end of an arrow has no meaning; hence it could not accidentally match some other end of an arrow in any meaningful way (as Higginbotham pointed out when he invented them). Obviative pairs are symmetric, but they too are relational by definition.

I shall remain neutral between these two approaches for this essay, although nothing in this essay would appear to require the second approach. The matter is taken up in Safir (2004).

### *2.4.2 Disjoint Reference?*

Recall now that Lasnik's original noncoreference condition required disjoint reference for an r-expression with respect to any c-commanding term, which means that the set denoted by a c-commanded r-expression cannot overlap with the set denoted by any of its c-commanders. I illustrated this with (5a), repeated below.

5a) ****They*** hate the man who forced **Tom** to hit *Harry.*

If *they* is indexed only to represent the group, then it will not have the same index of either *Tom* or *Harry,* and both *Tom* and *Harry* are free, hence not susceptible to Principle C (a partially acceptable reading for [5a] for this speaker). Only if *they* has a cumulative index, such that two of its indices match those of *Tom* and *Harry*, is the sentence excluded. In a theory with obviation stated as in (44), it is possible to mark *Tom* and *Harry* as obviative with *they* because they cannot share a value with *they*, presumably not even any subset of the values that *they* cumulatively has. There is no necessary role for indices in such an account.

However, it is not clear (especially for those who share my judgment of [5a]) that disjoint reference is the right characterization of the force of the noncoreference effect.[14] Some examples do not seem amenable to an extensional account of the sort Lasnik proposes, and F&M have gone further to claim that there "need not be any grammatical notion of overlap in reference" (p. 44). The examples in (50) are adaptations from those in Lasnik (1989, 102; but see also Chomsky 1973, 241).

50a) The officers expected the soldiers to leave.
b) The officers persuaded the soldiers to leave.
c) The officers thought that the soldiers should leave.
d) The officers demanded that the soldiers leave.

Lasnik judged (50a) to be starred although he notes that the judgment is delicate. F&M judge overlap possible in (50a) and (50c) but not in (50b) and (50d) and claim that these distinctions are not about binding theory. I find even (50d) acceptable, under an interpretation where the officers are among the soldiers, perhaps all of them as prisoners of war, but the officers are speaking for all the men when they demand freedom for all the men (especially with "be allowed to leave"). For (50b), by contrast, there is a two-way conversation, presumably involving individuals who are not self-persuading.

There are other cases where an overlap of sets is acceptable. In (51a, b), one individual is distinguished from the set to represent the others, whereas in (51c, d) the expression *one of them* is presumably not a pronoun (though *them* is), but a description of some sort.[15]

51a) ?John, Bill, and Harry thought that John would be their best representative.
  b) The three men thought that John (and Bill) would be their best representative(s).
  c) John, Bill, and Harry thought that one of them would be a good representative.
  d) The three men thought that one of them would be a good representative.

It seems where a subset is appropriately distinguished in some way from the full set, the overlap is fairly natural.

Higginbotham's (1992) distinction between "discriminating" and anaphoric uses of demonstrative terms may be useful here. The discriminating use in Higginbotham's sense "is one that distinguishes among several candidates a particular object as the one that one is talking about" (1992, 46). But he appears to restrict this usage to demonstratives accompanied by an ostensive indication, for example, *This chicken*, uttered by John as he points to the chicken he means to refer to, and occasional anaphoric uses of demonstratives, such as those in (52) (judgments mine).[16]

52a) ?*The typical narcissist* believes that *only that narcissist* admires *his* achievements adequately.
  b) ??*The typical narcissist* believes that *only that narcissist* admires *that narcissist's* achievements adequately.
  c) ?**Every boy* thinks that *that boy* should not be singled out.

I find all of these examples somewhat marginal, perhaps because each c-commanded demonstrative nominal requires emphatic stress, but insofar as these are possible, the discrimination is between the antecedent and any member of a contrast set. The discriminating use appears more congenial to the partitive examples in (51c, d) and those in (53) below, which don't seem to require any special stress.

53a) (*The*) *Young democrats* in that faction will tell you that one of *them* will be leading the country one day.
  b) (*The*) *Young democrats* in that faction insist that the oldest of *them* would make a good leader.

Similarly it is possible for a singular antecedent to overlap in reference with a c-commanded definite description, as in (54).

54a) *The squad leader/G.I. Joe* revealed that *his squad* would lead the charge.
  b) *The general* said that *the officers* would receive special treatment if surrender should be necessary.

These cases would seem to suggest that disjoint reference as a prohibition is too strong. However there is a noncoreference effect, and it appears to apply fairly consistently, at least between noncoarguments (on some special properties of coargument noncoreference; see 3.3.1), but only where the c-commanded r-expression overlaps in reference exactly with that of a c-commanding form. All of the following cases seem more straightforwardly excluded.

55a) **John, Bill, and Harry* thought that *John, Bill, and Harry* would be their best representatives.
  b) **John, Bill, and Harry* thought that *the three men* would be their best representatives.
  c) **The three men* thought that *the three men* would be their best representatives.
  d) **The three men* thought that *John, Bill, and Harry* would be their best representatives.

Moreover, all of the examples in (50) are unacceptable if the soldiers include all and only the officers.

We can summarize our results so far in (56).

56a) Incomplete overlap between a plural definite c-commander and a plural definite c-commandee is acceptable.
  b) Overlap between plural antecedent and a partitive c-commandee is acceptable.
  c) Overlap between c-commanding sets of proper names and subsets of those proper names is sometimes acceptable.
  d) Overlap between singular antecedents and plural definite descriptions is acceptable.
  e) Complete overlap between definite descriptions and contrastively stressed c-commanded definite descriptions appears possible.
  f) Complete overlap between c-commanding set of proper names and a c-commanded set of proper names is unacceptable.

Moreover, we have seen that there appears to be a discrimination effect along the lines discussed by Higginbotham for demonstratives, such that in every case where discrimination is not part of the meaning of the expression (e.g., in a partitive), some sort of distinction between subsets is highlighted (representatives selected from a group), or some contrast set is implied (as in the case of contrastively stressed, c-commanded r-expressions). Moreover, incomplete overlap cases do not require any extra stress; extra stress is only required for cases where overlap is complete, and some sort of discrimination other than set membership contrasts must be achieved.

If we concur with F&M that incomplete overlap between a c-commander and an r-expression c-commandee is not regulated by formal grammar, this set of distinctions would go unexplained. An alternative approach is presented in 2.5.

However, for the immediate concern of this section, the question is whether or not we need indices to represent relations of noncoreference. It appears that it is not necessary to use indices to capture disjoint reference, and indeed there are some awkward issues that arise if indices are employed, such as assuming that plurals have cumulative indices that may or may not match with the cumulative indices of c-commanders or c-commandees. On the other hand, it is not even clear that incomplete overlap of reference should, in fact, be excluded as a matter of formal grammar, and if not, there is no argument for or against the use of indices to represent noncoreference.[17]

### *2.4.3 Some Conclusions About the Representation of Coconstrual*

We have now traced some of the differences between coreference and dependence, and we have examined whether or not it is necessary to employ indices or arrows to represent dependency and/or coreference. Neither Lasnik's transitive obviations, nor disjoint reference, nor parallelism requires indices, as opposed to the strictly relational representation of dependency and, perhaps outside of syntax, the obviative pair relation.

Insofar as failure of dependency is crucial to what is captured by the BT generalizations, every potentially successful theory must express failure of dependency, but all such theories then require an account of the relationship between failed dependency and noncoreference. For both Higginbotham (1983, 1985) and F&M, the failure of dependency does not necessarily result in obviation, especially where the antecedent does not c-command. Higginbotham (1985), F&M, and Williams (1997) treat dependency relations as much more general and dispense with a positive c-command requirement for dependency altogether (a position I agree with here), in contrast to Reinhart (1983).[18] However, when c-command holds and dependency fails (e.g., due to Principle B or C), Higginbotham assigns obviation relations independently from the failure of dependent interpretation, while F&M bar covaluation as well as dependency. As pointed out in Safir (2004), however, F&M's theory predicts that there are anaphors that are exclusively covaluations, which does not appear defensible. Although my account of obviation has more in common with that of Higginbotham, I differ from his account in the next section where I argue that the relationship between failure of dependency under c-command and noncoreference is mediated by a principled competition of forms rather than principles B and C.

## 2.5 Obviated Dependency, Noncoreference, and the Competition of Forms

Recall that Reinhart (1983) and subsequently G&R require that if a variable (pronominal) is not employed where it could be, then the use of a name must mean that the speaker has some reason to avoid expressing coconstrual with bound reference. However, the point should be put more strongly.

57) If the dependent interpretation is not syntactically possible, then it is extremely difficult to accommodate a dependent interpretation.

From Evans' examples and those that others have raised, we have seen that it is possible to accommodate a coreferent interpretation, but recovering a bound interpretation from sentences like (58a, b) is barely possible, if possible at all.

58a) Every man named John thinks that John should be elected.
b) Every man named John painted John's wastebasket.
c) Every man named John raised John's hand.

Where the pronoun is available for dependent (bound) interpretation here (in place of the second mention of *John*), one must employ it to achieve the bound reading. Where *John* is used in place of the pronoun, it is taken to mean that "someone named John" should be elected, but it does not mean that every *x* such that *x* is named John thinks that *x* should be elected. Even (58c), which may be uttered in a situation where each man performs the gesture of raising his hand, is not really a bound interpretation, even though every individual is raising his hand, and since every individual in this case is named "John," it follows that the hand each man raises is a hand belonging to a man named John. What is peculiar about the interpretation of (58c) is that the context requires us to understand as if by accident that each hand corresponds to the individual who raises it. The value for *John's hand* cannot really be said to be dependent on *every man named John*; rather, the nature of the predicate describing the gesture requires this matching. Recall that names and epithets are in the same boat for such phenomena, even though epithets can be used as bound variables, as Lasnik pointed out.

59a) *Every bastard's* mother thinks *the bastard* is crazy.
b) **Every bastard* thinks *the bastard* is crazy.

60a) **Every bastard* raised *the bastard's* hand.
b) Every bastard raised a bastard's hand .

In (59a), just a slight modification of (24b), the bound variable interpretation succeeds because the quantified expression does not c-command it from an A-position, in contrast to (59b). (60a) shows, just as in (59b), that *the bastard* does not permit a bound reading. In the case of (60a, b) it is even more clear, since the gestural reading that expresses the sort of accidental correlation of hands and bastards is only achieved with the use of the indefinite, *a bastard's hand.*

The same point would appear to extend to Principle B phenomena, as in (61).

61a) John doesn't love just anyone. *John* just loves *HIMSELF/HIM/*him.*
b) It's not true that everyone loves his neighbor. All we can be sure of is that *everyone* loves *HIMSELF/*HIM/*him.*

While contrastive stress (marked by words in upper case letters) permits a bound reading when a SELF form is used in both (61a, b), stressing *him* only succeeds for (61a), where a coreferent reading is possible. However, when the antecedent is quantified, contrastive stress still does not permit a dependent reading.

The point of these examples is that it is not enough to say that avoiding the use of the bound form means that coreference, if possible, is intended to be circumspect. A stronger statement is required, but to make it, we have to factor out exactly how the dependency relation has failed. This may be achieved by (62).

62) Form to Interpretation Principle (provisional): If *x* c-commands *y*, and *z* is not the most dependent form available in position *y* with respect to *x*, then *y* cannot be directly dependent on *x*.

For present purposes, we only need know that pronouns are more dependent forms than epithets or proper names and that SELF forms in English are more dependent than simple pronouns. It would appear that FTIP in (62) is a consequence of formal grammar that renders certain dependent readings impossible. In the next chapter, this principle will be refined and explored in detail, including assumptions about which forms are more dependent than others and what renders a form "available."

However, FTIP still fails to predict that if the most dependent form is not used, then coreference is in any way affected, since FTIP only restricts dependent reference. There is no logical inference that the failure of a dependent reading requires the failure of a coreferent one. For this result we must rely on a descendant of G&R's Rule I, which I express informally as (63).

63) If *x* c-commands *y* and *y* is not the most dependent form available, then coreference between *x* and *y* is not expected.

Insofar as (63), like FTIP, also incorporates c-command, it would appear that (63) should also be a principle of formal grammar, and, moreover, one that is suspiciously similar to FTIP. It is possible, however, to factor out c-command from (63) if the interpretation of blocked dependence is considered carefully. Suppose we restate (63) as (64).

64) Pragmatic Obviation: If FTIP does not permit *y* to be interpreted as dependent on *x*, then *x* and *y* form an obviative pair.

The trick will be to ensure that the output of FTIP (62) does not supply to Pragmatic Obviation (64) a configuration; rather, it supplies a statement about the possible dependency relation between two nominals. If such a move is possible, it will serve to define the border between syntactic and pragmatic contributions to interpretation in a much more explicit and articulated way. In this account, the pragmatic principle in (64) does not refer to structures at all, but only to whether or not the output of syntax has marked two nominals (in relation to each other) in the relevant way. This is consistent with the alternative to indices discussed in 2.4.1, where it was pointed out that if indices and dependency arrows are not in the theory, what crucially must be maintained to account for BT effects is a record of obviation relations between nominal constituents, which is in any case necessary for record keeping in a discourse.[19]

In the FTIP account, then, failure to pick the most dependent form, given the condition of c-command, triggers Pragmatic Obviation. The interaction of these two principles derives the effects previously attributed to principles B and C of the BT or G&R's Rule I (which was for Principle C effects only) in a unified manner.

As noted earlier in the discussion of listener strategies, Pragmatic Obviation can be overcome where what is normally unexpected is taken to be expected. We have seen that some notion of discrimination may play a role in overcoming expectations of noncoreference for an obviative pair, and instantiation contexts are another loosely related set of cases where coreference is accommodated. Formatives like *even* have exactly the function of adjusting expectations, suggesting that the least likely candidate on a given scale is nonetheless the one that is salient. In this context, *even John* in (65a) indicates that John, though one would not expect him to be in this set, is also one of the individuals who has the property of considering John crazy, while (65b) also permits a dependent (bound) interpretation whereby John is one of the *x*s who consider *x* crazy.

65a) *Even John* says that *John* is crazy
b) *Even John* says that *he* is crazy

It is extremely important to note, however, that *a dependent interpretation for (65a) cannot be accommodated*, as can be illustrated in ellipsis contexts.

66) Almost every doctor is willing to say that John and Bill are crazy.
a) *Even John* says that *John* is crazy, and more surprising still, even Bill does.
b) *Even John* says that *he* is crazy, and more surprising still, even Bill does.

While (66b) permits a reading where each of the men thinks about himself that he is crazy, (66a) can *only* mean that even Bill thinks that John is crazy, not that Bill thinks that Bill is crazy. The fact that the first conjunct in (66a) permits coreference (however clumsily) but blocks the dependent reading follows from the failure to employ the most dependent form available in the first conjunct of (66a) (*John* is used instead of *he*); hence there can be no dependency relation between the subordinate *John* and the higher *John;* hence there is no dependency relation that could be copied in ellipsis. In (66b), by contrast, the dependent interpretation can be reconstructed because the first conjunct employs the most dependent form.

The significance of cases like (66a) is highlighted by the fact that Principle C effects are not normally preserved in ellipsis contexts, as illustrated in (67).

67) Alex is more certain that Lara loves Morgan than Morgan is.

The elided portion, *certain that Lara loves Morgan*, would be c-commanded by *Morgan,* and yet no obviation is observed. This is because the object of *loves* does not have to be evaluated as a name in the elision site of the second clause, if we adopt the "vehicle change" account of F&M. F&M propose that names in elided (unpronounced) constituents may be replaced with pronouns for the purposes of interpretation at LF (on vehicle change, see 4.3.4 and, for extensive discussion, Safir 2004). If so, the reconstructed elision is *certain that Lara loves him*, and FTIP will not induce obviation between *him* and *Morgan* since *him* is the most dependent form available in that environment (even though *him* does not depend on the subject *Morgan* in the second conjunct, but rather on object *Morgan* in the first).

It is significant that the use of the most dependent form does not *require* a dependent reading (unless the form in question inherently does). In an example like (66b), either a sloppy or a strict reading is possible. Where a term is inherently dependent, such as a SELF form, it will be generally required that the term be interpreted as dependent. The absence of a nondependent reading (which, as we will see in chapter 4, requires more subtle distinctions), however, is not a consequence of FTIP, which only determines that a dependent reading is possible for the pronoun in (66b).

Now that I have presented the FTIP and Pragmatic Obviation, let us reconsider our conclusions about disjoint reference. The relevant effect emerges where FTIP says the form employed for the posited coconstrual relation is not the most dependent one, and Pragmatic Obviation designates the relation between these two arguments as obviative. We concluded in the last section that complete referential overlap, absent stress or a discriminating interpretation, is not permitted between what we now call an obviative pair. It may be that complete overlap between the c-commander and the r-expression is worse because a pronoun fully coconstrued with its antecedent is possible in the environment in question and could successfully represent the same *nondiscriminating* meaning. Consider (68).

68a) ?/??*John* says that *John* and Mary make a great team.
b)**John* says that *John* and Mary play on the same team.

While (68b) is unacceptable in the way noncoreference cases generally are, (68a) is noticeably better, though how much differs from speaker to speaker. The difference could be that "John" as free agent is distinguished from the John who is part of a tandem. A pronoun in place of *John* is perhaps preferred because it would fully overlap with *John* but is not quite required since the reading is discriminating (reconsider [5a] now in light of note 14 to this chapter). Merely sharing a property with Mary (i.e., not being "combined" with her), as in (68b), does not discriminate the first *John* from the second; hence the obviative effect remains in force. Thus in both (68a) and (68b) the second *John* could be replaced by a more dependent term, namely, a pronoun. In (68b), however, the FTIP induces a Pragmatic Obviation that is not mitigated by a discriminating interpretation.

The same factors figure in the interpretive possibilities for (69).

69) John says that the men will defeat the women.

Even if the listener knows for a fact that John is one of the men who will be on the team that he predicts will beat the women, (69) is acceptable, as we would expect given that discrimination is respected. Moreover, (69) is acceptable even if it is the case that John means that in each individual singles tennis match, including those in which he expects to play, the man involved will emerge victorious. There is no preference for a pronoun, even one such as *they* in (69), if the use of the nominal is discriminatory.

Perhaps one more example will help to clarify the intuition concerning when the competition of forms has the result of an unmitigated Pragmatic Obviation.

70a) Now that ***their*** parents are dead, ***they*** can admit that *John's* mother insulted **Mary's** father at ***their*** wedding.
 b) Now that *his* parents are dead, *he* can admit that *John's* mother insulted **Mary's** father at ***their*** wedding.

Since there is discrimination as to which of *they* is in the relevant parent–child relation, (70a) is a situation where the expectation of noncoreference is suspended; hence the competition between the pronoun form and the proper names employed does not have obviative force. By contrast, (70b) is correctly predicted to yield noncoreference between *John's* and *he*, since there is no discrimination between *he* and *John's*. Thus, once again, a more dependent form is available in both (70a) and (70b), namely, a pronoun, so FTIP induces Pragmatic Obviation to declare an obviative pair in both cases between the c-commanded name and the pronoun that c-commands it. Discrimination, however, overcomes obviation; hence (70a) is acceptable, and (70b) is not.

They key to the account just presented, apart from appeal to discrimination, is that the competition of forms is crucial to unraveling the class of permitted coconstruals. Arguments of this kind, that is to say, arguments about when competition of forms is or is not in force, as well as arguments concerning the reason the force of Pragmatic Obviation is or is not suspended, play a major role in the chapters that follow.

At this point, a brief comparison with the G&R theory is perhaps instructive. Even if we were to add discrimination to G&R's theory of Rule I so as to account for (66) and (68–70), their theory still faces the almost c-command problem and would still treat principles B and C as fundamentally different (which, as argued in the next chapter more fully, would be a mistake). Moreover, as demonstrated earlier, epithets are susceptible to principle-C-type effects, as first pointed out by Lasnik. This is conceptually costly for Rule I, since the appeal of the theory is that bound interpretations are preferred to those that are not, yet epithets permit bound variable interpretations and so should not be susceptible to principle-C effects under Rule I. Either it must be stipulated for Rule I that variables are limited to pronominals or reflexives, or else a prohibition similar to Principle C is required to distinguish epithets from pronouns, just as Principle A distinguishes anaphors from pronouns. In the theory proposed here (and made more precise in the next chapter), the reason epithets are not available for dependent interpretations when they are c-commanded is that a more dependent form, a pronoun, is available in the same structure.[20] To the FTIP, it does not matter that a name or definite description has more (or different) information than a pronoun, only that a nominal in the position of the potentially dependent element could have allowed for a form more dependent than a definite description. It is the same reasoning that requires, for examples like (50), that *the officers* and *the soldiers* cannot overlap in reference completely, since in that case, a more dependent form is available, namely, a pronoun, and Pragmatic Obviation induced by FTIP would not be mitigated.

G&R's account of dependency–obviation also differs from mine in a number of other respects. One is that I distinguish two principles that they treat as one. They say that if one does not use a potential bound variable in a syntactic position where a bound variable interpretation is possible, then one must not intend for there to be a bound interpretation. However, this mixes intentions and dependency, and as illustrated earlier, a blocked dependent identity interpretation is not calculated on the intentions of the speaker or the pragmatics of the situation; no amount of context provided by the speaker or accommodation on the part of the listener can retrieve the bound (dependent) interpretation. That is why it must be a principle of grammar that excludes the dependent interpretation, rather than a pragmatic inference, since pragmatic inferences can be accommodated, as they can be for coreference.

The further advantage of separating FTIP and Pragmatic Obviation is that it is now no longer necessary to assume that a rule with pragmatic force, such as Pragmatic Obviation, need ever refer to properties of syntactic structure (such as c-command). All that Pragmatic Obviation needs to know is that for any two nominals, perhaps distinguished only by their thematic assignment and/or the predicates they are selected by, FTIP has blocked a dependent interpretation of one of them on the other.[21] Pragmatic obviation then marks them as expected noncoreferent. From this perspective, pragmatic principles use syntactic structure outputs as they will or do the best with what syntax provides, but pragmatic principles are not themselves subordinate to syntactic conditions. However, it is necessary to say that Pragmatic Obviation applies very specifically to the output of FTIP. Put another way, it does not matter if two elements are not in a dependency relation for any reason other than FTIP. Independence principle violations, for example, do not induce Pragmatic Obviation.

The essentials of my approach to dependencies, coreference and obviation are encapsulated in FTIP and Pragmatic Obviation (slightly reformulated in [73]), both of which I take to be universal. I assume the accompanying definitions of obviation (from Higginbotham 1985) in (44), slightly restated in (71), and of dependency in (72):

71) If X and Y are an obviative pair, then they are not expected to share a value.

72) X is dependent on Y if the value of X is a function of the value of Y

73) Pragmatic Obviation: If FTIP does not permit *y* to be interpreted as dependent on *x*, then *x* and *y* form an obviative pair.

Notice that neither (71) nor (73) makes any reference to structure. The definition in (72) is the intuitive notion of dependency we have been assuming since 2.1. Any two nominals that are not enjoined from coreference by Pragmatic Obviation can be coreferent, other things being equal, and any nominal can depend on another unless the FTIP or the Independence Principle blocks it. The Independence Principle overlaps with the FTIP in certain cases, but it also prohibits a wide range of dependencies that do not fall under FTIP.[22]

The centerpiece of this system is the FTIP, and it is my contention that the remaining universal principles conditioning anaphora are very few, in spite of the enormous range of variation in anaphoric patterns that is observed crosslinguistically. The most striking prediction of the FTIP is that there should be complementary distribution of potentially dependent forms, which predicts that Principle-B effects, like Principle-C effects, can be derived as a consequence of the distribution of more dependent forms (another departure from G&R and R&R, who treat principles B and C as fundamentally different). At this writing, the prevailing opinion is that any principle that predicts complementary distribution of this sort is not defensible, not only because there are contexts where anaphors and pronouns can apparently coexist, but also because there are contexts where an anaphor is excluded and a pronoun still will not do (Higginbotham 1985, 576; G&R 1993, 79–80, fn. 11; R&R 1983, 678; Lasnik 1989, 152; Safir 1992, 1997). It is the task of chapter 3 to show that the complementary distribution prediction is not only defensible, but indispensable if we are to understand the nature of anaphoric patterns.

3

# Competition and Complementarity

Throughout the history of anaphora in generative grammar, particularly since the advent of the Extended Standard Theory and later the LGB BT, the (near) complementary distribution of anaphors and pronouns has driven many theoretical proposals. However, theories designed to make robust complementarity predictions—those that have attempted to derive the distribution of one form from the mandated distribution of another—have typically foundered on both language-internal and crosslinguistic empirical grounds. In this chapter, I will try to rehabilitate the notion that complementary distribution in the pattern of anaphora should be derived by universal principles applying to select the "best available" form-to-interpretation match, rather than by mandating domains for each form in such a way that complementarity is accidental. For this to be possible, however, the nature of what counts as complementarity must be relativized both with respect to the nature of the formatives involved and with respect to the nature of the interpretations that are regulated. The more nuanced notion of relativized complementarity of form and interpretation that emerges from these considerations avoids many of the pitfalls of earlier derived complementarity theories while capturing generalizations that cannot be achieved otherwise. Moreover, this approach also permits us to eliminate Principle B and its descendants as an independent principle regulating pronouns in the theory of anaphora.

## 3.1 Complementarity Effects and Competition Theories

The distinction between theories that derive complementarity and those that permit it to arise as a result of overlapping prohibitions is easily misunderstood, and so I will attempt to put it in just the way I intend to use it.

A theory that derives complementarity between dependent forms mandates the distribution of only one form, α, and excludes β wherever β occurs without ever stating a condition specific to β. We have already discussed one such theory, namely, that of Reinhart (1983), that attempts to derive the obviation of names from the set of environments where bound pronouns can occur. The FTIP, proposed in the previous chapter, applies more generally to encompass contrasts between pronouns and pronoun-SELF forms as well, if we take the "most dependent" scale to include all varieties of nominals.

1) FTIP (provisional): If *x* c-commands *y* and *z* is not the most dependent form available in position *y* with respect to *x*, then *y* cannot be directly dependent on *x*.

Under the (to be justified) assumption that pronoun-SELF forms are more dependent than pronouns, whatever is permitted for the distribution of pronoun-SELF forms will exclude simple pronouns to represent the dependent reading, since pronoun-SELF forms win the competition for "most dependent" where they are available. Where pronoun-SELF forms are not available (due to a partial analogue to Principle A to be developed below), a pronoun is the most dependent form available and will win the competition with any r-expression in order to represent the dependent reading.

The view that a single principle, by its nature, regulates the effects of both Principle B and Principle C is by no means unique to me, nor is the notion that the principle in question is one that involves a competition to represent the relevant interpretation. I intend to make use of as much of the argumentation of my predecessors as still applies. However, Reinhart (1983a, 1983b), Pica (1984a, 1986), Levinson (1987, 1991), Burzio (1989, 1991), and Hellan (1988), among others,[1] suggest rather different ways for achieving a derivation of the distribution of pronouns from that of anaphors (or vice-versa), and I shall evaluate their approaches in detail. More profound questions of theoretical architecture concerning how the FTIP can be most successfully folded into theories for which competition is a fundamental property (e.g., the minimalist program or optimality theory) I reserve for chapter 7. The first order of business, however, is to illustrate the conceptual shortcomings of the family of theories that treat complementary distribution in the domain of anaphora as accidental and thereby motivate our search for an alternative.

### *3.1.1 Accidental Complementarity Theories*

A theory of accidental complementarity, like LGB BT, contains both positive and negative conditions that explicitly exclude what is not explicitly permitted. Complete overlap between the domain of the negative prohibition and that of the positive requirement need not arise, and there is no a priori expectation that complete overlap will or will not occur. A theory such as this can predict complementary distribution of referentially dependent forms when the domains of positive and negative conditions overlap, but complementarity should not be expected in the contexts where the domains for these conditions do not overlap. Huang (1983) argued, for example, that there are contexts such as that in (2a, b) where the domain for pronouns is narrower than that of anaphors with respect to a particular antecedent; hence both elements can appear in this environment.

2a) *The men* bought *their/each other's* pictures.
b) *These men* dislike pictures of *themselves/them.*

I shall return to a variety of cases like (2a, b) in a later section where complementarity breaks down, but of course (2a, b) were not seen as typical—indeed special reformulations of the LGB domains were necessary to permit them (as in Huang 1983; and Chomsky 1986b). The fact that the domains for principles A and B could be adjusted independently, as in Huang's account, only reveals how accidental to the theory complete overlap of principles A and B actually was.

Of course it seems natural to expect that anaphors require antecedents, since it is in their nature that they do not have interpretations unless they are assigned an antecedent sentence internally. What the syntax needs to say about them is not whether or not they must have an antecedent, but that the antecedent their nature requires must be found within the tree geometry. Potentially independent pronouns, by contrast, do not require linguistic antecedents, as Lasnik and Postal, for example, have established. That is one reason why Principle B seems particularly stipulative, in that it is a negative condition that forbids elements, elements that normally have no required relation with an antecedent, from having an antecedent in some local domain. Indeed the same sort of reservation can be raised with respect to r-expressions, which do not require a relation with an antecedent either and yet are forbidden certain antecedents. Given this conceptual reservation about Principle B (and its relation to the reservations we have about Principle C), we can ask just how well motivated the existence of Principle B is.

One argument for the existence of a negative prohibition like Principle B is presented by Lasnik (1989, 134–142). He points out that there are environments where neither pronouns nor anaphors can appear. If pronouns simply were to appear where anaphors cannot, then there should be no environments where pronouns are excluded as well as anaphors (unless no nominal can appear there). Lasnik cites examples like (3a) (his judgment, but see also Chomsky 1973, 241) to show that disjoint reference for the pronoun *me* is still in force even where no SELF form will do (as illustrated by (3b).

3a) **We* like *me.*
b) **We* like *myself.*

Cases like these appear to provide the strongest evidence for Principle B since they cannot be accounted for by the mechanism of derived complementarity. However, in 3.3.1 it will be demonstrated that these examples and related effects are accounted for by an independent principle that is not specific to pronouns. If cases like (3a, b) can be accounted for by a separate mechanism, the question remains whether there is any other supporting evidence for the independent existence of Principle B.

#### 3.1.1.1 THE PRO THEOREM

One feature of accidental complementarity accounts is that the principles that apply in specified domains allow for the possibility that there are environments where neither principle applies. Within LGB, this strategy was employed to predict that the pronominal anaphor PRO would have to be ungoverned, under the assumption that all and only governed elements have domains.

By contrast, derived complementarity theories typically require that the "most anaphoric" form available must be used in place of its competitors, but what does one use when no overt form is available? From this perspective, the assumption that PRO occurs in a Caseless position does not necessarily force a choice between derived complementarity theories and those in which complementarity is stipulated.[2] The accidental complementarity theory (in this case, the BT) only has an advantage if Caselessness is predicted by principles A and B.

Unfortunately for the LGB theory, establishing that a position is not governed is de facto circular on the definition of PRO, since the main diagnostic for an ungoverned position was that PRO could appear there. Other Caseless positions could be governed by prepositions or verbs or, in some languages, complementizers, but ungoverned infinitive positions had to be assumed to be headed by a node that mysteriously did not count as a governor (tenseless I) and the complement of a null complementizer that did not count as a governor (null C) but that blocked government from outside of the domain of that head (e.g., a C might not govern a subject PRO, but it would block government of PRO by a verb from the higher clause). Thus the ungoverned status of PRO in infinitives never shook off its ad hoc character, except for the prediction that ungoverned positions would be Caseless, hence without phonetic form.

Chomsky and Lasnik (1995) abandon the pronominal–anaphor theory of PRO because there is evidence that PRO is Casemarked (see also Burzio 1991, 102; Sigurðsson 1989; among others) and because they also abandon the theory of government. If we follow them in this, then there is no argument for stating both principles A and B on the grounds that we need them to predict the ungoverned status of PRO. Derived complementarity theories, however, depending on how the theory of case is integrated into them, are not necessarily challenged by the distribution of PRO (see also 6.1.3).

#### 3.1.1.2 ACCIDENTAL COMPLEMENTARITY AND LANGUAGE TYPOLOGY

If both positive and negative requirements must be stated, then the crosslinguistic variety of anaphoric domains and obviative domains requires extended accounts of positive and negative constraints, stated either as parameters or as lexical stipulations. For example, Manzini and Wexler (1987) propose that any sort of anaphoric domain that stands in a subset relation to others may be stipulated as a lexical property, and they add domains as empirically required (see chapter 6 for discussion). Although the subset relation they argue exists would represent a check on the proliferation of possible domains, it turns out that they still have to add a principle requiring that the domain where pronouns are excluded must match one of the anaphoric domains.

The stipulated domain theory reaches its extreme in Dalrymple (1993; see especially 39–40). She lists the following inventory of binding requirements; the first four are antecedent requirements and the remaining eight are domain requirements.

4a) Subject Binding Condition (must be bound by a subject)
b) Subject Disjointness Condition (must not be bound by a subject)
c) GF (Grammatical Function) Binding Condition (can be bound by any grammatical function)
d) GF Disjointness Condition (can't be bound by any grammatical function)
e) Coargument Binding Condition
f) Coargument Disjointness Condition
g) Minimal Complete Nucleus Binding Condition (e.g., in the domain of SUBJECT)
h) Minimal Complete Nucleus Disjointness Condition
i) Minimal Finite Domain Binding Condition
j) Minimal Finite Domain Disjointness Condition
k) Root S Binding Condition
l) Root S Disjointness Condition

There is nothing explanatory about this inventory of conditions, since if a new form of domain were to be discovered, it could simply be added to the list. However, what is even more troubling is that there is no reason given why for every positive constraint there is a corresponding negative one. For example, if some new domain for anaphors were to be discovered that had no negative counterpart, under this theory there would be no reason to be surprised. Surely this mirror image property is the sort of thing a theory should predict on principled grounds.[3] Dalrymple's approach, however, is just a radically descriptive implementation within the LFG (Lexical Functional Grammar) framework of the problem at the heart of the LGB assumptions (see, e.g., Everaert 1991, 90–91).

Of course theories that do not derive complementarity do not have to be quite so descriptive. For example, theories proposing that pronouns and anaphors must move at LF attempt to reduce the complementarity of the long-distance forms to the complementarity of more local domain restrictions (e.g., Pica 1987; Chomsky 1986b; Lebeaux 1984; Avrutin 1994; Hestvik 1992), and I will examine such cases in detail in chapter 5. However, even such theories as these, which may motivate long-distance anaphor movement in order to find an antecedent or perhaps to satisfy agreement requirements, typically fail to motivate parallel pronoun movement in any convincing way. Notice that these movement theories would make the right prediction if the distribution of nonanaphors were a derived consequence of the success of an anaphor that moves at LF.

A more general sort of problem for theories that do not derive complementarity is that they frequently are forced to hypothesize syncretisms wherever a pronoun seems to fill a gap in the paradigm of anaphors. For example, in languages where inherent reflexives are achieved for the third person with a form like Norwegian *seg*, which is always dependent, a potentially independent pronoun cannot be employed for this relation (5a). To mark inherent reflexivity for first person where *seg* cannot be anteceded by first person, one must use the accusative form of the first person pronoun (5b), even though the accusative form of the first person is also employed as an independent pronoun, as in (6).

5a) *Jon* skammer *seg/*ham.*
Jon shames him
"Jon is ashamed."
b) *Jeg* skammer *meg/*seg.*
I shame me
"I am ashamed."

6) Jon fortalte Ola om meg.
Jon told Ola about me
"John told Ola about me."

If Principle B is not to be compromised, then it must be assumed that *seg* is not a pronoun, but it must also be assumed that *meg* is not a pronoun in (5b), or else Principle B is again in trouble. If this were an isolated case, we might treat it as a syncretism by cross-classifying *meg* as a pronoun sometimes and as an anaphor others, but this just seems to miss the point. The pronoun fills in for a gap in the paradigm of anaphors. This sort of argument, which applies to a wide range of gaps in anaphoric and pronominal paradigms, was pioneered by Hellan (1988) and especially Burzio (1991, 1996), and I will be discussing a variety of cases in detail later in this chapter and, after some other assumptions are introduced, in 6.3.

### *3.1.2 Derived Complementarity Theories*

There have been several attempts to derive the distribution of pronouns as the complement of those domains where anaphors can occur and to derive the distribution of r-expressions from the domains where pronouns and anaphors cannot occur (with the relevant coconstrual), most notably, Hellan (1988), Burzio (1989, 1991, 1996), and Levinson (1987, 1991). Since the theory that I propose takes aims at the same target, it is important to begin by evaluating the hits and misses of previous approaches.[4]

#### 3.1.2.1 PRAGMATIC-BASED ACCOUNTS

Let us reconsider first the theory of Reinhart (1983a) because it has been misunderstood by some to have claimed to derive Principle B from pragmatic principles (e.g., see Higginbotham 1985, 575; Safir 1992, 38). Recall that Reinhart (1983a, 1983b) attempts to derive Principle C from a condition that says if it is possible to use a form that could be construed as a variable, then the use of anything else is obviative. This approach to obviation by competition remains at the heart of the FTIP proposed in the last chapter. However, Reinhart stops short of including the relationship between simplex pronouns and pronoun-SELF forms in the competition. Rather, she groups pronoun-SELF forms and simplex pronouns together as potential variables and then distinguishes the classes of elements that can be construed as variables by condition (7b) below (from Reinhart 1983a, 71), which is not part of her obviation mechanism.

7) Coindex a pronoun P with a c-commanding NP $\alpha$ ($\alpha$ not immediately dominated by COMP or S'). Conditions:
   a) If P is an R-pronoun, $\alpha$ must be in its minimal governing category.
   b) If P is a non-R-pronoun, $\alpha$ must be outside its minimal governing category.

Since both R-pronouns (e.g., pronoun-SELF forms) and simplex pronouns are elements that can be construed as variables, they obviate names. Given (7b), Reinhart does not assume that R-pronouns obviate pronouns but rather stipulates the difference.[5] Moreover, R&R and G&R both explicitly disavow any attempt to derive Principle B from obviation by more dependent forms, choosing instead a version of accidental complementarity with a Principle B descendant that was discussed (and partially critiqued) in chapter 1. I will return to the R&R account in 3.3.2.

On the other hand, Reinhart (1983a, 75–77) seems to suggest that while a pragmatic strategy of avoiding ambiguity does not account for obviation, perhaps a preference for the most explicit form does. She rejects an account on the basis of a pragmatic tendency to avoid ambiguity (specifically, Dowty 1980), since if this were the strategy, (8a) would be preferred to (8b) under the coreferent reading, contrary to fact, since *her* could be taken to refer to someone other than Zelda.[6]

8a) She bores Zelda's neighbors.
 b) She bores her neighbors.

Reinhart proposes, however, that a pronoun-SELF form is more explicitly dependent than a simple pronoun and that the strategy is always to choose forms supporting a bound reading because a bound reading is the best vehicle for a coreferent interpretation. Thus *Zelda saw herself* is preferred to *Zelda saw her* to support coreference, because *herself* is required to be dependent while *her* permits both bound and independently coreferent readings. This reasoning is probably the part of Reinhart's account that led some to assume she intended to derive Principle B from pragmatic principles, as if (7b) had not been stated. Even if we take this account to replace the distinctions between pronominal types in (7a, b), it is not clear that bound anaphora should be seen as a more explicit form of coreference. While the notion that bound readings are generally preferred to express coreference is perhaps defensible under some slightly different assumptions (see Safir 2004), I reject Reinhart's version of this view later in this chapter. However, the notion that a more explicitly dependent form might prevent a less explicitly dependent form from supporting the dependent reading will play a prominent role in the theory I propose.

In spite of Reinhart's (1983a) ambivalent treatment of the obviation approach to Principle B, Levinson (1987, 1991) takes his inspiration from Reinhart's pragmatic reasoning and attempts to derive BT principles B and C from A, or A and C from B (in his 1991 essay) by appealing to Gricean pragmatic maxims (see chapters

2 and 3 in Grice 1989), which he slightly modifies. The essential idea in Levinson (1987) is that there is grammatical specification of Principle A (the "A-first" theory), and Principle B is derived by Grice's first maxim of quantity, which mandates that the strongest statement consistent with what the speaker knows is what s/he will use. Thus a speaker will not say (9a) if the speaker knows it is possible to truthfully say (9b), since (9b) is a stronger statement, where the second statement would entail the first (a "Horn-scale," as Levinson calls it, referring to work by Horn, e.g., Horn 1988, 132–133).

9a) Some men came.
 b) Every man came.

Thus the hearer may presuppose that the speaker does not believe the stronger statement would be true if s/he hears the former one. There are two more maxims that Levinson employs. One is the M-maxim, which says that a more prolix (marked) form indicates that the less prolix (less marked) form is not applicable, and the other is the I-maxim, which says that the form with maximum informative value with minimum effort is what one would use if one could. For example, a pronoun (minimum effort, presumably) would be preferred for anaphora over a name if the name does not add information to the common ground about the discourse referent.

The Gricean account is applied to anaphors to derive Principle B in the A-first theory as follows: Assume Principle A. Levinson writes, "Wherever a reflexive (the semantically 'stronger' expression) could occur, the use of a pronoun (the semantically 'weaker' expression) will Q-implicate (imply by the maxim of quantity, [my explanation]) the inapplicability of a co-referential reading" (1987, 413). In a later article he adds, "Given a Horn-scale pair like <*himself, him*>, use of the weaker, less specific *him* will Q-implicate disjoint reference wherever the reflexive could have been used (if you had meant the stronger more specific co-referential sub-case, you should have used the form that encodes coreference)" (1991, 113). However both "the inapplicability of a co-referential reading" and "Q-implicate disjoint reference" are problematic accounts of what is going on.

First of all, it is not at all clear that noncoreference follows from nondependence, as discussed in chapter 2. Consider cases of contrastively stressed pronouns, such as (10a), where from the context it is clear that the expectation of noncoreference is suspended (for [10a]) and further, that coreference is required for (10b) and perhaps even for (10a), if it is accompanied by an appropriate pointing gesture.

10) I can't say whether or not John loves everybody, but you can bet.
  a) John loves HIM.
  b) John loves himSELF.
  c) #John loves himself.

Here both (10a) and (10b) are possible for most speakers, though most prefer (10b). Neither (10a) nor (10b) expresses a stronger statement than (10c), since the speaker is not committed to whether or not John loves anybody else, rather the speaker is stressing the one case for which s/he has enough knowledge to say that John loves at least one person for sure, namely, John. Use of the unstressed (10c) does not suggest John loves or does not love anyone else, but unlike (10a, b), (10c) does not limit the speaker's intimation of what s/he knows for sure. It could be claimed that (10a) and (10b) obviate (10c) by the M-maxim; however, if a stressed term is taken to be more prolix than a stressless one (even if the stressed term is, well, less prolix in the case of the pronoun), then something other than coreference is meant. But nothing other than coreference is meant; rather coreference and something else are meant. One might try to use the I-maxim to imply that failure to use the least energetic term, the unstressed one, must mean something other than coreference, but this is straightforwardly wrong.

The problem that arises here is not due simply to the breakdown in complementarity, since all of the reasoning in the last paragraph would hold true even if (10a) were not possible. In fact, (10a) is not acceptable without stress, and even with stress it is not acceptable with a bound reading, but only with a coreferential one. The distinction between bound and coreferential readings emerges sharply if the antecedent of the stressed pronominal is a quantified nominal, as in the contrast between (11a) and (11b).

11) It isn't quite right to say John loves no one at all, since we know for sure that
   a) **Everyone* loves *HIM*.
   b) *Everyone* loves *himSELF*.

That bound reference is possible in (11b) with stress but not in (11a) suggests that the bound reading is not what is possible in (10a); rather, (10a) permits coreference, as does (10b) (given what we take it to mean). The key point here is that (11b) still robustly obviates (11a), whereas (10b) does not obviate (10a). The competition of forms in (10), insofar as there is one, is a competition to represent the coreferent reading. This reading, and hence this competition, is not regulated by formal grammar. However, the competition between forms in (11a, b), a competition that determines which form can possibly represent the dependent–bound reading, is indeed regulated by formal grammar, as proposed in the previous chapter, by the FTIP. The output of the FTIP feeds Pragmatic Obviation.

12) Pragmatic Obviation: If FTIP does not permit *y* to be interpreted as dependent on *x*, then *x* and *y* form an obviative pair.

Obviative pairs are expected to be noncoreferent, but that expectation can be overcome, and environments of instantiation (see 2.2) like (10) and (11) are just the sorts of environments where expectations of noncoreference can be overcome (if the antecedent is not a quantifier). Thus Levinson's application of the Gricean system to obviation fails insofar as he does not distinguish dependence and coreference for the purposes of obviation. The same could be said of the half-hearted stab at deriving Principle B from Principle A in Reinhart (1983a, 1983b).

Although it is a smaller point, note also that disjoint reference, as opposed to noncoreference, does not follow from Q-implication. In cases like *The officers stated that the soldiers will leave*, where the officers are a subset of the soldiers, nothing is Q-, I-, or M-implicated at all. For these cases, this is a good result, as argued in 2.4.2, but it is less clear what would be predicted by the modified Gricean system for instances where *the soldiers* and *the officers* fully overlap. Levinson does not grapple at all with the problem raised by Lasnik (1989) for contexts where neither a pronoun nor a SELF form will do, as in (3a, b). Although the FTIP theory will also need a separate account of these latter cases, it is useful to point out, as Lasnik did, that none of the pragmatic reasoning of the sort Levinson proposes accounts for these cases of noncoreference.

Levinson (1991) takes a different tack toward reducing the binding conditions to pragmatic principles on the assumption that Principle B must be stated independently, but that Principle A is derivable. Pragmatic principles apply to the B-first theory as follows: Assume that a predicate involves noncoreferent roles in the stereotypical case (as suggested by Farmer and Harnish 1987) and mark the coreferent case with the SELF form. Where there is no clausemate relation, I-informativeness favors the maximally informative, minimally specified form, a pronoun, over the prolix one, the r-expression, for coreference (to derive Principle C effects). Reflexives are frequently marked with SELF or other "emphatic" portions over and above the pronoun portion, which induces an M-implication (marked form) that the expected (unmarked) disjoint interpretation is not in force.

This account has the same problems related to the dependence–coreference distinction that were discussed for Levinson (1987), with the slight twist that failure of disjoint reference is noncommittal between bound and independent coreferent interpretations. The B-first theory, however, is quite radical in its rejection of the central role of grammar in the derivation of anaphoric patterns. Levinson claims that disjointness between arguments is always taken to be "stereotypical." He is assuming either that there is an innate stereotype-forming mechanism that leads to the conclusion that disjoint reference for coarguments is unmarked, or he is assuming that the stereotype is innate. Neither assumption seems plausible.

Let us examine the hypothetical stereotype-forming mechanism. Predicates like *praise/bruise/scratch/proud of* and many others, depending on the culture, would appear to have no favored usage at all arising from stereotypical observation and induction. Also, verbs like *dress* might be thought of as stereotypically reflexive and are often marked inherently reflexive in languages that make the distinction. English, for example, allows for a null implied object for the reflexive interpretation. Nullity is surely the sine qua non of I-informativeness, the most reduced form available, which would presumably indicate that there has been no departure from stereotype. If we have nullity where our stereotype is a self-dressing situation, why not nullity for the stereotypical devouring situation, which is one that is stereotypically not reflexive? We do not have **John devoured* and understand this to involve disjoint reference—the sentence simply fails. It seems that nullity should favor the stereotype, whatever it is, and yet for English and many other languages, a null argument more typically implies reflexivity. Moreover, if stereotypes can be formed in either direction based on the notional nature of the verb, we might expect some language to have a "contrary to expectation marker" that implicates by the M-maxim that the I-maxim is not in force, thus indicating for some verbs coreference and others noncoreference. To my knowledge, no one has ever discovered such a marker of antistereotypical coreference relations. For verbs like *cut* it seems more plausible to say that there is no commitment one way or the other as to whether animate coarguments are disjoint or coreferent; hence no stereotype should favor either possibility, but such a conclusion sinks the B-first theory.

The cases Levinson takes as evidence for his B-first theory are interesting in and of themselves (I will return to them in a later section) but do not confirm his view. He notes that some languages lack reflexive forms, marking reflexive readings with pronouns that can be independent in other contexts. Following Faltz (1977), he points out that there is a frequently observed historical development from languages with only pronouns to a stage where an emphatic marker is added to a pronoun to indicate coreference, and eventually pronoun + emphatic marker becomes a reflexive (see notes 2 and 50 of chapter 6 for references). The new reflexive then enters into the M-implication relation, Levinson reasons. In languages without reflexives, then, it is not clear how the stereotype is ever overcome to yield a reflexive interpretation, yet Levinson reports that there are languages that are fully ambiguous as to reflexivity or not for sentences of the form pronoun-V-pronoun. In other words, where there is no pragmatic implication of obviation, the stereotype should hold quite generally. Once a reflexive form develops, his stereotype has the appropriate work to do, ensuring that the more prolix form is used to mark coreference, contrary to stereotype.

There are a number of other problems with Levinson's 1991 account, some pointed out in the running commentary he responds to with one of his anonymous reviewers, whom he nicknames "Bite." Bite points out (Levinson 1991, 128, fn. 26) that in ECM environments, pronoun-SELF forms are required in place of pronouns, but since the infinitive subject in (13) is not a coargument with *Carol*, there is no stereotypical preference for disjoint reference.

13a) *Carol* considered **her/herself* to be lucky.
b) *Carol's* father considered *her/*herself* to be lucky.

The prediction would be that a pronoun should be available for the coreferent reading (by I-informativeness) in both (13a) and (13b). To stipulate that the reflexive must have a local c-commanding antecedent is to reintroduce Principle A, so it would appear that the B-first theory is disconfirmed. Levinson concludes instead that English operates on grammatical rules but that the functional explanation of stereotype formation is the underlying motivation for the pattern. The leap between functional motivation and rule of grammar seems vast and unexplained, even if the proposed method of stereotype formation were plausible.[7]

I will henceforth reject any Gricean account of the core anaphora patterns and continue to assume that if one of the locality conditions of the LGB BT is to be derived from the other, it cannot be that the locality condition on anaphors is to be derived from a universal coargument disjoint reference condition, which appears untenable.[8] Moreover, if a competition theory of anaphora is to be correct, it would appear to be one based on competition to represent the dependent interpretation, not on competition to represent a coreferent one. On the other hand, I will try to make use of any argumentation about complementarity that transcends Gricean assumptions.

#### 3.1.2.2 DERIVED COMPLEMENTARITY IN AN ARTICULATED ANAPHORIC PATTERN

One of the early attempts to derive all complementarity effects from a single principle is that of Hellan (1988), who investigates the highly articulated anaphora pattern of Norwegian. The Norwegian pattern lends itself to a theory where some anaphoric elements obviate others, and the anaphoric ones obviate the nonanaphoric ones. Let us consider some basic features of the Norwegian anaphoric pattern and Hellan's account of it.

The niches for potentially dependent forms are intricately shaped in Norwegian (and in Mainland Scandinavian generally) by fairly strict clausemate restrictions on SELF-type forms (in Danish and Norwegian, *selv*, in Swedish, *själv*), on the subject orientation of SIG-type forms (in Danish and Swedish, *sig*, in Norwegian, *seg*), and on the potential for compounding of pronouns and SIG forms with SELF forms. Consider how a principle of complementary distribution derives the right effects in coargument contexts where SELF forms are the most dependent forms, then SIG, then pronouns.

First, for any clausemate antecedent, a compound SELF form should be favored over any simplex SIG or pronoun form, as illustrated in (14). The subject orientation of SIG, which for now we stipulate, excludes it (and SIG-SELF) where it is anteceded by a nonsubject, but anywhere the subject is antecedent and SIG-SELF is possible, pronoun-SELF is predicted not to be available, since pronoun-SELF is less dependent than SIG-SELF, assuming the latter contains two dependent elements. SIG should obviate any pronoun in the same position, as we already saw for inherent reflexives in (5a).

14a) Vi fortalte *Jon* om *ham selv/*ham/*seg/*seg selv.*
"We told Jon about himself."
b) *Jon* fortalte meg om **ham selv/*ham/*seg/seg selv.*
"Jon told me about himself."

What is of particular interest from our point of view is that complementarity predicts obviation of one dependent form by another (e.g., SIG obviated by SIG-SELF, pronoun-SELF obviated by SIG-SELF) as well as obviation of pronouns by anaphors. This is not a state of affairs easily captured in more than a descriptive way in any accidental complementarity theory (e.g., Dalrymple 1993), yet the negative prohibitions follow from the range of possible mandated relations if a principle enforcing complementarity is assumed.

Hellan's own account of this pattern is very close to the one proposed here (and is part of the inspiration for it), but the differences are interesting. His Complementarity Principle is given in (15):

15) If the NPs E and F both have the capacity of being bound and E contains an anaphoric element missing in F, then the domain of E and F are disjoint.

Hellan continues, "Complementarity is presumably a phenomenon devised at [sic] reducing ambiguity . . . . From studies of other languages [fn. omitted], we also know that complementarity is far from 100% enforced at a universal basis. So our real expectation from [the Complementarity Principle] would be that it serve for the central cases only, and perhaps could be asserted as a kind of markedness principle" (1988, 135). However he then rejects a pragmatic approach, arguing that (15) is a rule of grammar "even if it is clearly functionally or pragmatically motivated" (1988, 142), because the factors that perturb the pattern are part of formal grammar (1988, 136).

The presence of anaphoric elements, that is, SELF and SIG forms, that are not present in potential competitors will set up an obviative relation given (15). For example, SIG-SELF is more dependent than pronoun-SELF. While this works well for the data given above, Norwegian is just like English with respect to Principle C effects, yet the Complementarity Principle will not derive Principle C; where pronouns obviate names, pronouns do not have anaphoric subparts by comparison with names (for example, *John* and *him* both lack anaphoric subparts). Some stipulation to the effect that r-expressions are less dependent than pronouns is required to extend the force of Hellan's (15) to Principle C effects, but if such a stipulation is made, (15) approaches the force of the FTIP (where Hellan's use of "binding" implicates c-command).

I concur with Hellan's claim that the Complementarity Principle should not merely be formulated as a markedness principle. Otherwise any number of unspecified factors might obscure this pattern, and apparent exceptions that arise are, well, exceptions. Hellan pursues a number of apparent breakdowns in the pattern to show that the Complementarity Principle is in fact upheld, once sensitivity to other syntactic factors is understood to contribute to the competition of forms, and I will explore a number of these effects in the chapters that follow. However, one case suffices to illustrate the nature of Hellan's justifications for (15) as a principle of grammar.

Hellan notes that the coargument condition on SELF forms is insufficient to distinguish predicates that are inherently reflexive (e.g., [5a]) from those that are reflexive but not inherently so (e.g., [14]). Some condition on grammatical linking must account for this difference presumably, but whatever the condition is, it has the effect of excluding SELF forms in this environment. Hellan's point is that the thematic restriction limits the input to the syntactic competition to select the form that has the most anaphoric parts, but his Complementarity Principle is still selecting the best form from among those that compete. Thus, in cases like (5a), *seg* triumphs over a pronoun although both forms might have represented the interpretation in principle. (This is a line of argument I extend considerably in chapter 4.)

Consider Frisian, a slightly different sort of case, as Frisian, like English, lacks SIG forms, but Frisian SELF forms are still not possible in inherent reflexive environments (as in all Germanic languages save English). It is correctly predicted by the FTIP that Frisian will then employ the next most dependent form available to represent the dependent reading, and so in Frisian, a pronoun is used to represent the inherent reflexive, even though the pronoun in question is one that is otherwise employed for independent reference. Compare the Dutch example in (16b).[9]

16a) Willem skammet him/*himsels. (Frisian)
Willem shames him
"Willem is ashamed."

b) Willem schammt zich/*hem. (Dutch)

The notion that the Complementarity Principle must be syntactic because the forms that influence the nature of the competition are syntactic does not follow. It could be argued that the syntax makes available whatever is possible in a given syntactic environment, and then a pragmatic principle chooses between the syntactic structures as a matter of appropriate usage, as in Levinson's approach. I am assuming that the FTIP is syntactic because its effects are indefeasible and sensitive to c-command. However, I endorse Hellan's notion that any process that influences the syntax to limit the availability of forms is part of the input to the relevant Complementarity Principle, and we shall see numerous instances of it.[10]

#### 3.1.2.3 MORPHOLOGICAL ECONOMY AND REFERENTIAL ECONOMY

During the same years that Chomsky (1995b) was first looking into the effect of economy principles on the computation of syntactic form, Burzio (1989, 1991, 1996) was developing an economy principle designed to derive complementarity in the distribution of anaphoric relations. The analytic intuition that Burzio set out to capture is exactly the one I have been attempting to exploit here; he writes the following: "The obligatoriness of anaphors up to availability will yield the 'Principle B' effect. An analogous assumption that (bound) pronouns are obligatory up to availability will yield the 'Principle C' effect" (1991, 93). Burzio's first version of the idea is that anaphoric readings should be achieved using the barest morphological forms available in a given syntactic context, and the result of the competition of forms would be the only form that could be used without inducing disjoint reference.

In part, the heart of Burzio's reasoning stems from the observation that the LGB theory of anaphors is essentially circular. Principle A requires an anaphor to be bound in its local domain, but in practice, it is also stipulated that anaphors are elements that satisfy the locality restriction of Principle A, which is, moreover, parametrically elastic in many accounts (e.g., Manzini and Wexler 1987). To avoid circularity, Burzio reasons, susceptibility to Principle A must be determined independently from satisfaction of Principle A. He proposes that morphological forms are anaphoric if they are unspecified for syntactically relevant features. An unspecified element will be inherently dependent on something for its content, capturing our intuition that anaphors require antecedents. Pronouns, by contrast, have morphological features but no idiosyncratic content, while R-expressions have both features and content. Given the complementarity intuition, the step is then short to the theory of Morphological Economy:

17) Morphological Economy: A bound NP must be maximally underspecified.

Although locality conditions, a form of Principle A, must still limit the distribution of anaphors, Morphological Economy then does the rest of the work, obviating pronouns and names where anaphors are available and obviating names where pronouns are available.

The obviation of pronouns in this theory succeeds best for the Romance languages, where LGB BT always failed to capture what is going on. In French, for example, coargument reflexivization involves, for the third person, a form that is underspecified for number and gender.

18) Jean et Marie se parlent.
Jean and Marie SE speak
"Jean and Marie speak to themselves." or "Jean and Marie speak to each other."

For each person, singular and plural, in French, there is an independent pronoun, but only third person reflexively interpreted predicates require a form, *se*, that is not otherwise identical to an independent pronoun and that cannot exist without an antecedent.

19a) Jean me parle.
"Jean speaks to me."
b) Je me parle.
"I speak to myself."
c) *Je se parle.
"I speak to myself." or "I speak to him."

For examples like (19b), the LGB BT straightforwardly predicts disjoint reference, unless it is stipulated that French, like Norwegian and many other languages, allows first- and second person forms to be ambiguous between pronouns and anaphors.

An LGB traditionalist might be comfortable with assuming that first person and second person have the general property of lacking distinct reflexive forms in many languages, but as Burzio demonstrates convincingly, such a retreat would miss the point. Burzio proposes that the relationship of antecedent to bound form induces an agreement relation. Agreement of the bound form with all features of its antecedent is simple agreement, but of special interest here is the relation Burzio calls "pseudoagreement," which holds when an underspecified form agrees with its antecedent only with respect to the features it has values for. For example, the *se* form is unspecified for gender or number, and Burzio assumes that it is also unspecified for person. He proposes that languages like French permit pseudoagreement for only third person forms, not for first or second person forms. Thus pseudoagreement makes available (possible in this syntactic position) an underspecified *se* form for third person, and Morphological Economy ensures that it is employed to represent the bound reading.

Crosslinguistic variety in the patterns of pseudoagreement suggest that it would be insufficient to shore up the accidental complementarity theory by simply assuming that languages like French allow syncretisms of first and second person accusative independent and reflexive pronouns. Burzio points out that impersonal subjects require a *soi* form to support a coargument reflexive interpretation on a prepositional object, but the *soi* form is not used to form simple third person reflexives in the same context; rather an independent pronoun is employed.

20a) Victor a honte de *soi/lui.
b) Gianni ha vergogna di *lui/sé.

Whereas Italian permits the underspecified form to support a reflexive reading for third person as well as impersonal, French limits the impersonal cognate to impersonal antecedents. The Complementarity Principle applies accordingly (as first pointed out by Pica 1986, 197). In Italian, where pseudoagreement is more general, the *sé* form is less specified and hence obviates the potentially independent third person pronoun, while in French, as in (20a), where *soi* is not available for nonimpersonal antecedents, the third person independent pronoun is not obviated. Compare what must be said in the LGB theory: Either French violates Principle B in cases like (20a), or the third person prepositional object pronoun must be treated as a syncretism of anaphor and pronoun, just as the first and second person forms are. As syncretisms abound with each form of pseudoagreement that is not permitted, the appeal of the accidental complementarity theories diminishes. By contrast, derived complementarity approaches deduce the obviation pattern from the permitted pseudoagreement without new stipulations about the forms involved (i.e., both theories must say that *soi* is impersonal, but the BT must add that it is optionally anaphoric). The most underspecified form available is the one that is employed to represent the bound reading.

I shall return to pseudoagreement effects in 3.2.1, adducing additional cases as well as others pointed out by Burzio, but for now those presented suffice to show the superiority of the derived complementarity approach. However, Morphological Economy faces some serious counterexamples, whether it is based on the minimal use of features or morphological complexity. For example, complex forms seem to obviate less complex ones in many of the Germanic languages, as we see, for example, in Norwegian where compound SIG-SELF forms obviate SIG forms. Moreover, SELF forms in many Germanic languages can be inflected for plurality, casting doubt on the criterion for anaphorhood based on total lack of features. After all, pronoun-SELF in English is mostly an anaphor (see 5.4), and where it is, it is limited by Principle A, yet it is not maximally underspecified if the SELF portion of the form agrees with respect to plurality.

Burzio (1991, 94) does not ultimately resolve the problem of the plural marking on SELF forms, but instead attempts to reformulate his economy condition as in (21).

21) Referential Economy: A bound NP must be maximally underspecified referentially.

Thus the hierarchy anaphor >> pronoun >> R-expression may now be understood as a referential hierarchy. The term *referential* remains obscure but is presumably an indication of how much semantic content a term has. Featureless elements are still assumed to be the least referential, but this proposal permits Burzio the leeway to say that pronoun-SELF compounds are anaphoric because the pronoun is not the head of the construction; hence it is thematically deficient, while the head of the construction does not inflect (except for number).[11]

The successes and failures of Burzio's scalar notion of "referentially underspecified" must be compared with the scalar notion "most dependent" to be developed below, but Burzio's idea that there is a scale and that the competitor available that scores highest on the scale is favored in a given environment is the same idea that is built into the FTIP. Unlike Hellan's approach, which assumes that SELF and SIG are anaphoric and then favors forms with the most anaphors in them, Burzio's approach generalizes beyond obviation between anaphors or between anaphors and pronouns to obviation between pronouns and names, neither of which contain anaphors.

However, Burzio's reliance on the notion that anaphors are featureless, the driving force behind his definition of anaphors and his Morphological Economy idea, is a weakness of the account. Reciprocals are far from featureless, yet they obey essentially the same locality restrictions as SELF forms (themselves problematic where SELF is plural) in many Germanic languages. The same assumption forces Burzio to assume that pseudoagreement is a rule with language-particular exceptions (e.g., first person can agree with a featureless element) rather than assuming that an anaphor has agreement features that allow it to compete or not with other forms for person, number, or gender. For example, in Danish, unlike in Norwegian and Swedish, the SIG form for possessives, *sin*, only obviates pronouns when its antecedent is singular (Vikner 1985, 53, fn. 13). In (23b) Danish *sin* is not acceptable and hence does not obviate the plural nonanaphoric pronoun (which is also well formed in (23b) where *deres* does not refer to *John og Mary*).[12]

22a) *Jon* fortalte om *sin/*hans* nabo. (Norwegian)
Jon told about SIN/his neighbor
b) *Jon og Marit* fortalte om *sin/*deres* nabo.[13]
Jon and Marit told about SIN/their neighbor

23a) *John* læste *sin/*hans* artikel. (Danish)
John read SIN/his article
b) *John og Mary* læste **sine/deres* artikler. (Danish)
John and Mary read SIN/their paper

Rather than saying that pseudoagreement fails to have a Danish exception for plurals, it seems simpler to say that Danish *sin* has a feature for singular. A simpler statement of agreement with an antecedent is then possible.[14]

24) Antecedent Agreement: The morphological form of a dependent cannot have an agreement feature that conflicts with its antecedent.

To posit (24), however, it is necessary to assume that SIG forms are not featureless in Danish, but they are still anaphors in that they must have antecedents, and that they are "more anaphoric" than full pronouns. The statement that SIG is more underspecified than a full pronoun is compatible with Morphological Economy, but the claim that SIG has feature specifications ought to mean that it can occur independently as full pronouns do (unless it competes with something less specified), and this is false. I shall henceforth assume, with Reinhart (1983a, 1983b), that an anaphor is necessarily (but not sufficiently) a term that cannot be used deictically, as SIG cannot, but I reserve further discussion of the matter until 3.2.3, and chapters 5 and 6.[15]

### *3.1.3 Some Conclusions About Existing Derived Complementarity Theories*

The accounts of Burzio, Levinson, and Hellan all manage to capture, with varying degrees of success, these central intuitions: (a) that complementarity in the anaphoric pattern should be derived and (b) that competition between forms within the same syntactic environment results in the success of one form to the exclusion of others. Theories of this type permit an explanatory account of antisubject orientation and antilocality, as well as exceptions to the antilocality and (as we shall see) antisubject orientation where no anaphoric form is available. Unlike Levinson, Burzio and Hellan treat the principles that enforce the complementarity effect as a rule of grammar. The theory I shall make precise in the next section is thus deeply indebted to these previous accounts, particularly those of Burzio and Hellan.[16]

None of the above accounts successfully relates the failure of dependence in c-command environments to expected noncoreference, either because the right line between syntax and semantics is not drawn, as in Levinson's papers; because failure of dependence with and without c-command are not sufficiently distinguished (and hence obviation is not correctly limited), as in the case of Hellan; or because the matter is so backgrounded as to not be seriously considered (Burzio).

All of these derived complementarity theories are challenged by syntactic environments where more than one form is acceptable and by environments where no form is acceptable, as in Lasnik's cases illustrated in (3). While Burzio and Hellan attempt to address some of the overlaps of distribution (in ways that will be explored further below), none of these theories accounts for Lasnik's cases, which many have taken to be the strongest evidence for Principle B. As a result, many researchers do not believe that the complementarity accounts have met the requisite burden of proof.

In the next section, the FTIP is more precisely crafted to require that dependent interpretations be represented by the most dependent forms available in the syntactic context. The theory that emerges is in the lineage of Reinhart, Hellan, Burzio, and Levinson, though it differs from all of these with regard to what counts as "available" both for interpretations and for forms and with regard to how the principles in question are situated in a theory of grammar driven by principles of economy.

## 3.2 Deriving Complementarity: A New Proposal

Let us now suppose that the range of complementary distribution is too wide to be accidental and that it is indeed understood as a reflex of a competition between potentially dependent forms where the winner obviates the losers. If such a theory is to be successful, the class of interpretations regulated must be made precise; the principles and morphological properties that regulate the competition must be discovered and detailed; and contexts where not even the optimal form will do, or contexts where more than one form is possible, must be shown to be only apparent challenges to the theory.

The bare bones of the proposal are already in place. They are the FTIP and Pragmatic Obviation. In the remainder of this chapter, my focus will be on the FTIP and all of the syntactic and morphological mechanisms and principles that interact with it, especially those that appear hidden in imprecise formulations. The FTIP is sensitive to c-command, to a scale detailing the degree of dependency for given morphological forms, to a syntactic context that must be held constant while forms are compared, to a notion of availability restricted by syntactic context, and to a notion of dependent interpretation. The output of the FTIP is a relation: A given position may be marked as incapable of representing a dependent reading with respect to a particular antecedent in the structure. Then Pragmatic Obviation assigns the obviative pair relation when dependence is blocked by FTIP.

The definition of c-command I employ is a version of the "first branching node" idea, now simplified by recent developments in phrase structure assumptions, such as binary branching and unique specifiers. I assume heads without sisters c-command nothing (though their maximal projections or extended projections may c-command something) and that sisters are not in a c-command relation with each other, though these are fine points that will not play a role in my discussion.[17]

25) C-command: X c-commands Y if X is a sister to Z and Z dominates Y.

The notion "interpreted as dependent on *x*" means, as discussed in chapter 2, that the value of *y* is a function of the value of *x*, but in this work I almost always mean by this "identity dependent," which involves a complex notion of identity, or a family of notions, to be examined further and explicated in chapter 4, but among these are included distributed, collective, guise, proxy, and (perhaps) reciprocal readings.

We also want to distinguish exhaustive dependence on an antecedent from cases where part of a larger phrase is dependent on an antecedent, such that the larger phrase is dependent on the antecedent in a more extended sense. In (26), *his doctor* is dependent on *every patient* because a portion of *his patient*, namely, *his*, is dependent on *every patient*.

26) *Every patient* loves *his* doctor.

Recall that c-commanded dependent epithets are treated as r-expressions, and independent of their semantic content (which is typically richer than that of a pronominal), they lose in competition with pronominals. In other words, we want *him* to outcompete *the old fool* in the right structural context. However we do not want *his doctor* to losc in competition with *himself* (or *him*) in (26), which would be possible if we do not require of the alternatives that they yield the same interpretation, given that *himself* is a more dependent form than any r-expression, including the whole expression, *his doctor*.

27) FTIP

If a) X c-commands position Y,

b) *z* is the lexical form or string that fills Y,

c) *w* is a single form more dependent than *z*,

d) both *w* and *z* could support the same identity-dependent interpretation if Y were exhaustively dependent on X, then (the referential value for) Y cannot be interpreted as identity dependent on X.

The revised version of FTIP in (27) now identifies only those substitutions that take position Y and put in it a single form that would replace all of Y, as if Y had no internal structure. This inaugurates the competition to represent Y if the relevant reading, where Y exhaustively depends on X, is to be a possible reading for the sentence. Consider how it would apply in (28a–c).

28a) *He* loves *her father/Bill.*
 b) *Every patient* loves *his* doctor.
 c) *Every patient* loves *the fool's* doctor.

In (28a), if *he* (X) c-commands the object of *loves* (Y) and if *her father/Bill* (*z*) is not the most dependent form available in position Y (rather *himself* is), then Y represented by *z* cannot be interpreted as exhaustively identity dependent on X; that is, *her father/Bill* is obviative with *he*. For the same reason, (28b) is not reflexively interpreted, but *his* successfully competes with, for example, *the fool's*, as in (28c), to represent the identity-dependent interpretation for the genitive. Of course, values for *his doctor* are dependent on *every patient* in (28c), but only the genitive is in an *identity-dependent* relation with *every patient*. In this book I am only concerned with dependent interpretations that involve identity matching (but see Safir, 2004, for a theory of simple dependency relations based on the Independence Principle of 2.4), and this is what I mean by *identity dependent* (but see the appendix to chapter 6 for a discussion of reciprocals).

Another qualification of my notion of dependency involves the potential variety of identity-dependent interpretations. There are instances where it would appear that we would want to distinguish which forms compete based on the species of identity-dependent interpretation that is involved, as in some cases of collectivity/distributivity distinctions. Complicating the issue is that it is not always clear in many cases whether it is distinguished interpretations or dissonance of syntactic features that is involved (or both). For example, one area of English usage that is in flux suggests that dissonance of features is not always involved. Consider the statements in (29).

29a) *Everyone* thinks *he/she* is smart.
 b) *Everyone* thinks *they* are smart.
 c) $\forall$x (*x* thinks *x* is smart)

In the last 30 years, attempts to remove sexist presuppositions from English have resulted in a tendency for speakers to avoid using (29a) with *he*, formerly the supposedly unmarked pronoun, to represent the proposition in (29c), opting instead for the genderless but plural, *they*. The awkwardness that arises for many speakers born before 1960 (based on my anecdotal survey only) arises from the tendency to treat (29b) as either a failure of Antecedent Agreement or an attempt to represent a different proposition, namely, one whereby each member of the group thinks the whole group is smart. However, (29b) as a representation of (29c) seems to be gaining ground over the number-conservative speakers.

It would appear that if (29b) is ever to be grammatical with the reading of (29c), Antecedent Agreement must be softened as a principle by adding the "unless" clause.

30) Antecedent Agreement: The morphological form of an identity-dependent form cannot have an agreement feature that conflicts with its antecedent unless there is no dependent form that agrees and can represent the identity-dependent reading.

The dependent distributed reading in (29c) is now representable only by a plural, since a gender prohibition has rendered the singular forms unavailable, but the unless-clause is required because the dependent has a feature that conflicts with its antecedent. After all, if the collective reading is considered an identity-dependent one, and it is not easy to characterize it otherwise, then it is also necessary for number-conservative speakers to distinguish the collective dependent reading by using a form that induces a mismatch of features with the antecedent (singular antecedent, plural dependent).[18, 19] What cases like (29) show is that we must be careful to distinguish among identity-dependent readings in deciding which forms are competitors, a matter pursued further in chapters 4 and 6.[20]

### *3.2.1 Limiting Availability*

The FTIP evaluates a form with respect to a given potential antecedent. Not every dependent form is available to compete with others when we consider what the given antecedent is. In (31) for example, the most dependent form available is *herself*, but *herself* is not available with respect to *Gloria* although it is available with respect to *Shana*. We do not want *herself* to outcompete *her* in a position where *herself* is excluded by Principle A, which I assume still is in force.

31) *Gloria* says that Shana loves **herself/her.*

This raises the question of what factors enter into the calculation of "availability with respect to *x*."

Let us suppose that some principle (or set of principles) determines the scale of what is most dependent in a given language such that we have a scale for Germanic as in (32), where SIG stands for all of its Germanic cognates, as does SELF.

32) SIG-SELF >> pronoun-SELF >> SIG >> pronoun >> r-expression

Obviously, the morphological inventories of the various Germanic languages differ, either because they lack a certain form, lack a corresponding form with all its features, or treat a corresponding form as having different features (and hence a different position on the scale). While English and Frisian lack SIG and SIG-SELF, the Mainland Scandinavian languages have all of the forms, and German lacks pronoun-SELF and even SIG-SELF in a form relevant to the scale (see 3.3.3). If we think of a fuller scale as what is morphologically possible, then morphological gaps in any particular language, or even gaps in a morphological paradigm within one language, predict shifts in what is available for competition, a matter I will return to repeatedly. However, given such a scale and a language-specific morphological inventory (hopefully derived from principles of scale formation; see chapter 6), how do we determine, for a given syntactic context, which of these forms is available with respect to some c-commanding *x*?

Given that there are empirically attested limits on the distance between an anaphor and an antecedent that can license it, an analog of Principle A is required in this theory, and I have formulated it as Local Antecedent Licensing.

33) Local Antecedent Licensing (LAL): An anaphor must be c-anteceded in Domain D.
34) Domain D (provisional): The domain for X is the minimal maximal projection containing X and a sister to X.
35) X c-antecedes Y if X covaries with Y and X c-commands Y.

I distinguish the notion "c-antecede" in (35), which is just a statement of the binding relation without indices, from the broader notion "antecedent," which does not require c-command. In typical cases an anaphor is both c-commanded by and dependent on its antecedent, but as we shall see in 4.1, the use of "covary" in (35) is necessary (and must be more precise), as there are certain atypical contexts where LAL is satisfied, and yet the anaphor is not dependent on its c-antecedent. The definition of Domain D in (34) is adapted from LGB and mildly updated and simplified to be consistent with current assumptions, including binary branching and the elimination of government, and will suffice for presentation until it is reevaluated in chapter 5 (where the parallel between A-movement and anaphor binding is abandoned). Given the VP internal-subject hypothesis, if a verb is a sister to its complement, then the minimal maximal projection dominating the complement and its sister is VP, where SPEC-VP contains the subject; that is, the (trace of) subject in VP is in the same domain as the verb's direct object. If V takes an IP complement, then VP counts as the minimal maximal projection for SPEC-IP of the IP complement, if IP does not count as a maximal projection, but not if the complement of V is CP. This will permit us to distinguish control infinitives and tensed clauses, which I will provisionally assume are CPs, from ECM complements, which I will assume are IPs.[21]

I further assume (provisionally) that the content of SPEC-PP, if it is not PRO, is within the domain of the selecting V, either because thematically related prepositions incorporate into V or because prepositional objects move to a SPEC position of V or a functional projection above V at LF. While I will not explore these latter two hypotheses except briefly in 3.3.4, the consequence of this assumption that will matter is that prepositional objects can be bound by VP-internal subjects, especially given the characterization of Domain D in 5.1.

From the perspective of the theory of availability, both LAL and Antecedent Agreement intervene to limit the class of elements that are available with respect to a given antecedent in a given syntactic structure. Thus in (31), *herself* is not available with respect to *Gloria* because an anaphor cannot be licensed in this position, and in (36), *herself* is not available because it would not satisfy Antecedent Agreement.[22]

36) **He* killed *herself.*

In languages like Norwegian, where the SIG form *seg* is not marked for number, *seg* will obviate third person pronouns whether they are plural or not. This obviation occurs because where SIG is available, it is more dependent (being an anaphor) than an independent pronoun. In Danish, *sin* is marked for number (singular), so Antecedent Agreement only permits it to obviate singular third person pronouns.

There is some reason to believe that "third person" is really [-personal] marking (which is a version of an idea originally due to Benveniste 1966), whereas SIG is either unmarked for person, or also [-personal], depending on the language. SIG [-personal] or SIG unmarked for person would obviate other "not personal" pronouns by virtue of being anaphoric. We then expect that SIG unmarked for person also obviates independent pronouns that agree with their antecedents for first or second person. In other words, we must treat pronominals as [+/-personal], but if a pronominal is [+personal], it is distinguished further for first or second person. Pronouns that are [-personal] are then what we would call "third person."

Separating the feature values in this way is motivated, as Burzio (1991) notes, because it is quite generally the case that in a language in which a SIG form (which I use more generally now to mean an underspecified anaphoric pronominal) can be anteceded by first person, then it can be anteceded by second person and vice versa. Moreover, in a language where a SIG form is anteceded by first or second person, it can always be anteceded by third person. On the other hand, it is not the case that a language in which a SIG form can be anteceded by third person predicts that it can anteceded by a first or second person pronoun, and the Mainland Scandinavian languages are good examples of this.[23] Languages such as Russian and Hindi have SIG-like forms unmarked for [+/-personal] and in these languages, such forms permit first, second, or third person antecedents, as illustrated in (37a, b, and c) for Russian *sebja* (from Timberlake 1979b, 124, 127). Faltz (1977, 118) adds that Wappo, a language in the Yukian family (Campbell 1997, 132–133), behaves similarly. The [-personal] feature predicts this grouping of the facts.[24, 25]

37a) *On* dal ej umyt' *sebja* i vypil kruzku moloka.
he let her wash self and drank mug milk
"He let her wash him and drank down a mug of milk."

b) Tetja Frosja *vy* dadite u *sebja* perenocevat
Aunt Frosja you let by SEBJA stay overnight
"Aunt Frosja, will *you* let (us) stay overnight with *you*?"

c) . . . *menja* poprosjat xotja v dvuk slovax rasskazat' o *sebe*/*obo *mne*
me ask if only in two words tell about SEBJA/about me
" . . . (they) would ask me to talk about myself if only in two words"

From the perspective of FTIP, both LAL and Antecedent Agreement are factors that intervene on the most dependent scale to knock out some competitors that would otherwise be available in the syntactic context with respect to the antecedent. Factors that have this effect I will call *scalar intervention factors*. Each time a scalar intervention factor intervenes in some way to knock out a competitor, the competition theory makes robust predictions about what sort of form can stand in for a more dependent one that is not available. Each one of these factors can now be taken to illustrate another argument against accidental complementarity theories, which allows us to place these arguments in the context of the current proposal.

Language-particular morphological gaps provide one set of such arguments. A morphological gap in a language L, in this informal sense, is either a case when a morphological form common to the same language family is missing in L, or there is a paradigm gap, such that a form corresponding to a possible feature set otherwise distinguished in the language is missing. Morphological gaps interact with the other scalar interventions, in that a missing agreement feature value on an anaphor or pronoun will render it compatible with more potential antecedents; that is, it enters more competitions. Highly specific agreement feature matrices tend to limit competition by disqualifying forms that cannot have conflicting features with their antecedents, while less specific agreement matrices extend competition. This we see in the case of Russian above, where the anaphoric form *sebja* is underspecified for the feature [personal], and as a result it is in the same competition as first and second person pronouns. Thus *sebja* may be expected to obviate first and second person pronouns to represent reflexive readings, since it is more dependent (it is an anaphor and the others are not), although the facts need more study. By contrast, first and second person pronouns are employed for the dependent readings in Mainland Scandinavian where SIG is too feature specific ([-personal]) to be in competition with the [+personal] pronouns.

The way inherent reflexivity is marked can also be a scalar intervention factor in many languages. As we have seen, most Germanic languages do not mark inherently reflexive predicates with SELF forms, but only with SIG forms. However the restriction is stated, it will have the right effect with respect to FTIP if it disqualifies SELF forms in these environments as competitors with SIG forms. This form of scalar intervention is discussed in more detail in chapter 4.

Subject orientation is a particularly interesting scalar intervention factor for a number of reasons, though I postpone the analysis of what brings it about to the next section (and more particularly, 5.2.4). The effect on the available class of competitors is the same as usual: If anaphors are somehow designated as subject-oriented, it then follows that pronouns, which are less dependent, will be antisubject oriented in the same environments. On the other hand, where a subject-oriented anaphor is disqualified from competition by a scalar intervention factor such as LAL violation, the antisubject orientation effect for pronouns disappears. We have already seen evidence for this in Norwegian with respect to the distribution of SIG-SELF vs. pronoun-SELF, in that wherever SIG-SELF is possible in the coargument domain, pronoun-SELF is not (as in [14], repeated below as [38]).[26]

38a) Vi fortalte *Jon* om *ham selv/*seg selv.*
  b) *Jon* fortalte meg om *seg self/*ham selv.*

Moreover, in Danish examples like (23a, b), the antisubject orientation of pronouns in the local domain is suddenly lifted where the competitor is unavailable, as in the case of *sin*, which is inherently singular in Danish, anteceded by a plural.

As we saw in the last section, the choice of form to represent a particular species of dependent reading can involve a separate competition, and in this sense, distinctions between dependent readings with respect to a given antecedent can have the force of a scalar intervention factor. An interesting example from Russian that combines a scalar intervention with the subject-orientation effect is discussed by Avrutin (1994, 97). Avrutin notes that in (39) the distributed interpretation is only available for *svoi*, not the pronoun *ix*, which must be interpreted as collective. However, in (39b), where *svoi* is unavailable (presumably because it cannot move far enough at LF; see chapter 5), *ix* can have either interpretation (collective or distributed). Also, *svoi* is available for the distributed interpretation in (39c).[27]

39a) [*Amerikanskie turisty*] opisali *ix/svoi* goroda.
American tourists described their/SIG cities
b) [*Amerikanskie turisty*] skazali [čto Ivan posetil *ix/*svoi* groda].
American tourists said that Ivan visited their/SIG cities
c) [*Každy student*] poprosil Ivana PRO pročittat [*ego/svoju* staju].
every student asked Ivan to-read his/SIG article

In Avrutin's account of this phenomenon, both *svoi* and *ix* must move at LF into the domain of *Amerikanskie turisty* in (39a), but only *svoi* must move so far in (39c) (to find an antecedent). This means, however, that the option for *ego* to move so far as *svoi* does in (39c) is not excluded, predicting that PRO could antecede *ego*, which would be out of the domain of PRO (for Principle B) after movement, a prediction Avrutin (113, fn. 35) realizes is false. This problem disappears as an artifact of his assumption that the pronoun permits long movement if pronouns do not move at all but are obviated for this reading where an anaphor (that can move) is available.

We are by no means finished with subject-orientation effects, as so far we have not examined any of the analyses proposed to account for them, but we will return to them in 3.2.2. and 5.2.4. We shall also return repeatedly to scalar interventions, both those already mentioned and others, as the variety of anaphora is examined in more detail, but these cases serve to illustrate some of the effects that are naturally accounted for by a competition theory that derives complementarity. Now it is necessary to consider some very particular properties of the theory proposed here.

### *3.2.2 Calculating Availability*

To this point we have concluded that the competition between morphological forms to represent the dependent reading is regulated by a most dependent scale that is determined outside of any particular syntactic context. In any given syntactic context, only those forms that are configurationally permitted, either by principles of agreement or movement, and so forth, compete to support the dependent interpretation. Only the most dependent form of those available in the given syntactic context can be used to represent the dependent interpretation. It is now very important to be precise about the mechanism that computes for any given derivation that the most dependent form has in fact been employed. What is required is a reliable algorithm that tests each syntactic context to ensure that no more dependent form could have been used without violations arising from some scalar intervention factor. Thus the algorithm needs to compare possible derivations that differ only in the choice of morphological form to represent the dependent reading, while the dependency relation between the two nominals in question is held constant. The algorithm in (40), which relies on some key assumptions of the minimalist program, is intended to achieve this result.

40) FTIP Algorithm: The input is a given numeration and the resulting LF that contains a nominal A potentially dependent on and c-commanded by a nominal B. Substitute the next most dependent form for the lexical content of A (the target) in the given numeration. If the new test numeration permits an LF to be derived that permits the same dependency relation without crashing, then a dependent reading on B for the target form is unavailable, but if the test derivation crashes, then repeat the process with an even more dependent form substituting for the target until there is no more dependent form to be tested. If there is no substitution of a more dependent form for the target that permits the derivation to converge, then the dependent reading is indeed available for the target.

To understand exactly what is meant by a numeration, an LF, convergence, the same dependency relation, substitution, and exactly how the algorithm succeeds, it is necessary to clarify key notions.

As discussed in chapter 1, one of the goals of the minimalist program (MP) is to avoid positing syntactic levels that are not required for either phonetic interface or interpretive interface. This means that the LGB levels of S-structure and D-structure can no longer be appealed to as points in a derivation where general principles hold. The level of D-structure, the level where morphological forms are inserted into trees, no longer exists. In its place is the notion that a derivation begins with a numeration, which, as discussed earlier, is a selection of morphological forms from the lexicon that will be used in a derivation. Then tree building operations of merge and move build syntactic trees node by node, building in forms from the numeration until there are no forms left. When there are no forms left, the derivation may be spelled out at any point, which means that a syntactic tree is submitted to the phonetic interface. However the tree may still be operated on by rules adding structure or moving structure as long as no new lexical items are introduced.[28] The result of these covert operations (covert because they are subsequent to the point where the syntactic structure is submitted to the phonetic interface), that is, when all tree-building is complete, is an LF (i.e., it is syntactic form that meets the interpretive interface).

The formation of the tree is regulated by principles of economy that apply either by comparing successful derivations to see if the most economical derivation has been employed or by evaluating each operation performed in the course of the derivation to ensure that that operation is the most economical move among the possible ones that might have been made at that point in the derivation. In the MP, all such economy principles of the former type only compare converging derivations. Derivations converge if all conditions are met (other than economy principles) when an LF is formed on the basis of a given numeration. Otherwise, derivations that converge could be blocked by derivations that do not converge.

For example, within the MP, it is always more economical not to move at any given point in a derivation. However, if a feature is unchecked at LF, the derivation will fail Full Interpretation and crash. In such a case, Full Interpretation cannot be satisfied by any derivation without movement. If derivations without movement always compete with those that have it, then derivations that do not converge will block any one that could. If, however, we limit our comparison to derivations based on the same numerations that converge, then a derivation that includes movement may turn out to be the most economical *convergent* derivation. If there is a way to check a feature without movement, then it is more economical not to move, other things being equal. Only the most economical derivation for a given numeration is grammatical.

The FTIP also involves a competition between converging derivations, but it must also compare convergent derivations that differ only with respect to the dependent form employed. To determine which form is the most dependent one that leads to a convergent derivation with the relevant interpretation, the FTIP runs test derivations with forms that are more dependent than the one in the given sentence. Since the hierarchy of dependent terms is very small, there are very few derivations to test to know if the given form can support a dependent reading on the posited antecedent.

Now we must ask what the "same dependency relation" means in this formulation. Recall that a form is only evaluated by the FTIP with respect to a given antecedent, or else a SELF-form in English could be licensed by a nominal that c-commands it but does not antecede it, as in (31), repeated here.

31) **Gloria* says that Shana loves *herself/her*.

Once we allow comparisons between different derivations, we need to keep constant the relations between antecedents and potential dependents that may not occur in comparable positions in converging LFs. More specifically, what needs to be kept track of is the selectional relation assigned by the selecting head to the antecedent, as well as the selection or the theta relationship that defines the dependent. Like obviative pairs, the relation involved does not involve an actual index, since it is a binary relation between a nominal and its selector, not an index that could be compared with any other index or that could accidentally correspond to some other index. It is not clear whether or not theta assignments are part of the numeration input or whether they are only established at the interface, but for the purpose of the FTIP algorithm, all that matters is that when test derivations are compared with the given numeration, the resulting test LF preserves the same theta or selectional relations of the antecedent and the dependent as those of the given numeration, and every other member of the numeration is the same for the given LF and the test LF. Crucially, no other property of the given LF is compared with the test LF.

To see how the FTIP algorithm works, consider (41) and (42).

41) Given input:
   a) Numeration: he, loves, him
   b) LF (simplified): [*he* [loves *him*]]

42) Test:
   a) Numeration: he, loves, himself
   b) LF (simplified): [*he* [loves *himself*]]

The given input contains the target *him*, which bears the patient theta role to *love* with the numeration index of *love* (here omitted), identifying the value of *him* as that of the lovee of that particular instance of the verb *love*. *He* is similarly the lover of this particular instance of *love* and is the antecedent with respect to which *him* is evaluated. We then replace *him* with the next most dependent form available, which on the scale for English is *himself*, and as it turns out, there is a derivation for (42) that does not crash. Thus (41b) is not an LF that can represent the most dependent interpretation, though, of course, a coreferent interpretation is not ruled out, if the expectation created by Pragmatic Obviation is somehow overcome.

The same procedure applies to (43).

43) Given input:
   a) Numeration: he, loves, George
   b) LF (simplified): [*he* [loves *George*]]

In this instance the next most dependent form is a pronoun, and so the numeration in (41a) with its resulting LF in (41b) would be the test derivation, and this derivation does not crash either. Thus (43b) cannot represent the dependent reading, even though in this instance it is obviated by a form in a numeration that itself would fail to represent that reading (by comparison with [42]). After all, all that FTIP determines is whether or not the dependent reading is available for the target, and the test in (41) is sufficient to show that it is not. By this algorithm it is rarely necessary to compare more than one test derivation with the given one, but even if there are cases where there are as many as two test derivations, the nature of the comparison derivations is always fully determined by a limited class of substitutions.

The same reasoning applies to (44a, b).

44a) *John* expects *himself/*him* to win.
   b) *John* expects Mary to love *him/*himself.*

Where LAL still permits *himself* to find an antecedent, *himself* still obviates a pronoun, as in the ECM environment in (44a) since there is a test derivation with *himself* that will converge, and *himself* is more dependent than *him*. By contrast, in (44b), a derivation based on the same numeration and theta-assignment relations for antecedent and dependent will not converge with *himself* substituted for *him*, so (44b) with *him* can still represent the dependent reading.

Of course *him*, as opposed to *himself*, does not inherently require anaphoric licensing; where a pronoun is the most dependent form available, it does not *require* the dependent reading; rather it simply permits it. If the most dependent form available has been employed, namely, the pronoun in (44b), FTIP does not induce Pragmatic Obviation even if the pronoun happens not to be dependent on *John* but merely coreferent with *John*. By contrast the availability of the independent reading is an awkwardness in the G&R account, insofar as they contend that bound reference is always to be preferred to independent reference if there is a choice. If so, one would expect strict readings in elision contexts to be heavily marked; for example, *Bill loves his mother and Harvey does too* should heavily favor the reading where Harvey loves his own mother (sloppy, dependent reading), rather than the one where Harvey loves Bill's mother (strict, independent reading), but both readings are possible (as pointed out at the end of 2.2).

As it is formulated, the FTIP algorithm permits a single form to replace a target consisting of some number of forms in the given numeration, as in the case of *his* replacing *the old fool* as long as identity-dependent interpretation is maintained. The replacement relation in test derivations is asymmetric, in the sense that no group of forms, unless they constitute an idiom (hence a single selection for the numeration), can replace any target; that is, nonidiomatic, multiform strings are not in competition with single forms, but single forms can compete with nonidiomatic, multiform target strings. I assume that the FTIP algorithm never substitutes the absence of a form (the numeration otherwise constant) for one or more forms in the numeration, nor do I permit the FTIP algorithm to replace the absence of any form with the presence of one. I accept, however, that there exist phonetically null forms that can play a role in competitions (at least in principle), a matter I postpone until 6.1.3. In other words, the FTIP algorithm only allows test derivations where one form replaces another in the numeration or where one form replaces a set of others. (This means that what counts as one form for the purposes of the FTIP algorithm needs further elaboration, and the issue is examined in chapter 6.) The limitation on forms used for test substitutions is advantageous because it restricts the class of competitors (and hence possible empirical outcomes) and helps to keep competition computations simple.

It is also important to stress that the FTIP algorithm does not require that the LFs of the given and test numerations be the same in order for obviation to occur. All that matters is that the test numeration be checked as to whether or not it results in an LF where the same dependent identity relation can hold. This particular property shows to best advantage as we reconsider the antisubject orientation cases from the perspective of the movement analysis originally proposed by Pica (1987) and Chomsky (1986b), which was developed from Lebeaux's (1983) proposal that anaphors move covertly.

Pica suggests, for example, that SIG-type morphemes (including their possessive varieties) move at LF to a position in proximity to their antecedents. Let us assume, for example, as in a number of proposals (see 5.2) that the movement in question adjoins the SIG morpheme to I, in which case the most local c-commanding element is the SPEC-IP associated with the I that is adjoined to. This can account for subject orientation since the direct object no longer c-commands the SIG-form (in this case SIN), as illustrated in the schematic example in (45a) for sentences like "Jon told

Olaf about his book" (where for presentational purposes I assume a trace left by movement, but see 5.1).

45a) *Jon* [$_{I'}$ *sin*-I [$_{VP}$V Olaf [$_{PP}$ P [$_{DP}$ *t* N]] ]]
  b) **Jon* [$_{I'}$ *hans*-I [$_{VP}$V Olaf [$_{PP}$ P [$_{DP}$ *t* N]] ]]

As mentioned in 3.1, however, it is plausible to assume that anaphors may move to find a domain where they can be licensed, but it is much less plausible to argue that pronouns must move to a domain where they can be disjoint, as in (45b). In fact, the implausibility of this movement is related to the implausibility of Principle B, since pronouns, by their nature, do not require a syntactic antecedent. Just as Principle B is derived by the FTIP under the assumption that pronouns cannot represent the dependent reading where pronoun-SELF forms, which are more dependent, are available in English, so should antisubject orientation be derived from the distribution of available SIG forms. The FTIP algorithm makes this possible without the drawback of having to assume that pronouns must move as SIG forms do.[29]

The derivation of antisubject orientation from subject orientation is illustrated with the schematic example in (46b) along with its numeration in (46a). To test whether or not there is a more dependent form than the pronoun that can converge and be identity dependent on *Jon*, we need to replace the pronoun in the numeration with a more dependent form and see if that derivation results in a convergent derivation expressing identity dependence on *Jon*.

46a) Jon, I + past, tell, Olaf, about, pronoun, article
  b) *Jon* [$_{I'}$ I + past [$_{VP}$ tell Olaf [$_{PP}$ about [$_{DP}$ *hans* article]] ]]

As is evident from the possibility of (45a), a SIG form in place of the pronoun leads to a derivation that converges, permitting the same dependency relation, and so the pronoun cannot be identity dependent on *Jon* in (46b). Pragmatic obviation will then treat *Jon* and the pronoun as an obviative pair.

It is important to note that no theory that simply compares LFs will achieve the right result because it is not obvious that the LF in (46b) is comparable with (45a); (46a) and (46b) are not structurally identical since (46b) lacks LF movement (unmotivated LF movement of the pronoun was proposed precisely to achieve the structural parallel). This is why the FTIP algorithm is designed to compare only numerations that can converge, not the resulting structure. No other account of these facts achieves this result while preserving the advantages of movement of SIG (on which, see also 5.2.4).[30]

The FTIP as implemented by the FTIP algorithm is reminiscent of the economy principle of the MP, but it is by no means an economy principle. It is not even the case that the FTIP ensures the most efficient representation of a dependent reading (and we will see why in 3.3.3) but only evaluates whether the form in question can support the dependent reading in this particular context. In a given context, the use of less dependent forms to represent the dependent reading might be regarded as costly, but this theoretical inference does not seem to lead anywhere, particularly since I have argued that failure to use the most dependent form is not always costly in the same way; that is, it does not contribute to obviation unless there is c-command by the potential antecedent. What is similar to economy is the notion of competition, which also plays a central role in optimality theory, but the question of how the competition proposed here fits into broader theoretical architectures is postponed until chapter 7.

### *3.2.3 The Most Dependent Scale*

Recall that Burzio's reasoning began with the observation that defining an anaphor as any element that must be bound in D is circular for Principle A. However, in the system developed here, pronouns can be bound locally if no anaphor is available, and so it cannot be said our definition is circular. On the other hand, our identification of anaphors susceptible to LAL does rely on lexical marking. We have seen that there are problems, probably insurmountable ones, that lead us to abandon feature underspecification as a criterion for anaphorhood (and recall that Burzio was also forced to abandon it in favor of some notion of "referentiality"). On the other hand, whether or not an element can be used deictically does seem to be a criterion for anaphorhood.

In English, for example, there is no discourse context where it is possible to point out an individual not seen before and exclaim *Himself!*, thereby identifying that individual as the one under discussion. Suppose one is blindfolded in a room full of men one has never seen, and when the blindfold is removed, one must randomly pick one man to receive a prize. Even with an accompanying pointing gesture, one cannot use pronoun-SELF in this situation, but the use of *him*, *that man*, *the man with the bandana*, or if you happen to know his name (perhaps he is wearing a name tag), *Jake*, will all succeed in this environment. Names, demonstratives, definite descriptions, and pronouns all have *deictic potential* in this sense, and even an indefinite description can be used where an unfamiliar individual is spotted on the beach, for example, *a man!* Neither *x*-SELF nor SIG can be used in this fashion in this scenario, so both of the latter forms *lack deictic potential*, which I will assume is a *necessary* condition for status as an anaphor (i.e., form susceptible to LAL).[31] As we shall see in 5.3, 5.4, 6.1, and 6.2.2 (see also note 35 of this chapter), however, elements lacking deictic potential are not always anaphors. In other words, *anaphors are a lexically marked subset of the class of forms that lack deictic potential.*

Note here that our diagnostic test for the necessary property of anaphors is indifferent to the morphological class of the element diagnosed. We may assume that a form is pronominal if it represents only of a bundle of grammatical features, has no idiosyncratic lexical or semantic content, and might be required to have some nominal character.[32] Thus it is possible that a pronominal may be diagnosed as anaphoric, and in this sense, SIG may be thought of as an anaphoric pronominal, while other anaphors, for example, SELF forms, are not pronominal (as discussed in 6.2).

Now suppose that the organization of the most dependent scale conforms to the following generalization:

47) Between any two anaphors, the more referentially specified one is more dependent, whereas among nonanaphors, the more referentially specified one is less dependent.[33]

This statement may seem paradoxical, but it follows a plausible logic once the distinction between anaphors and nonanaphors is assumed. Elements that can be independent are more easily identified the more specific they are; hence potentially independent elements are less dependent on context the more content they have (speakers have more information to exploit as they look for an antecedent). By contrast, elements that can't be independent and have more specific readings tend to occur in a subset of the environments that a more general term can appear in, other things being equal. For example, SELF forms cannot represent indistinctness readings in languages that have SIG forms (as we shall see for Dutch, for example). Thus SELF is more specific than SIG, at least in Dutch. In contexts where the SELF form is not available, the SIG form can support the indistinctness reading. By this reasoning, SELF-forms are always more dependent than SIG, since the class of readings they can support is smaller. I return to such rankings in chapter 6.

Thus SIG is less dependent than X-SELF, and both of these are more dependent than pronouns, which are, in turn, more dependent than names and descriptions. I also assume the SIG-SELF is more dependent than pronoun-SELF in those languages that have the contrast, probably because it has two anaphoric elements, and pronoun-SELF has only one (reminiscent of Hellan 1988), but that will depend on morphological distinctions that I postpone until chapter 6. I assume SIG taken by itself is certainly more dependent than a pronoun, but this is because SIG, besides lacking deixis, is an anaphor and hence always more dependent than a nonanaphor. It may be that underspecified pronouns favor designation as anaphors, since their lack of specific content impoverishes their deictic potential, but this tendency does not play a role in my system. This yields the scale for Germanic, for example, in (48).[34]

48) SIG-SELF >> pronoun-SELF >> SIG >> pronoun >> r-expression

In Romance, independent pronouns in the first and second person can represent the reflexive reading, while French *se* can be anteceded by third person, but *se* cannot form reflexive readings for first or second person because it is [-personal] (not unmarked for person, as in Russian). It is not clear whether or not clitic pronouns are necessarily more dependent than tonic ones for this scale, but they do appear to be in a competition, since wherever a clitic form is possible, a tonic form is generally not possible without special stress. This seems true in general, but it is independent of any c-commanded dependency relation (see also Cardinaletti and Starke 1994) and thus not relevant to our most dependent scale (but see 6.1.1).

49a) Vous vous critiquez. (French)
You you criticize
b) Je vous/*se critique.
I you/him criticize
c) Elle se critique.
She SE criticizes

If we assume that *se* is an anaphor (it must be bound by *elle* in [49c])[35] and has no interpretation in (49b) (since it lacks deictic potential), then *se* is more dependent than the other third person clitic pronouns, which can be independent. This leaves us with the scale in (50), with *se* crucially more dependent than the other pronominals. Where *se* cannot match features with its antecedent, it is not available, as with first and second person antecedents, in which case the independent clitic pronouns are employed to achieve the dependent reading.[36]

50) *se* >> independent clitic pronouns/tonic pronouns >> r-expressions

Those familiar with French will now wonder about the status of pronoun-MÊME and how it fits on this scale. This matter we will postpone until 6.2.3, although the basic approach to adjunct anaphors will be sketched in the next section.

The richness of the world's morphologies makes available a much wider range of possible anaphoric types than just these, however, and so quite a number of other possibilities and analytic distinctions have to be considered that have consequences for the most dependent scale in any given language. These issues are examined in chapter 6. However, it is to be hoped that the construction of a most dependent scale for any given language should be deducible on principled grounds, once the subset of forms lacking deictic potential that are lexically marked as anaphors is distinguished.

## 3.3 Where Complementarity Does Not Rule

Complementarity in the pattern of anaphora is not always easy to discern because, as a matter of unanalyzed fact, potentially dependent items are not in complete complementary distribution with respect to a purported antecedent, even a c-commanding one. Complementary distribution under c-command fails in at least three possible ways. First, there are instances where more than one form can be found in an apparently identical structural environment c-commanded by an apparent antecedent. Second, there are languages in which there is no apparent complementarity of forms because only one form can represent the relevant reading wherever that reading is found. Finally, there are syntactic contexts where no form will do—the most dependent competitor available appears to be unable to represent the relevant reading, and no other form is permitted to do so. All three of these scenarios are empirically represented in relatively well studied languages. I will strive to present an account of each sort of scenario on principled grounds, preserving the competition theory proposed here.

The account I propose is further constrained by the Universalist Hypothesis, defended in chapters 5 and 6, where that hypothesis is presented in more detail. The essential idea, first discussed in this form in Safir (1996c) but with many historical antecedents cited there, contends that all statements specific to anaphora are universal; hence all variation in the domains of anaphora must follow from lexical properties. Lexical properties are in turn constrained in that the only sort of designation a lexical item can have that is specifically relevant to anaphora is whether it is an anaphor or not. If it is an anaphor, it is constrained by LAL, which has the same domain in every language. If anaphors differ, it must be with respect to lexical properties that are attested independently of any anaphoric phenomena. If this hypothesis is correct, it is not possible to invent a lexical property to permit a special domain for a quirky anaphor—rather it must be demonstrated that the quirkiness follows from a lexical property, such as stress, agreement, morphological structure, and so forth, that is also a property of nonanaphors. Independently motivated properties may conspire with universal principles and other independent properties of a given grammar to allow a domain for an anaphor that superficially exceeds that permitted by LAL (but not at LF) or that requires a domain smaller than that permitted by LAL.

The theory of availability presented thus far has been thoroughly consistent with the universalist outlook. FTIP and Pragmatic Obviation are universal, and variation between languages has been discussed so far in terms of the lexical inventories in a given language and features assigned to the potentially dependent items, like person, number, gender, Case, ability to bear stress, and so on, as these interact with the most dependent scale built for a given language on general principles. If these do not suffice, the Universalist Hypothesis forces us to add another anaphora-specific universal principle but then holds our feet to the fire to show how this universally available mechanism plays a role in other grammars. Given the Universalist Hypothesis, then, my options for solving the complementarity failures discussed so far are notably limited.

### *3.3.1 Where No Form Will Do*

Veterans of the anaphora literature will know that the main club used against derived complementarity theories over the years has been the observations originally put forward by Lasnik (1989, 151) that there are contexts where no form is adequate to form a dependent relation, as in (3), repeated below.

3a) **We* like *me.*
 b) **We* like *myself.*

As noted earlier, if pronouns are always available where anaphors are not, then there should be no environments where pronouns are excluded as well as anaphors. Only an explicit prohibition like Principle B can exclude *me* in (3a), Lasnik reasoned, given his judgment that disjoint reference for the pronoun *me* is still in force in (3a) even where no SELF form will do (as illustrated by [3b]). Such cases will never follow from the FTIP without some further statement. I will refer to such cases as "the residue of Principle B."

However, we have seen a considerable amount of evidence emerge against Principle B (and we are not done). Apart from the conceptual objection (why should an independent form be required to have a domain in which it cannot be dependent?), FTIP-regulated scalar interventions frequently produce environments where pronouns could appear within a domain that is generally too local to be consistent with Principle B, as long as more dependent competitors are not available.

It is thus time to scrutinize Lasnik's examples more closely. First of all, it is noted by G&R (1993, 81), by F&M (1994, 43–46), and by R&R (1993, 676–677) that Lasnik's description of the facts needs to be more nuanced. Many speakers accept (3a) with what we called in the last chapter a "discriminating interpretation," one where the first person plural represents a group, not a set of distributed individuals, and so the direct object, though a member of the group, is an entity distinguished from its antecedent.[37] By contrast, a reading whereby each member of the first person plural group is such that that individual likes the first person singular is generally rejected, since the obviative effect, whatever it is, seems to disdain exact matches between the antecedent and the dependent in these close quarters.

R&R choose to illustrate the difference in the effects with examples like (51).[38]

51a) *Both *John* and Mary love *him.*
b) *Both *John* and Mary love *himself.*

Since *both John and Mary* requires that each of them have the *love* relationship individually with *John*, it is not the case that they love him as a collective, so the interpretation that many find acceptable for (3a) is not available in (51). (Notice that *John and Mary bought the house* may involve them buying it together, but not *Both John and Mary bought the house*, which suggests two different transactions).

In the R&R system, neither *him* nor *himself* will do in (51); *himself* fails to agree with its syntactic antecedent (the full conjunct), and *him* fails because of their partial decomposition of Principle B, stated in (52).

52) Reflexive Interpretation Principle (RIP): If a predicate is interpreted as reflexive, it is marked reflexive.

In the R&R notational system, a predicate is interpreted as reflexive if two of that predicate's arguments are coindexed (although it is not obvious that coindexation for them means one identity depends on the other in this case—see the introduction to chapter 4). For a reflexive relationship to hold, one of the arguments of the given predicate must be marked with SELF (in English), so in an example like *John loves him*, the reflexive interpretation (where *John* and *him* are coindexed) is blocked because there is no SELF on *him* to mark the predicate *love* as reflexive. However, (52) won't apply to rule out (51a), since the syntactic subject of (51a) involves conjoined arguments, only one of which is coindexed with a syntactic argument of *love*, so it is not the case that *John* is a syntactic coargument of *him*, even though the distributed reading of the subject would seem to require *John* to be in a self-loving relationship. For this reason, R&R state their RIP on the hypothesized "semantic level," something more nuanced than an LF, which is a form in which each of *John* and *Mary* is a direct coargument in a proposition with *him*, as shown informally and schematically in (53).

53) Both (*John* loves *him*) and (Mary loves *him*)

At this purported semantic level, *John* and *him* are direct coarguments, but the predicate at that level is not morphologically marked as reflexive. Since there is no reflexive form that can satisfy agreement and a pronoun won't do to meet the reflexive-marking requirement, neither form is available.

R&R introduce a second principle that rules out pronouns too close to their antecedents, the Chain Condition, discussed in chapter 1, which is intended to catch the spillover of noncoreference effects for pronouns beyond the coargument domain, namely, in the ECM environment.

54) *John* considers *himself/*him* (to be) brilliant.

In these environments *him/himself* is not a coargument with *John*, so the RIP does not apply. If *him* is to be excluded, a prohibition with a larger domain must do the work, and R&R believe it is the same principle that regulates the links of A-chains and permits raising, for example, in a syntactic position comparable to *himself/him*. Although they do not pursue it, they make a clear prediction that (55) should be acceptable with a pronoun, and in this I think they are correct, as the additional contrasts in (56a, b) and (57a, b) also show, though a split dependent anteceded by a quantified nominal is always very awkward.

55) Both *John* and Mary consider *him* (to be) brilliant.

56a) *Both *every Republican* and *his* wife overvalue *him/himself.*
b) ?Both *every Republican* and *his* wife overvalue *his* contributions to mankind.

57a) *Both *every bankrupt* and *his* wife blame *him/himself* for wasting money.
b) ?Both *every bankrupt* and *his* wife blame *his* mother for wasting money.

Since *John* in (55) is not a syntactic antecedent to *him*, but only at the semantic level (given a semantic decomposition like that in [53]), it will avoid the Chain Condition but avoid the RIP also, which is restricted to coarguments. Similarly, *him* cannot be dependent on *every Republican* in (56a) and (57a), but in (56b) and (57b), where *his* is not a semantic coargument with *every Republican*, the relevant relationship is possible, and similarly for *every bankrupt* and the respective pronouns in (57).[39]

Although I reject the way R&R account for it, the distinction between the coargument domain and the ECM domain for anaphors is important in my alternative to RIP and for essentially the same reasons. While the FTIP derives Principle B effects wherever a SELF form is available, including ECM environments, there are availability effects peculiar to coarguments in many languages, effects that are induced by specialized reflexive argument markers. I will explore a variety of these effects in chapter 4. From the perspective of the FTIP, it could be argued that RIP could be adapted to rule out just Lasnik's cases, having the effect of a scalar intervention that rules out nonreflexives in certain environments where reflexives are unavailable. If no point on the scale is left, the interpretation is simply blocked—it is unrepresentable.

While appeal to a scalar intervention is attractive to rule out these cases, RIP does not have the right properties to do the job. For example, R&R's RIP will fail in all the environments where first and second person coargument pronouns lack reflexive forms (such as SELF) and yet support reflexive readings, as in Romance. Like the LGB account, the R&R account can be shored up with a large number of hypothesized syncretisms (or abstract reflexive markers), but the same sort of stipulative escape will have to be used for noncoargument cases of paradigm gaps, with a similar lack of predictive force. Moreover, the syncretisms will have to be marked for two separate morphological feature values for this to work in R&R's theory. First person pronouns in Romance will have to be optionally reflexive-markers/non-reflexive-markers to escape RIP, and they will have to be optionally +/-R to escape the Chain Condition, which will exclude +R marking on independent pronouns when they are in the relevant domain (which includes the coargument domain as well as the ECM subject).[40] These inelegant syncretisms are of just the sort that result from inflexible mandated outcomes, as opposed to those that involve competitions relativized to syntactic context.

Another unattractive feature of the R&R proposal is the proliferation of levels. In addition to the syntactic level, the one at which distributive predicates are not decomposed and at which the Chain Condition and Principle A (their analog) applies, they hypothesize a level of formal grammar at which complicated semantic decompositions must be possible to create clausemate relations that do not exist in syntax proper (a position I confess to endorsing in Safir 1997). It seems especially out of place that a morphological condition should hold at such a level; indeed it is the morphological condition expressed as RIP that forces representations of the sort we see in (53), duplicating the predicate and theta-assigning relations so that the morphological condition can do its work. Thus even if we are to make the interpretation of distributivity part of the solution, the intervention of affixal morphology at this point in semantic interpretation seems very unnatural.

Let us consider what we need. We are searching for a restriction on coarguments that captures the residue of Principle B first pointed out by Lasnik and more precisely delineated by G&R and R&R. On the one hand, it appears that a principle that requires reflexive morphology is too strong, but on the other, what seems right about the intuition behind the R&R analysis is the shift of focus away from pronounhood per se. We can see this if we look at some effects where what is involved is not a restriction on morphology, but a restriction on a particular kind of interpretation.

Consider German *sich*, which is not intrinsically a reflexive marker, since it can also be interpreted as reciprocal and which does not evidence number agreement. Yet (58b) cannot mean what (58a) also fails to mean (nor can **John und Mary sehen *ihn***, where *ihn* is a [-personal] pronoun), though *sich* is unmarked for plurality.

58a) **John* and Mary saw *him.*
b) John und Mary sehen sich. (German)
"John and Mary see themselves/each other."
but not "John and Mary see John."
c) Die Frauen und die Männer sehen sich.
"The women see themselves and the men see themselves."
"The women and the men see themselves."
"The women see each other and the men see each other."
"The women and the men see each other."
but not "The women see themselves and the men see each other." (or vice-versa)
and not "The women and the men see the women/the men."

Notice that in (58c) *sich* can be applied with reciprocal force to each conjunct, thereby permitting an interpretation (among other more salient ones) such that the women see each other and the men see each other without it being the case that any men saw any women. Thus it is even more striking that (58c) does not allow *sich* to apply to only one conjunct of the subject, or even to apply to each conjunct of the subject differently, such that the women saw themselves and the men saw each other.

Now one might respond to the previous argument by noting that if *sich* is an anaphor, the exhaustivity effect we see may be a function of its being an anaphor rather than its being a coargument. However, the same sorts of distinctions arise for first person plurals, where the form that supports the grammatical interpretations is the same form that serves as an independent pronoun.

59) Wir Onkeln und wir Väter kritisieren uns zu viel.
we uncles and we fathers criticize uns too much.
a) Each of the uncles and fathers are self-criticizers.
b) Uncles criticize uncles as a group and fathers criticize fathers as a group.
c) Each uncle criticizes the other uncles (but not the fathers) and each father criticizes other fathers (but not uncles).
d) Uncles criticize fathers and fathers criticize uncles.
e) *Uncles criticize other uncles and each father criticizes himself.
f) *Each uncle criticizes himself, but fathers criticize themselves as a group.

Here again we see the failure of coargument interpretations with mixed forms of dependency, and unless we assume that *uns* is syncretically anaphoric just to save Principle B (or R&R's RIP), we must conclude that the dependent interpretation requires a consistent and exhaustive form of dependency.

Whatever restricts the dependency interpretation in (51a) but not (55) is imposing the same conditions on the interpretations in (58b, c) and (59e, f). An informal statement of this condition appears in (60).

60) Coargument Dependency Constraint (CDC): If A is identity dependent on B and A and B are coarguments, then for any distributed interpretation of B, A depends on every distributed atom of B in the same way.

Since we need (60) independently of any Principle B for (3) and (51), (51a) is no longer evidence for a Principle B specifically geared to pronouns or reflexive interpretations, and it is certainly not a reason to abandon a derived complementarity account.[41] Moreover, as it is stated, CDC requires a semantic analysis that will ensure that distributivity is respected, but it is not clear that this requires any special level of representation more complex than any analysis of semantic distributivity requires independently (i.e., no decomposition into two clauses). More specifically, it does not require introducing a level of grammar that must pass a morphological test, as R&R and Safir (1997) assume. Rather the CDC applies wherever in the derivation distributivity is interpreted, rather than at any independently stipulated level.

As is the case generally, once certain dependencies are blocked, no subsequent semantic interpretation can reinstate one of the prohibited dependencies.

It is still necessary to address the cases that Lasnik originally raised, but now we must reconsider their force. For cases like those in (61) ([61a = 3a]; [61b, c] were discussed by F&M 1994, 38–46; and R&R, 1993, 676–677), which many speakers accept, it appears that something much less rigid than Principle B is required.

61a) *We* will vote for *me*.
  b) *We* elected *me*.
  c) Felix and *Lucie* authorized *her* to be their representative.

Part of the discussion in the latter references concerns the mismatch between distributed and collective interpretations, such that coreference is not necessarily blocked by rule if the interpretation of the plural is collective. While this is part of the story, it would appear that coargument relations between antecedent and anaphor or pronoun are also sensitive to the nature of the relation between the subject and the object. Consider the cases in (62), where collectivities coconstrued with singular coarguments seem particularly natural.[42]

62a) When Larry and Maurice were sued, Larry defended/represented them.
  b) Harvey's team had been harshly criticized, so when he scored the winning goal, he felt he had vindicated them.
  c) In those days, every man who met Celia imagined them walking down the aisle together.

63a) When Larry was sued, he represented/defended him. [*Larry* = he (*him*]
  b) Harvey had been harshly criticized, so when he scored the winning goal, he felt he had vindicated him. [*Harvey* = he (*him*]
  c) Every man who met Celia imagined him walking down the aisle with her. [*Every man* (*him*]

The contrast between (62) and (63) confirms the general approach to pronoun/anaphor distribution in terms of a principle of complementarity. Coreference is successful for the pronouns in (62a, b), where no reflexive form is available because agreement with the antecedent is not possible.[43] If (62c) receives a split anaphora interpretation, where *them* denotes one of the men and Celia, there is no SELF form that could represent it and agree with both antecedents, so SELF is not available for these cases either. Thus a pronoun is successful in each case as the most dependent available form. Where the subject is undistributed and singular and the object is undistributed and singular, nothing intervenes to permit a pronoun to support the dependent reading over the SELF form, so the relevant interpretations in (63) are ruled out by FTIP.

Cases like (62) contrast with those in (64) where the predicate cannot take subparts of a group and the whole group as role players without logical or pragmatic inconsistency. Examples where collectives act on patients that are one of their number tend to fail if such notions are not taken into account. Compare (64a, b).

64a) They hit him.
b) The dog and the cat groomed him.

Where *him* is one of *they* in (64a) or in (64b) where *him* is the cat, the acts in both sentences could be collective, but coreference is strongly dispreferred just the same. If one looked only at (64a, b), the disjoint reference account based on Principle B might still seem defensible, but comparisons with examples like those in (62) show that principles like Principle B in Lasnik's sense of it are inappropriately general because they are insensitive to differences between predicates.[44]

Perhaps the force of the effect is related to how naturally discrimination, in the sense of chapter 2, can be employed. Discrimination was not applied to pronominal cases in chapter 2, but many of the same sorts of effects may be observed when appropriate examples are constructed. Thus (65), from Berman and Hestvik (1997, 8) is possible:

65) *John and Mary* were experiencing marital strife, so *they* called Bill to discuss the situation. They talked about *them* for the rest of the evening.

In (65), it is possible that John, Bill, and Mary can be construed as *they* and that John and Mary could constitute *them*. However, (65) cannot mean that the three of them as individuals talked about the three of them as individuals, or that the three of them as a group talked about the three of them as a group, or that any two of them collectively talked about the same tandem, or that any two of them individually talked about the same two of them individually. The cases that are not permitted are precisely those where a more dependent form is available to express the same meaning (e.g., *themselves*), as predicted by the FTIP.[45]

To summarize, Principle B and the RIP of R&R must be rejected for three reasons.

A) Most of these distributions are redundantly accounted for by FTIP.
B) Where there is a general restriction against coargument dependency, the relevant restriction does not appear to be specifically about pronouns or about reflexive morphology.
C) Cases like (3) that were part of what originally motivated Lasnik's disjoint reference notion do not seem to be sufficiently general to support a predicate blind principle like Principle B or RIP.

The ground formerly covered by Principle B in the LGB theory and by the Chain Condition and RIP in the R&R theory are now covered by the FTIP, which generalizes across competitions between different anaphors, between anaphors and pronouns, and between pronouns and referring expressions. The CDC accounts for the residue of Principle B without specifically restricting pronouns or any morphological class. Instead it restricts the distributivity of coargument dependencies, and it does so without introducing morphological conditions on semantic interpretive levels of a derivation. Further arguments against Principle B will accumulate as my presentation unfolds, including in the very next subsection.[46]

### *3.3.2 Where One Form Does All*

Any theory of morphology will allow for the possibility that the lexical inventory of a language may lack forms corresponding to those generally found in most other languages. If so, we should expect that it is possible for a language to lack forms classed as anaphors. No theory with a firm Principle B or RIP can account for such a language without assuming that apparent pronouns are anaphors in the domain of Principle A, and every anaphor in the language just happens to be homophonic with an independent pronoun. Otherwise there is no way to say "John sees himself" without violating Principle B. A competition theory of derived complementarity, however, as Levinson argues, simply predicts that all of the functions of anaphors will be subsumed by the next most dependent elements, namely, pronouns. This reasoning is thoroughly consistent with both the FTIP and the Universalist Hypothesis.

Although I postpone discussion of the range of crosslinguistic morphological distinctions and the resulting predictions until chapter 6, it is worth noting that Levinson (1991) has assembled reports of a number of Australian and Austronesian languages and European-influenced Creoles that appear to lack anaphors. The same may be said of a language closer to home, namely, Old English, which appears to have permitted transitive sentences with pronominal objects to be understood as reflexive, as in (66) reported by Visser (1963, 439; cited in Levinson 1991, 139, fn. 37; but see van Gelderen, 2000, for numerous examples, references, and discussion), which he claims could be understood as noncoreferent, reflexive or reciprocal.

66) Hi gecyston hi. (Old English)
They kissed them
"They kissed them/themselves/each other"

In most of these languages, a form typically called *emphatic*, usually a relational anaphor (e.g., SAME, SELF), is used to disambiguate wherever the reflexive interpretation is underdetermined by context, just as in the German cases with *sich*. In the Germanic languages that element is a SELF form. Faltz (1977), Levinson (1991), Keenan (1994), and especially van Gelderen (2000) present a great deal of evidence (and references to earlier accounts) for the evolution of so-called emphatic reflexives into canonical reflexives, a view quite compatible with the approach taken here, insofar as the system shifts at the point the body part reflexive (see chapter 6) becomes conventionally integrated into the most dependent scale because pronoun-SELF forms an idiom.

### *3.3.3 Where More Than One Form Will Do*

The FTIP would be counterexemplified if forms of unequal dependence on the scale could support the same dependent reading in the same structural context. This is a very strong claim and one that faces a wide range of apparent counterexamples. I will adopt three principal strategies to account for such purported counterexamples, listed in (67), which correspond to factors that regulate the competition of forms.

67) Strategies for apparent noncomplementarity of distribution:
  a) Interpretations are distinct.
  b) Forms tie on the most dependent scale.
  c) There are distinct numerations (apart from the target).

By (67a), I mean that in some instances, where it is possible to tell, overlaps in the distribution of forms actually involve the representation of distinct interpretations, interpretations that may happen to allow the some of the same inferences in some contexts. Such cases typically involve distinctions between dependent and coreferent readings that can be disambiguated where the antecedent is quantified. In other instances, I will argue that more dependent elements, particularly SELF forms in the Germanic languages, can be promoted to discourse-sensitive pronominal status where they have no potential syntactic antecedent in principle, exploiting earlier work of Safir (1992, 1997) and of Reinhart and Reuland (1991, 1993). Where SELF forms are so promoted, they tie on the most dependent scale with their pronominal counterparts, though other factors may influence the use of one or the other. Finally, there are cases where a single surface string could be derived from distinct numerations. Such cases arise where the predicates involved assign thematic roles differently, or the morphology of the potentially dependent form is ambiguous.

I begin with the strategy in (67a), which is based on the idea that apparent overlaps can sometimes represent different interpretations. These typically involve cases where the interpretation of the antecedent can crucially influence the choice of dependent element. For example, consider the Danish example in (68) from Vikner (1985, 52).

68) *Kun Peter* bad Susan om PRO elske *sig/ham.* (Danish)
  only Peter asked Susan to love SIG/pronoun
  a) Only one person asked Susan to love Peter, and that was Peter.
  b) Only one person asked Susan to love him, and that was Peter.

In (68) it appears that *sig* and *ham* appear in the identical structural context, and if *sig* is more dependent than *ham*, then *sig* should obviate *ham*, marking *ham* and *kun Peter* as an obviative pair. However, there is evidence that the right result has been achieved. Vikner (1985) points out that examples like (68) have the bound interpretation (68b) with *sig* and (what has been called) the coreferent interpretation (68a) when *ham* is employed—an interpretation where *ham* does not depend on *only Peter*. While this result is fully compatible with FTIP, something must be said about Pragmatic Obviation, which does not render the interpretation in (68a) contrary to expectation in this instance, even where *kun Peter* is replaced simply by *Peter*, and there is no obvious way to know if the reading is bound or not. It appears that the force of Pragmatic Obviation may be softened as the distance between the antecedent and the potentially dependent pronoun increases, but the issues need more study.[47]

Vikner's example is actually a version of an argument based on Icelandic from Anderson (1986), which is in turn a version of an argument from Thráinsson (1976) as reported in Sells (1987, 467).

69) *Aðeins Jón* telur að María elski *hann/sig*. (Icelandic)
"Only John believes that Mary loves him."

The bound reading of (69) requires the more dependent form; that is, (69) with *sig* implies that there is no other person, such as Olaf, who believes that Mary loves Olaf, while (69) with *hann*, the pronoun, does not support this inference. However, if *hann* is employed in (69), then it should be inferred that there is no person who is not John who believes Mary loves John. From this perspective, some apparent failures of complementarity evaporate on the basis of independently required distinctions of dependent interpretation.[48, 49]

Other apparent problems arise in ECM contexts, such as the resultative small clauses noted by R&R (1993, 710, fn. 51), citing earlier work by Voskuil and Wehrmann (1990).

70a) Münchhausen trok [zichzelf uit het moeras]. (Dutch)
b) Münchhausen trok [zich uit het moeras].
"Münchhausen pulled himself out of the swamp."

Here there is a difference as to whether Münchhausen has pulled himself out by his own hair, which is the reading intended in the story and which must be represented with *zichzelf*, or one where the result of Münchhausen's pulling (something else) is that he is out of the swamp, which is the reading available with *zich*. There is much more to be said about such cases of dependent interpretations with different meanings, but I set them aside until 4.3.3.

Now let us consider the second strategy. The examples in (71) illustrate a particular set of domains where SELF forms and pronouns overlap in English.

71a) The men insisted that the evidence would show that everyone other than themselves/them should be prosecuted.
b) Al knows that Alice believes that Sam and he/himself should be prosecuted.
c) Muriel admitted that her boyfriend had taken naughty pictures of her/herself.

In the works cited, exclusion predicates, conjunctions, and picture nominals are identified as environments where there is no potential antecedent for a reflexive interpretation. In those environments, it is possible for pronoun-SELF forms to be treated as pronominals, in which case they have roughly the same status as simple pronouns (they are neither r-expressions or anaphors), although they are subject to various perspective or contrastive effects; see Baker (1994), Zribi-Hertz (1995), and Safir (in preparation).

This second strategy, as it applies to (71a, b, c), would mean that SELF forms promoted to discourse dependents have the same status on the most dependent scale as pronouns. Such a claim requires at a minimum a clear algorithm that distinguishes anaphoric cases from discourse-dependent ones and that identifies which sorts of anaphors can be promoted in this way (not all varieties of anaphors can) and in exactly what sort of circumstances (the Universalist Hypothesis requires that the promotion algorithm apply universally where its requirements are met, since it is a process that applies to anaphors as such). The matter is examined in 5.4, where my discussion is based on the intuition that anaphors are permitted to find antecedents asyntactically if they are arguments of predicates that do not semantically permit a possible coargument antecedent. Thus both the pronoun and the SELF form are acceptable dependents of *every boy* in (72), although there are presumably matters of contrast or emphasis or point of view that might tease them apart.

72) *Each boy* insisted that Mary could love no one but *him/himself.*

Finally there are cases where apparent failures of complementarity arise because the numerations involved are distinct, hence not in competition, although the surface strings may appear identical but for the difference in a potentially dependent form. One such case is that of Mainland Scandinavian and Dutch inherently reflexive verbs that also permit a transitive reading. Verbs such as these allow either a SIG form or a SIG-SELF form, but it is plausible to claim that the thematic assignments in these cases are different and that thematic assignment is part of the numeration, either in the form of a lexical distinction between the verbs selected (most likely in this case), or perhaps in terms of the properties that constitute theta assignment.

73a) *Jon* vasket *seg*. (Norwegian)
"Jon washed."
b) *Jon* vasket *seg selv*.
"Jon washed himself."
c) *Jon* bad meg vasket *seg/*seg selv*.
"Jon asked me to wash him."
d) *Jon* skammer *seg/*seg selv*.
"Jon is ashamed."

One sort of approach to these cases is to say that the SIG form is a nonargument whereas the SIG-SELF form represents an argument. If so, the verb is detransitivized in (73a, d), but not in (73b), in which case the verb meaning "to wash" can be selected from the lexicon in either of two forms (an option not available for the verb meaning "to be ashamed"). The result is that the numerations for (73a, b) are distinct, hence the FTIP algorithm does not evaluate them as competitors. For much more discussion of such cases, see chapter 4.

Another way in which forms may overlap in distribution is if the forms themselves have more than one internal analysis that is distinguished by the comparison of numerations. For example, SELF forms in English, Dutch, and Norwegian are in competition with SIG forms to represent the reflexive reading, but for the most part, not in German, where the addition of the SELF form is either emphatic or disambiguating. Recall example (58c) where the form *sich* was multiply ambiguous between distributed and collective reflexive readings as well as between a reflexive reading and a reciprocal one. Compare (74), which is unambiguously reflexive and for most speakers, unambiguously distributed; that is, John saw John and Mary saw Mary (see note 37 to this chapter).

74) John und Mary sehen sich selbst. (German)
"*John and Mary* see *themselves*."

If *sichselbst* is treated as a single morphological form, it should be in competition with *sich* to represent this very specific reading, such that the use of *sich* should be obviated for this particular interpretation, but this is not the case; *sich* in (58b) permits the same interpretation that is assigned to (74).

The reason both forms can represent the same reading is that *sich* does not obviously form a single morphological entity with *selbst* in German. If so, the two lexical items *sich* and *selbst* are not submitted to the FTIP algorithm such that *sich selbst* could obviate *sich*, because test numerations only introduce comparisons where a single form can be substituted for the target. If so, *sich selbst* is not in competition with *sich*. This sort of situation frequently arises where an emphatic or adverbial form disambiguates an anaphoric dependency that supports more than one reading, and we shall see other instances of it (see 6.2.3).

If we were to assume that an FTIP competition is constituted to apply between any and all elements that can achieve a particular interpretation, then German *sich* and *sich selbst* in (74) would have to be in competition to represent the distributed interpretation; Instead, I have formulated the FTIP competition to determine only whether or not the dependent interpretation is available for a given class of forms, in which case, the competitors are relativized to a single substitution for each test numeration. This is an important point because it shows that the competition does not seek the most efficient representation of the relevant interpretation if it is a question of evaluating different combinations of forms, be they sentences or phrases (e.g., *His mother loves Leo* does not compete with *Leo is loved by his mother*, even if one were to assume they had the same meaning).

### *3.3.4 Dependent Forms in PPs*

It is not often obvious whether a given sort of empirical breakdown in complementarity is to be explained by one strategy or the other, or whether more than one of the strategies in (67) are relevant. One very complicated class of cases are those PPs that permit either pronoun or pronoun-SELF to appear in English. Consider the examples in (75–77), which are taken from R&R (1993, 686).

75a) *Lucie* explained Max to **her/herself.*
b) Lucie explained *Max* to **him/himsel*f.
c) *Lucie* explained **her/herself* to Max.

76a) *Max* saw a ghost next to *him/himself.*
b) *Max* put the book next to *him/himself.*
c) *Max* pulled the cart towards *him/himself.*

77a) *Lucie* said that I explained Max to *her/*herself.*
b) *Lucie* said that Max saw a ghost next to *her/herself.*

Although their system is different, many of the remarks of R&R (1993, 663–664, 686–688) can be translated into appropriate statements within the approach taken here.[50]

For example, R&R remark that when a preposition is thematically tied to the predicate that selects it, the preposition is invisible for the purposes of obviation; that is to say, coargument antecedency results in obviation of pronouns by pronoun-SELF. Locative PPs and some directional PPs, whether they are selected as locations by a predicate or added as adjuncts, seem to form their own domains insofar as pronouns are not excluded when anteceded by a clausemate antecedent. This is so whenever these prepositions assign a thematic role autonomously (since the matrix predicate merely selects for a location or a direction, not a nominal).

There are a number of ways of capturing the thematic–adjunct distinction, such as assuming that thematically related P of PP is incorporated covertly, extending the domain of the PP into that of the VP. If the movement is triggered by a feature, then it is a feature that one numeration has and the other does not, with the result that strategy (67c) permits a superficial empirical overlap. Alternatively, as Hestvik (1991) argues (following the references he cites, including unpublished work in LFG by Bresnan), the adjunct and thematic cases may differ according to whether or not the PP has an internal subject, which would once again mean the numerations would be distinct (if we take PRO to be a selection from the lexicon, as in 6.1.2)—cases of overlap would then just be cases where a controlled PRO subject of PP is optional.[51] On the other hand, if we allow to PPs form a separate domain, some of which do not have subjects, the possibility of promotion to discourse dependent (as in 5.4) also arises in (76), permitting overlap by strategy (67b).

The strategy of assuming that the subject of a domain may be optional seems appropriate for some PPs in DP. Consider (78).

78) *John* took a picture of *him/himself.*

If (78) is interpreted idiomatically (i.e., *x* photographs *y*), then *him* is excluded with coconstrual for most speakers, possibly because there is a PRO subject of *picture of himself.* However, if *take* is interpreted in the sense of "carry away, remove," then either *him* or *himself* is possible, consistent with the lack of a subject PRO for the nominal *picture of him/himself* (see Safir 1999, 596, fn. 10).[52]

This quick review of the variety of analyses addressing complementarity breakdowns in PPs is far from conclusive but may be taken as sufficient for my general program, in that most of these analyses are consistent with the operation of the FTIP algorithm within the competition theory proposed here by one or another of the strategies in (67).

There are many other sorts of cases that appear to counterexemplify the complementarity between dependent forms, and only the reader can judge whether the challenges faced by the competition theory are met with independently motivated proposals. I have faced as many of these challenges as I am aware of in the chapters that follow.

## 3.4 Summing Up

The goal of this chapter was to establish that only a derived complementarity approach to the pattern of anaphora can provide an explanatory account, and I have made a case that the particular competition theory I have proposed is the best mechanism for achieving that explanation.

More specifically, I have established a scale of relative degree of dependency for morphological forms and a principle, the FTIP, that determines whether or not a dependent interpretation is supported by a given form in syntactic context. Where the FTIP does not permit a dependent interpretation to be supported, the antecedent and prospective dependent form an obviative pair, which, according to Pragmatic Obviation means the members of the pair are expected to be noncoreferent. The distinction between coargument dependencies and noncoargument dependencies so far is limited to the operation of CDC for the purposes of this chapter, but I will have more to say about these issues in chapter 4.

The notion of availability presented here is embedded in the architecture of the MP even though the FTIP competition is argued not to be an economy-based competition (but see chapter 7). The FTIP regulates the competition of elements on the most dependent scale as it interacts with a given numeration and a given dependency relation between selected arguments or forms. The algorithm that computes the FTIP compares numerations with successful outcomes for the dependent identity interpretation in question—it does not compare LFs. This is an advantage when the comparison class must include competitors that do not share the same LF, as in the case of antisubject orientation, which is derived from the distribution of subject-oriented anaphors.

I presume that the FTIP, CDC, LAL, and Pragmatic Obviation are all universal, and that what is available in any given environment depends on the morphological inventory of the language and the scalar intervention factors (including those among the universals) that limit what the competing forms are in a given case. Thus my approach is resolutely syntactic, not based on any appeal to the functions sentences serve or any competition to represent purported functions—rather I take the perspective that the functions sentences can serve, particularly the coconstruals they allow, are largely determined by the competitions that define their syntax.

In the remaining chapters I explore further aspects of anaphora that affect the FTIP competition. Although not all of the proposals that are to come depend crucially on the reasoning of this chapter and chapter 2, the principles presented in these two chapters will serve as my default assumptions as I address the wide variety of issues that arise.

4

# Coargument Coconstrual and the Varieties of Dependent Identity

In the last two chapters I have distinguished dependent-identity readings from independent coreference, proposing that the FTIP exclusively and directly regulates the former. In this chapter I distinguish a variety of fine-grained distinctions between dependent-identity relations that can arise when arguments of the same predicate are coconstrued, and I explore the consequences these differences have for FTIP competitions. Moreover, in many languages, the forms that achieve coargument coconstruals are marked with special morphology that cannot be employed for noncoargument coconstruals. The sensitivity of certain forms to the coargument relation also has consequences for the FTIP and for the theory of coconstruals, which this chapter explores. However, as our examination unfolds, it will be established that there is little or no evidence to posit a semantic notion of reflexivity distinct from dependent identity.

Turning now to terminology, by *coargument relations* I mean relations between arguments semantically selected by the same argument-taker as instantiated in the lexical argument structure of that argument-taker. Since *John's discussion of himself* involves an argument-taker, *discussion*, that is not obviously a predicate (its truth value is not obviously determinate), I do not assume all argument-takers are predicates. A *reflexive interpretation* is descriptively defined as a coargument coconstrual. I assume without direct argument (there will be indirect arguments) that there is no utility in extending the term *reflexive interpretation* to noncoarguments, since in that case the notion reduces to one for which we already have a name, namely, dependent identity. Thus I avoid the term *long-distance reflexive*, which I do not believe to be of any further use.

We have already seen one interpretation relation that seems to be conditioned by coargumenthood, namely, the CDC, which accounts for the difference between (2a) and (2b), as well as for the missing interpretations for (3) discussed in the last chapter.

1) CDC: If A is identity dependent on B and A and B are coarguments, then for any distributed interpretation of B, A depends on every distributed atom of B in the same way.

2a) *Both *John* and Mary love *him*.
b) Both *John* and Mary consider *him* (to be) brilliant.

3) Die Frauen und die Männer sehen sich. (German)
   a) "The women see themselves and the men see themselves."
   b) "The women and the men see themselves."
   c) "The women see each other and the men see each other."
   d) "The women and the men see each other."
   e) not "The women see themselves and the men see each other." (or vice-versa)
   f) not "The women and the men see the women." (or vice-versa)

The CDC, however, does not regulate a particular class of forms, and it does not distinguish between specific types of dependent interpretations, except that a dependent form cannot depend on different atoms of its coargument antecedent in different ways. This condition was shown not to hold of noncoarguments, as illustrated in (2b). If only for this reason, the coargument coconstrual relation does seem to have a special status.

There are, of course, a variety of argument-takers that place idiosyncratic thematic restrictions on the form and interpretation of their coargument coconstruals, and most of these predicates are typically referred to as *inherently reflexive*; I reserve my discussion of them for 4.3. There are also languages that mark coargument dependency with a verbal affix, both for reflexive and reciprocal interpretations, and in some of these languages, there is no contrast in form between inherent reflexives and thematically unrestricted reflexives, though noncoargument anaphora may be marked in a different fashion. The issues that arise in the analysis of these languages are reserved for 4.4. However, it is clear that affixal reflexives and inherent reflexives treat the coargument coconstrual relation in a very particular way that seems to be different from what we have described as dependent identity generally. We must ask then, the following question: If there are interpretive differences between reflexive interpretation and noncoargument dependent identity, what theoretical significance do these differences have?

In answering this question, it seems prudent to avoid positing special semantic relations of dependency for anaphors that are not attested for anaphora that is not morphologically marked. Indeed all of the relations to be examined in this chapter deserve to be examined through this heuristic filter. On the basis of chapter 2, I assume without further argument that dependency relations and identity relations are independently necessary semantic relations outside of formal grammar.

In this light, is interesting to note that Reinhart and Reuland (1991, 290–294) introduce a very important assumption about reflexivity that does not necessarily follow from the coargument relation, nor from dependency, nor from identity, in that they speak of "reflexive predicates." A predicate is semantically reflexive in their view if two of its arguments are coindexed. Although coindexation is always dependency in the G&R theory, R&R appear to treat identity among coarguments as symmetric covariation, in that they allow for the possibility that a subject could be reflexively marked to indicate covariation with a direct object that is not reflexive in form, as in (4a) and (4c). This is so because they assume that c-command is not relevant to coargument relations of reflexivity.[1] Rather they assume symmetric covariation, as formulated in (5).

4a) **Himself* loves *John.*
b) *John* loves *himself.*
c) **Himself* loves *him.*

5) Reflexivity in R&R: $\lambda x(R(x, x))$

By contrast I have explicitly been assuming that *himself* is not only covariant with *John* where they are well-formed coarguments, as in (4b), but also that *himself* depends on *John*. If the relation is dependent identity, then the rather popular description of the logical form of reflexivity they rely on in (5) (see Bach and Partee 1980, 9), namely, symmetric covariation, is inadequate.

The FTIP only addresses dependent interpretations, and assuming a dependency relation, (4a, c) are excluded because FTIP determines that neither *John* nor *him* is the most dependent form available with respect to the c-commanding *himself,* and so the object cannot depend on the subject, and as discussed in chapter 2, failure of dependency cannot be accommodated. Moreover, LAL requires a c-antecedent for an anaphor (see 3.2.1) and in (4a, c) it has none.[2] Finally, in 2.5, it is suggested, following Higginbotham (1985), that an element cannot be dependent on a node it c-commands (which I have called the Independence Principle), and if so, this would be sufficient to eliminate (4a, c) without obviation or reliance on LAL or FTIP, but only if the relationship is asymmetric dependency.[3]

If the relation involved in (4b) *is* dependency rather than just symmetric covariation, then the reflexivity relation is less unlike noncoargument relations, which also can involve dependent identity rather than only covariation. Since my reduction of principles B and C under FTIP is based on the view that the semantic reflexivity of predicates (as in R&R's Principle B) involves the same sort of asymmetric dependency as that found in the noncoargument cases, I have a lot at stake. In 4.1 and 4.2, I argue that the standard cases of reflexivity involve dependent-identity interpretation. In fact the centerpiece of the R&R approach to anaphora, the notion of "reflexive predicate," turns out to have no special theoretical standing. Abandoning reflexive predicates turns out to have a liberating effect, leading us to put much more emphasis on FTIP as the central anaphoric principle.

## 4.1 Reflexivity and Dependency

An argument that the reflexivity relation, at least in languages like English, is an asymmetric dependent-identity relation, may be illustrated by adapting a sort of example originally introduced by Heim (1993).

6) *Every woman* thinks that only *she* respects *her* husband.

It is possible that (6) could describe (a) a set of women who believe they are husband respecters or (b) a woman like Sally, who believes that her (Sally's) husband is not respected by other women. For both interpretations, *she* and *her* covary, but in the latter case, both *she* and *her* are each directly dependent on the matrix subject, while for the husband-respecter interpretation, *her* is dependent directly on *she*.

With careful choice of examples, it is possible to illustrate exactly the same dependency distinction which, in the case of coarguments, can actually be disambiguated by the choice of SELF form or pronoun, where the latter choice is somewhat degraded for some speakers (for a similar example, see Fox 1998, 141).

7a) *?Every woman* thought that *only she* voted for *her.*
b) *Every woman* thought that *only she* voted for *herself.*

Both the third person feminine pronouns in (7a) covary with the choice of woman, but in (7a), for any choice of woman, that woman thought she got a total of one vote (her own). By contrast, (7b) strongly favors an interpretation where each woman thought that no other woman was a self-voter, leaving open, however, the possibility that our candidate may have gotten more votes than her own. Following Heim (1993), Reinhart (1997), and Fox (1998), I take it that both *she* and *her* are directly dependent on *every woman* in (7a), whereas in (7b), *herself* is dependent only on *only she* in the most accessible reading. Notice that a theory representing anaphora based on symmetric indices without dependency diacritics would not be able to characterize these distinctions.

Now it has been suggested that the difference between (7a) and (7b) is dependent on *she* rather than on *only she*. Higginbotham (1980b, 698) has so argued to account for cases like (8) (originally due to Geach 1962).

8) Only Satan loves Satan.

It would appear that (8) is a Principle C violation if *only Satan* is coreferent with *Satan*. Higginbotham argues that such cases involve coreference between *Satan* embedded in *only Satan* and the direct object *Satan*, whereby the embedded *Satan* does not c-command the object. If so, the contrast in (7a, b) has only to do with the strictness of c-command.

However, it does not appear that potential antecedents like *only DP* should be decomposed as antecedents for the purposes of c-command, nor do SELF forms always have to be dependent on those antecedents that meet their syntactic antecedency requirements, even in environments where they are not promoted to discourse dependents (see 5.4).

9a) *Every Democratic candidate* insisted that *only she* expected *herself* to win.
b) *Each candidate* insisted that everyone except *her* thought *she* would lose.
c) *Each candidate* insisted that no other candidate expected to win.

In (9a), both covariant readings are possible, including one where *herself* is dependent directly on the quantified antecedent and not on *only she* (which entails [9b]), and one where *herself* depends on *only she* (which entails [9c]), that is, where each candidate expects it of herself that she will win. However, if c-command distinguished *she* from *only she* for these two interpretations, the SELF form would not have a c-commanding antecedent for the interpretation entailing (9b).[4]

The facts in (9) settle some issues and raise others. The examples were introduced to show that *only DP* could satisfy the structural c-command requirement that licenses a SELF form and still permit both dependent readings. I take it to be settled now that the difference between (7a) and (7b) is not a distinction of c-command but is rather based on which c-commanding antecedent is the one a form depends on. Settled also is the conclusion that reflexivity, at least as it affects the distribution of SELF forms in languages like English, can denote asymmetric dependency for coarguments, not just codependency on an identical antecedent, a form of covariation. However two new questions now arise. First, why do examples like (9a) permit two readings, while (7a) and (7b) each permit only one reading? Second, how does the theory permit antecedency requirements for SELF forms to be met independently of asymmetric dependency?[5]

Let us take the second question first. Recall the formulation of LAL, repeated below, where it is assumed, as pointed out in 3.2.1, that the term c-antecedent requires c-command and a form of covariation that we may now characterize as symmetric codependency of the sort described in (10b) (in cases where X and Y are both dependent directly on Z).

10a) LAL: An anaphor must be c-anteceded in Domain D.
b) If X is a *c-antecedent* of Y, then X c-commands Y, and either Y is dependent on X, or X is dependent on Z, and Y is dependent on Z.

I assume for the form *himself*, as I do for all other SELF forms in English, that it is an anaphor in this environment, since examples like (11) are excluded.

11) ?**Every woman candidate* insisted that only the men expected *herself* to win.

In (11), the requirement that *herself* be dependent is met because it is dependent on *every woman candidate*, but the latter antecedent is local enough to license *herself* under LAL, so the sentence crashes. In the case of (7b) and (9a), by contrast, *herself* is locally c-anteceded within Domain D by a *codependent* c-commander, and so the anaphor is licensed, but the SELF form in (9a) is also *asymmetrically dependent* on an antecedent outside of Domain D.

The formulation in (10b) makes an interesting prediction for examples like (12) that no other approach has ever addressed. In (12), *each athlete*, a non-c-commanding constituent in (12), can be what the c-antecedent of *himself* is dependent on.

12) *Each athlete's* wife suggested that *only he* had expected *himself* to win.

Thus (12) allows the codependent covariation interpretation, where each athlete's wife suggests her husband was alone in predicting he would win, and a locally dependent interpretation where each athlete's wife believes that only her husband was confident of victory and that the other athletes did have that confidence.

Now let us take a step back and consider how the FTIP computes the results for (7a, b), augmented with dependency arrows in (13a, b). Recall that the FTIP runs entirely on dependency relations and LAL is a scalar intervention that indirectly limits the availability of dependent forms. In (13b) the SELF form is dependent on the antecedent in the domain of LAL. In this instance, the most dependent form available, *herself*, can be dependent on its coargument subject, and *herself* is not excluded by LAL. Thus use of *her* for the most local dependent interpretation is obviated.

13a) *Every woman* thought that *only she* voted for *her.*

b) *Every woman* thought that *only she* voted for *herself/*her.*

Here we encounter a potential problem, however. Though *her* is dependent on the matrix antecedent, *every woman* in (13a), *only she* can be the c-antecedent of *her*, but that means that a SELF form is also available for the reading in (13a), since c-antecedent is locally available. Thus the SELF form should obviate a pronoun, even for the reading of nonlocal dependence. This is the wrong result, since (13a) with a pronoun is possible and in fact required for the relevant interpretation.[6] It would be the right result, however, if we were considering (9a), where both interpretations are indeed available. In terms of FTIP, it appears that some other scalar intervention must knock out the nonlocal dependent interpretation in (13b) without knocking it out for (9a).

The obvious distinction between (13b) and (9a) is that the most local antecedent of the SELF form in (13b) is a coargument, whereas the most local antecedent of the SELF form in (9a), which is an ECM environment, is not a coargument of the ECM complement subject *herself.* It would appear that when the SELF form is a coargument of its antecedent, it *must* be semantically dependent on it as well as be syntactically anteceded by it. To enforce the coargument-dependent interpretation in these environments, I introduce the Locally Reflexive Principle.

14) Locally Reflexive Principle (LRP): An identity-specific anaphor is dependent on its coargument antecedent, if it has one.

By distinguishing identity-specific (i.e., specifically identity-matching) anaphors from reciprocals (for which participants in the relation denoted by the predicate do not match), I am adding to the universally available lexical inventory from which particular languages can choose a subset of forms. For now, I do so arbitrarily, including SELF forms as identity specific (which are always a subset of lexically marked anaphors), but in fact whether a form can be an identity-specific anaphor, as opposed to an anaphoric pronominal that permits different sorts of readings (such as German *sich*), can often be derived, or largely derived, from its lexical composition (see chapter 6). Here it will suffice to point out that *sich* is not a form that marks dependency specific to identity, since it also permits reciprocal interpretation, while SELF forms never permit reciprocal interpretation.[7, 8] As demonstrated in note 2 of the appendix to chapter 6, reciprocals don't show the same sort of coargument limitation blocking codependent covariation (e.g., *The men thought they were taller than each other* permits a wide scope of reading).

Now let us return to (13a, b) and (9a). The reasoning about (9a) remains unaffected by these considerations, since LRP does not intervene in that case. Rather in (9a) we simply have an anaphor that is licensed by a sufficiently local c-commanding covariant DP and that can be dependent on any other c-commander, thus permitting both readings. The difference for our account arises for (13b), where LRP now ensures that the SELF form, if it is used, must depend on its c-antecedent because its c-antecedent is a coargument. Thus the LRP acts as a scalar intervention to render the SELF form unavailable for the long-distance dependent interpretation. Now compare (13a), where the pronoun unambiguously supports the nonlocal dependent interpretation. Since the SELF form is unavailable for the nonlocal reading, the pronoun, as the next most dependent form available with respect to *every woman*, becomes the bearer of the nonlocal dependent reading. The pronoun cannot support the local dependent reading, however, because the FTIP algorithm determines that SELF is available with respect to the more local antecedent; hence the pronoun is obviated for the dependent interpretation. Now the readings for (13a, b), (9a), and the two readings for (6) (which share the relevant structural properties of those in [9a]) are all derived.

It is important to understand that though I posit LRP as a universal, it may not have anything to apply to in some languages, since it is both possible and attested that a language may, as a gap in its morphological component, lack any identity-specific anaphor. As pointed out in 3.3.2, there are a number of languages where otherwise independent pronouns may be used to achieve reflexive readings with coarguments when there is no anaphoric form available. This is one respect in which the LRP makes very different predictions from the R&R RIP. LRP does not require that reflexive interpretations *have* to be marked by reflexive markers, as RIP does. Note further that R&R's requirement that a syntactic predicate must be reflexive if it is marked reflexive (their Principle A) is violated by the cases I have discussed here, since there is no sense in which the so-called syntactic predicates are reflexive—the SELF form is not dependent on a coargument. Only a weak appeal to coindexation without dependency could salvage the syntactic predicate idea, but to do so drains from it any intuitive appeal to a broader sense of coargumenthood.

There are languages that seem specifically sensitive to LRP in that they have identity-specific anaphors that are even more specifically restricted to coargument antecedents. I reserve the term *reflexive marker* for anaphors that can only participate in coargument coconstruals (which does not hold for English *himself*, but may hold for Norwegian *ham selv*, for example; see 3.1.2.2). Abe, as discussed in Koopman and Sportiche (1989), provides evidence for the existence of a pure reflexive marker, never used for noncoarguments. Abe has two sets of pronouns that Koopman and

Sportiche refer to as the *O*-pronoun series and the *n*-pronoun on the basis of their morphophonology. The reflexive morpheme, which consists of a portion meaning "body" (*-se*) and a pronoun (drawn from either of the two sets of pronouns), must be coconstrued with a coargument (see Koopman and Sportiche 1989, 564, ex. 20) and cannot receive an acceptable interpretation when it is embedded within a complement nominal or even a PP (see their ex. 21).

Before I extend the independent motivation for the LRP, some of the results of this subsection concerning reflexivity are summarized in (15).

15a) The reflexivity relation, as examined thus far, consists not only of covariance of identity between coarguments, but also of asymmetric dependent identity.
  b) SELF forms are licensed by their c-antecedents, but they are not always dependent on their c-antecedents.
  c) A SELF form is an identity-specific anaphor, and other anaphors are not identity specific (e.g., *sich*).
  d) The LRP requires an identity-specific (matching) anaphor to be dependent on a coargument c-antecedent if it has one.
  e) Some forms are specifically sensitive to LRP.

On the basis of what I have said so far, it would appear that at least the asymmetric-dependency relation in (16), where R is a predicate, must be part of what counts as reflexivity for LRP.

16) *x* R *x*

If this is all there is to reflexivity, then it is not semantically different from dependent-identity relations that do not involve coarguments. A question that remains open and that I return to in 4.2 is the following: In what sense is the second argument of R somehow a dependent function of its antecedent "*x*"? However, before I do, it is useful to present further arguments supporting the coargument effect enforced by LRP.

### *4.1.1 More Evidence for Coargument-Conditioned Dependent Identity*

Consider the instantiation paradigm based on Evans (1980) in (17) where the property of hating Max is ascribed to instances of *everyone*. This property is applied to a number of instantiations, including Max. I assume that *him* is consistently dependent on the first mention, as is possible in my account given that c-command is not required for a dependent interpretation.

17a) Everyone hates Max.
  b) John hates him.
     Bill hates him . . .
  c) Even Max hates him.
  d) #*Even* Max hates *himself.*

In this paradigm, (17d) is deviant because it has only the meaning that *Max* is a self-hater, that is, the meaning where *himself* is dependent on *even Max*, but being a self-hater is not the property that the rest of the paradigm instantiates. The LRP straightforwardly supplies us with a reason as to why *himself* cannot be treated as independently covariant in (17d), since *himself* is a coargument of *even Max*

The deviance of (17d) within the instantiation paradigm is not simply a function of the fact that *himself* must be locally dependent, however. If the instantiation context is strong enough, *himself* can have a codependent, covariant interpretation (dependent on the first mention of O.J.) that is independent of *even O.J.* as long as it is c-anteceded, as is illustrated in the paradigm in (18).

18a) Everyone expects O.J. to be acquitted.
b) Bill expects him to be acquitted.
Sarah expects him to be acquitted.
c) *Even O.J.* expects *him* to be acquitted.
d) *Even O.J.* expects *himself* to be acquitted.

In (18d), *himself* permits a reading independent of *even OJ*, adding even O.J. to the list of people who think O.J. will be acquitted. Some find (18d) more acceptable than a pronoun (18c) for this interpretation, but the FTIP does not regulate a competition between forms representing a dependent interpretation where there is no c-command (both depend on the first mention), so if there is a difference, the FTIP does not predict it or require it. The locally dependent interpretation is, of course, available for (18d), but it would be as deviant in this discourse as it is in (17). As a control, however, (19) shows that in a different paradigm, the dependent interpretation for the sentence in (18d) is possible.

19a) *Everyone* expects *himself* to be acquitted.
b) *Even O.J.* expects *himself/*him* to be acquitted.

The O.J. paradigms in (17) and (18) show once again that syntactic antecedence for LAL does not require a most local dependency relation unless, as the LRP predicts, the anteceded term is a coargument of its antecedent. Moreover, there is no account of these facts within a theory that expresses the force of Principle A as the formation of a reflexive predicate, as R&R do, since there is no extended sense of coargumenthood between *O.J.* in (18a) and *himself* in (18d).

## 4.2 Reflexivity and Identity

Up to this point, I have focused on how coargumenthood and asymmetric dependence are crucial to the reflexive relation, but I have avoided discussing what I mean by *identity* in the reflexive relation. What constitutes a relation of identity between two entities is too profound a metaphysical issue for me to grapple with here, and even an attempt to define identity independently for the representations I propose seems too difficult. Rather I will take a resolutely empirical approach to the notion of identity as it relates to reflexive interpretations, adducing no more or less to it than our linguistic intuitions commit us to, already a formidable task. This section explores some of the empirical effects that appear to reflect conditions on how identity is interpreted in linguistically represented coconstrual relations.

To narrow the inquiry, at least at first, let us restrict ourselves to thematically unrestricted reflexivity between coarguments of a predicate P, such that if $x$ is an anaphor object of P anteceded by its coargument $y$, then $x$ receives the same theta assignment and selectional restriction that it would if it were neither dependent nor even coconstrued with $y$. In short, we are setting aside inherent reflexivity and reflexivity induced by nonargument affixes in what follows, at least until 4.4.

We can put the question slightly more precisely by asking (a) What constitutes identity of a dependent with respect to its antecedent? and (b) Do noncoarguments treat dependence of identity differently than coarguments do?

### *4.2.1 Proxy Readings*

Recent work by Reuland (1997), Jackendoff (1992), Lidz (1996), Rooryck and vanden Wyngaerd (1997, 1998), and others has refocused attention on contexts where reflexive readings hold for reflexive marker arguments that are not extensionally coconstrued with their antecedents. Such cases arise where the dependent is in some way a representation or representative of its antecedent and typically require a set of background assumptions for the relevant interpretations. Consider some of the relevant cases based on similar examples from the literature on coreference over the years.

20) Original and Likeness:
  a) *Marlene Dietrich* admired *herself* but thought *she* ought to have been dressed differently.
  b) *Fidel Castro* bumped into *himself* (and broke *his* arm).
  c) At the costume ball, *Marlene and Fidel* kept running into *themselves*.
  d) *Hitchcock* liked *himself* in that movie.

Imagine for (20a, b) that Marlene Dietrich and Fidel Castro are in a wax museum (see Jackendoff 1992) such that Marlene is admiring a statue of herself, and Fidel is clumsily damaging his own likeness (not experiencing a fractured bone). In the case of (20c), assume that Marlene and Fidel are constantly running into people in Fidel or Marlene costumes (see Rooryck and vanden Wyngaerd 1997). In these cases, the SELF form is not even coreferent with its antecedent extensionally, though it is clear that the reflexive allows for an interpretation where the referent of the SELF form is clearly dependent on its antecedent, such that the identity of the SELF form referent is a function of that of its antecedent. The example in (20d) (discussed by Fauconnier 1994, 36) may be understood in the following context: Hitchcock makes a movie about himself in which his persona is played by Orson Welles, and the director makes a cameo appearance as a man at a bus stop. Example (20d) could describe how Hitchcock is satisfied by how he is portrayed by Welles, or how Hitchcock himself portrayed the man at the bus stop, but in neither case does the referent of *himself* = Hitchcock extensionally, but rather represents his persona in one way or another.

21) Author and Work:
   a) *Grisham* will be reading *himself* in Swahili soon.
   b) Looking up at the scoreboard, *Sosa* saw *himself* in second place.

In cases like (21a) (see especially Nunberg 1979), it is Grisham's novel, translated into a language he presumably does not know, that represents him in some way, while in (21b) the baseball player Sammy Sosa is presumably looking at his home run statistics, not at his image or his own body.

22) Representative Vehicle:
   a) *Alice* rolled the dice and then moved *herself* three spaces.
   b) *Patton* positioned *himself* between the Germans and the sea.

In (22a) we could imagine that Alice is represented in the board game by a tin thimble that marks her position on the board, and in the situation described, she is moving the piece that represents her ahead three spaces. In (22b), we may imagine Patton in a chateau nowhere near either the Germans or the sea as he is positioning his army in the field (for similar examples, see Jackendoff 1997, 56–57).

These examples do not exhaust the varieties of such relations, but they will do to illustrate the phenomenon. Reuland (1997, 26) remarks, "[The SELF form] expresses a relation between an $x$ and an f($x$) which bears a systematic resemblance to $x$, but can be distinguished." The term I will use for this resemblance is *proxy interpretation*, and (16) could serve as its representation. It would be a mistake, however, to see the formula in (16) as motivated by proxy interpretation, since proxy interpretation is not peculiar to coargument interpretations. Noncoargument relations show the same sorts of effects:

23a) As they strolled through the wax museum, *Fidel* could not help thinking that *he* would have looked better in a uniform, and **Marlene** could not help thinking that **she** would have looked better without one.
   b) The masquerade ball was a bit disconcerting. It seemed to *Marlene* that everywhere *she* looked, either *her* nose was too long or *her* chin too weak.
   c) *Hitchcock* thought *he* looked insufficiently bald in that scene (as played by Welles).
   d) *Grisham* claims that *he* is even more suspenseful in Swahili.
   e) *Alice* thought *she* was positioned to win until the Red Queen knocked *her* into the bushes.
   f) *Patton* realized that *he* would be vulnerable to a flanking movement.

Jackendoff (1992, 5) points out, moreover, that the asymmetry goes in only one direction, insofar as (24a) cannot be interpreted to mean (24b), but rather (24c) (which is pragmatically quite difficult).

24a) *Ringo* and I were drunk in the wax museum. I clumsily started bumping into statues as I danced, and then *Ringo* toppled over and fell on *himself*.

b) #*Ringo's* statue fell on *Ringo*.
c) *Ringo* fell on *his* statue.

In (25a), where there is no coargument relation involved, it is again quite difficult to construe *he* as the biblical David and *David* as the statue even though the sentence makes no contextual sense construed the other way. Compare (25b), which, though awkward, is acceptable.

25a) In Michaelangelo's time, *David* indicated how handsome *he* was thought to be.
b) In Michaelangelo's time, the statue of *David* indicated how handsome *he* was thought to be.
c) In Michaelangelo's time, *he* indicated how handsome *David* was thought to be.

This is expected if the proxy reading is susceptible to the Independence Principle (introduced in 2.5), which prohibits a constituent from depending on anything it c-commands. Example (25a) is one case where the Independence Principle applies to a case where FTIP (or Principle C) does not overlap it. By contrast, both the FTIP and the Independence Principle rule out (25c). The Independence Principle rules it out not because *David* in (25c) is noncoreferent with *he*, but because *he* as a proxy cannot depend on *David*, as is the case with the tokens reversed in (25a). FTIP rules out (25c) because *he* c-commands *David*, and because *David*, if it is to depend on *he*, is not the most dependent form available. Given the Independence Principle and the FTIP, there is no need to appeal to a syntactic constraint holding at a conceptual level, as Jackendoff (1992, 1997, 55, 73–74) does, but rather it is possible to say that proxy readings are dependent readings and are not available where the dependent interpretation is syntactically prohibited.

Note also that the fact that proxy relations are dependency relations provides additional evidence against the symmetric interpretations of reflexivity proposed by R&R (as in [5]). If they were right, then (24a) should be ambiguous, contrary to fact, between interpretations where proxy acts on person, on the one hand, and where person acts on proxy, on the other.

But where does this leave us? We have made no progress on what identity means, but syntax seems sensitive to a proxy relation, conditioned by dependency, which results in noncoextensional coconstrual. The proxy reading does not choose between coargument relations and noncoargument relations and thus does not reveal any special content to a notion of reflexivity that is over and above a dependent-identity relation. In 4.2.3 I return to this relation, however, since certain choices of grammatical form are sensitive to it.[9]

### *4.2.2 Guise*

Now let us reconsider a class of examples discussed by Lakoff (1968, 1996) that were introduced in 2.4, where it is possible to create situations in which, by placing the perspective of one in the shoes of another, apparent coreference relations are confounded. I employ the term *guise* now to descriptively refer to the readings in (26) where one person's perspective is put in the shoes of another and is represented by a nominal form.[10]

26a) If I were you, I'd hate myself.
b) If I were you, I'd hate me.
c) If John were in Bill's place, he'd hate himself.
d) If John were in Bill's place, he'd hate him.

The first person examples are particularly interesting, since even where it is clear that the FTIP does not permit a dependent interpretation, a coreferent one of some sort must be held to exist in examples like (26b), where first person is indexical. The relation in (26b) is not reflexive, since it does not involve dependence, while (26a) permits a dependent interpretation by FTIP (the most dependent form is employed) and must be interpreted as dependent by LRP since *myself* is an identity-specific anaphor.

To clarify, the guises of *I'd hate myself* in (26a) are the same, which is to say that "I as you" would hate "I as you," but the guises in (26b) for *I'd hate me* are not the same, since "I as you" is said to hate "me." My proposal about these readings is summed up in (27).

27) If A cannot depend on B and B cannot depend on A, then guise A denoted by A is distinct from guise B denoted by B.

The claim that one guise must be able to depend on the other in order for them to be coextensive is enough to account for (26b, d) since the subject cannot depend on what it c-commands (by the Independence Principle), and the object, if it is to be dependent on the subject, must not be represented by a pronoun, which is not the most dependent form available (by virtue of the FTIP). We can confirm that the distinctions in (26) are determined by the pattern of dependence, as illustrated by the absence of a sloppy reading for (28) (as discussed in 2.4).

28a) Speaker A: If I were him, I would hate me.
b) Speaker B: Yeah, if I were him, probably no more than I would.

Speaker B's response must mean that, under speaker A's hypothetical, speaker B would also hate speaker A, not that if speaker B applied the hypothetical to himself, such that speaker B had the perspective of *him*, speaker B would hate speaker B. This is because there is no dependency to copy into the elision site in speaker B's utterance, so the position of the elided pronoun in (28b) can only depend on the reference of *me* (crucially not its first person form, since the referent of first person has shifted along with the speaker).[11]

Both interpretations are available for (29), although the sloppy one is favored.[12]

29a) Speaker A: If I were him, I would hate myself.
b) Speaker B: Yeah, if I were him, probably no more than I would.

In (29b), a sloppy interpretation is possible because *myself* with a coargument requires the dependent interpretation. Since the SELF form is dependent, the guise of the object is identical to that of the subject. It is also possible for (29) to have a strict interpretation, one which matches that of (28), but that is due to the option of applying vehicle change in the elided VP to replace the reflexive-marked form with a simple pronoun, as discussed briefly in 2.5 (but see also 4.3.4 and especially Safir 2004). If a pronoun is copied in the elided VP complement position, then FTIP predicts that the most dependent interpretation is not available from the first conjunct, so a distinction in guise is unavoidable by virtue of (27), since no dependency of object on subject can be copied.

The contrast between guise interpretations and proxy interpretations is instructive. Proxy interpretations are failures of coextensive coreference that nonetheless satisfy the requirements of identity, whereas guise interpretations do not maintain distinctness from their antecedents under dependency. For example, the distinctness of coconstrual evidenced by dependent proxy interpretations can be preserved under sloppy identity in elision contexts (as well as under strict interpretations, for those that permit strict interpretations in these environments).

30a) Alex hoped his likeness would be more prominently displayed than Joe's, but unfortunately, as they entered the gallery, Joe saw himself before Alex did.
b) Grisham expects to read himself in Spanish translation before Le Carré does.
c) Patton deployed himself between the two armies more quickly than Montgomery would have.

The proxy readings persist in the hypothetical identity examples, which shows that proxy and guise readings exist independently and can overlap.

31a) Grisham to polyglot Le Carré:
If I were you, I couldn't bear to read me/myself in Spanish.
b) Marlene Dietrich to Patton at Mme. Tussaud's, where he is dressing the statues as part of a promotion:
If I were you, I would dress me/myself as a general.
d) Melissa to Felicity as they play croquet:
If I were you, I would knock me/myself out of bounds.

Recall now that the dependent reading, which a proxy interpretation requires, can be blocked, either because the potential proxy c-commands what it depends on or because the FTIP does not permit a dependent interpretation because the form employed is not the most dependent one available. Where dependent interpretation is blocked by FTIP within each of the consequents above, that is, in those cases where a pronoun rather than a SELF form is employed, the *guise* must be distinct from that of the subject, and the proxy cannot be a proxy of the subject, yet the pronoun can still get a proxy interpretation by depending on the first person in the *if* clause. By contrast, wherever the SELF form is employed, guise does not shift, and the proxy reading falls on the antecedent of the SELF form. Thus precisely where guises are psychologically coconstrued with their antecedents, proxies are extensionally distinct. Ultimately, however, the guise of a proxy behaves just as other guises do with respect to the perspectives they represent, while the proxy of a guise behaves just as other proxies do with respect to the functions of their antecedents that they represent.

The point of this discussion is not to reveal the ultimate nature of the proxy function or the meaning of guises, though one would like to know these things, but rather to understand the relations between dependency and identity, since dependency is syntactically conditioned, and identity relations sensitive to dependency will thus show evidence of syntactic conditioning. Why it is that proxies must be dependent is intuitively clear insofar as they are functions of the things they are dependent on. One might similarly assume that an individual with *x*'s perspective is a function of *x*. Why an individual *y* independently coconstrued with *x* (when both are first person, for example) does not permit G(*y*) (guise of *y*) to have the same value as G(*x*) is less obvious, since in these cases Pragmatic Obviation, presumably overcome by person, does not prevent covaluation. The evaluation of the semantic identities that the guises represent reduces to the familiar Fregean problems I do not claim to have solved. The point, however, is that in cases like *If I were him, I'd hate me*, the guises in the consequent are not dependent on one another as enforced by FTIP in syntax, even though they each may be covalued with first person.

The relationship between dependency and guise readings permits us to put some extravagant claims made by antiformalist linguists in perspective. Lakoff (1996), for example, claims that the choice of anaphor is sensitive to a conceptual split he takes to be the essence of the different readings in (26a, b). The conceptual distinction he proposes is between the "subject," which represents one's subjectivity, and the "self," which roughly corresponds to one's body/place.[13] It is true that the difference between the SELF form and the pronoun distinguish between the readings in (26a, b), but the reason is entirely formal and not at all a function of the meaning of pronouns or SELF forms. This is easily demonstrated when the readings available for (32) are considered.

32) If I were you, I would ask Marilyn to marry me.

This is ambiguous between the two readings (Marilyn is asked to marry the *I* of *if I were you,* or Marilyn is asked to marry the *you* of *if I were you*), which we would not expect if the actual meaning of *x*-SELF were at stake. The distinction between these two readings is that one must piggyback on a form that must support a dependent reading, and the other piggybacks on a form that need not. Lakoff's (1996, 98) claim that "the use of anaphoric pronouns is based on this split" is true only if one pays attention to the formal syntax of the sentence, and not to which particular form the syntax (specifically FTIP) determines to be the bearer of the dependent reading. This does not explain our sense of shifting perspective or the nature of the metaphor involved, which Lakoff explores, but it shows that whatever the distinction semantically consists in, it is not independent of structural considerations, but rather exploits a distinction provided by the formal grammar.

Similar objections may be raised to conclusions based on examples discussed by Nunberg (1979), Abusch (1989), Sag (1981), and Fauconnier (1994) where individuals are known and referred to by something that characterizes them. For example, in the restaurant sentences originally discussed by Nunberg, for example, *The ham sandwich says he wants a cup of coffee*, the person who ordered the ham sandwich is the one referred to. These cases, which Abusch calls *reference shifters* (and Nunberg calls *deferred reference*), are not proxy readings, since the ham sandwich is not a function of the one who orders it (though one might claim that the one who orders the ham sandwich is a function of the sandwich). Rather they appear to be nothing more than epithets that happen to employ inanimate nominals as descriptions. Much is made of the fact that a replacement of *he* with *it* in our example is unacceptable, but this seems merely to be a function of whether or not the antecedent is taken to be an epithet for some animate individual or just a literal description. More to the point here, however, is that when such cases participate in reflexive readings, the individual denoted by the ham sandwich is not extensionally distinct from the SELF form that depends on it; for example, *The ham sandwich squeezed too hard and covered himself with mayonnaise* can only mean that the customer was soiled. If *itself* replaces *himself*, then it can't mean that the sandwich was over-lubricated by the customer (who is denoted by *ham sandwich)*. The reflexive readings are always dependent ones, as Abusch points out, but the point from my perspective is that for the epithet cases these dependent readings are coextensional. Cases that Abusch (1989, 3) mentions that are not coextensional, such as *Andy Warhol imagined himself hanging in the Louvre next to Leonardo,* are proxy cases in my account and unremarkable in that respect.

Thus, though there is obviously a considerable pragmatic contribution to the interpretation of epithets, proxies, and guises, patterns of dependency still restrict their use, and it is therefore an overstatement to conclude, as Nunberg does, that "it is much cleaner and simpler to suppose that the grammar of the language places no restrictions on deferred use, leaving it to pragmatics to sort out individual cases" (1993, 31). Much more research into the distribution of guises, proxies, and epithets is required, particularly as they occur in languages with different inventories of anaphors and reflexive affixes. More of what is at stake is examined in 4.3 and chapter 6.

### *4.2.3 Exhaustivity*

Another property of dependent readings that is remarked on from time to time is exhaustivity, which comes in at least two varieties. One variety of this is the claim, which I describe as *exhaustive dependency,* that if the antecedent is divided into an n-tuple of atoms, the dependent depends on every atom of its antecedent. The CDC is a constraint on coargument interpretations that appeals to this notion. Another variety of exhaustivity, *exhaustive antecedence,* is that for every atom of the dependent, there is an antecedent that corresponds to it.[14]

The second variety of exhaustivity might seem at first to be largely a matter of agreement. Thus examples like (33) fail because the agreement features of the SELF form disagree with its antecedent.

33a) He loved *themselves/?them (as they were in their younger years).

b) He considers *themselves/them to be a happy couple.

As (33b) shows, this is not a coargument property but a property of anaphors, and further, it is not a property of pronouns. The acceptable, though somewhat marginal dependent collective reading of (33) with the pronoun, as mentioned in 3.3.1 (see also note 38 to this chapter), is one where an individual loves the group as a group, and the group includes that individual (see Antecedent Agreement as described in 3.2).[15] Cases like (33b), similar to cases discussed by G&R (1993, 83), have embedded predicates that require a plural subject, and so if we know that Jack is speaking of his life with his wife Jill, (33b) with a pronoun might grammatically report Jack's perspective. By introducing quantified antecedents in a carefully controlled setting, it is possible to show that the collective interpretation of the couple can be dependent. (The context for [34a] assures that the universals are selected from individuals in the study who have had spouses of 50 years).

34) Individuals married for 50 or more years were interviewed for a research project on the future of marriage. Each participant was asked describe how well s/he got on with his/her spouse.
  a) *Every husband* considered ***?them/*themselves*** to have been a happy couple, but **every wife** believed ***them/*themselves*** to have been cursed beyond words.

We have seen (in chapter 2) that split antecedents are possible, but partial dependency involves a dependency of a plurality on an antecedent that involves less atoms than the plurality it antecedes. What these examples show is that pronouns do not need to be exhaustively anteceded, although the dependency of the pronoun exhausts the atoms of its antecedent; for every couple there is a unique husband. The anaphoric SELF forms do not permit this relation, but pronouns do.

The same sort of fact also holds for split dependents, as in (35) (where such examples require that the pronoun must receive contrastive stress).

35a) ?***Every couple*** had expected *him/*himself* to earn more money than **she** would.
  b) In 1960, *almost every couple*, even when the spouses were interviewed separately, suggested that *her* aspirations should always be the ones to be sacrificed if it would suffice to avoid open conflict.

Once again, the dependent pronouns are exhaustively dependent on their antecedents, since there is one wife and one husband for each of the couples in (35a), varying pairwise and exhausting the antecedent, while there is likewise a frustrated wife for every couple in (35b). As in (35b), subparts of the antecedent atoms need not be used as antecedents, however, and once again we see that pronouns can represent these relations (where the CDC does not intervene), and anaphors cannot.

It then comes as no surprise that anaphors, elements susceptible to LAL, which cannot be partial or split dependents, require also the much stronger exhaustivity relation even when they are not coarguments.

36) *The men* considered *each other/themselves* to be trustworthy.

There is no reading for (36) with the SELF form where *themselves* is only anaphoric on a (plural) subset of the men, or where *each other* only involves reciprocal relations on a (plural) subset of the men. Since plural agreement would be satisfied in either case, we now see that the exhaustivity requirement is not sufficiently accounted for by Antecedent Agreement. Thus, for languages that employ identity-specific anaphors to mark reflexivity, it may be impossible to tell whether or not exhaustivity is a requirement of a reflexive marker itself rather than the reflexive relation; the effect of it would be masked by the requirement of anaphors that they be exhaustively anteceded and exhaustively dependent. See 6.3.4 for some interesting exceptional cases.

### *4.2.4 Reflexive Interpretation: Some Preliminary Conclusions*

We have no evidence so far that the coargument reflexive relation is anything more than one of dependent identity, but it is certainly nothing less. The evidence that the dependent reading is syntactically sensitive is robust, which shows that symmetric covariation is always an inadequate characterization. Although certain properties of identity appear to be elastic (in the cases of guise and proxy readings), the identity relations that are sensitive to dependency are always sensitive to it in the same way, at least where reflexivity is achieved by an identity-specific anaphor (although the same could be said for reciprocals).

This result would appear to be welcome. We know that there are morphological consequences to coargument reflexivity, in that there is a narrowing of possible interpretations by comparison with situations where a SELF form is anteceded by a noncoargument. However, no special reflexive relation has been presented to this point that would distinguish dependent identity between coarguments from what is independently interpreted for dependent identity between noncoarguments. Proxy, guise, split dependents, and partial dependents—while they all involve varieties of dependence on an antecedent, all do so for both coarguments and noncoarguments, with the notable exception of the CDC. As we explore the domain of inherent reflexivity in 4.3 and also those languages that mark thematically unrestricted reflexivity on the predicate instead of on a complement argument in 4.4, we shall have to reexamine these conclusions and admit of a potential augmentation of the identity relation.

## 4.3 Idiosyncratic Reflexivity and Indistinctness

Reflexive interpretations are signaled in essentially two ways. Either one of the arguments of a predicate is marked to indicate it is to be coconstrued with another argument of that predicate, or else the predicate itself bears an affix that indicates two of its arguments are coconstrued. Up to this point I have focused my attention on languages like English (or Abe) that mark arguments with identity-specific anaphors to indicate reflexive interpretation, but in languages that have both identity-specific anaphors as well as pronominal anaphors (like German and Dutch, for example), not all reflexive interpretations employ the identity-specific anaphor—rather the idiosyncrasies of the lexicon play a role. In the latter case, it is more difficult to defend the view that all reflexive interpretations are only dependent identity interpretations, and so I will introduce an additional notion of semantic identity that I call *indistinctness*.

*Inherently reflexive predicates,* as I shall refer to them here, are those predicates that involve coconstrual between coarguments but are interpreted as reflexive in a fashion that is either noncompositional or that results in a thematic interpretation not evidenced if the same predicate is not reflexive. In languages that mark arguments to indicate reflexivity, it is often the case that inherent reflexives are not argument marked in the way that thematically unrestricted reflexives are, and in the rest of 4.3 my discussion stays close to these distinctions.

There are a number of ways of classifying the varieties of inherently reflexive predicates (see, for example, Everaert 1986, 188–189; Geniušiene 1987) in terms of their syntactic or semantic properties. The classification that follows is descriptive, incomplete, and in 4.3.1 and 4.3.2, entirely based upon English, but the purpose of it is to consider just enough variety so as to render accessible the most salient properties for analysis that will be developed in comparison with other languages in 4.3.3 and 4.4.

### *4.3. Inherent Reflexives in English*

As a baseline, we must consider predicates that are not inherently reflexive, and these are examples like those in (37), typical for English, in that they involve a two-place predicate, like *praise*, *hit*, or *ransom*, all verbs for which the same thematic relations can be expressed when the subject and the object are distinct individuals. I shall refer to cases like these as *thematically unrestricted transitive reflexives,* or TUT-reflexives, for short.

37) TUT-reflexives:
   a) *Sally* slapped *herself*/Patty.
   b) *Prentiss* praised *himself*/Pruitt.
   c) *Ron* financed *himself*/Anscombe.

We immediately see a contrast when we compare examples like those in (37) with those in (38), which are also common in English, though less so than those in (37). The examples in (38) permit an interpretation akin to passive voice, as in Gil got verbed where Gil may not be the volitional cause (agent) of his being *verb*ed.

38a) *Hannah* hurt *herself* (by stepping on Burt's toe).
   b) *Minka* incriminated *herself* (by bleeding on Adrian's shoe).

The passivelike interpretation is not required for these cases and tends to be missing when there is no reflexive relationship between the subject and object. Cases like (38) have the flavor of unaccusative verbs, as if only one thematic role is involved, even though the verb is syntactically dyadic. Insofar as the volitional agency of the subject is suppressed, I shall call them *devolitional reflexives,* encompassing a class that probably has a number of subclasses, such as cases like (39).

39a) *Carmen* communicated *her* irritation.
  b) *Carmen's irritation* communicated *itself*/?her hostility.

Whoever asserts (39b) is not committed to the proposition that Carmen made her irritation known intentionally. These cases do not always take a direct object that is not a SELF form easily, although it is not impossible, but we also see the apparent promotion of object to subject.[16]

Verbs that permit volitional agents and occur with direct objects freely but that are nonetheless thematically restricted when reflexive are what I will call *gestural reflexives,* exemplified in (40).

40a) *Steve* stretched (*himself*)/Cheever.
  b) *Dora* draped *herself*/Olaf across the sofa.

Examples like (40) are slightly less common and appear to indicate a gesture performed by an individual in and of itself and not involving anyone else, much as coughing or smiling, the sort of relations typically described by unergative verbs. Gestural interpretations are very typically expressed in possessed body part descriptions, as in (41), which suggests a relationship, one often noted in other contexts in the literature, between inalienable possession and reflexivity.

41a) *Alice* shrugged *her* shoulders.
  b) *Loren and Brian* batted *their* eyes.
  c) *They* caught *their* breath.

Further semantic distinctions that seem to characterize the array of possibilities can be distinguished (see in particular Geniušiene (1987, ch. 3), but one classificatory fact that particularly stands out is that some predicates require a SELF form in order to have any sort of interpretation, or else require it to have an idiomatic interpretation. These predicates are typically called *obligatory reflexives,* and they are somewhat diverse in English.

42a) *Bill* perjured *(*himself*)/**his* secretary.
  b) *Proserpine* prostrated *herself*/**her* daughter before Hades.
  c) *Beverly* behaved (*herself*)/*Sid.
  d) *This* lends *(*itself*)/*that/*Bill to interpretation.
  e) *He* forgot *himself*/#Margo. (Idiomatically: "He acted inappropriately.")
  f) *Pruitt* prides *himself*/*Ida on *his* manner of dress.

While (42a, d) appear to involve specific idioms, which unlike (42e) do not have another interpretation with a distinct object, (42b) appears to involve gestural interpretations that in this case just happen to be obligatorily reflexive, and (42f) involves a psych predicate, which is a class frequently represented by inherent reflexives in other languages (as in the case of "to be ashamed," which we have employed for Norwegian and Dutch in earlier examples). The examples in (42) give the impression even more strongly that they are not transitive, and so we have to ask how the SELF form functions within the argument structure of the predicate it is associated with.

The variety of possibilities is perhaps underappreciated in the literature. For example, there is evidence to suggest that SELF in (42c) is not a direct object, but a manner adverb. Examples like (42c) cannot just describe a situation in which Beverly behaved in any way at all, but rather one in which she behaved in a manner appropriate to our hopes and expectations of her. Otherwise, *behave* always has a manner adverbial. Here the manner adverbial corresponding to "meeting our hopes and expectations" is *herself*, which is employed idiomatically to achieve this reading and is comparable to *Beverly behaved*. Indeed *Beverly behaved herself well/badly/in an unseemly manner* is odd because the manner adverb relation is already saturated (though *herself* is resistant to modification, as Marcel den Dikken [personal communication] points out, such that **Beverly behaved quite herself* is not possible). Thus these are not reflexive readings at all, but are more like adverbial ones. In other cases, the SELF form clearly cannot have an adverbial role, even for a predicate that requires an adverb.

43a) *John* conducted *himself*/*Mary/ badly.
b) **John* conducted *himself*/Mary.
c) *John conducted (badly).

These facts suggest that one of the factors we must weigh in the analysis of inherently reflexive verbs is not only whether or not the reflexive marker corresponds to an argument position, but whether or not it corresponds to an adjunct (adverbial) role.

Predicates like *dress* and *shave*, on the other hand, permit both overt SELF forms and distinct objects. When *dress* and *shave* are zero-marked, they have an idiomatic character. As Geniušiene (1987, 191) points out, when one speaks of how one dresses, it could describe what sorts of clothes one wears, which is not obviously a reflexive interpretation, or it could describe what one puts on first, which could be a reflexive interpretation of some sort. The use of the SELF form in (44) can serve to disambiguate between these readings (although the "what one wears" interpretation is not completely lost for [44a], at least for this speaker). By contrast, *shave* in (44b) only describes the manner in which Sherman performs the act of shaving, not the style of his facial hair, although the latter interpretation is at least marginally improved by including *himself*.

44a) *Darren* dresses (*himself*) fashionably/step by step.
b) *Sherman* shaves (*himself*) fashionably.

It is clear, however, that if one states that Sherman shaves, it cannot mean he shaves anyone but himself, unless the shaving in question is not grooming (e.g., some carpenters trim the boards, and others shave).[17]

While both the obligatory reflexives in English and the zero reflexives tend to be idiomatic, there is at least one productive class of obligatory reflexives that shows up similarly in other languages. These are cases which involve resultative interpretations of secondary predicates.

45a) *Loughren* laughed *himself*/*Sylvia silly.
b) *Kara* cried *herself*/*Celia to sleep.
c) *Drummond* drank *himself*/*Deirdre drunk.

These predicates in English seem to be those that have unergative intransitive counterparts, even though some, like (45c), can be transitive with selectionally distinct objects (i.e., *Drummond drank wine/#himself*).

This list is by no means complete,[18] but it will serve for the purposes of presentation in that most of the difficult issues that arise for my theory and others may be examined in light of the inherent reflexives so far discussed (although I will introduce other varieties as presentation requires).

### *4.3.2 English Inherent Reflexives From the Perspective of FTIP and LRP*

Since the classes of inherent reflexives are diverse, it is not likely that a single solution will apply to all of them. Moreover, there are virtually no theoretical proposals in generative grammar providing a comprehensive account of how the syntax of inherent reflexives in English should be analyzed, probably because the whole class has been regarded as relatively unsystematic and lexically idiomatic. This is by no means the case for a wide variety of other languages (see note 18 to this chapter), but it permits us to develop our FTIP/LRP account in a relatively uncontested environment.

With respect to the FTIP, obligatory reflexives require the selection of a nominal, and SELF forms are available to be selected (i.e., no scalar intervention renders them unavailable), so English is unproblematic. Where SELF forms are available, they outcompete any other form to represent the dependent-identity reading, if that is what is semantically required.

Null reflexives like *dress* and *shave* are unproblematic if we assume that they select a specific null morpheme more dependent than a SELF form, a null form that is not otherwise licensed by transitive predicates in English (which is a lexically stipulative "easy way out"). Predicates that license the null form will then permit the SELF form to be outcompeted. The availability of such a form must be a different lexical selection than the *dress* that takes an overt direct object, or else the SELF form could never represent a dependent reading, but it clearly can, just not one that is idiomatically restricted in the way that the null reflexive *dress* is.

Other matters are not so simple. The LRP requires an identity-specific anaphor to have a reflexive interpretation when it is anteceded by a coargument. But do inherent reflexives represent dependent readings? If the SELF form does not represent a thematic argument, what is it exactly that is semantically, as opposed to syntactically, dependent?

For example, if the SELF form of *behave oneself* is not a coargument of the subject of *behave*, then the LRP does not apply. Moreover, since *behave* has only one true argument, it arguably does not qualify as reflexive at all. This result is now likely for all of the obligatorily reflexive verbs. They select the SELF form as an idiom, often with a special reading, probably because the SELF form is an anaphor that, unlike pronouns, never permits independent reference. For most of these idiomatic cases, then, the SELF form is neither an argument nor a reflexivizer and there is no dependent interpretation, although the anaphoric form is still regulated by LAL and satisfies FTIP (which does not require dependent interpretations where it does not block them).

Where SELF forms are not exclusively required, yet the semantic interpretation appears to be binary, hence reflexive, and also idiomatic, the nature of the identity relation is often less asymmetric. Consider the gestural reflexives, such as *drape oneself*, where it appears that the idiomatic interpretation arises as a result of the relations that actors bear to their bodies, such that the actors and the bodies they use to function are necessarily indistinct entities with respect to the predicate involved. By contrast, a verb like *punch* does not involve the object of *punch* as an indistinct part of the agent of punching, though the fist of the agent has this property. For the *drape oneself* cases, it seems more appropriate to say that the reflexive favors a reading not (only) of dependence, but of *thematic indistinctness*.

46) Thematic Indistinctness: If A and B are semantic roles of a predicate P and if B is a necessary attribute of A determined by P, then coconstrual of A and B requires that they are thematically indistinct.

I use the term *semantic role* instead of *thematic role* in (46) since a thematic role is a semantic role assigned to an argument position in syntax (by definition, I assume), whereas a semantic role is not always so assigned. Controversies abound as to whether or not any given imaginable semantic role is represented in syntax, however abstractly, but whatever *semantic role* turns out to mean, thematic indistinctness will apply to those cases represented in syntax as well as to those that are perhaps only represented semantically in the lexicon.[19]

In fact, I take thematic indistinctness be an augmentation of the identity relation, rather than an identity relation itself. Although I will not explore it here, thematic indistinctness seems to be part of what the inalienable possession relation is typically about. As defined in (46), *Hannah* and *her hand* are not precluded from being thematically indistinct for the gestural interpretation of *Hannah raised her hand*. In this case, it is possible that two theta roles are assigned, even though the semantic roles are thematically indistinct. However, thematic indistinctness does not imply that "Hannah" is equivalent to her hand. By treating thematic indistinctness as a relation independent of identity, we both avoid positing special semantic relations between anaphors and their antecedents that are not attested for nonanaphors, and we can continue to maintain that reflexivity is just a name for a dependent identity relation between coarguments, one that can be augmented by the thematic indistinctness relation.

From this perspective, many of the devolitional reflexives (e.g., *hurt oneself*) are just readings readily permitted for these transitive predicates where experiencer and injured party are indistinct. Some gestural verbs also permit transitive readings when coconstrual is with an unexpected extension of oneself, but in such cases it is not obvious that the interpretation is gestural in the intended sense

47) *Mr. Fantastic* stretched *himself* around the criminals.

Since the famous elasticity of this superhero is not a necessary property of just anyone who stretches, such cases do not appear to exemplify thematic indistinctness, and if languages distinguish such cases in the form of the anaphor chosen, this might be a case that would favor an anaphor that did not entail thematic indistinctness. Perhaps further from indistinctness are cases like (39b), where *Carmen's irritation*, her experience, is also understood as a message emanating from her. For (39b) we may take *itself* to represent a form of proxy interpretation, since what is communicated (the fact that Carmen is irritated) is not necessarily of the same form or nature as the experience or sensory state that Carmen is in.

48a) *Carmen* communicated *her* irritation.
b) ***Carmen's** irritation* communicated *itself/?**her*** hostility.

It may be that (48b) requires some sort of account of the apparent argument promotion (insofar as *Carmen* is evaluated as agentlike), but this seems orthogonal to our concerns.

We may now regard proxy readings as more radical versions of thematic distinctness under identity: Wherever thematic distinctness (and dependency) is possible, proxy interpretations are possible (as long as they can be contextually justified). Where thematic indistinctness is required (by dependent form or by predicate), proxy interpretations are impossible by definition. This pattern, as we shall see in 4.3.3, is quite generally attested.

It can also be established, at least for English, that indistinctness readings for reflexives are also creatures of the dependent reading. Recall that first person guise readings distinguish between covalued (simple pronoun) and dependent readings (SELF form). In (49b, c, d) ([49a] is a TUT-reflexive included as a control), notice that only the dependent readings allow the thematically specific readings (in [49b–d]).

49a) If I were a Republican, I wouldn't criticize me/myself.
b) If I were O.J., I wouldn't have cut me/myself.
c) If I were Yogi, I wouldn't have stretched me/myself during the seventh inning.
d) If I were Valachi, I wouldn't have incriminated me/myself.

SELF forms, which must be dependent here, sustain the special thematic flavor of the reflexive interpretations, but that special thematic flavor (e.g., devolitional, gestural) is lost when the relation is not the dependent one (i.e., when the pronoun is used instead of the available SELF form).

### *4.3.3 Inherent Reflexives in More Articulated Argument-Marking Systems*

In our discussion of English, we have considered how certain predicates may impose thematic indistinctness on the relation between SELF forms and their antecedents. It is also possible that certain morphological forms can impose a form of indistinctness between noncoarguments. With this possibility in mind, let us turn to a class of languages that overtly mark TUT-reflexives differently from inherent ones.

As mentioned earlier, all the Germanic languages that have both SIG forms and SELF forms employ the SIG form for inherently reflexive readings in almost every instance.[20]

50a) Jon skammer seg *(selv). (Norwegian)
Jon shames SIG (SELF)
"Jon is ashamed."
b) Hij heeft zich/*zichzelf geschaamd. (Dutch)
He has SIG/*(SIG-SELF) ashamed
"He has been ashamed."

Within the approach proposed by R&R, if the interpretation of a predicate is reflexive, and they assume inherent reflexives are interpreted as reflexive, then that predicate must be reflexive marked. R&R assume that there is some phonetically null marker of reflexivity in Dutch and many other languages that reflexive marks an inherently reflexive predicate. From their perspective, the use of a SELF form for an inherent reflexive was deemed redundant, since the phonetically null marker does this work; hence a non-SELF form is used. However, since I do not share their assumption that reflexively interpreted predicates must be reflexive marked, I do not need to posit a null reflexive marker that is otherwise unnecessary. Moreover, I do not conclude with them that the identity-specific SELF form would be redundant in these contexts.

From the point of view of FTIP, if SELF is available in these contexts, and we assume it is more dependent than SIG, then SELF ought to outcompete the SIG form—but this is the wrong result for these cases, unless there is some sort of scalar intervention that excludes SELF forms in the context of inherent reflexives. In the previous chapter, I suggested that such a scalar intervention does occur, and now it is time to pay the promissory note.

Suppose that there are anaphors that cannot represent any argument necessarily indistinct from its antecedent. TUT-reflexives, by definition, do not require indistinctness between their coarguments: It is possible for the object of *kill* to be distinct from *Karl*, even though a TUT-reflexive may also be understood as involving indistinct roles in *Karl killed himself* (committed suicide). Suppose that SELF forms are not available (outside of English) where thematic distinctness is not a lexically available interpretation, as is the case with inherent reflexives. Where SIG and a SELF form would normally compete, SIG is then obligatory (for a thematically restricted interpretation) because SELF forms are not available for readings of indistinctness in principle. In other words, SIG, being less specifically conditioned in this respect, is the only anaphor available and thus wins the competition for the indistinct dependent interpretation. This account, then, relies on a distinction like that between collective and distributed dependent interpretations (see note 38 of chapter 3), or like that between reflexivity and reciprocity, which are cases in which different dependent interpretations may delimit different sets of competitors in an otherwise identical syntactic environment.

The fact that the SIG form in inherently reflexive environments is often analyzed as a nonargument is probably not accidental. If the SIG element does not represent an argument, then it could not in principle represent a referential value distinct from what it depends on. However, nothing I have said requires that these inherent reflexive environments treat that SIG-form as a nonargument. In this respect, my account underdetermines analyses of the diathesis of inherently reflexive predicates, only requiring of them that if they mandate a dependent form for whatever reason, that form must not be able to represent anything thematically distinct from what it depends on. Otherwise, the dependent element will be represented by a SELF form, where a SELF form is available. This approach is quite consistent with the Dutch facts, such as those reported by ter Meulen (1998):

51a) Jan schaamt zich/*zichzelf/*Marie.
Jan shames SE/*SE-SELF/*Marie
"Jan is ashamed."
b) Jan haat *zich/zichzelf/Marie.
Jan hate *SE/SE-SELF/Marie
"*Jan* hates *himself*."
c) Jan verbaasde zich/zichzelf/Marie.
Jan surprised SE/SE-SELF/Marie
"*Jan* surprised *himself*."

For (51a), indistinctness is required, whereas for (51b), it is not possible. In the case of (51c) we must ask if there is a possible indistinctness interpretation with a distinguishable thematic effect. Ter Meulen remarks, "SE-surprise (*zich-verbazen*) is the ordinary state of being surprised by some unspecified external cause, whereas SELF-surprise (*zichzelf-verbazen*) means one surprises oneself by one's own, perhaps subconscious actions, like one may surprise anyone else" (1998, 5).

By setting aside the issues of the argument status of SIG forms in inherent reflexive contexts, many of the thorny (though very interesting) questions about the lexical and syntactic representation of the diatheses of reflexive predicates need not be explored, at least not for the purposes of understanding how the pattern of anaphora emerges. This division of labor relieves the discussion of anaphora from some of the analytic freight that previous approaches to these predicate classes has been required to carry (in other words, those concerned with the diatheses of inherently reflexive verbs will be disappointed). From the perspective of FTIP, it does not matter whether or not French *se* corresponds to an object argument or subject argument, where in the latter case, accompanying dethematization permits the syntactic subject position to be filled by movement from the object position (e.g., Marantz 1981; Cinque 1988). All that matters is whether or not a pronominal of some sort is required, and if it is dependent, what sort of elements compete to permit a dependent reading.

On the other hand, I agree with Everaert (1986, 65), who suggests that a truly explanatory account of the distribution of SIG forms in inherent reflexives should not require extra stipulations about these elements where they appear as noncoarguments to their antecedents.[21] As remarked earlier, SIG forms generally do not have coargument antecedents, except where they support inherently reflexive predicates, but instead are available in a wider, but still bounded domain, which differs somewhat across the range of Germanic languages (this sort of pattern will be explored outside the Germanic family in chapters 5 and 6). Simply put, we now expect that if a SIG form is to be available where a SIG-SELF form also competes, one of the strategies for overlapping distribution must be in force. If SELF forms are allergic to obligatorily indistinct interpretations and SIG forms, simply lack the allergy, then the appearance of a SIG form coconstrued with a coargument will indicate a necessarily indistinct interpretation, while the appearance of a SELF form indicates such an interpretation is not required.

Fortunately, the apparent overlap in distribution between SIG and SELF forms has been studied by a variety of scholars in recent years, most notably Reuland (1997, 2001), Lidz (1996), Pica and Snyder (1997), ter Meulen (1998), and Rooryck and Vanden Wyngaerd (1997, 1998). drawing on some of the work evaluated in 4.2.1 on what I now call *proxy readings*. Reuland (1997; see also R&R, 1993, 710, fn. 51) draws (52) from earlier work by Voskuil (1991).

52a) Münchhausen trok zichzelf uit het moeras. (Dutch)
b) Münchhausen trok zich uit het moeras.
"*Münchhausen* pulled *himself* out of the swamp."

As mentioned in 3.3.3, the reading achieved by *zichzelf* is the one whereby Münchhausen has pulled himself out by his own hair (the reading intended in the story). This is exactly what we expect where a proxy is involved, as in our Mr. Fantastic example, where Münchhausen acts on himself as "other." This is much like pulling someone else out of the swamp. However, *zich* must be used to represent the reading he did not intend, which is that Münchhausen simply got out of the swamp. Where there is a choice between *zich* and *zichzelf*, *zich* only wins the competition if it favors the thematically indistinct interpretation, which, by hypothesis, is not representable using a SELF form. Where Münchhausen is acting on Münchhausen, the most dependent form available is *zichzelf*, since it is not disqualified for that meaning by the restriction relating to thematic distinctness.[22, 23]

If overlaps between SELF forms and SIG forms generally correlate with necessary thematic distinctness or the absence of it, then these apparent violations of complementarity are no threat to the FTIP. Moreover, if the overlaps can indeed be handled this way, we have also met Everaert's desideratum, in that the factor that distinguishes *zich* from *zichzelf* in the inherent reflexive cases is the same one that accounts for their distribution wherever they compete.

It is worthwhile to stress, however, that the use of *zich* where *zichzelf* is normally a competitor, even in the resultative contexts, always comes with thematic restrictions, typically unspecified agency interpretations or loss of volition. These restrictions often appear to reflect lexical choices of distinct but homophonic lexical predicates (even if the predicates are formed by productive lexical processes). It is the difference in lexical predicate that requires the indistinctness reading, which in turn determines the availability of the SELF form. Thus, from the perspective of 3.3.3, this apparent breakdown in complementarity is ultimately due to homophonic but distinct numerations, which leads to competitions for distinct dependency relations.[24, 25]

A number of other cases discussed by Rooryck and Vanden Wyngaerd support the same scalar intervention effect, which removes SELF forms from contention where the indistinctness is required but favors SELF forms to support proxy readings, as in their Dutch examples (1997, 53–57).

53a) Op het gemaskerd bal konden Sally en Freddy zichzelf/*zich zien zonder spiegel.
"At the masquerade, *Sally and Freddy* could see *themselves* without a mirror."
b) Dorian Grey zag zichzelf/*zich op het schilderij zoals hij werkelijk was.
"*Dorian Grey* saw *himself* in the picture as *he* really was."

54a) Freddy sneed zich.
"*Freddy* cut *himself*."
b) Freddy sneed zichzelf.
"*Freddy* cut *himself*."

55a) Loes danste zich naar de top.
b) Loes danste zichzelf naar de top.
"*Loes* danced *herself* to the top."

56) García Márquez heeft zichzelf/*zich nooit vertaald.
"*García Márquez* never translated *himself*."

57) Sally waste zich/zichzelf.
"*Sally* washed *herself*."

In (53a), the relevant interpretation is one where Sally and Freddy see people who are portraying them, in which case they are viewing proxies, and proxies are represented by a SELF form. Similarly, where Dorian Grey sees his "real self," only the SELF form will do.[26] In the case of (54a, b) and (55a, b), the distinction is one of volition, which is lacking where *zich* is employed but not where *zichzelf* is. In another typical proxy context, only the SELF form is possible in (56) to represent the author–work relation. Although the contrast is not necessarily one of volition, the choice of anaphor in (57) seems to permit subtle distinctions along the same lines, which suggests, as Rooryck and Vanden Wyngaerd (1997) also point out, that the English null reflexive, in those limited cases in English where it is possible, corresponds to contexts where *zich* is used for these verbs, whereas (57) with *zichzelf* corresponds to the corresponding verb with a SELF form in English.

Rooryck and Vanden Wyngaerd's discussion of these differences of interpretation focuses on what they take to be the doubling effect of the SELF form rather than the indistinctness relation that the SIG form is permitted to represent. As they put it, "Whenever a predicate allows for the interpretation of the antecedent as a 'duplicated' i.e. a spatiotemporally different entity, the complex anaphor *zichzelf* is required" (1997). This way of putting it, though correctly focusing on the distinctness issue, seems backward from the perspective I have been developing here. It is not a special property of the SELF form that permits the proxy reading—independent pronouns typically allow it too—but rather it is a special property of the SELF form that it cannot represent the indistinct reading (except in English; see below). In other words, the necessarily indistinct reading is a scalar intervention that eliminates SELF forms from competition. SELF forms outcompete SIG forms where both are available, and so SELF forms represent proxy readings, which they are not prevented from representing. Thus SIG forms remain the most unmarked forms, as they are generally.[27]

There is an important and very familiar sort of advantage to viewing the problem in terms of a competition to represent this particular dependent reading (necessary indistinctness). Like German *sich*, Dutch *zich* cannot be anteceded by first or second person pronouns, and so in all the inherent reflexive environments where *zich* is employed for third person, pronominal forms that are otherwise independent are used to represent first and second person inherent reflexivity, as illustrated in (58).

58a) Wij wassen ons.
we wash us
"We wash."
b) Zij zien ons.
they see us
"They see us."
c) Jullie vergissen je.
you forget you
"You are wrong."
d) Ik was je.
"I wash you."

The competition theory is not forced to endow these pronouns with special *zich*-like properties (as Rooryck and vanden Wyngaerd, 1997, 1998, are forced to do by a mysterious process of "anaphorization"),[28] nor must they be treated syncretically as optional anaphors. The ability of otherwise independent pronouns to represent the indistinct dependent interpretation follows in the competition account because they are the most dependent forms available (not marked for resistance to required indistinctness, as SELF forms are). The same approach permits us to account for Frisian inherent reflexives, which are formed with an otherwise independent pronoun in all persons since Frisian lacks a SIG form, and the SELF form, though anaphoric, is not available for the indistinctness reading.

The odd language out in the Germanic family, from this perspective, is English, which, like Frisian, lacks a SIG form and yet does not form inherent reflexives with pronouns but instead employs SELF forms. The difference is easily described if we stipulate that *English* SELF forms are not prohibited from representing indistinctness interpretations, and if so, they will always defeat pronouns where they compete as the most dependent form for that dependent reading.[29] One would hope that this stipulation about a lexical form in English can be related to other distinctions between English SELF and SELF in the rest of Germanic. I postpone this discussion until 6.2.3, where the morphological properties of anaphors are discussed.[30]

There is a further advantage to viewing the pronominal forms (including SIG) as the default winner of a competition to represent the indistinct interpretation, as illustrated for Norwegian in (59).

59a) Yeats lese seg selv på engelsk og så gjorde Hamsun det på norsk.
"Yeats read SIG-SELF in English and then Hamsun did in Norwegian."
b) Siden han visste at Le Carré var flerspråklig, bad Grisham Le Carré om ikke å lese seg på tysk.
"Knowing Le Carré was a polyglot, Grisham asked Le Carré not to read SIG in German." [SIG = Grisham's writing]
c) Le Carré synes at folk skulle lese ham kun på engelsk.
"*Le Carré* thinks that people should only read *him* in English."

These are author–product proxy readings, where that reading is represented by the most dependent available form in each instance.[31] In (59b), for example, *seg* embedded in an infinitive can be anteceded by the higher subject rather than the object-controlled PRO subject of the infinitive (a possibility not available in Dutch for *zich*); hence *seg* is available in this environment, while a SELF form is not. Similarly in (59c) where no SIG or SELF form is available with respect to the antecedent *Le Carré*, a nonanaphoric pronoun permits a proxy reading. A theory that treats SIG as having the special requirement of indistinctness would have to be domain restricted for this interpretive condition, and that domain restriction would be over and above that which applies to it as an anaphor.

If we step back from the details for a moment, what is established here is that SELF forms typically require "distinctness in principle" with their antecedents, while SIG forms and pronouns are unmarked in this respect. That SIG forms are the generally unmarked forms is consistent both with their wider distribution and with the claim of the previous chapter that among anaphors, more specifically restricted forms are typically more dependent. The distinction between SIG and SELF forms is, moreover, orthogonal to identity-specific marking or reflexive marking. Since we have rejected R&R's RIP, nothing requires reflexive readings to be represented by reflexive forms, so no otherwise unmotivated null morpheme needs to be posited to mark inherent reflexives as reflexive—a welcome result.

With respect to the question of what constitutes reflexivity as the term is applied to coargument coconstruals, we can conclude that both indistinctness and exhaustivity restrictions are separable aspects of such readings, but only exhaustivity, insofar as it is enforced by the CDC, is an ineliminable property of reflexivity. These distinctions and those pertaining to reflexive markers raise issues as to the nature and the number of distinctions that can be marked in the lexicon, but these are postponed until chapter 6. However, there is little motivation, if any, for the existence of an independent, semantic notion of reflexivity.

### *4.3.4 On the Distribution of Sloppy Readings*

Insofar as sloppy readings are dependent ones, the distribution of sloppy readings for reflexives in ellipsis contexts can be used as evidence that reflexivity is a dependency relation. What we have determined so far (in 4.2.2) is that proxy readings can succeed in ellipsis environments whether they are anteceded in the sentence or not, but neither proxies nor guises succeed where they cannot depend on their antecedents. These results are quite independent of the indistinctness facts.

My reasoning in this subsection depends on my assumption, mentioned in 2.4.3, that the strict reading arises in ellipsis contexts by means of *vehicle change*. Vehicle change, first proposed by F&M, is the option to represent a deleted nominal as a pronoun at LF, regardless of the form its overt antecedent has. F&M justify vehicle change on the basis of examples like (60), where a name within the (bracketed) ellipsis should be ruled out by FTIP (Principle C, in their account), but no violation arises if the last *Daphne* is replaced by a pronoun at LF.

60) Dorian despises *Daphne's* mother more than *Daphne* does [despise *Daphne's* mother].

The effect of vehicle change on cases like (61), which favors a strict interpretation, is to replace a SELF form with a simple pronoun.

61) *Clinton* tends to praise *himself* before even Hillary can [praise *him*].

A vehicle change pronoun cannot represent the reflexive reading in the second predicate, since it is not the most dependent form available in English to represent that dependency, but a SELF form could, and only a gender mismatch disfavors it. Parallelism is preserved, however, if *him* depends directly on *himself* for its antecedency. Thus the strict reading is possible where *him* is anteceded by the reference of the nominal that occupies a parallel position in the first conjunct. Vehicle change is restricted to replacing nominals with pronouns and nothing else. Otherwise, replacing a pronoun with a SELF form at LF would license a reflexive reading for the elided predicate in (62).

62) *Bill praised *Hillary* before *she* could [praise *herself*].

The vehicle change analysis assumed here is defended at length in Safir (2004).

Now consider (63).

63a) *Kurt* cut *himself* before Didier did.
b) *Mr. Fantastic* stretched *himself* before Galacticus could.
c) Sean shaved before Bevan did.
d) *Loughren* laughed *himself* silly before Balfour could.

In (63a) and (63b), both strict interpretations and thematically unrestricted readings are available, but the strict interpretations lack the thematically restricted readings (in both conjuncts). This is unsurprising, since indistinctness is required for the thematically restricted readings, and the strict readings involve distinct coarguments by their very nature. There are no strict readings for (63c, d) because these predicates do not have thematically unrestricted reflexive readings. After all, the thematically restricted interpretation of the verb is a particular lexical choice, as discussed in the last section.

This suggests that what prevents thematically restricted reflexives from permitting sloppy readings has nothing directly to do with the availability of strict interpretations in parallel structural positions, but rather has to do with a failure of parallelism, such that the antecedent VP must contain the same sort of verb type that the ellipsis site would. For example, if the first conjunct in (64) does not have the thematically restricted interpretation, then the second cannot have the thematically restricted interpretation, either, even under a sloppy reading.

64a) *Kurt* cut *himself*, and then Ben did.
b) *Jeter* flung *himself* onto the couch before Posada could.

In other words, if (64a) describes what Kurt did to impress the general, then Ben cannot be nonvolitionally cut, and likewise, if the famous Derek Jeter flings his proxy, a bobble-head souvenir doll, onto the couch, then it cannot be that Jorge Posada gesturally flops heavily onto the couch. Notice that both strict and sloppy readings are available with the thematically unrestricted interpretation, and in (64b) those interpretations are proxy readings (see also [59a] for Norwegian). Thus it appears that the limitations on thematically restricted interpretations has to do with matching lexical choices of parallel homophonous predicates, and not directly with a parallel pattern of dependencies.[32]

Our predictions for Dutch are now fairly clear. Wherever *zich* is anteceded by a coargument, there will be no strict reading.[33] We have observed that *zich* anteceded by a coargument could only win the competition if the reading it represents is one of indistinctness. A strict reading in the ellipsis context could only arise by vehicle change and hence the substitution of an independent pronoun instead of *zich*. Since the pronoun is not the most dependent form available, it would be obviative with respect to its subject; hence it could not be indistinct from it. The following examples illustrate that *zich* always enforces a sloppy reading when it is in an indistinctness reading with its antecedent, but if the same verb allows a thematically unrestricted reading with *zichzelf*, a strict reading is possible, since vehicle change can replace the SELF form without having to satisfy indistinctness (examples from Sells, Zaenen, and Zecs 1987, 182, 184).

65a) Hans verdedigde zich beter dan Peter/*hem.
"*Hans* defended *himself* better than Peter/*him*."
b) Zij heeft zichzelf beter verdedigd dan hij.
"*She* defended *herself* better than he (defended *her*)."

The distribution of sloppy readings also enables us to distinguish the behavior of SIG in contexts where it is not competing with SIG-SELF. As we saw earlier, where

SIG does not compete with SIG-SELF, SIG can support proxy readings. Similarly, where SIG does not compete with SIG-SELF, SIG can support strict readings. Lidz (1996, 118) has examples for Norwegian drawn from work by Hellan and by Hestvik.

66a) John vasket seg bedre enn Per.
John washed SIG better than Peter
"*John* washed *himself* better than **Peter** washed **himself**/**him*."
b) John vasket seg selv bedre enn Per.
John washed SIG-SELF better than Peter
"*John* washed *himself* better than Peter washed himself/*him*."
67) John hadde hort meg snakke nedsettende om seg, og det hadde de som stod rundt også.
John had heard me talk deprecatingly about SIG, and it had those who stood around too
"*John* heard me talking deprecatingly about *him*, and **those who** were standing around also heard me talking that way about *him*/**them**."

In (67), for example, *seg* would not be licensed overtly in the elided position where it would have to be represented (i.e., those standing around [hear me talking that way about *x*]). Since we have distinguished the sloppy–strict contrast from the proxy–indistinct contrast, the availability of strict readings for SIG where it does not compete with SIG-SELF is independent evidence in support of the FTIP, once again showing that competition between anaphors is regulated by the same principles that regulate distinctions between anaphors and nonanaphors.

## 4.4 Affixal Reflexivity

I now turn to those languages that signal the reflexive interpretation of a predicate with a nonpronominal marker on the verb. I begin by clarifying the affix–pronoun distinction as it pertains to reflexive readings, and then I address the issue of whether derivations including affixal reflexive markers ever compete with argument-marked reflexive numerations.

Unlike the Germanic cases where SIG forms have a pronominal function independently, languages like Finnish employ an affix that does not correspond to any pronoun and presumably cannot be replaced by a pronominal affix (the affix alternates as *-utu-/-yty-* depending on vowel harmony), as illustrated in the examples in (68) drawn from Sells, Zaenen, and Zecs (1987, 177).

68a) Jussi pese-yty-i.
"Jussi washed himself."
b) Jussi puolusta-utu-i.
"Jussi defended himself."

In Finnish, the reflexive affix occurs as a general strategy for representing reflexive readings, even for TUT-reflexives.

At this point we need some assumptions about just how reflexive affixes achieve the reflexive reading. It could be that the affix changes the thematic assignment of the predicate argument structure without changing the binary semantic relation, such that detransitivization is understood as two semantic roles assigned to a single argument position.[34] This would be an adicity shift in the predicate, leaving out an anaphoric marker, marking it on the predicate, or marking it on a lexically selected anaphor that does not receive a thematic role. Alternatively the affix could license a null form not otherwise possible in the position of the complement argument. However, these possibilities are beside the point for our immediate concern here.

The logic of the question, from the perspective of the FTIP, is fairly clear. If the affix inducing a reflexive reading is adicity reduction that induces required indistinctness, then the argument marker that would compete with the adicity reduction marker, supposing that were possible, would have to be capable of representing the indistinct interpretation. If the argument marker cannot represent indistinctness, then the verbal affix and the argument marker are not in competition for the same readings. Similarly, if the verbal affix permits the distinctness reading and the argument reflexive marker does or does not support the same readings, then the argument reflexive marker will or won't compete with the verbal affix accordingly. Finally, if there is a thematic restriction not involving adicity reduction imposed by the verb when it bears the verbal affix and that restriction is not imposed when the argument-marked reflexive is employed, then it is also possible that the two markers would not, in that situation, compete. However, if both markers permit the same reading, then the FTIP predicts that they are in competition. Unless we stipulate a tie on the most dependent scale, noncomplementary distribution of these markers constitutes a counterexample to the FTIP.

A few more details about Finnish permit us to illustrate how empirical evidence can be brought to bear on the issue. The Finnish *-utu-/-yty-*, according to Sells, Zaenen, and Zecs (1987, 177–179) is not pronominal or at least never corresponds to a pronoun in that morphological position (unlike Dutch), and it is not limited to expressing reflexivity (it is also used for inchoatives and "mediopassives"). Moreover, *-utu-/ -yty-* does reduce the adicity of a predicate, since *-utu-/-yty-*affixed predicates pattern with intransitives, not with transitives, when they are further affixed with a causative morpheme.

Given this much information, we can make an interesting prediction about ellipsis interpretation. Since the *utu/-yty* affix is not a nominal, it cannot be vehicle-changed to a pronoun. We then correctly predict that *-utu-/-yty-*affixed predicates should never allow for strict readings in ellipsis contexts, or for distinct objects.

69) Jussi puolusta-utu-i paremmin kuin Pekka/*Pekkaa.
 John defend-refl-past better than Peter-NOM/Peter-PART
 a) *John* defends *himself* better than **Peter** defends **himself**. (sloppy)
 b) **John* defends *himself* better than Peter defends *him*. (strict)
 c) **John* defends *himself* better than he does Peter. (object comparison)

The fact that *-utu-/-yty-* is not exclusively a reflexive marker is not an issue within the approach adopted here, but we do need to know whether or not the affixal reflexive marker would compete with an argument reflexive marker, all else constant.

It appears that Finnish permits us to answer this question, since Finnish also has an argument-marked reflexive form, *itse*, which usually appears with a possessive suffix as in (69) (from van Steenbergen 1991).

70) Pekka näki itsensä.
Pekka saw ITSE-POSS
"Pekka saw himself."

Reflexive readings achieved with *itse* remain transitive, as *itsensä* can be replaced with a pronoun (obviative with the subject). Insofar as this is possible, we then expect reflexive readings formed with *itse* to permit strict, sloppy, and object-comparison readings. The strict reading should be possible, along with the sloppy one, because vehicle change can replace *itse*-poss with a pronoun, and the object-comparison reading should be possible because *itse* does not enforce indistinct coargument antecedent readings, or it would not permit the strict reading either. These predictions exactly match those reported in Sells, Zaenen, and Zecs (1987, 178, fn. 9), although they do not provide the examples.

Now we must conclude for Finnish that the affixal readings do not compete with the pronominal ones because more than one morpheme is involved in the difference between the two numerations, insofar as the adicity, not just the reflexive markers, of the verbs in the two cases is different. Thus we predict, apparently correctly, that the affix and the anaphor can support reflexive readings for the same predicate in many cases, but distinctions between them arise where the interpretation requires or does not permit thematic indistinctness.

Compare Finnish *-utu-/-yty-* with the Chichewa affix *dzi-*, which, as reported in Sells, Zaenen, and Zecs (1987, 187), forms reflexive readings when it is embedded in a verb's morphological complex.

71) Alenje a-na-dzi-lum-a.
hunters SA-past-DZI-bite-indic
"The hunters bit themselves."

In an ellipsis environment, however, all three interpretations available for the corresponding sentence in English are available in Chichewa.

72) Fisi a-ma-dzi-kond-a kuposa mkango.
hyena SA-habit-DZI-love-indic more-than lion
"*The hyena* loves *himself* more than the lion loves himself."
"*The hyena* loves *himself* more than the lion loves *him*."
"*The hyena* loves *himself* more than *he* does the lion."

For these readings to be possible, we predict that *dzi* must not detransitivize the predicate it attaches to and that it must correspond morphologically to a position in which a pronoun could be well formed, or else vehicle change could not apply to it to produce a strict reading. As Sells, Zaenen, and Zecs remark, "Not only are reflexive pronouns incorporated into the Chichewa verb but so are non-reflexive pronouns.

. . . The rules that change valence . . . are marked by suffixes that are part of the stem while the prefixes are not part of the stem and never change the valence of the verb . . . " (1987, 187). This supports our assertion that vehicle change, rather than an indexing formula, is crucial for the strict reading (where a sloppy one is possible with an anaphor) and makes the strong empirical prediction that no affixal reflexive will ever permit a strict reading unless an independent pronominal form can appear in the same lexical slot.[35]

There is, however, an issue of competition that arises in work by Lidz (1996) and that is potentially challenging for the FTIP. Lidz contends that lexical reflexivity competes with transitive "near reflexivity" to represent reflexive readings, and that the lexically reflexive ones (not always reduced adicity structures) are always considered more economical vehicles of a reflexive interpretation. In languages like Kannada, which is his paradigm case, the lexical structure is represented by a verbal affix *-koL* (sometimes realized morphologically as *-koND*) that does not correspond to a position where a pronoun could occur and is associated, according to Lidz, with thematic properties of the argument structure not specific to reflexivity. A TUT-reflexive is represented by the obligatory appearance of the *-koL* affix on the verb and an anaphoric pronominal in argument position, *tann* (which I will not designate as "self," as Lidz does, because I take SELF forms to have very particular properties not in evidence here).

73a) Hari-yu tann-annu hode-du-koND-a. (Lidz, 1996, 19)
Hari-NOM TANN-ACC hit-pp-REFL.PST-3SM
"*Hari* hit *himself.*"
b) *avanu tann-annu hoDE-d-a. (Lidz, 1996, 55)
he TANN-ACC hit-pst-3ps
"*He* hit *himself.*"

Notice that unlike the other cases we have discussed, two elements are necessary to instantiate a well-formed reflexive, both the *-koL* affix and TANN. TANN appears where an argument otherwise would (since *-koL* is not a detransitivizer, as other evidence is adduced to show). Moreover, TANN must be locally (typically coargument) bound where *-koND* appears in the same clause, but otherwise TANN may be bound at a distance (Lidz, 1996, 55).

74a) shyaamu raamu tann-annu hoDE-du-koND-a anta heeL-id-a.
Shyamu Raamu TANN-ACC hit-pp-REFL-PST-3sm that say-pST-3SM
"Shyamu said that *Raam* hit *himself.*"
b) shyaamu raamu tann-annu hoDE-d-a anta heeL-id-a.
Shyamu Raamu TANN-ACC hit-PST-3SM that say-PST-3SM
"*Shyamu* said that Raam hit *him.*"

If we think of TANN as an anaphoric pronominal, not as a SELF form, then it is not an argument reflexive marker in Kannada (though it appears that a complex form, *tann* + case + *taane*, can create TUT-reflexive readings without the affix).[36] The question that now arises is why (73b) is not sufficient to represent a reflexive interpretation. Lidz takes this to be the result of a competition between representing reflexivity in the lexical structure versus representing reflexivity in the syntax by means of a syntactic chain, and following a line of thought suggested in Reuland (1997), he argues that the lexical representation is always favored as a more economical representation of this interpretation.

The conclusion is odd, however. It would appear that the required presence of *-koL* is morphologically quite uneconomical insofar as the TANN form is still present in (73a) and must still be bound. Rather it seems reasonable to suppose that the presence of *-koL* in constructions where it is not participating in a reflexive reading (including middles, impersonals, and certain inalienable possession constructions, among others) is a requirement independent of anaphora. According to Lidz, these are cases where the argument structure of the predicate in question is marked as not being linked to an "external cause," a notion I accept only for the sake of argument. If the unlinked external cause requires the *koL* form, and reflexives, by Lidz' hypothesis, are instances of an unlinked external cause construction, then there is no reason to believe that there is any competition between lexical reflexive marking and the syntactic variety. The *-koL* affix just appears where it is semantically required (perhaps to signal indistinctness; see note 36 to this chapter), and just one such case is on a predicate for which one of its arguments is dependent on its subject. Thus the failure of (73b) is due to the absence of *-koL*, not to any antilocality condition or property of TANN, which simply must be bound wherever it appears. From the perspective of FTIP, Kannada is a language that lacks reflexive marker altogether and uses the anaphoric pronominal TANN to effect reflexive readings when a nominal must be present.

Although my sample is admittedly tiny, it would appear at first blush that there are no serious challenges to the FTIP from purported reflexive affixes, once cases are considered in detail. In many instances, there is no competition because the verbs that these affixes attach to are different lexical selections than the verbs, which have their internal arguments saturated by reflexive-marked arguments (e.g., "wash" in Dutch or Norwegian). In other instances, the purported affixes function essentially as pronouns, as in Chichewa, and compete with other pronouns, much as in Germanic. In languages such as Kannada, it would appear that the purported reflexive affixes are not reflexive affixes at all, and their presence is not due to reflexivity as opposed to more general properties of predicate argument structure. If there are affixes not corresponding to pronominals that form reflexive readings in the absence of an overt direct object, and these affixes compete with argument anaphors that appear only where the verbal affixes for some reason cannot, then there is a better case for competition between an argument reflexive-marker and an affixal reflexive-marker. I leave the empirical matter open, but I will assume henceforth that there is no such case.

## 4.5 Summary and Conclusion

We have now established that the semantic content of reflexivity is just a composite of properties otherwise found to hold of other, noncoargument coconstrual relations. Reflexivity is an instance of a dependent identity relation that just happens to hold between an argument and its coargument antecedent. Dependency is certainly a widespread property of natural language grammar relating noncoarguments as well as coarguments, and the notions of identity that hold among coarguments are not unknown in relations between noncoarguments, as is the case for proxies and guises.

What is peculiar to coargument relations is the CDC, introduced in 3.3.1, and the LRP, introduced in 4.1, which require coargument dependency for identity-specific anaphors when there is a choice of antecedents. Both of these constraints narrow the class of interpretations possible, and neither one has broad pervasive effects. The LRP, for example, only shows its force in languages that have identity-specific anaphors. As it is defined in this chapter, the thematic indistinctness relation is uniquely a coargument relation, but it is not necessarily a reflexive relation, as it also applies to inalienable body part interpretations that arise from gestural interpretations (for example). The coincidence of indistinctness and reflexivity produces the sorts of interpretations often associated with adicity reduction, and no special definition of reflexivity should include such restrictions as a general property (e.g., as in the case of ter Meulen, 1998, or the observationally limited definition in Salmon, 1992). It is possible that some cases of control involve nonclausemate indistinctness relations, but I will not pursue the matter here (but see note 26 to chapter 6).

We have also concluded that anaphoric forms are not all alike with respect to the dependent-identity interpretations they can represent. Specialized forms (like SELF) tend to be more dependent than less specialized forms (like SIG; as suggested in 3.2.3), yet the less dependent form often emerges as the winner in FTIP competitions to represent a variety of interpretations if the more specialized form is not available. Crucially, it is assumed that FTIP competitions are relativized to the type of dependent-identity reading that is involved. Although I have distinguished identity-specific anaphors from pronominal anaphors and argument reflexive markers as a subset of identity-specific anaphors, as well as reflexive affixes, I have not mined the internal morphology of these elements for factors that could determine such distinctions, a task that is begun in chapter 6.

Finally, by treating reflexivity as a composite of dependency relations that may also hold among noncoarguments, our theory gives reflexivity no special semantics distinct from coargument dependent identity and rejects the notion of "reflexive predicate" as a theoretical entity. These results are no accident in my theoretical program because wherever the role of dependency relations regulated by c-command is extended, the force of the FTIP and the Independence Principle are maximized.

## Appendix to Chapter 4: On C-Command

Over the years there have been a variety of formulations of the *command* relation that establishes the superiority of one constituent in relation to another for the purposes of anaphora and scope, among other things. Historically, the command relation has been stated on formal properties of trees, as in the work of Lees and Klima (1963), Langacker (1969), Reinhart (1976), and Aoun and Sportiche (1981) (or even on derivational properties of trees, as in the work of Epstein (1999)). The command relation has also been stated on formal properties of argument structures, most recently Williams (1994) and Pollard and Sag (1994), the second of which explicitly draws on the relational grammar literature, specifically Johnson (1977), or on thematic hierarchies (e.g., agent, theme, goal) as in the work of Jackendoff (1972). These theories differ as to the role trees play in the theory, if any, and so it depends on the theory as to whether any trees exist in the theory or whether they exist but are not used for this purpose.

In the text, I have assumed and will continue to assume that the command relation, more specifically a form of c-command, is a structural one that is read off of a structural tree, but there are gaps and unclarities that arise in my reliance on this structural notion, and so in this brief appendix I explore what is at stake for my theory where the predictions of c-command are called into question.

I assume that the structure of a tree arises in the course of a derivation by virtue of the formation of phrases out of the lexical building blocks provided by the numeration, as discussed in chapter 2. The formation of phrases by Move and Merge, as discussed in Chomsky (1995b), is consistent with X'-principles and theta-assignment requirements. Thus if *Chava kissed Benny* is the sentence we are deriving, the numeration consists of the unordered set {*Chava*, *kiss*, *Benny*, past}, and the derivation proceeds roughly as follows (irrelevant details suppressed).

1a) [kiss Benny]
b) [Chava [kiss Benny]]
c) [past [ Chava [kiss Benny]]]
d) [Chava [past [t [kiss Benny]]]]

The first three steps involve Merge, which forms a new constituent from a combination of two selections from the numeration or from two already-formed phrases or from one of each. Move applies to create (1d) from (1c). I assume that the subject position is defined as SPEC-IP, which is what *Chava* would be in (1d), if *past* is an I. The theta theory will tell us in one fashion or another that *Chava* is the external argument of the VP, since it is merged with the already formed verb + object in (1b), and also that *Benny* is the internal argument, however that thematic role is semantically characterized.

Now the question we need to consider is what is at stake for anything said here if some thematic relations of command are better represented by a nonstructural notion rather than a structural one. Let us first make a distinction between internal arguments of a predicate and the external one. All theories of command concur that in a transitive sentence like *Chava kissed Benny*, *Chava* commands *Benny*. In such cases, the agent has primacy over the patient, the nominative over the accusative, the relational subject over the relational object, and the structural subject over the structural object.

Questions begin to arise when the external argument or structural subject or relational subject is promoted to that position by movement or by advancement (e.g., the highest rated argument on the thematic or obliqueness scale is treated as subject in the absence of a higher ranking argument). In these instances the question arises as to whether the superficial subject commands an anaphor that must depend on it. Typical cases in English, based on examples from Postal (1971), are the following.

2a) ??Vincent was implicated by himself.
b) ??Bush seemed to himself to have been elected.
c) ??He worries himself.

One might argue that the oddity of (2a, b, c) arises because a thematically lower element on the hierarchy agent >> goal/experiencer >> theme is the antecedent of an argument higher on the thematic hierarchy, along the lines of Jackendoff (1972, 148; see also Wilkins 1988).

Like Pollard and Sag (1994), I reject the thematic account for (2a, b) since the oddity with *himself* is not general to other anaphors for such positions.

3a) The men were implicated by each other.
b) The men seemed to each other to have been rejected by the voters.

Moreover, if the *by*-phrase or the experiencer phrase were to command the subject position, we would not expect the success of the bound variable interpretations in (4a, b) and the failure of such interpretations for (4c, d) (I reject a linear approach to weak crossover; see Safir 2004).

4a) *Every man* was implicated by *his* brother.
b) *Every successful student* seems to *his* mentor to be insufficiently grateful.
c) **His* brother was implicated by *every man*.
d) **His* student seems to *every successful mentor* to be insufficiently grateful.

The results in (4) are important because all theories of command agree on the general statement in (5).

5) If *x* commands *b* then *x* commands any subpart of *b*.

After all, the disputes about whether or not command should be represented in trees has to do with what representation best provides a natural expression of the command relations between coarguments. Once that is settled, the command relations between subparts of coarguments have been taken to follow from the relations between coarguments.

Turning now to psych predicate cases like those in (2c) (which Pollard and Sag do not discuss) the judgments are less clear, at least in the case of (6a).

6a) ?The men worry each other.
b) Every student worries his mentor.

However, the psych cases would be predicted to differ in just this way if we take into account the thematic properties of psych verbs in relation to the Independence Principle. Since the experiencer must be animate, under any reading where the subject is not agentive, the resulting relation between subject to object for cases like (2c) resembles one between a proxy and the entity it depends on. If we apply Jackendoff's (1992) wax museum scenario to the examples in (7), then they are odd precisely because we expect the experiencer to be animate. If the inanimate Castro depends on the animate one, then *Castro* corresponding to the statue in (7a–c) will be excluded because it c-commands the animate being it depends on, violating the Independence Principle. This is particularly clear for (7d), which is ill-formed if *Castro* denotes the wax statue and the person "Castro" is the one who has misapplied his cigar (whereas [7d] would be acceptable if Castro were an animate wax figure with an ill-advised appetite for cigars).

7a) ?**Castro* worries/upsets/pleases *himself.*
 b) ?**Castro* seems to *himself* to be melting.
 c) **Castro* was melted by *himself.*
 d) **Castro* was melted by *his* cigar.

While all three of these cases are explicable under the Independence Principle account of the restrictions on proxy readings, the passive case cannot be purely a matter of proxy interpretation, because, as we have already seen, that pattern of dependency is unacceptable even without proxy interpretation. It might be argued, however, that (2b), the raising case, is similar to a proxy interpretation like the one intended for (7b), since *seem* applied reflexively is alienating in some sense: It is Bush the candidate who seems to Bush the person that he has been elected? If so, the form representing Bush the candidate, if it is to depend on Bush the person, should not c-command the form representing Bush the person.

Thus there is ample evidence for a structural account of the relation between the subject as antecedent and those arguments that depend on it, once animacy restrictions on particular arguments are integrated with the requirements of proxy interpretations. It is not clear that theories such as those of Pollard and Sag (1994) or Williams (1994) will significantly differ in their predictions about what is a subject from the standard structural view, especially in sentential contexts (small clauses aside). I will assume that the remaining differences are not significant with respect to subjects and conclude that for the relationship between subject antecedents and dependent internal arguments, the c-command account is at least as adequate as any other account of command and has the advantage of making the proper predictions with respect to the Independence Principle.[1] This view will be further defended in 5.2.4 with regard to subject orientation of anaphors, at which point structural assumptions become crucial to my account.

Matters are less clear where internal arguments are involved, but I believe the issues are clarified by similar considerations. Some classic cases of asymmetries of anaphora among internal arguments are those pointed out by Postal (1971), as illustrated in (8) and (9). Consider both cases in terms of the proxy reading, that is, where the curator of the wax museum is presenting (or talking about) the statue of Castro to the man Castro.

8a) ?The proprietor showed *Castro himself.*
 b) *The proprietor showed *Castro* to *himself.*
 c) *The proprietor showed *himself* to *Castro.*
 d) *The proprietor showed *himself Castro.*

9a) The proprietor talked to *Castro* about *himself.*
b) *The proprietor talked to *himself* about *Castro.*
c) *The proprietor talked about *Castro* to *himself.*
d) *The proprietor talked about *himself* to *Castro.*

Now suppose that prepositions such as *to* and *about* in these examples can be incorporated, such that their direct objects share the c-command domain of the verb as well as the preposition; in other words, assume that the objects of these prepositions can c-command the contents of the prepositional phrase that follows after (as in a long line of reanalysis proposals for passive, such as those proposed by Hornstein and Weinberg 1981). Under this interpretation of what c-commands what, (8a, b) and (9a, c) should allow for *himself* to satisfy LAL with *Castro* as its antecedent. However, of these four examples, only (8a) and (9a) are acceptable. Once again we can appeal to the notion that where Castro is the goal or experiencer, he is animate; hence the proxy must depend on the animate. The object of *about* or the "shown thing" is the dependent proxy in an identity relation with the other, animate internal argument. If the not necessarily animate version of Castro must always depend on any animate one in the same sentence (when there is one), then (8b) and (9c) are ruled out by the Independence Principle, since in these cases *Castro* must depend on an argument that it c-commands (in [9c], *Castro* c-commands *himself* after P-incorporation of *about*).[2]

Now let us return to the relation of experiencers to the clauses that follow in raising contexts. Notice my discussion above allows for incorporation but does not require it in the absence of anaphora. With that in mind, consider (10a, b).

10a) *They seem to *him* to like *John.* (Lasnik 1999).
b) *It seems to *him* that they like *John.*

In (10a, b), *him* only c-commands *John* if the preposition *to* obligatorily incorporates into *seem*, an assumption that does not appear necessary. If the incorporation is necessary, we expect an FTIP effect of the principle-C sort, just as we apparently see in (10a, b), but this result is not expected if the incorporation is optional. If the incorporation is not optional, then a variety of c-command problems arise with respect to the intervention of an A-position in the derivation of raising for cases like (11).

11) *They* seem to *each other/themselves* [*t* to be angry]

In such a case, *themselves* ought to create an FTIP violation if *they* is reconstructed into its lower position of origin, or in some more representational theories of chains that employ indices, *themselves* might intervene in the construction of the chain. The latter situation does not arise as a problem for minimalist accounts, since the chain formation relation does not involve coindexation, and if A-traces neither reconstruct nor constitute copies, then this should not be a problem either (I will argue in chapter 5 that A-traces do not have to be copies). The oddity of (11) with *themselves* is explicable in terms of the Independence Principle as described above, but the problem here is the effect in (10).

The effect in (10) may follow, however, from an independent property of propositional attitude complementation that is proposed in Safir (in preparation). There it is argued that propositional attitude verbs introduce, as a property of their complementation, an attitudinal operator with scope over the clausal complement. The attitudinal operator is controlled by the perspective holder of the attitude, in this case, the experiencer argument of the raising verb. This control relation is not restricted by c-command, as it is a local relation between the perspective-holder argument and the propositional argument (e.g., the object of unincorporated *to* can count as the controller of the operator). If any dependent argument in the scope of this attitude marker is a position subject to FTIP competition with respect to the c-commanding operator, then pronouns will obviate names in examples like (10a, b).[3]

I have been assuming, for the cases discussed above, a relatively conservative set of grammatical-linking relations, insofar as I have not assumed that the objects of experience that appear as surface subjects are, or are not, underlying subjects. Since I do not assume reconstruction effects are mandatory in A-chains (see 5.1.3), what the underlying positions are may not matter for the points I am making, but it remains to be seen whether pertinent issues will arise depending on what structural mappings of thematic linking are predicted to be within a given theory. However, what is crucially different about my approach is that the semantic effects that have been expressed in terms of thematic or obliqueness hierarchies in other theories and expressed in terms of coargument relations are characterized here in terms of the proxy relation. The proxy relation is not restricted to coarguments, as demonstrated in 4.1.3.1, and thus coargumenthood is not significant factor in my account of the apparent c-command failures I have treated in this appendix.

The cases discussed so far do not exhaust the range of c-command issues, but they serve to suggest that there are principled reasons as to why some of the evidence against structural approaches is not consistent across all forms of anaphoric relations and obviations, and that these principled reasons are best understood in terms of relations that are regulated by structural conditions, such as FTIP and the Independence Principle.

5

# Anaphors and Domains

One of the proudest achievements of the Extended Standard Theory of the 1970s was the conclusion that the domain of anaphora and the domain of movement are determined by identical principles. Going against the grain of most work within the principles and parameters approach, I argue in this chapter that the conflation of the domains for A-movement and anaphora should be abandoned on both conceptual and empirical grounds. Rather I will argue that the domain in which anaphors are anteceded is smaller than the domain of the well-formedness condition on chain links that restricts movement and that A-traces are not anaphors. I shall also sketch and defend a typology of extended well-formedness domains for anaphors based on how these forms can be covertly moved into the narrow domain of LAL, but my main reason for doing so is cashed out in the next chapter, where competitions between anaphors with overlapping availabilities is garnered as evidence for the FTIP.

Over the years, the view that A-traces are anaphors has been widely challenged for a variety of reasons. Many have pointed out that "reflexive" anaphors and reciprocals work differently in other languages and, in particular, that reflexives could be bound across specified subjects and tensed Ss (e.g., Kuno 1972). Even in English, many pointed out that reflexive SELF forms (Zribi-Hertz 1989; Reinhart and Reuland 1991; Safir 1992) and even reciprocals (according to Pollard and Sag 1992) could be bound across great distances in certain environments, or even appear without antecedents. However, most binding theorists of the 1980s did not budge from the view that the core analysis was correct and addressed the apparent counterexamples with a variety of strategies.

One strategy led to the hypothesis that the long-distance anaphors are in fact locally bound at LF, after covert LF-movement, with the result that the locality domain of Principle A can be maintained as universal. Apparent differences in the domain of anaphors was argued to result from the sort of LF-movement a given anaphor permits, such that the typology of anaphors is a reflection of the typology of movement.[1] Another strategy led many to deny that some of the long-distance anaphors are really anaphors; hence they should not be expected to be subject to the same principles. Combined with the first strategy, supposed cases of unbounded anaphora that do not respect restrictions on overt movement might then be expected to have a variety of properties that are notably unlike those of syntactic anaphors. These strategies for preserving the locality that originally motivated the LGB BT are as legitimate as the independent motivation that supports them, and I argue in this chapter that both strategies deserve to outlive the theory that spawned them.

The key to this system, then, is that the domain of LAL is universal and unparameterized, while the differences in the distribution of anaphors at a distance from their antecedents is a result of how they can covertly move. In light of the FTIP, every extension of the domain of anaphors makes a dependent form available for FTIP competition, which also should predict patterns of obviation. In other words, the distribution of an anaphor may turn out to be a subset of the range of positions where it is available. Further discussion of the competitions forms enter into and the degree to which the morphology of anaphors can be used to predict their varied distributions is reserved for chapter 6.

## 5.1 Distinguishing the Domain of Movement From the Domain of Anaphora

A central contention of Extended Standard Theory (Chomsky 1973) is that movement respects the Specified Subject Condition and the Tensed S Condition and that the domains in which reciprocals and reflexives are bound, as well as those within which pronouns are disjoint from any antecedent, are identical. Within the LGB framework, A'-movement, movement to operator positions, was distinguished from A-movement (typically passive and raising, but also middles, subjects of ergative verbs, and a variety of other constructions), and only A-movement was assumed to be regulated, like reflexives and reciprocals, by opacity conditions. This parallel is enshrined in the BT as Principle A, where a "governing category" notion had replaced the opacity conditions of the 1970s.

1) Principle A: An anaphor must be bound in its governing category.

A similar view, persistent during the same era, maintains that the formation of "movement" chains is just the base generation of null anaphors in the positions posited by movement theorists; Principle A simply extends to base-generated empty anaphors (see, for example, Koster, 1997, and earlier work cited there). In arguing that traces (or more neutrally, the extraction sites) are not anaphors, I am also arguing against approaches like Koster's as well as the LGB standard, R&R, and any other approach that conflates the locality of anaphors and A-chain links.[2]

Since I adopt the view that covert movement brings apparently distant anaphors into a local licensing domain, the argument against the A-trace/anaphor parallel I raise here abstracts away from the controversies about long-distance anaphors. Rather I am asking what the most local domain for Principle A could be.

A priori, a theory that conflates the domain A-chain links with the local domain of anaphora licensing has always been attractive because apparently different classes of phenomena are reduced to the same principle. If we are to reject such a theory, it either must be argued that there are strong empirical reasons to have separate principles (i.e., a single one does not capture the correct generalizations), or else that there are conceptual reasons for distinguishing the two principles (the principles are different in kind). I will conclude that the correct approach is to distinguish two principles on both empirical and conceptual grounds.

### *5.1.1 Movement Requires a Bigger Domain Than Anaphora Does*

As mentioned above, apparent long-distance anaphora is reduced to local anaphora on the assumption that (certain) anaphors can move at LF, or can move further at LF, than others, but the proposal that anaphors move at LF was not originally posited to account for long-distance anaphora. Rather the idea that SELF anaphors in English move at LF was intended to capture the difference between (2a, b) (Lebeaux 1983, 1984; Chomsky 1986b).

2a) *The men* expect *themselves* to win.
 b) **The men* expect that *themselves* will win.

Mechanically speaking, the proposal is that anaphors must move, much as Romance clitics are argued to do overtly, from an argument position to a position adjoined to some projection of the verb. If SELF forms are required to move in this way, the empty category principle, which, among other things, blocks movement of the subject of a tensed clause (especially when it does not pass through Spec-CP) will block movement in (2b) but not in (2a). If SELF cannot move, then it cannot reach the domain in which it could be licensed, besides failing to abide by whatever principle requires it to move. The necessity of SELF movement is not independently motivated, but assuming it is necessary permits the appropriate distinction to be made.

There is a key difference, however, between assuming that movement delivers an anaphor to the domain in which it can be bound and assuming that the domain in which movement chain links are well formed is the same as, or different from, the anaphoric one. The standard approach is to say they are the same domain. In chapter 3 I formulated Domain D in a fashion that permits us to preserve this assumption, as in (4).

3) Local Antecedent Licensing: An anaphor must be c-anteceded in Domain D.

4) Domain D (provisional): The domain for X is the minimal maximal projection containing a head that c-commands X.

The definition in (4) is carefully crafted to permit SELF forms in examples like (5a) to be anteceded in a clause higher than the one they appear to be in on the surface, where IP is stipulated not to be a maximal projection. This exploits the parallel with raising to subject, as in (5b) and the de facto raising to subject brought about by passivization of *expect* in (5c).

5a) *The men* expect [*themselves* to be lucky].
b) *The men* seem [*t* to be lucky].
c) *The men* are expected [*t* to be lucky].

Chomsky (1995b) proposes, however, that at LF, ECM subjects, anaphoric or not, are raised to a Case position in the matrix clause, as in (6) (subscripts illustrative of movement history).

6a) The teacher considers the boys to be lucky.
b) [ the teacher] $[_{XP}$ considers$_i$ $[_{YP}$ the boys$_j$ $[_{VP}$ $[_V$ t$]_i$ $[_{IP}$ t$_j$ to be lucky]]]]

If this raising-to-object style of analysis is correct, the ECM complement subject, *the boys*, raises to a functional projection above VP at LF to get Accusative Case (and the verb moves at either LF or in syntax, though this is not crucial to this account). Thus the ECM infinitival subject lands in the same clause as the matrix subject simply by principles of Case attraction. By the same reasoning, the structure of (2a) at LF is (7).

7) [ *the men*] $[_{XP}$ expect$_i$ $[_{YP}$ *themselves*$_j$ $[_{VP}$ $[_V$ t $_i]$ $[_{IP}$ t$_j$ to win]]]]

The effect of Case attraction in (7) is sufficient now to distinguish (2a) from (2b) without introducing a special assumption requiring SELF forms to move. *Themselves* need not move in (2b) since it receives case in the lower clause, and given the principle of least effort (or its descendants), it will not move unless some other feature requires it to.[3]

If anaphors do not move because they are anaphors but are excluded if they do not end up close enough to their antecedents, then we need a notion of "close enough to their antecedents" and that is what Domain D of LAL is. Given that the domain of LAL in (4) is rigid, *themselves* is not licensed in (2b) and is correctly excluded. Moreover, (8a) (with its LF in [8b]) is also excluded, since the movement of *themselves* does not deliver it to the domain of its antecedent.

8a) **The men* say Ernie expects *themselves* to win.
b) [ *the men*] say Ernie $[_{XP}$ expects$_i$ $[_{YP}$ *themselves*$_j$ $[_{VP}$ $[_V$ t$]_i$ $[_{IP}$ t$_j$ to win]]]]

Thus the assumption that SELF forms must move because they are SELF forms appears unnecessary, since movement to satisfy case requirements determines whether or not anaphors can be delivered into the domain of LAL.

In this account, the assumption that the domain of anaphora and the domain of A-chains is the same is now no longer motivated by the distribution of lexical anaphors. The LGB account extends the domain of Principle A to include the surface position of the anaphor in (2a), a requirement that is not necessary at LF *except to include the trace of A-movement within the domain of anaphora.* This reasoning about (2a) is familiar, since it is exactly the same as that which motivates movement for long-distance anaphors, where extending the domain seems ad hoc if the anaphor can be brought closer by movement. A smaller domain than that required by movement will suffice for LAL at LF, namely, the one in (9), where no stipulation excludes IP as a maximal projection.

9) Domain D: The domain for X is the minimal maximal extended projection containing X.

I intend the notion of "extended projection" in the spirit of van Riemsdijk (1990, 1998) and of Grimshaw (1989) as including every maximal projection dominating a lexical head (V, N, A, C and P).[4] Thus, for example, all the daughters of nominal nodes above N (e.g., DP) will be in the same extended projection of that N up until a projection of some other lexical element dominates, which in the case of a direct object would be V'. If it is possible to eliminate functional projections, as Chomsky (1995b) suggests, then perhaps the notion of "extended" could be elided from (9), but I will keep it for now.

As we have already pointed out in 3.3.3, PPs present a complex variety of possibilities as to how anaphors contained in them can receive a local antecedent. Even as Domain D was formulated in (4), it required a special extension for prepositional objects. Our new formulation of Domain D (9) does also, at least for those cases where the preposition in question is seen as assigning a semantic role that is not independent of the verb (e.g., English *count on*) and where the PP has no "subject" of its own. In these cases, I will assume that the P counts as part of the lexical head of the verb, somewhat extending the notion of "lexical head of an extended projection" (perhaps by means of incorporation). This seems formally clumsy but intuitively appropriate. Rather than extend my discussion, I will not try to improve on it here.

What is more important is the difference between (9) and (4) with respect to examples like (7). For (4), both *themselves* and the trace of *themselves* in (7) are in the same domain as the matrix subject, but by the reckoning of (9), *themselves* is in the same Domain D as the matrix subject, and the trace of *themselves* is not. Moreover, the trace of *themselves* is not in the same Domain D as *themselves*. Only if we assume that the trace of *themselves* is an anaphor do we have to loosen Domain D to ensure that *themselves* can antecede it. Thus the domain that anaphors require is smaller than the domain required for chain links.

### *5.1.2 Lower Chain Links Are Unlike Anaphors*

From this perspective, the motivation to match the domain of chain links and that of LAL comes down to the plausibility of assuming that traces are anaphors. It seems inescapable to say that since traces can't be pronounced, they can't be deictic. However it is not at all obvious that null categories are appropriate candidates for the failure of deixis test, since there is ample evidence that empty categories are not all alike in the way they are treated by the principles of anaphora. In the rich literature on this topic, there is evidence from null subject languages and resumptive pronoun languages that empty categories can be pure pronominals as well as variables and anaphors (as in LGB and Chomsky, 1982, for example). If we are to extend the Domain D regulating anaphors just to include A-traces (but not A'-traces, for example), it is time to reconsider how good the evidence is that A-traces should be treated as anaphors.

The question becomes more acute if movement is copying, a view recently revived in the MP. Recall now some of the properties of derivations in the MP discussed in 2.4.1, particularly the numeration indices. A derivation begins with a selection of forms from the lexicon, assigning each of these a numeration index (e.g., multiple selections of *the* would have different numeration indices). Movement consists of copying the lexical forms and their numeration indices (along with the constituent that contains them) into another position, hence doubling the moved constituent. Most literally taken, movement of *the men* in (10) involves leaving a copy of *the men* in the position from which movement has taken place, thereby doubling *the men* in the structure.

10a) The men seem to be guilty.
b) seem [$_{IP}$ the men to be guilty]
c) *The men* seem [$_{IP}$ *the men* to be guilty]

It seems implausible that the lower copy of *the men* should be treated as an anaphor in any sense (it is a referring expression), so if there is any reason to leave the lower copy in the structure, then the assumption that the lower copy is an anaphor is immediately called into question.[5] However, it is often assumed within minimalism that A-traces are deleted or converted to anaphors (e.g., Hornstein 1995, 186).

If A-traces are deleted, then what restricts them is not the domain of anaphora but the operation of movement itself. We have already seen that there must be a locality restriction on the output of movement by anaphors that is independent of the operation of movement, as illustrated by (8) and (2b). Thus the assumption that lower A-chain links are deleted requires that we establish the domain for chain links separately from the domain for anaphors, which are evaluated in their landing sites.

Moreover, there is evidence from lowering structures that lower A-chain links are sometimes preserved as copies. Examples like (11) are well known (for recent references, see, e.g., May 1985; Lebeaux 1998; Hornstein 1995).

11a) Some senator is likely to speak at every rally.
b) likely $\forall$x(rally(x)) ($\exists$y(senator(y)) (speak-at(y, x)))

Among other interpretations, it is possible to interpret (11a) to mean (11b), in other words, that it is likely that at every rally, some senator or other will speak. In the earliest literature on the topic, it was suggested that *some senator* lowered into the complement clause of *likely* at LF, but with the advent of copy theory, the lower scope interpretation in (11b) can be achieved by using the lower copy in situ. If this is done, then there is no reason to view the lower copy as an anaphor, unless it is to justify the extension of the LAL domain to include traces. From the point of view of the anaphor-based domain, the reasoning for extending the domain to include traces is circular.

Now we must ask what the status of a trace can be if it is not a copy, as it apparently must not be for the unlowered interpretation of (11a) ("there is a senator such that s/he is likely to speak at every rally"). There are at least three possible answers to this question, one of which is of particular interest here.

One answer is the one that is generally assumed in one form or another, namely, that the lower trace is deleted (movement does not have to leave a copy). A disadvantage of this account is that the thematic connection between the trace and its antecedent must then inhere in the moved constituent, rather than by virtue of a chain. A similar approach is not possible for operator variable relations, such as wh-movement or QR, and so the move operation for A-movement would become more dissimilar from A'-movement in this account.

Moreover, it is not obvious that deletion of traces at LF is independently motivated. For most other contexts where deletion of copies has been proposed, it has been assumed that given Full Interpretation, the extra copies could not all be interpreted at LF without creating chaos. It has been pointed out, however, that deletion is not necessarily justified by Full Interpretation since trace copies can be determined to be indistinct from other copies within the same numeration given all proliferated copies will bear the same numeration indices, differing from each other only in terms of their structural relations. This sort of account has been explored by Nunes (1999), Cresti (1996), Fox (1999) Brody (1995),[6] and Safir (1999), particularly for A'-chains and the traces in them, but if the same holds for A-chains, then all that such an account must appeal to is that when one structural position is interpreted, everything bearing the same numeration index has then been interpreted at the point where that is done. If this is the right account (see Safir, 2004, for various wrinkles), then the case that A-traces are not anaphors in general is already made.

Rather than deleting the copy, a second option would be to insert something else in its place, and this was the option adopted in the LGB theory, such that A-traces were identified as anaphors. From our perspective, such an operation is essentially akin to vehicle change, if vehicle change is not restricted to introducing pronouns. There are at least two reasons to reject the vehicle-change-to-anaphor idea. Consider (12).[7]

12a) *Max* loves *himself* even more than Bill does.
b) Max loves *Bill* even more than *he* does.

For (12a), we are assuming that the second conjunct could be reconstructed with either a SELF form or with a pronoun, yielding sloppy and strict readings accordingly (see 4.3.4 and Safir 2004). For (12b), if vehicle change introduces a pronoun, it cannot be one dependent on *he*, since that could only arise if *Bill* in the first conjunct were dependent on *Max*, which is of course blocked by FTIP, and so no dependency arrow connecting *Bill* to *Max* can be copied. If a reflexive reading is a coargument-dependent one, then we predict that the second conjunct containing the elision cannot have a reflexive interpretation. If, however, vehicle change could introduce an anaphor in this environment, then the anaphor would be c-anteceded by *he* (also dependent on *Bill*) and thus (12b) would be well formed with respect to LAL. This is clearly the wrong result.

There is also a conceptual reason for restricting vehicle change to substitution of a pronoun. By discarding Principle B, the term *pronoun* has no more than a descriptive status. In fact, the only distinction between pronouns and anaphoric pronominals, as we will see in chapter 6, is that anaphors (a subset of elements that lack deictic potential) are specially marked as such to be susceptible to LAL. If we take seriously the notion that anaphors are marked as such (as are pronominal anaphors, see 6.1.2), then replacing a referring expression or an anaphor with an unmarked pronoun loses information, but does not add any.[8, 9] By contrast, replacing a referring expression or a pronoun with an anaphor *adds* information, namely, a feature specification for anaphorhood. Just such an addition should be excluded by Chomsky's inclusiveness condition, which was discussed and slightly modified in 2.4.1.

The third answer, now apparent, is that A-traces can undergo vehicle change to pronouns. Notice that there is nothing to exclude a pronoun in the position of a trace in the context of (13).

13) John was killed t

Replacing a copy with a pronoun loses information about the string but does not add to it if pronouns merely consist of grammatical features specific to nominals but not specific to particular lexical items. Recall that there is no Principle B to prevent binding of a pronoun within the domain that corresponds to that of LAL, and no anaphor is available in the environment of an A-trace, given the inclusiveness restriction on vehicle change, unless the A-trace is itself the trace of an anaphor. In other words, a null pronominal trace is the most dependent form available most of the time; hence the status of most A-traces is usually that of a pronoun.

The optional availability of vehicle change for A-chain traces is in fact crucial within the account of LAL assumed here, as there are contexts like (14) in which an A-moved anaphor cannot leave a copy at the tail of the chain that fails to undergo vehicle change.

14) *Spector* expects [$_{IP}$ *himself* to be considered [$_{IP}$ *himself/pro* to be the winner]].

If the copy of *himself* is left behind, then that lower *himself* is not licensed by LAL, given the domain in (9), since a projection of the lowest IP (an extended projection of the verb *be*) dominates the lower *himself.* The only way that (14) can be grammatical is if vehicle change applies to the lower *himself,* changing it to a pronoun. The result satisfies FTIP, since a pronoun is the most dependent form available where an anaphor is not licensed by LAL. The higher *himself* will raise to the highest clause to get Case, also leaving a pronominal trace behind.[10]

Finally, it is demonstrated in Safir (2004) that a variety of A'-movements leave anaphoric copies only if the moved constituents are anaphors themselves. Unless we are to needlessly heighten the differences between A- and A'-chains, this is another strong reason to assume that vehicle change is restricted to pronominal substitutions.

We can thus conclude that there is no reason to assume that A-traces are anaphors unless their antecedents are. Indeed there is ample evidence suggesting that A-traces generally are not anaphors, but that in any case, their properties need not be stipulated but instead will follow from copy theory and the distribution of vehicle change, which permits unpronounced nominals to be evaluated as pronominal.[11]

### *5.1.3 More on Subordinate Chain Links as Pronouns*

I have proposed that the tail of an A-movement chain (speaking descriptively) can be a null pronoun inserted by vehicle change. The possibility then presents itself that vehicle change could occur before spell out and that resumptive pronouns could be their overt spell out (I have explored this matter in detail for A'-chains and their traces in Safir, 2004, which I will not review here).

In using the term *A-chain* descriptively, I am assuming two things about them: first, that they are the result of movement, and second, that they are the result of movement into an A-position to which no theta role is assigned. Still speaking descriptively, I will assume that an A-position is any SPEC position other than SPEC-CP (assume that QR is adjunction, leaving a trace or copy, to a maximal projection that already has a specifier), keeping in mind that I will simply change the description if one were to point out A'-movement to say, SPEC-DP. In short, we are looking for cases where one expects A-movement, and what one finds is an overt pronoun in the position of the trace.

There are cases that appear to meet this description, namely, apparent raising from finite sentences, which has been purported to be found in Turkish, Greek, and Balkan.

Soames and Perlmutter (1979, 154–163) argue, on the basis of work by Joseph (1976) on Greek, that raising to subject is possible with verbs corresponding to *seem, appear, be likely* and *begin* when these verbs occur with *na* subjunctive clauses as complements. In *na* clauses, the subordinate verb agrees in person and number with its subject as in (15a). Theta theory requires that the matrix subject has moved, but if it is A-movement, then the chain should be broken by a tensed clause. The same argument is made for raising to object (parallel to English ECM contexts), where an accusative in the matrix clause would appear to have its thematic role assigned in the complement *pos*-clause, yet the subordinate verb appears with agreement corresponding to the accusative-marked nominal in the matrix clause. Finally, a verb corresponding to English *let* also takes a *na* complement from which raising to object appears to be possible.

15a) I kopeles fenonde na ine fliaros simera.
the girls seem/3pl SUBJ be/3pl talkative today
"The girls seem to be talkative today."
b) Olos o kosmos θeori ton yani pos ine eksipnos.
Everybody considers John/ACC COMP is smart
"Everybody considers John to be smart."
c) O yanis mas afise na ksekurasθume.
John/NOM us/ACC let SUBJ rest/1pl
"John let us rest."

Soames and Perlmutter (1979) argue specifically that this sort of raising leaves a pronominal copy that, like other pronominal subjects in Greek, is dropped by normal pro-drop; that is to say, Greek is a null subject language where stressless subjects are not pronounced. However, where emphasized, the pronouns can surface, and when they do, they are nominative.

16a) O filos mu fenete na kerdizi to pegnidi mono aftos.
the friend my seem/3sg SUBJ be-winning the game only he/NOM
"Only my friend seems to be winning the game."

b) Olos o kozmos θeori ti Maria pos mono afti ine eksipni.
Everybody considers Maria/ACC COMP only she/NOM is smart
"Everybody considers only Mary to be smart."

c) I Maria mas afise na ksekurasθume mono emis.
Maria/NOM us/ACC let COMP rest/1pl only we
"Maria let only us rest."

Since the raised nominal cannot be theta-assigned in the matrix, a chain must relate it to its theta position, but if the tail of the chain is a pronoun, then Principle B should rule it out, if the domain of anaphora and the domain of A-chain links is the same. Similarly, in the R&R theory, the generalized Chain Condition should not permit a full pronoun to be a subordinate chain link, unless the pronoun in question bears the ad hoc [-R] feature, which is otherwise not required for nominative pronominal subjects in Greek. There is a little wiggle room here, since one might plausibly argue that the emphatic cases would overcome a principle-B effect in any case, but the larger point, that traces can leave pronominal lower chain links, must still be accepted, if one is to treat the emphatics as lower chain links.

Of course a number of questions about this construction remain unanswered by the Soames and Perlmutter proposal. Within the LGB framework, a trace in a finite subject position would be an empty category principle (ECP) violation, and given the reasoning that led to splitting the ECP from the theory of anaphora,[12] it would appear that the pronoun saves a structure that would otherwise be ruled out by conditions not specific to anaphora. The uncertain status of the ECP within the MP leaves the matter in limbo.

If the Soames and Perlmutter account is right, then we have further evidence that A-chains can leave pronominal chain tails, just as A'-movement can, a point made for similar structures in Turkish by Moore (1998). In this case, what we have proposed as a possibility in covert syntax is thus apparent on the surface in languages like Greek and Turkish.[13]

We can conclude, then, that subordinate A-chain links can act like pronouns rather than anaphors in some environments, and so the assumption that A-traces are inherently anaphors incorrectly restricts their distribution.

### *5.1.4 Summary of the Case for Separating Movement From the Domain of Anaphora*

I have presented three forms of argument against the notion that the domain of A-movement is to be identified with the domain of anaphora. First, if movement is a vehicle for anaphors to get close to their antecedents, then it is not clear what is to be gained by extending the domain of anaphora to encompass the sites from which movement takes place. By not weakening the locality restrictions on the domain of anaphora in this way, the domain of anaphora turns out to be quite compact, as stated in (9). It will be argued further, in 5.2.5, that this compact domain makes a striking prediction about the range of possible anaphors. Second, the tails of chains are not like anaphors in principle if movement is copying, except where the moved element is itself an anaphor. Finally, there is some evidence that some A-movement leaves a pronominal residue rather than a copy or an anaphor. If the condition on chains is identified with the domain of anaphora (or Principle B), then this is exactly what is not expected.

Naturally, the assumption that Domain D is clause bound and that A-movement is not raises the question as to what determines these two domains. It could be that the domain in (4) is descriptively correct for A-movement but may exist as it does by virtue of some theory of shortest move that distinguishes clausal and interclausal A-movement, assuming that filled specifiers cannot normally be moved across. Thus the apparent opacity sensitivity of anaphors is just an artifact of the way that movement delivers anaphors into the domain of LAL.

The next question natural question to ask is whether or not the domain of LAL can be reduced to some other independently necessary requirement, since a derivation of this domain from something else would of course be desirable. I do not, however, foresee this result as attainable from my present perspective. It is argued in 6.2.3 that relational anaphors, anaphors that are not pronominal, do not normally move except for Case reasons, and if so, it is not expected that a relational anaphor will be in a SPEC-Head relation with its antecedent to satisfy agreement. Perhaps recent proposals in Chomsky (2000, 2001), which treat agreement as a less local relation, may be appealed to, but even if they are, at least two sorts of matters would remain unexplained. First, many of the possessive anaphors that respect LAL agree with the nominal heads they possess (MS SIN, the genitive version of SIG, agrees in gender, for example), so it is not obvious that they formally lack agreement—quite the contrary, it is just that some do not show agreement with their antecedents.[14] Secondly, as will be discussed in 5.2.4, many languages permit datives to license anaphors just in case they are in subject position, but these datives do not agree with the verb they are associated with (see also Hindi ergative subjects). In the latter case, then, movement of an anaphor to the position of the head T or an Agr node would not achieve agreement with the features of the subject.

If LAL cannot be reduced to agreement, however, it is still not obvious that there is a more promising way to derive LAL or its domain from something else, and so I leave the matter for future study. I shall briefly return to the relation between movement and anaphora in 7.3, but for more detailed discussion, see Safir (2003, 2004).

## 5.2 Bounded Domains

Let us return now to the hypothesis, mentioned earlier, that the typology of movement plays a crucial role in the distribution of anaphora, but only indirectly, as the means by which anaphoric elements are transported into the very local domain of anaphora where they may be anteceded. Since many anaphors are not superficially close to their antecedents, this movement must be covert, as was first hypothesized by Lebeaux (1984), Pica (1987), and Chomsky (1986b), but the proposal is only interesting insofar as covert movement is restricted in some independently motivated way. A plausible restriction that we shall adopt as a working hypothesis is that no type of covert movement should be posited unless there is a form of attested overt movement it corresponds to (on theories where all movement is overt, see note 19 of chapter 2).

17) There is no form of covert movement that is not attested for overt movement.

Thus a key determinant of the typology of anaphoric domains is the independently motivated typology of movement relations.

The limitation of the typology of anaphors imposed by (17) is consistent with the Universalist Hypothesis (UH; discussed briefly in 3.3 and more fully in chapter 6), which requires that all principles and properties pertaining to anaphora be universal and invariant. The UH rules out any variation in the domain of Principle A. It does not rule out the possibility, exploited here, that nonanaphoric properties of anaphoric forms may vary, such that independently attested properties of nonanaphors may also be attributed to anaphors. Thus additional nonanaphoric properties of different anaphors may account for their differing distribution.

Following this logic further, if covert movement cannot render the domain of LAL accessible to a purported anaphor and the purported anaphor is empirically acceptable, then it must not be an anaphor at all, even if it lacks deictic potential. Elements of the latter sort are often considered syntactically unrestricted (see Thráinsson, 1991, 59, where this position is explicitly defended), and I will refer to them a little more neutrally as *UD-forms* (UD = unbounded dependent). As is well known, many UD-forms have been shown to be susceptible to logophoric or perspective effects (e.g., as first proposed by Kuno 1972), but others are more influenced by stress and contrast (e.g., Baker 1994). The neutral term *UD-form* abstracts away from these additional factors, some of which are addressed in 5.3–5.4. There are contexts, however, where it is difficult to sort out the force of explanations based on conversational perspective from one based on syntactic form, but apart from brief comments in the next chapter, the issues are not addressed here (but see Safir, in preparation, for a more comprehensive approach to perspective effects).

Our strategy, then, must be to show that syntactic properties restricting anaphora are fully absent when a purported anaphor is anteceded from a position inaccessible for LAL or for the typology of movement. For example, many of the UD-forms appear to share with syntactic anaphors an affinity for subject antecedents. This affinity has been one reason that the movement account proposed by Pica (1987) to account for subject orientation in Scandinavian, which is generally bounded by tense islands, was extended to languages like Chinese, to be discussed below, where the relation between the dependent and its antecedent is unbounded, but the antecedent is generally thought to be necessarily a subject.

Since I do assume that subject orientation arises by covert movement to a landing site that provides only a subject as local antecedent, issues of locality of movement are indeed also to be related to issues of subject orientation. However, the subject sensitivity of bounded domains tends to be much stricter than it is for UD-forms, especially if we define *subject* narrowly:

18) The *syntactic subject* of $\alpha$, $\alpha$ a lexical category, is any $\beta$ such that $\beta$ is the SPEC of an extended projection of $\alpha$, and $\beta$ is in an A-chain relation with SPEC-$\alpha$.

Thus any claim that a given inherently dependent element is "subject oriented" means that its antecedent must fit the definition in (18) at some point in the derivation.[15] Any purported anaphor that can be anteceded over a long domain (one that crosses a specified subject) is either subject oriented or else not an anaphor in the sense of LAL; in other words, it is a UD-form. Such forms do not always need c-commanding antecedents or even sentence-internal antecedents and are hence inaccessible by movement, but discussion of these properties and others I reserve for 5.3.

Some further terms will be useful. Syntactic anaphors that are superficially outside the domain of LAL but not separated from the LAL domain of their antecedent by a specified subject have what I will call *short-bounded domains* (sometimes I will just call them *short domains*). Syntactic anaphors subject to LAL but separated from the domain of LAL by an intervening subject will be said to have *long-bounded domains*. These domains are "bounded" in the sense that they are subject to conditions attested for overt syntactic movement. Finally, there are reflexive-marked morphemes, as discussed in chapter 4, that must have a coargument antecedent and hence inhabit a subset of positions in the short domain. Given these distinctions, along with the existence of UD-forms, I will henceforth avoid the terms *long-distance anaphor* and *long-distance reflexive*, which are now insufficiently specific and misleading.

Three last caveats: First, I postpone all discussion until chapter 6 of any causal connection between the morphology of dependent forms and their covert movement potential, though I shall make suggestive remarks from time to time where there is no major distraction to the main line of argument. Second, I present the typology of movement in a largely descriptive way, not attempting to derive the locality conditions on the variety of movements from deeper principles restricting movement operations.[16] On the other hand, any I movement restriction I do propose will be motivated on the basis of evidence not peculiar to anaphora, consistent with the Universalist Hypothesis. If my conclusions are correct at this level of abstraction, I hope they will contribute to the enterprise of deriving the class of locality domains from deeper principles, but this task is beyond the scope of my inquiry. Finally, readers should keep in mind that this chapter tracks the availability of the different anaphors, not their ultimate distribution, which may be restricted by the FTIP competitions a given anaphor enters into. Once again, these issues are postponed until chapter 6, where the consequences of the distinction between domain and availability is examined in some empirical detail.

### *5.2.1 Motivating Covert Movement*

Why should anaphors ever move? One might suppose that the motivation for covert movement need not be any more complex than the need of anaphors to participate in convergent derivations. If, on the surface, they are outside the Domain D that includes their antecedent, they don't survive; hence, it might be reasoned, they must move covertly if it will suffice to permit them to converge at LF. But if this is so, it is surprising that overt movement specific to anaphors (distinguishing them from nonanaphoric pronominals) is not attested.

Rather it would appear that if anaphors move, it is because they have properties in common with nonanaphors that cause them to move. Indeed this is just what the Universalist Hypothesis requires: If anaphors differ from one another, it must be with respect to lexical properties that are attested of nonanaphors. Direct objects, if versions of the MP accusative-case-assigning theory are right, must move to a higher specifier, but that movement is not specific to anaphors. Clitic anaphors in languages like French move overtly, but in this they are just like nonanaphoric clitic pronominals. The varieties of long-distance anaphora should thus be a reflection of the typology of long range, but bounded, dependency relations, whether they are represented as movement, as I assume here, or whether typology of long-bounded dependencies is accounted for by some other sort of device that captures the locality effects (see note 16 of this chapter).

Now let us consider the variety of familiar overt movements. Since LAL accounts for locality within a clause, we are interested here in movements that are interclausal. I am assuming that the moved element always c-commands its extraction site and that this movement is restricted by limitations on chain formation, such that syntactic islands are respected. The following sorts of movements are candidates for anaphora delivery, though I shall have nothing to say about scrambling.[17]

19a) A-movement
 b) Head movement
 c) A'-movement
 d) Scrambling

We have already seen that A-movement can transport an anaphor into Domain D, as in the case of English Accusative Casemarking. The latter account makes only the otherwise Caseless subject of a complement clause a candidate for antecedence in the domain of LAL and hence derives the specified-subject effect for accusatives, since a complement of the embedded verb would not move to the matrix for Case if a lower position were available. Thus case-driven A-movement accounts for the short domain of English SELF anaphors.

The specified-subject condition is not derived for movements not motivated by case, however, and so this much of the OB opacity effect, where it holds, remains a condition on the way chains are formed or a condition on the distance between chain links, depending on the theory. Scrambling aside, it is not clear that there are other movements to A-positions that require discussion here.

### 5.2.2 *Head Movement and the Short-Bounded Domain*

When we turn to head movements, there appear to be two sorts to consider. Those described as cliticization, most typically of pronominal elements, which can travel interclausally, and head-to-head movements, which are strictly local and appear to involve lexical heads moving into, or adjoining to, the heads of their functional projections, respecting the strict locality of the head movement constraint (see references in Li 1990; Travis 1984; Baker 1988). The latter sort of movement is not of direct interest to us in this chapter (see note 32 of chapter 6), but clitic movement is, insofar as it can transport a form to a higher LAL domain. Clitic movement is typically taken to be a variety of head movement where the clitic represents either the head of DP or the head of NP, but if clitics are phrasal, it will not affect my reasoning in this section (for more details, see 6.1).[18]

What we know of overt interclausal cliticization of argument pronominals, however, seems to indicate that it is very limited. In French, for example, cliticization can apply across clauses, applying, for example, to the subject of the subordinate clause in (20a). An intervening subject appears to block the process, as discussed by Kayne (1975), unless the subject of the complement clause is somehow gotten out of the way or a restructuring verb is involved. In (20d, e) it is rendered dative by whatever process the causative–infinitive construction permits (either V or VP fronting or complex predicate formation, etc.), but where nothing suppresses the lower subject, the clitic cannot climb, as illustrated in (20c).

20a) Paul la laissera manger les gâteaux.
Paul her-ACC let-FUT eat the cakes
"Paul will let her eat the cakes."
b) Paul laissera son fils se/te/la dénoncer.
Paul let-FUT his son SE/you/him denounce
"Paul will let *his son* denounce *himself*/you/him."
c) *Paul se/te/la laissera son fils dénoncer.
d) Elle le fera manger à Jean.
She it-ACC make-FUT eat to Jean
"She will make Jean eat it."
e) Jean se fera connaître à Marie.
Jean SE make-FUT to-know to Marie
"Jean will make Marie know him."

Oversimplifying somewhat, this variety of clitic movement cannot occur across an accusative or nominative subject, though it can across a dative subject, which becomes possible in these environments because of the morphosyntax of causatives in French, whatever analysis one adopts for that process. To put it another way, the domain of clitic movement is expanded by morphosyntactic predicate formation, not necessarily by the pattern of case assignment. For our purposes, all that is important is that clitic movement of this variety does extend the range of a potential anaphor more than our account of A-movement does, once the peculiarities of the Romance causative structure are taken into account.[19]

The other key distinction between case-driven short domain and the clitic domain is that overt clitic placement of *se* accounts for the strict subject orientation of *se*, as opposed to the reciprocal and *lui-même,* which can be anteceded by objects, as illustrated by the contrasts in (21) and (22) (from Kayne 1975, 371; for sparse comments on the domain of reciprocals, see the appendix to chapter 6).

21a) La psychiatrie a révélé *Jean* à *lui-même*.
"Psychiatry revealed Jean to himself."
b) *La psychiatrie *s*'est révélé *Jean*.
"Psychiatry revealed Jean to himself."

22a) Je présenterai *ces filles l'une* à *l'autre*.
"I will introduce those girls to one another."
b) *Je *se* présenterai *ces filles*.
"I will introduce those girls to one another."

If *se* targets I (or AgrS or TP, according to the relevant theory) as its landing site, as illustrated in (22), then the only antecedent for *se* in the domain of LAL at the surface is the subject, since within the extended projection of the verb, only the subject c-commands *se* (indices are used descriptively here to mark chain relations).[20, 21]

23) $[_{IP}$ Jean$_i$ $[_{I'}$ se$_j$ + I $[_{VP}$ t$_i$ $[_{V'}$ présenterai t$_j$]]]]
Jean SE will-introduce
"*Jean* will introduce *himself*."

Thus clitic movement of *se*, a movement that also applies to nonanaphoric clitics, is enough to account for its distribution outside the domain of LAL and for its subject orientation.

Once we allow for an overt variety of clitic movement, we may expect that covert cliticlike movement might be available for forms that do not have the overt placement of clitics high in the verbal extended projection. In such a language, an overt pronominal form would act covertly as a clitic and, if it is an anaphor, it will be subject oriented and sensitive to morphosyntactic predicate formation (overt or covert).

German *sich*, for example, unlike French *se*, can appear in direct object position or in prepositional object position, but like *se*, *sich* is always subject oriented ([24c] from Everaert 1986, 243).

24a) *Peter* hilft *sich/*ihm*.
Peter helps SIG/him
"Peter helps himself."
b) *Peter* spricht über *sich/*ihn*.
"Peter speaks about himself"
c) *Die Leute schlagen *dem Fragenden ihn/*sich* als Vorhandlungsführer vor.
"The people proposed the questioner himself as the principal negotiator."

Cases where *sich* is bound in a clause higher than its thematic assignment seem to require embedding in an appropriate sort of PP in certain causative constructions, as in (25a) as opposed to (25b), where the preposition *über* is a separable prefix rendering *sich* a direct object in the complement clause. In (25c) (from Reis 1976, 31, 29, 30; cited in and translated by McKay 1985, 18, 19), the dative-marked prepositional object cannot have a matrix antecedent.[22, 23]

25a) *Hans* lässt die Müdigkeit über *sich* kommen
"Hans lets tiredness overcome him."
b) *Hans* lässt die Müdigkeit *ihn/*sich* überkommen.
"Hans lets tiredness overcome him."
c) *Hans* liess boshaft wie *er* war die Leute stundenlang nach *ihm/sich* rufen ohne zu reagieren.
"Hans, malicious as he was, let people call him for hours without reacting."

Thus German *sich* contrasts with English SELF forms both in that it is subject-oriented, and it permits a larger domain (compare, *"*He* let people call *himself*"). The difference between the domain of *sich* and that of English *self* may be captured by a parallel with French clitic movement if we assume that covert clitic movement from prepositional object position is possible in German for *sich* and that certain causative constructions permit the domain of covert clitic movement to pass a specified subject.

The suggestion that clitic movement has a covert counterpart that permits PP extraction while the overt form doesn't violates our working hypothesis that we should not posit covert movements that don't correspond to overt ones, but there are, in fact, occasional examples of overt clitic movement in French that allow preposition stranding, as illustrated for the clitic *lui* in (26) drawn from Kayne (1975, 141).

26a) Jean court après Marie.
"Jean is running after Marie."
b) Jean lui court après.

It could be that some principle usually applying to spell-out to prevent P-stranding does not affect covert movement, a view suggestively supported by occasional overt parallels like (26). In other words, there is an overt model for P-stranding clitic movement, even if it is not as fully general as it is in its covert form.[24, 25]

The distribution of Dutch *zich* makes an even stronger case for a covert parallel to the overt clitic movement of Romance. *Zich* is not possible as a direct object unless an argument of the verb is dethematized, since it is in competition with *zichzelf* in object position and loses, but like German *sich*, *zich* can be a prepositional object, depending on the relation of the PP to the main verb (see 3.3.4).

27a) *Jan* zag *zichzelf/*zich*.
Jan saw ZICH-SELF/ZICH
"Jan saw himself."
b) *Jan* zag een slang naast *zich*.
"Jan saw a snake near himself."

Unlike *zichzelf*, but like French *se* and German *sich*, *zich* must have a subject antecedent, as illustrated by (28a, b) (from Koster 1986, 328–329). While the antecedent of *zichzelf* in (28a) is ambiguous in Dutch, *zich* (28b) can only have *Jan* as its antecedent.

28a) Jan raadde Peter zichzelf aan.
Jan recommended Peter ZICH-SELF part.
"*Jan* recommended Peter to *himself*."
b) Jan raadde Peter [de vrouw naast zich] aan.
Jan recommended Peter the woman near ZICH part.
"*Jan* recommended the woman near *him* to Peter."

In causative constructions and some perception verb constructions, but not in infinitives generally, *zich* can find an antecedent beyond an intervening logical subject, as illustrated in (29) (from Koster 1986, 340, where the whole clause is embedded to abstract away from verb second).

29) . . . dat *Marie* Peter aan *zich* liet denken.
. . . that Marie Peter of ZICH let think
" . . . that Marie let Peter think of her."

Everaert (1986, 31–34) even argues that Dutch *zich* is a clitic, but one that does not necessarily attach to the verb as in Romance. Modifying Everaert's examples slightly, (30a–c) illustrate that *zich* in PPs, like reduced pronouns in PPs (e.g., *me*), cannot be conjoined with another nominal, while full pronominals (e.g., *mij*) can.[26]

30a) **Jan* liet Marie voor *zich* en Hans werken.
"Jan let Marie work for himself and Hans."
b) Jan liet Marie voor *me/mij en Hans werken.
"Jan let Marie work for me and Hans."
c) **Jan* zag een slang naast *zich* en Hans.
"Jan saw a snake near himself and Hans."
d) Jan zag een slang naast *me/mij en Hans.
"Jan saw a snake near me and Hans."

If Everaert's suggestion is correct, then the only difference between *zich* and *se* is covert versus overt movement, modulo some minor distributional differences between overt and covert clitic movement.

Reinhart and Reuland (1991, 301–304), suggest an account close to this one based on a head movement of SIG anaphors (and German *sich*, Dutch *zich*, and French *se*). They propose that SIG is motivated to move in search of an agreement configuration (but see 5.1.4), and they assume that the movement in question is very local, such that the SIG anaphor ($SIG_j$) adjoins to the verb that selects it. They then propose to relate SIG forms to higher subjects by virtue of the morphosyntax that applies to infinitival complementation (seemingly putting into form a suggestion of Koster 1986, 340). The analysis requires the verb selecting SIG to head-adjoin to I and then to a higher verb, which in turn head-adjoins to I. SIG agrees with the features of the highest verb. The domain of anaphora for SIG will then be determined by the domain of verb-raising to form complex predicates, and they then correlate the well-formedness of *zich* to environments where verb-raising is possible in Dutch.[27]

Whatever its merits for Dutch (see note 27), a variety of problematic analytic questions arises for this hypothesis should it be extended to all SIG forms in other languages, such as Mainland Scandinavian (MS). Tenseless verbs in MS would have to raise past overt complementizers (or whatever forms such as *å* are) as well as I, which would mean that a lexical category adjoins to a functional category, which then adjoins to another lexical category. This is just the sort of head movement that Li (1990) argues is a form of improper movement and does not exist. Neither is it clear that there would be any reason for the verb-raising in MS, other than to extend the domain of SIG under this theory.

It seems preferable to distinguish the MS (and Hindi and Russian) cases from the Dutch (and German and French) cases on principled grounds, such that the latter cases involve domains where the covert movement of a form is extended by the morphosyntax of complex predicate formation that clitic movement is overtly sensitive to, while the domain for the former set of cases, cases that cross clausal domains not easily rendered as unified predicates, is motivated by something else. I conclude, then, that an anaphor may have a domain extended not only by covert A-movement, as in the case of English ECM, but by covert clitic movement, as in the case of German and Dutch.

#### 5.2.2.1 DUBIOUS COVERT MOVEMENT

MS SIG can be anteceded not only in a higher clause, but also across a series of infinitives with complementizers (as in [3a]). This distribution does not correspond to the set of launching sites for any form of overt pronominal clitic movement I am aware of. Thus we must look elsewhere for an overt movement analog that corresponds to these cases, and we must do so respecting the restriction imposed by (17), which does not permit us to invent covert movement relations for anaphors for which there is no overt analog.

There are, however, analyses such as that of Pica (1987, 1991) that posit a form of LF head movement that does correspond to what we know of overt head movement. Pica proposes that complex anaphors are XP constituents while simplex anaphors are X° elements.[28] Under the assumption that like adjoins to like, XP constituents can adjoin to maximal projections, which means that a complex anaphor embedded in a PP can be anteceded by the direct object, since the anaphor can adjoin to the PP (although it is not clear why it moves at all). Thus in (31c), *hinanden* could adjoin to the PP constituent [*om*-trace] at LF, permitting *dem* to c-command *hinanden*.

31a) *Jeg fortæller *Hans* om *sig*.
"I tell Hans about himself."

b) Jeg fortæller *dem* om *hinanden*.
"I tell them about each other."

c) Jeg [$_{VP}$ fortæller *dem* [$_{PP}$ *hinanden*$_i$ [$_{PP}$ om $t_i$]] ]

However, *sig* does not have this option, since it must be interpreted as an X°; hence it must move to a head position. Pica stipulates that the head position it moves to is

INFL (Pica 1987, 488) on the supposition that *sig* lacks features perhaps obtainable in association or agreement with INFL. In INFL position, its local antecedent is SPEC-IP, hence subject orientation. Up to this point, Pica's proposal is not unlike the covert clitic movement that I proposed in the previous section (inspired by Pica's analysis).

However, to permit elements like *sig* to travel over long distances, Pica proposes, "The Specified Subject Condition can be overcome through a cyclic head movement from INFL to INFL through the head position C of CP (COMP). This position serves as an escape hatch for $X^o$ anaphors when C is empty at LF (but not for $X^{max}$ reflexives for which such movement is impossible). . . . " (1987, 490). Covert head movement accounts differ in detail as to whether *sig* (or its supposed counterparts in other languages) must adjoin to every intervening head on its way to adjoin to I[+tns], or must adjoin only to the intervening Is and Cs, but all assume that the adjunctions are just stopping points leaving behind nodes of the form [ $[_x$ [t] $x^o$], that is, a complex head containing a trace of some sort, if a trace is left at all.

Interclausal head movement across intervening subjects and across other appropriate landing sites is not supported by analogy with any attested overt phenomenon, however. Moreover, excorporation of adjoined heads, crucial to the possibility of moving beyond the most local available landing site, does not seem defensible either.[29] Finally, the fact that SIG only travels across tenseless domains does not follow from nor is it shown to be related to this mechanism.

Once the analogy with head movement fails and the analogy with the more specific process of clitic movement fails, all that remains about this movement that is "head specific" is the claim that simplex, as opposed to complex anaphors, are the ones that move (see note 28 to this chapter). Even though I reject Pica's account of head movement, it must be pointed out that the proposal for German *sich* in the previous section and MS SIG in the next section relies on what I take to be the essence of Pica's analysis, which is that it unites subject-orientation and movement domains.

Most of the objections I have raised to SIG movement as head movement also extend to work on Chinese *ziji* inspired by Pica's analysis of MS (e.g., Battistella 1989; Cole, Hermon, and Sung 1990; Cole and Sung 1994;[30] and to a slightly lesser extent to the operator movement account of Huang and Tang 1991), though for Chinese the movement approach seems even more problematic. These analyses either treat the long-distance relationship as nonisland-bound head movement or nonisland-bound operator movement, but as illustrated in 5.3, there is evidence that neither c-command nor sentence-internal antecedents are always required for Chinese *ziji*. Huang and Liu (2001) continue to support an unbounded LF head-movement account that does not correspond to any form of overt movement, as do Cole, Hermon, and Lee (2001), though they tie the syntactic movements to the satisfaction of conditions on logophoric interpretation. I return to these matters in 6.3.3.

To summarize, the varieties of covert head movement that have been proposed to account for the distributions of Dutch *zich*, MS SIG, Chinese *ziji,* and Japanese *zibun* rely on forms of head movement, agreement, or percolation that are not independently motivated by overt (or covert) analogues, in that these processes are either hypothesized to be specific to anaphors or are de facto restricted in their application to anaphors. Moreover, in the case of Chinese *ziji* and Japanese *zibun*, which do not appear to be island sensitive, it is not clear that there is any locality restriction based on head movement that provides a revealing account of their full distribution.

### *5.2.3 A'-movement and Tense Domains*

A'-movement within the LGB framework classed movements that land in SPEC-CP or that adjoin to maximal projections as having distinct properties, most notably, the ability to ignore large classes of filled specifiers of intervening projections in a general way. Restrictions like subjacency and ECP, extended or not to adjunct islands, or successor theories, such as relativized minimality, were assumed to hold of such movements, and evidence of the operation of these constraints were later taken to be the hallmarks of covert counterparts to these movements. Thus long-distance anaphora, if it is movement related, should be conditioned by the same constraints as overt A'-movement is, in the best case.[31]

One promising overt analog to the sort of movement our theory would appear to require is suggested by instances where the movement of operators appears to be sensitive to a domain bounded by the lowest clause-containing tense. For example, consider Hindi interrogative wh-phrases, which do not move overtly to clause-initial position or to a position outside of the clause in which they appear (unless they are scrambled in the manner of -wh phrases). As in other wh-in-situ languages, interrogatives are still possible because the wh-phrases are construed to have scope over a clause at the interpretive level, and LF-movement has been proposed as a device that renders these interpretations possible (e.g., Huang 1982). What is of special interest to us is that Hindi interrogative wh-phrases cannot be construed higher than the domain bounded by the lowest clause-containing tense (see, for example, Dayal, 1996, and references cited there).

32a) tum [kahãa jaanaa] caahtee ho.
you where to-go want
"Where do you want to go?"
b) tum jaante ho [ki vo kahãa gayaa].
you know that he where went
"You know where he went." (not "Where do you know he went?")
c) maiN nahiiN jaantii huuN ki usne kis-kii kitaab paRhii.
I not know-FEM-PR that he/she-ERG who-GEN book read
"I don't know whose book he read."

Moreover, Hindi has properties similar to Norwegian (33a, b) and Russian (34a, b), mentioned in chapter 3, in that it has an anaphoric form sensitive to just such a tensed domain:

33a) *Jon* bad oss forsøke å få deg til å snakke pent om *seg*.
Jon asked us try to get you to talk nicely about seg
b) **Jon* var ikke clar over at vi hadde snakket om *seg*.
Jon was not aware that we had talked about him

34a) *Každy student* poprosil Ivana PRO pročittat *svoju* staju.
every student asked Ivan to-read SIG article
b) **Amerikanskie turisty* skazali [čto Ivan posetil *svoi* groda].
American tourists said that Ivan visited SIG cities

35a) *siitaa-ne* raam-ko [PRO *apnii* kitaabe˜ paRhne] d̃ii.
Sita(SU) Ram(DO) self's books(EDO) to-read gave
"Sita allowed Ram to read her books."
b) **siitaa-ne* kahaa [kii raam-ne *apnii* kitaab phe˜˜k dii].
Sita(SU) said that Ram(ESU) self's book(EDO) throw gave
"Sita said that Ram threw away her book."

The parallel between wh-in-situ and anaphora, noted by Dayal (1993) and by Safir (1993), shows that sensitivity to the tensed domain is not peculiar to anaphora.[32, 33]

The other question that arises in this connection concerns the landing site of the purported movement. Even if tense-restricted operator movement is what is determines the locality effect, the subject-orientation effect is only accounted for if the landing site of movement places the anaphor in a position where only the subject is a possible antecedent. Given the tense restriction on this movement and the absence of wh-morphology (wh-morphology probably requires SPEC-CP as a landing site), it is plausible to assume that tense-restricted operator movement adjoins to TP or to a projection immediately subordinate to TP. In either case, the result would predict subject orientation, as the only c-commander within the extended projection would be a SPEC that meets our definition of syntactic subject, in whatever projection that is found in or above TP in the IP system.[34]

The apparent shortcomings of this account, both of which are shared in parallel fashion with the accounts I criticized on other grounds, include the apparent lack of overt, tense-restricted movement to the landing site I have designated and the lack of any intrinsic relationship between the kind of movement involved and tense. On the other hand, the account proposed here forges stronger parallels with attested overt phenomena and in so doing removes the motivation for increasing the domain of LAL parametrically in order to extend it to these anaphors.

Upon closer inspection, the first apparent shortcoming may be based on the too hasty conclusion that overt movement does not proceed through a TP-adjoined position. Consider the fact that tense-restricted operator movement is not totally unfamiliar in English. English *tough*-constructions, and *worth*-constructions, for example, appear to be limited in a similar way, and according to Stowell (1986), who considers a range of such constructions (for *worth,* see also Safir 1991), these are to be analyzed as pre-LF (overt) A'-movements of null operators. Both constructions support parasitic gaps, which are not generally supported by LF movement.

36a) ?Alex is tough to persuade Amina to talk to.
b)? *Alex is tough to persuade Amina that she should talk to.

37a) Artem is worth trying to get to know.
b) ?*Artem is worth showing that you like.

38a) Carlos is too dangerous to ask to anyone to talk to.
b) ?*Carlos is too dangerous to ask that anyone should talk to.

39a) ?Ada is easy to avoid without insulting.
b) ?A pen pal is worth writing to without ever meeting.
c) ?This linguist is too smart to talk to without being convinced by.

Like the proposed anaphor-operator movement and the tense-restricted Hindi interrogative interpretation, the movement relation in question is, in any case, superficially invisible. However, it is possible to determine that the landing site of movements like those in (36–39) is higher than the subject, since the subject must be disjoint from the trace of operator movement as determined by whatever derives strong crossover (as pointed out by Chomsky, 1982, 31, especially for cases like [40]).

40a) ?*Carlos* is too careful PRO/**PRO* to expose *t* (as a terrorist).
b) *Carlos* is too careful *PRO* to expose *himself* (as a terrorist).

For predication and interrogation, then, we must assume that the final landing site of the tense-sensitive operator is SPEC-CP, but I contend that movement to SPEC-CP takes place only as the last step after movement to a position in the highest TP below the relevant SPEC-CP. Tense-sensitive anaphor operators do not move for the last step since they are not required to by whatever forces wh-movement to SPEC-CP for interrogation and the predication of clauses (as in *tough*-movement or relative clause formation, etc.).

There is some evidence that may favor cyclic movement to TP by tense-sensitive operators as opposed to SPEC-CP to SPEC-CP movement of the sort typical of wh-movement across tensed clauses. Note that infinitives frequently allow argument extraction across a wh-island, for example, as illustrated by (41a–c), which are acceptable for many English speakers. Even those who accept (41a–c) typically find their tensed counterparts in (42a–c), respectively, much degraded.

41a) $\text{Who}_j$ were you wondering $\text{what}_i$ to give $t_j$ $t_i$ ?
b) $\text{What}_i$ was Astrid asking $\text{how}_j$ to serve $t_i$ $t_j$ ?
c) Which $\text{animal}_i$ did she tell you $\text{how}_j$ to feed $t_i$ $t_j$ ?

42a) ??Who were you wondering what you gave?
b) ??What was Astrid asking how she should serve?
c) ?Which animal did she tell you how you should feed?

Facts like these led Chomsky (1986a, 37) to treat infinitives as weakened barriers to movement. If extraction in (41a–c) proceeds by adjunction to TP in the lower clause because it is an infinitive, and then it proceeds by adjunction to TP in the highest clause, the intervening SPEC-CP does not occupy a position that is a relativized minimality antecedent-blocking movement of the operator. When movement proceeds out of a tensed sentence, however, adjunction to TP is somehow blocked (at present, I have no proposal to offer as to why), and movement must proceed directly to SPEC-CP, where the filled SPEC-CP is a relativized minimality antecedent that gets in the way of extraction.

If I am correct to conclude that adjunction to [-tense] TP but not to [+tense] TP is what permits overt extraction from a subordinate clause to avoid stopping in SPEC-CP of the lower clause, then there is independent evidence that operator movement out of infinitives proceeds via adjunction to TP (as also suggested by Davison 2001).[35] The posited covert movement of tense-sensitive anaphors to TP-adjoined position is just a case where the operator has not taken the last step and moved to SPEC-CP.

The reason that I assume that movement to SPEC-CP does not take place is very important. Movement of an anaphor to SPEC-CP would place it in a position where it could never have an antecedent in the domain of LAL. SPEC-CP is a position that is not immediately dominated by an extended projection of the matrix clause (it is rather immediately dominated by CP), so an anaphor in SPEC-CP must find an antecedent within the CP that contains it. It would appear that LAL predicts that (barring reconstruction) no anaphor could covertly move to SPEC-CP and be well formed.

I have less to say about the prospect that we will discover an interpretive relation between SIG anaphora and the domain of temporal interpretation. Rooryck and vanden Wyngaerd (1997) attempt to establish such a relation by arguing that Dutch *zich* is necessarily interpreted as covarying with the "time slices" of an individual to yield what I have called the *indistinctness reading*. They attribute proxy readings to identification with an individual where the time slices do not necessarily covary, as in the case of *zichzelf* anaphora. If such a correlation were correct, we are at least in the ballpark of understanding why SIG forms should be tense sensitive, insofar as the domains in which a form is dependent require that its value must interpretively match the temporal situations that include its antecedent.

Unfortunately for this idea, it was shown in 4.3.3 that SIG forms can indeed support proxy readings (in Norwegian, for example) where they do not compete with SELF forms (recall that unlike SELF forms, SIG forms permit the indistinctness reading, but they do not require it). Yet even under proxy readings, Norwegian *seg* still is sensitive to locality effects.

43a) Siden han visste at Le Carré var flerspråklig, bad Grisham Le Carré om ikke å lese seg på tysk.
"Knowing Le Carré was a polyglot, *Grisham* asked Le Carré not to read *SIG* in German." [SIG = Grisham's writing]
b) Le Carré synes at folk skulle lese ham/*seg kun på engelsk.
"*Le Carré* thinks that people should only read *him/*SIG* in English." [him/SIG = Le Carré's writing]

I conclude that whether or not the indistinctness reading is describable in terms of time slices, the distribution of this interpretation does not predict the relevant domain restriction on SIG forms.

It also appears to be a general feature of long-bounded domains that the form of movement involved need not be maximal, which is to say that the operator–anaphor can stop in any lower TP compatible with FTIP. Thus the following cases are all ambiguous as to whether the highest subject or the lower one is the antecedent. (I have employed possessives in the lowest clause to avoid FTIP effects obviating the operator anaphor, e.g., SIG SELF in MS obviates SIG as a direct object anteceded by the subordinate subject; [44a,b] is from Kidwai 2000, 83).

44a) professor$_i$ poprosil assistenta$_j$ [PRO$_j$ citat svoj$_{i/j}$ doklad].
professor asked assistant read SVOJ's report
"The professor$_i$ asked the assistant$_j$ to read his$_{i/j}$ report."
b) sita$_i$ -ne ram$_j$ -ko [PRO$_j$ əpni$_{i/j}$ kitabēpər.$^h$ne] dī.
Sita (SU) Ram (DO) APNI's book to-read gave
"Sita allowed Ram to read his/her books."
c) Nils bad Jens (om aa) lese boken sin.
Nils asked Jens (for to) read book SIN
"Nils asked Jens to read his book."

Finally, I have been careful to speak of the tense-restricted operator movement as covert, not necessarily as LF-movement, although I assume that LAL applies at LF. This leaves open the question of whether covert movement that determines the extended pattern of anaphora is the result of LF-movement of the form in question, the result of overt movement that leaves a copy such that only the lower copy is pronounced, or the result of overt movement in pre-LF syntax of a null operator as suggested for Stowell's cases above (and extended to wh-in-situ, in the form of null operator licensing, by Watanabe 1991) and as mentioned in note 14 to this chapter.[36]

Setting aside the details, I conclude on the basis of the parallel with Hindi interrogatives and English tense-restricted operator movement that the domain of MS SIG, Russian *svoi,* Hindi *apne*, and so forth results from tense-restricted covert-operator movement to TP-adjoined position that renders these anaphors subject oriented.[37]

### *5.2.4 Strict Subject Orientation*

Consider again the definition of a syntactic subject, on which our notion of syntactic subject orientation is based.

45) The *syntactic subject* of α, α a lexical category, is any β such that β is the SPEC of an extended projection of α, and β is in an A-chain relation with SPEC-α.

This definition identifies syntactic subject positions independently of their semantic role, their discourse role (see the discussion of UD-forms), or Casemarking, as most purely formal accounts do, and so it should be no surprise that elements that qualify as subjects are sometimes neither nominative nor agentive and generally don't agree with verbs when they are not nominative. In the case of passive, for example, or for an ergative verb like *arrive*, the direct object presumably moves through SPEC-VP, where no theta role is assigned, on its way to whatever the SPEC of the highest functional position is (presumably what counts as SPEC-IP). By virtue of moving through SPEC-VP, the underlying direct object will count as a subject.

This predicts that if a language L has accusatives that function thematically as the subject of a clause (assuming a small clause analysis of predication of an object or a form of raising to object analysis) and L has subject-oriented anaphors susceptible to covert clitic or operator movement, then such accusatives in L should be able to antecede strict subject-oriented forms. This prediction appears to be correct. For example, it extends to composite subject-oriented anaphors in languages like Icelandic (and MS) where the SIG-SELF anaphor outcompetes SIG locally.

46a) Sie uberliessen *die Kinder sich/*ihnen*. (Grewendorf 1992, 52)
they left the children SIG/them-DAT
"They left the children to themselves."
b) Sálfrœđingurinn gerđi *Harald* stoltan af **honum sjálfum/sjálfum ser*.
The psychiatrist made Harald-Acc proud-Acc) of him SELF/SELF SIG
"The psychiatrist made Harald proud of himself." (Maling 1986, 54)

Under the assumption either that [*Harald* stoltan af *sjálfum ser*] is a small clause lexically headed by the adjective, a fairly standard assumption within the principles and parameters tradition, *Harald* will count as the syntactic subject of *stoltan af* and hence be eligible as an antecedent just in case the tense-sensitive movement can stop in a functional projection of the small clause. The assumption that *die Kinder sich* must count as a small clause in German is more controversial but not semantically unnatural. See both Maling (1986) and Grewendorf (1992) for further examples not all of which are congenial to this analysis,[38] as compared to Everaert (1986) and Toman (1991), who explicitly support the small clause analysis as licensing subject-oriented forms (Toman for Czech; see also den Dikken, 1995, for extensive discussion of triadic verbs and the small clause analysis).

However, even if the small clause analysis is correct, the abstract head of the small clause is not obviously inhabited by tense since there is no overt inflection. Here we can do no better than Reinhart and Reuland (1991, 319, fn. 14): "In order to allow subjects of small clauses as antecedents of SE-anaphors we have to assume that small clauses carry Agr too," or at least tense, in my analysis. As in their account, I must assume that the landing site for tense-restricted operator movement is cyclic in the TP-adjoined position (and not necessarily an agreement position) such that any intervening strict subject antecedent is in a position to be an antecedent for the anaphor. This analysis of the accusative subject paradigm, as in the case of ECM, we often see for causatives, perception verbs, and sometimes epistemics.

Returning now to the variety of syntactic subjects, Franks (1995, 253–255) points out that the Russian anaphors *sebja* and *svoi* (possessive form) are oriented toward datives that are arguably structural subjects, although he finds the diagnostics for syntactic subjecthood inconclusive. Moreover, some predicates that take genitive arguments also permit them to antecede anaphors, as in (47).

47a) mne žal' sebja.
me-Dat sorry SEBJA-Acc
"I feel sorry for myself."
b) mne svoix nagrad nečego stydit'sja.
me-Dat SVOI awards nothing to be ashamed of
"There is no reason for me to be ashamed of my awards."

48a) u nego ne ostavilos' vremeni na sebja.
at him-Gen Neg remained time for SEBJA
"He didn't have any time left for himself."
b) malo u menja svoix boljaček.
few at me-Gen self's sores
"I don't have enough of my own pains as it is."

However, in all of these cases, it would appear that the absence of a nominative subject allows for the possibility that the case that is assigned may be assigned to an argument that has originated in or passed through SPEC VP, and if so, even these cases involve strict subject orientation.[39]

Icelandic is another language that has nonnominative subjects both in tensed and untensed sentences. As Zaenen, Maling, and Thráinsson (1985, 450; 1990, 107) show, the dative nominal in (49) is a subject, in that it can be passivized, but it also antecedes a SIN form rather than a nonanaphoric pronoun within the clause.

49) *Honum* var oft hjálpađ af fore drum *sínum*/**hans*.
he-DAT was often helped by parents SIN/his
"He was often helped by his parents."

Similar effects are found in Hindi, where subjects of tensed sentences may be ergative, be marked with a postposition, or else be nominative (agreeing with the verb), yet both sorts of subjects can antecede *apne* as shown for nominative in (50) where the plural subject agrees with the verb (compare [35a]).

50) raam aur sitaa apnii kitaab baaNT rahee haiN.
*Ram and Sita their* book distribute-PROG aux-PL-PR
"Ram and Sita are distributing their book."

A straightforward prediction of this analysis is that no tense-sensitive operator or covert clitic anaphor will take split antecedents, since any landing site they reside in provides a unique antecedent. This claim appears correct, in that it is only the subject that antecedes the anaphoric forms in (51) (a plural, nonanaphoric possessive pronoun is required for the split antecedent for Norwegian, Hindi, and French).

51a) Nils introduserte Jens til deres/*sin revisor.
"Nils introduced Jens to their/SIN accountant"
"*Nils* introduced *Jens* to *their* accountant."
b) raam-ne sita-ko apnii nai TV ke baare meN bataayaa.
Ram-ERG Sita-DAT APNII new TV about told
"*Ram* told Sita about *his*/*their new TV."
c) Jean a demandé à *Georges* de *PRO se* critiquer.
Jean past-asked to Georges to PRO SE critique
"Jean asked *Georges* to criticize *himself*/*themselves."

Failure to take split antecedents does not follow for elements that do not move in this way, since anaphors that don't move are still c-commanded within Domain D by more than one antecedent. Anaphors like English pronoun-SELF, for example, should permit split antecedents that are both plurals, but a good test is frustrated by the role of SELF forms as reflexive markers with coarguments. On the other hand, the Norwegian example in (51a) shows that precisely this interpretation is possible for pronouns, which is only possible if they do not move in the way that SIG forms do. Notice, moreover, that the FTIP predicts that the pronoun in (51a), though locally anteceded, is not antisubject oriented.

The issues surrounding whether or not some dative subjects are "subjects all the time" in some larger sense of "subject" I will not address here. Recent debates have renewed interest in differences among dative subject constructions (for a richer presentation of the issues, see Moore and Perlmutter 2000), but I concur with Sigurđsson (2000) that there is no interesting, wider, universal notion of subject that should be appealed to to make these distinctions. How an argument comes to satisfy my definition of strict subject by passing through a main predicate specifier may involve more subtle argumentation, however (see note 39 of this chapter). I shall assume henceforth that anaphors subject to LAL are strictly subject sensitive due to their landing site within the domain of LAL, whether the movement that places them there is covert clitic movement or covert tense-sensitive operator movement.[40]

### *5.2.5 A Summary of Covert Movement Into the Domain of LAL*

We have posited three sorts of movement into the domain of LAL, A-movement, clitic movement, and tense-sensitive operator movement, and we have rejected several other proposed covert movements. Anaphors that have Case properties of the relevant sort will be driven to A-move into the domain of LAL, as is the case for an English SELF form when it occurs in the subject position of an ECM complement. Forms that have the status of clitics at LF will be driven by whatever motivates the movement of overt clitics and will move across analogous domains, as in the case of Dutch *zich* and German *sich*. Tense-sensitive operators move to SPEC TP (or thereabouts) for reasons that remain mysterious but that parallel the equally unexplained tense sensitivity of in situ questions in Hindi and tense-sensitive null operator movements in English. Hindi *apne*, MS SIG, and Russian *svoi* are all anaphors that are delivered into the domain of LAL by tense-sensitive operator movement.

I have rejected long-distance head movement as a possible account of MS SIG or of Chinese *ziji* and Japanese *zibun* because the movement in question bears no resemblance to overt head movement of any sort. I have also rejected A'-movement to SPEC-CP as a mechanism for delivery into the domain of LAL, since SPEC-CP simply doesn't reach the domain of LAL. If such an anaphor existed, it would be, like wh-movement, sensitive to islands but unaffected by tense bounding. I know of no such anaphor. This is straightforwardly predicted by the formulation of the domain of LAL that I have proposed.

Finally, I have established strict subject orientation as a sufficient condition for anaphorhood, as opposed to UD-form status. This last point will be clearer once we examine the general properties of UD-forms.

## 5.3 The Distribution of UD-Forms

I have just argued that long-bounded domains are syntactically conditioned by the properties of movement applying to forms sensitive to LAL, and I have suggested that not all forms lacking deictic potential are anaphors in this sense (following, e.g., Thráinsson 1991). Elements lacking in deictic potential that are not subject to LAL are not anaphors by definition, and so nothing requires them to end up in a domain where their antecedent is local. Thus we would expect the relation between a UD-form (recall that this is a term meant to suggest the description "unbounded dependent form") and its antecedent to be syntactically unrestricted by tense or islands. We can press the difference further by positing that if a moved constituent always c-commands the position it moves from, as is usually assumed, then there is no reason that elements outside the domain of LAL should require that their antecedents c-command them, or even be contained in the same sentence. To put it simply, I will argue that UD-forms need not be syntactically restricted, and if not, the distributional properties in (52a–e) are what we would expect of them.

52) Distributional Properties of UD-Forms:
  a) They can be anteceded beyond the domain of the tensed or indicative sentence.
  b) They can appear as the subject of a tensed or indicative sentence.
  c) Their antecedent can be outside of a relative clause in which they are embedded.
  d) They do not always have to have a c-commanding antecedent.
  e) They do not always have to have a sentence-internal antecedent.
  f) They typically permit split antecedents.
  g) They are sensitive to discourse perspective effects.

The properties described in (52a–f) are essentially those of independent pronouns, but what distinguishes UD-forms from independent pronouns is, first of all, that many UD-forms are not morphologically pronominal (see 6.2.3); second, that some UD-forms are not restricted in the short-bounded domain (as pronouns would be under Principle B, but not necessarily under the FTIP, depending on what they are in competition with); and third, that UD-forms are much more sensitive to inferences about conversational participants with respect to their antecedents than most free-standing pronouns are.

For the last of these reasons, these forms are often called *logophors*, but I choose to reserve this term for a more restricted class of cases involving the scope of verbs of saying and belief, so I will not use it here. An examination of the antecedency conditions on UD-forms, those that originate in both syntax and discourse, deserves a lengthy discussion, one that is beyond the scope of this book, and so I defer those issues to Safir (in preparation), where they are addressed in detail. To further limit the goals of this chapter, I confine myself to illustrating, with a limited set of examples, the UD-form properties in (52), postponing until chapter 6 the question of how UD-forms participate in the most dependent scale when they enter into FTIP competitions, although it will serve to assume they tie with pronouns. (Recall that c-command by an antecedent is not required for dependency, a matter discussed in chapter 2 and elsewhere.) Now let us examine the forms in question.

Among the forms that I characterize as UD-forms, many have received careful study in the literature. Among these are included *taan* from Malayalam, *kendi-si* (inflected *kendi*) from Turkish, *ziji* from Chinese, and *zibun* from Japanese (see also 6.3 for further discussion of these forms, excepting *kendi-si*). All of these elements can be anteceded beyond the domain of the tensed or indicative sentence, as in (53) and can appear as the subject of a tensed or indicative sentence, as in (54).[41]

53a) [[ma*nt*Ri *t*an-te bhaarya-ye *n*uḷḷu*nn*-a*t*ə] seenaa-*n*aayakan kaṇḍe*nn*ə]
minister TAAN-Gen wife-Acc pinch-nominal army-chief saw COMP
raajaawə wicaariccu.
king thought
"The king$_i$ thought that the army chief$_k$ saw the minister$_j$ pinching TAAN's$_{i,k,j}$ wife."

b) Hasan [Zeyneb-in [Ali-nin kendi-sin-i sev-diğ-in-i] bil-diğ-in-i]
Hasan Zeynep-Gen Ali-Gen KENDI-3s-Acc love-Ger.-3s-Acc know-Ger.-3s-Acc
san-iyor.
think-Progr.
"Hasan$_i$ thinks that Zeynep$_j$ knows that Ali loves KENDI-SI$_{i,j}$."

c) Zhangsan renwei [Lisi hai-le ziji].
Zhangsan think Lisi hurt-Asp ZIJI
"Zhangsan$_i$ thinks Lisi hurt ZIJI$_i$." (Huang and Tang 1991, 263)

d) John-ga [Bill-ga Mike-ni zibun-no koto-o hanasita to] itta.
John-SB Bill-SB Mike-IO ZIBUN-GN matter-DO
"John said that Bill told Mike about ZIBUN." (literally, "about ZIBUN's matter"; Katada 1991, 289)

54a) [*t*aan waliya aaḷ aaṇə e*nn*ə] raaman-ə *t*oo*nn*i.
TAAN great person is COMP Raman-Dat seemed
"It seemed to Raaman$_i$ that TAAN$_i$ was a great man."

b) Ali Oya-ya [Ankara-ya kenilerin-in gönder-il-eceğ-in-i] söyle-di.
Ali Oya-Dat Ankara-Dat KENDI-3pl-Gen send-Pass-Fut-3s-Acc tell-Past
"Ali$_i$ told Oya$_j$ that they$_{i+j}$ would get sent to Ankara."

c) Zhangsan shuo ziji kanjian-le Lisi. (Huang and Liu 2001)
Zhangsan say ZIJI see-Perf Lisi
"Zhangsan said that he saw Lisi."

d) Taroo wa zibun ga tensai da to motte iru.
Taroo ZIBUN genius is that thinking is
"Taroo thinks that he is a genius." (Kuno 1987, 138)

These two properties do not make the case on their own, especially since overt wh-movement in many of the languages that have it can move across tensed sentences, and it has been argued that the subject position of a tensed sentence is not opaque to movement in some languages. In particular, Huang (1982) has argued that the subject position of a Chinese indicative is properly governed and hence available for covert extraction.

Moreover, it might appear that (54a–d) conform to a generalization recently discussed by Woolford (1999) and Rizzi (1990a) (see 6.2.3 and 6.3.1) that languages with overt subject–verb agreement do not permit subject anaphors in finite sentences. Jayaseelan points out, however, that the fact "that the Malayalam verb has no agreement morphology does not seem to be relevant to the binding possibilities in [(53a)]. Tamil, Telugu and Kannada (sister languages of the Dravidian family) have rich morphologies of subject–verb agreement and yet permit long distance binding" (1997, 188, fn. 3). For Turkish, Kornfilt (2001) merely states that singular agreement for (54b) is preferred, not required, which would appear to violate the anaphor-agreement generalization. This is not surprising if *kendi-sin* is not an anaphor, as Enç (1989) and Kornfilt both argue (for further discussion, see note 46 of chapter 6).

Stronger evidence against a movement account for this set of forms is that they can be related to antecedents outside of islands. For example, where discourse-perspective restrictions are taken into account, these forms do not always have to have a c-commanding antecedent (55) or, in some of these cases, not even a sentence-internal antecedent (56).[42] It is thus unsurprising that they can have antecedents outside of a relative clause in which they are embedded (57) (I have no example available for Malayalam).

55a) raman-te kalpana [sii*t*a *t*an-te kuttikal-oodə samsaarik'k'aru*t*ə ennə aanə.
Raman-Gen order Sita TAAN-Gen children-to should not speak COMP is
"Raman's$_i$ order is that Sita$_j$ should not speak to his$_i$/her$_j$ children."

b) Oya-nun *kendi-sin-i* beğen-diğ-i] *Ahmet*-çe bil-in-iyor-du.
Oya-Gen KENDI-3s-Acc admire-Ger-3s] Ahmet-by know-Pass.-Prog.-Past
"Oya's admiring *him* was known to *Ahmet*."

c) *Zhangsan* de xin biaoshi [neiben shu hai-le *ziji*].
Zhangsan's letter indicate that book hurt-Asp ZIJI
"*Zhangsan's* letter indicated that the book hurt *him*." (Huang and Tang 1991, 281, fn. 4)

d) [Yosiko-ga *zibun-o* nikundeiru] koto]-ga *Mitiko-o* zetuboo-e oiyatta.
Yosiko-SB ZIBUN-Obj be-hating COMP-SB Mitiko-Obj desperation-to drove
"That Yosiko hated *her* drove *Mitiko* to desperation." (Sells 1987, 453)

56a) aartum sahaayik'k'illa e*nnə* *raaman-ə* manassilaayi t*aan* ini ottak'k'ə aaṇə
no one will not help COMP Raman-Dat. realized TAAN from-now-on alone is
"*Raman* realized that no one would help. *He* was alone from now on."

b) *Ali* hakkinda Ahmet ne düşün -üyor? Ahmet *kendi-sin-i* çok
Ali about Ahmet what think-PROG? Ahmet KENDI-3ps-Acc very admire
beğen-iyor-muş.
PROG-rep.past
"What does Ahmet think of *Ali*? (They say that) Ahmet admires *him* very much."

c) *Zhangsan* zhe ren yi-xiang hu-li-hu de guo shenghuo.
Zhangsan this person all-along muddled DE spend life
Jushuo you yihui lian *ziji* fan-le-fa dou bu zhidao.
It-was-said have once even ZIJI commit-Asp-law even Neg know
"*Zhangsan* has always been absentminded. It was said that *he* once broke the law without even knowing it." (Lee 1996)

d) *Taroo* wa totemo kanasigat-tei-ta. Yosiko ga Takasi ga *zibun* o hihansita
Taroo Top very sad-Prog-past Yosiko Subj Takasi Subj ZIBUN OBJ criticized
noni bengosi-nakat-ta kara da.
though defend-not-past because Cop
"Taroo was very sad. It is because Yosiko did not defend *him* though Takasi criticized him." (Sells 1987, 455)

57a) *Ahmet kendisin-i* gör-meğ-e gel -en herkes -e
Ahmet kendisi-ACC see-INF-DAT come-Rel.Part. anyone/everyone-DAT
yemek ikram ed-iyor.
meal offering do-Pres.Progr.
"*Ahmet* offers a meal to anybody/everybody who has come/comes to see *him*."

b) *Zhangsan* bu xihuan [niexie piping *ziji* de ren].
Zhangsan not like those criticize ZIJI rel person
"*Zhangsan* does not like those people who criticize *him*." (Huang and Tang 1991, 271)

c) *Taroo* wa *zibun* ni ai ni kita hito ni wa, dare-demo syukuzi o dasu.
$\text{Taroo}_i$ ZIBUN to see to came people whoever meal offer
"*Taroo* offers a meal to anybody who has come to see *him*." (Kuno 1987, 255)

Covert-movement accounts of these phenomena can only hope to capture (57) by arguing that movement at LF is not subject to island conditions, a possibility pursued in Huang and Tang (1991) and still maintained in Huang and Liu (2001). Insofar as c-command and sentence-internal antecedence are not respected, the appeal of this approach is limited to its purported derivation of subject orientation. The subject-orientation effect is not as strict, however, as it is in MS, where *sig* can only have a c-commanding syntactic subject, and of course (55) and (56) are not consistent with it.

As argued earlier, covert movement brings an anaphor to a position where only the syntactic subject of a clause can antecede it, and so split antecedents are not possible for covert movement of clitics and tense-sensitive operators. If UD-forms are not derived by movement, nothing in the nature of their domain rules out split antecedents for them. Most UD-forms permit split antecedents, as illustrated in (58) ([58a] from Jayaseelan 1997, 191; [58b] from Kornfilt 2001; and [58c] from Kitagawa 1986, 377).

58a) raaman sii*t*a-k'k'e *t*aŋŋaḷ uḍe makkaḷ-e kaaniccu-koḍu*tt*u.
Raman Sita-DAT TAAN-GEN children-ACC showed gave
"*Raman* showed Sita their children."

b) *Ali Oya-ya* [Ankara-ya *kendi-lerin-in* gönder-il -eceǀ-in] -i söyle -di.
Ali Oya-DAT Ankara-DAT KENDI-3pp-GEN send-PASS-FUT-3s-ACC tell PST
"*Ali* told Oya that they would get sent to Ankara."

c) Gakutyoo ga Gakubutyoo ni [aru gakusei ga kinoo zibun-tati o kokusosita to tugeta.

president-NOM dean-DAT some student-NOM yesterday ZIBUN +PLU-ACC sued COMP told.
"*The president* told *the dean* that some student sued *them* yesterday."

Movement to the domain of a unique antecedent will be problematic for any LF-movement account of split antecedency.[43]

While the UD-forms illustrated above diverge from one another with respect to a number of properties, I contend that the core of their syntactic behavior is evidenced by these contexts, and one simple conclusion is consistent with these results: UD-forms are not anaphors, or else they are anaphors that allow usages where they are not anaphors and are therefore not subject to LAL. Thus UD-forms need not move covertly to the proximity of their antecedents. Moreover, since dependency may be achieved without c-command, there is no reason that these elements must be anteceded by c-commanders or even have an antecedent in the same sentence.

Moreover, by separating out UD-forms with their characteristic core set of properties from the behavior of anaphors, our characterization of anaphors acquires more teeth and addresses Burzio's (1991) concern, echoed by Huang that "to argue that a long-distance reflexive is a pronominal simply because it violates binding condition A is circular" (2000, 104). This is not true of the analysis proposed here, given the distinction between strict subject orientation and discourse or logophoric antecedence, and by the generalization that anaphors are never crucially sensitive to logophoric or discourse effects in their bounded domains. This means that any form that has a life both as an anaphor and a UD-form will evidence different interpretive restrictions in the two domains independently of Principle A, a matter I return to in 6.3.

## 5.4 Promotion to UD-Form

There is another variety of elements, elements that are anaphors in the short-bounded domain, that may also have the distribution of UD-forms under certain specific syntactic conditions. Recall in 3.3.3 I introduced some contexts in which SELF forms appear in positions from which covert movement is dubious and where they are not in complementary distribution with nonanaphoric pronouns. Cases like (59) are generally called picture nominals, and those in (60) involve contrastive predicates.

59a) *The great dictator* has been known to arrest people who fail to put pictures of *himself* on their walls.
b) *Stalin* felt put upon. The descriptions of *himself* that were circulating were most unflattering.
c) Janet informed *Peter* that unflattering pictures of *himself* were hanging in the post office.
d) Pictures of *oneself* hanging in the post office tend to upset *one's* children.

60a) *Selena* insisted that Charlie would trust no one except *herself.*
b) People such as myself have never been admitted.

c) In *Arthur*'s opinion, Lisa should trust no one other than *himself.*
d) Andy told *Erica* that no one would expect that Zack and *herself* would be on time.
e) *North* was sure that Bush would not hire any CIA director who would prevent people like *himself* from making secret deals.

Nonsubject antecedents, antecedents outside relative clauses, non-c-commanding antecedents, or antecedents missing altogether are all possible for these SELF forms, which is a clear indication that they are not behaving as anaphors with respect to Principle A or its analogs (e.g., LAL).

By developing work by Safir (1992, 1997), Pollard and Sag (1992, 1994), and Reinhart and Reuland (1991, 297–298; 1993), it appears possible to predict when English SELF forms can be used as UD-forms sensitive to perspective effects. The essential intuition behind these accounts is that if a SELF form can find no potential antecedent within its coargument domain at all, not even one that fails to match its features, then that SELF form is exempted from anaphoric status.

There are notable differences between the proposals mentioned, but for reasons of space I will not enter into them. The key intuition I exploit here is that a SELF form can only be anteceded by an argument that is in an asymmetric thematic relation to it. One way of cashing this out is to rely on a condition like (61).[44]

61) Promotion of an Anaphor to Discourse-Sensitive UD-Form: An anaphor can be promoted to a discourse-sensitive dependent if it does not participate in a complete thematic complex.

The essential idea of (61) is that the picture nominals do not express all of the potential arguments of the picture nominal, and so picture nominals without prenominal genitives are not complete thematic complexes. Verbs that have only one argument, where that argument is represented by a SELF form, are complete thematic complexes; hence the SELF form is not promoted to UD-form and will be regulated by LAL. However a SELF form in a contrastive relation is not part of a complete thematic complex either because the relation between the two arguments of a contrastive predicate is not thematic at all. None of the contrastive predicates introduce a thematic role that corresponds to any semantic role in an event or situation, such as agent, patient or goal, or experiencer. Instead, these predicates introduce a distinction internal to a nominal that bears one of these relations. Now all of the contrastive predicates (similarity predicates and exclusion predicates), as well as all of the picture nominals, will fall under (61).

There is an interesting prediction that follows from promotion to UD-form, but to see it, we must consider some Norwegian data. In (62a) and (62b), notice that pronoun-SELF is well formed in picture nominals and contrastive environments, respectively.

62a) Mary fortalte mennene om noen bilder av henne/henne selv/*seg selv. (N)
"*Mary*$_i$ told the men about some pictures of *her/herself.*"

b) Carl sa at Marie hadde snakket med alle andre enn ham/ham selv/*?seg/ *seg selv.
Carl said that Marie had talked to all others than him/himself/SIG/SIG SELF
"*Carl* said that Marie had talked to everyone but *him/himself*."

Where this is possible, notice first that SIG SELF is unavailable, probably because SIG is inherently strictly subject sensitive. Pronoun-SELF does not face the same difficulty, and so pronoun-SELF can be promoted to UD-form. Now if antisubject orientation only arises from competition with a subject-oriented form, then it is predicted that pronoun-SELF in these environments is not antisubject oriented, and indeed the antecedent for pronoun-SELF in both (62a) and (62b) is a subject. Moreover, since neither pronoun nor pronoun-SELF is an anaphor in this environment, it is not clear that they are in competition, aside from discourse effects that favor one or the other; hence both can occur.

## 5.5 Summing Up

The essential goal of this chapter has been to develop a disciplined typology for anaphors that establishes what the structural boundaries are for the availability of a given anaphor or class of anaphors. Insofar as I have argued that the domain of LAL is not reduced to a movement domain but is instead more restricted than a movement domain, I have had to invoke the typology of movement to deliver anaphors into the domain of LAL. The range of variation in the domain restrictions on dependent forms is thus reduced to the typology of movement and LAL. That typology presents us with short-bounded domains, driven by case or morphosyntactically conditioned clitic movement, and long-bounded domains, driven by tense-sensitive operator movement, but no domain corresponding to tense-insensitive wh-movement, as the latter sort of movement could never bring an anaphor into the domain of LAL.

There are, moreover, a variety of forms lacking deictic potential that are not conditioned by any bounded domain. These latter forms, UD-forms, are sensitive to restrictions on discourse perspective or contrast but are not restricted by conditions on movement, indeed if they are conditioned by any syntactic conditions at all. The apparent overlap in subject orientation that UD-forms appear to share with tense-sensitive operator forms has been argued to be illusory, the latter being strictly syntactic and the former being violable in the right discourse conditions. Further complicating the picture, some anaphors may be promoted to discourse-dependent UD-forms if their immediate syntactic environment provides no complete thematic complex, even though the same forms act unexceptionally as anaphors in almost all other environments. A more complete typology would explore the discourse and syntactic conditions that may restrict UD-forms, but I defer to Safir (in preparation), where the relevance to anaphora of person, perspective, logophoricity, and contrast are examined in detail.

One of the most interesting predictions of the FTIP is that the availability of an anaphor or UD-form is frequently distinct from its distribution, which is determined by the available competitors. For this reason I have been able to formulate the long- and short-bounded domains without ever accounting for the fact that many anaphors cannot appear in portions of the short-bounded domain (like MS SIG). Some of the characteristic patterns of anaphora that emerge where the distribution of a form does not match its availability are the subject of the next chapter.

# 6

# Competitive Narrowing and Morphological Form

As remarked in the previous chapter and as explored in chapters 3 and 4, the force of the FTIP is measured by the mismatch between the domain in which a form is available on the one hand and its overt distribution on the other. This chapter explores some results that only the FTIP permits us to achieve, and then the system is exemplified by a number of analyses of particular languages with respect to their inventory of potentially dependent forms.

The first of these results concerns the relationship between the lexical properties and morphological structure that a form has and its availability. In earlier work (Safir 1996c) I attempted to establish a typology of anaphors based on their morphology, and then I sought to predict, as much as is possible, the distribution of a given anaphor from its morphological makeup. In its strongest form, the position I took was that there could be no aspect of the distribution of an anaphor $\alpha$ that did not follow from invariant principles A–C, designation of $\alpha$ as an anaphor, and lexical properties of $\alpha$ of a sort also assigned to nonanaphors. I dubbed this strategy the *Universalist Hypothesis* (UH), and I shall expand upon it below. However, that approach assumed that no other principle, such as the FTIP, could narrow the distribution of one form on the basis of its relation to other forms. As a result, too much burden was placed on the morphological properties internal to a given anaphor to predict its full distribution. I shall refer to theories of this type as *rigid internalist* approaches, because they propose that establishing a form's inner nature should directly predict its distribution.[1]

The main result of this chapter then is to refute the rigid internalist position championed in my work and that of others (e.g., Faltz 1977; Pica 1987; Reinhart and Reuland 1991, 1993) in favor of the hypothesis that the internal properties of potentially dependent forms does not predict their distribution directly but only serves to predict their availability to participate in FTIP competitions. The advantage of such a *mediated internalist* approach is that the classes of possible anaphors that emerge are less varied. For example, differences between cognates across languages may not be due at all to lexical distinctions between the cognates, but rather may be accounted for by the differing competitors they face in their respective languages. This is what I call *competitive narrowing*.

The mediated internalist position is supported whenever the domain in which a form is available is wider than its distribution. In the last chapter, this distinction was assumed so that I could focus on the range of possible domains in which anaphors are available without worrying about domain holes. A *domain hole* is my descriptive term for cases where bounded domain of an anaphor or the distribution of a UD-form has a gap in it that corresponds to the portion of its available range where it is obviated by a competing form. Rigid internalist approaches to anaphoric domains might attempt to stipulate why a form like MS SIG, for example, might be allergic to local domains (aside from lexical reflexivity) but be permitted in a wider domain. By contrast, a mediated internalist approach only expects the lexical properties of SIG to determine its bounded domain—the FTIP predicts the size and nature of the domain hole. Gaps between availability and distribution have already been presented in chapters 3 and 4, but the gaps in question were not examined, as they will be here, from the perspective of an explicit internalist theory of availability for anaphors and pronouns.

To vindicate the mediated internalist position, however, it must be demonstrated that there is a portion of a form's distribution that is not accounted for by its intrinsic morphological properties and should not be. Part 6.3 illustrates these results by means of a set of case studies. Hopefully the most general conclusions reached for these cases can be extended to the far richer variety of competitive narrowing cases that I do not explore.

It should be expected of any internalist account that it should limit, by general principles, the distribution of anaphors and pronouns and the inventory of possible forms, both language internally and crosslinguistically. A variety of approaches to anaphora have targeted this goal, often formulating complex feature matrices of the varieties of anaphoric properties to predict the range of possible forms (see, e.g., Sportiche (1983); Enč (1989); and Thráinsson 1991) or else introducing parametric paradigms, applied to the lexicon, to define the range of possible domains consistent with the perceived empirical variation (see, e.g., Manzini and Wexler 1987; and Yang 1983). These approaches, however, permit otherwise unmotivated stipulations about domains specific to anaphora to be added to universal grammar as they become empirically necessary (as illustrated in 3.1.1.2 with respect to the typology of Dalrymple 1993; see also Safir 1987; and Hermon 1992).

The approach I develop here is more like that of Everaert, who proposes that "the differences in syntactic behaviour between types of lexical anaphors should follow from intrinsic properties of these anaphors rather than from parameters in the binding theory" (1986, 216; see also Everaert 1991, 114). Although Everaert's statement still leaves the possibility that lexical properties assigned to anaphors might be a class of properties that other morphemes don't share, I think it is in the spirit of his idea that even the properties that anaphors have, besides being anaphoric, should be independently motivated properties that nonanaphors share. While I have more in common with Everaert's rigid internalist approach, the mediated approach I ultimately adopt opposes his, not by adding parameters, but by taking account of competitive effects that restrict internalist tendencies.

This perspective on the typology of anaphora is, of course, a reflection of a more general view that the world's grammars are the varied outcomes of principled interactions between invariant universal principles and the universally limited inventory of lexical properties. Languages exploit the lexical inventory differently, and different patterns result (for the general idea, see Borer 1984a). Moreover, any typology we propose must be learnable within the natural course of language acquisition, and one that allows a child to infer the full range of abstract syntactic generalizations from frequently occurring lexical items would be eminently learnable.

With these considerations in mind, I propose to limit the hypothesis space for universal properties of anaphora in the following way (adapted from Safir 1996c).

1) The Universalist Hypothesis:
a) All statements specific to anaphora are universal.
b) The only lexical properties specific to anaphoric principles are
   i. to be syntactically anaphoric (i.e., subject to LAL, more dependent than pronouns for FTIP).
   ii. to be an identity-specific dependent form

As suggested in chapters 3 and 5 where the UH is briefly introduced, LAL, LRP, and the most dependent scale for FTIP are all sensitive to lexical specifications and are all universal. Pragmatic obviation, the CDC, and the Independence Principle are universals that do not specifically refer to lexical properties, and I shall have nothing to say about them in this chapter.

The inventory of lexical designations permitted by the UH is outlined in (1b). This ensures that "is an anaphor" has the same syntactic interpretation universally for the FTIP no matter what lexical item we apply it to. However, this does not mean that there are no independent criteria that contribute to anaphoricity. For example, we can impose lack of deictic potential as a necessary condition to have the syntactic property described in (1bi.). This is not a sufficient condition, since UD-forms lack deictic potential but are not anaphors in the sense of LAL (see 5.3). It is also necessary to know whether or not a given form is a pronoun or not on the most dependent scale in order to derive Principle C effects, but the property of being a pronoun may be completely derivable from its internal properties. The designation in (1bii.) is necessary in certain relatively specific cases as discussed in chapter 4, where reflexive markers are a subset of identity-specific anaphors (see note 32 of this chapter on incorporation). I shall argue that identity-specific anaphor status is largely predictable from internal factors.

The UH as formulated in (1) ensures that every lexical stipulation or diacritic I introduce must be supported by evidence independent of our principles of anaphora. For example, variations of local availability cannot be stipulated by special domain statements parametrically variant and specific to anaphora, as in the Manzini and Wexler (1987) approach, for example. Nor can I introduce features or feature matrices peculiar to dependent forms to categorize the class of domain sensitivities, as in the approaches of Sportiche (1983) and Thráinsson (1991).

We do expect, on the other hand, that anaphors and UD-forms may vary in the way lexical expressions do, insofar as they may bear or fail to bear grammatical features (e.g., person, number, gender, Case, etc.); insofar as they may differ in meaning (e.g., with respect to reciprocity or collectivity or resistance to indistinctness); and insofar as they may differ in their internal composition, both morphologically (e.g., being simplex, consisting of compounds or adjuncts, or consisting of stems with varieties of affixation) and relationally (having an internal argument structure or not). I have already appealed to differences in dependent readings and feature composition in determining which elements compete with respect to the FTIP in chapters 3–5.

It is useful to keep in mind that there is a certain diachronic flow of forms reported in the literature, which may be seen as a progression of grammaticalized forms up the most dependent scale that is fueled by loss of specificity. The more conventionalized a term becomes, the more it loses its specifications of deixis independent of the immediate conversation. For example, *Bill Clinton* is a more conversation-independent term than *the former president* in picking out the individual "Bill Clinton," and terms like *the man* are less informative still and capable of drifting into pronominal status, as in the case of German *man*. Pronouns, then, may have an independent definition as forms that have lost all semantic content independent of grammatical features. It is also common to discover pronouns that have crossed a line in their loss of deixis such that they become anaphoric, which is to say that they have become lexically marked as susceptible to LAL. Section 6.1 explores the synchronic state of being a pronoun or a pronominal anaphor.

Another diachronic source of anaphors results from grammaticalization of forms that disambiguate dependent coconstrual readings, readings often marked by nonspecific anaphoric pronominals. For example, French *l'un l'autre*, whether or not it is itself an anaphor (see the appendix to this chapter), is an adjunct that distinguishes between reflexive and reciprocal interpretations of the anaphor *se*. In languages like English, *each other* has come to occupy an argument position and is lexically marked as an anaphor. Many linguists (e.g., Faltz 1977; Keenan 1994) have argued that SELF forms as anaphors derive historically from adjunct uses (such as emphatic usage) and have evolved into argument nominals.[2,3] Anaphors like these, which retain some of their reading-specific character, typically retain more morphological structure and a relational semantic meaning that has not entirely bleached away. Forms of the latter sort, *relational anaphors*, thus differ from pronominal anaphors in having some residue of semantic argument structure. I reserve discussion of them for 6.2.

## 6.1 Pronominal Status

The FTIP scale distinguishes pronouns from nonpronouns in order to derive principle-C effects, but the distinction between anaphors and nonanaphors is enough to derive Principle B. Thus our only need to distinguish pronouns from other forms is their place on the most dependent scale. In the best case, however, no special +/(feature need be hypothesized to determine pronominal status if pronominal status is a direct result of a form's internal properties. This is the position I adopt here.

As just suggested, a form is pronominal if it consists only of a bundle of grammatical features with no idiosyncratic lexical or semantic content, and it might be required to have some nominal character. More crucially for our discussion, pronouns, as opposed to forms like SELF explored in 6.2, do not have a relational argument structure of any sort (Safir 1996c). Rather pronouns (may) reside in argument positions as placeholders, the way proper names or definite descriptions do, but without the semantic content of proper names or descriptions apart from grammatical features.[4] On the other hand, pronouns do not have to count as thematic arguments, or else expletive pronouns, which most typically have the form of thematic pronouns, would have to be different sorts of entities, even though they participate in pronominal paradigms in many languages. Moreover, pronominal clitics frequently double overt arguments in the world's languages, but it does not seem to be universally the case that the clitic is the one to be treated as the argument (if indeed it ever is).[5]

The range of features that pronouns may bear is an empirical matter, but it typically includes person, number, gender, Case, animacy, human, perhaps definiteness or distributivity, and any other grammatical specification that is active in a given language and applied to nonpronominal nominals as the latter participate in agreement or concord relations. Apart from agreement and concord features, pronouns vary, as other lexical items do, with respect to whether or not they cliticize (obligatorily or optionally) to other heads or move overtly in the manner of operators like *who* and *what*. In some languages, relative pronouns that appear to move are indistinguishable from phonologically identical ones that remain in situ in nonrelative clause contexts (e.g., see Wiltschko, 1998, on German and Demirdache, 1991, on Hebrew and references cited in these sources). And of course, some pronouns are posited to be phonologically null, as in null subject languages, and this introduces the possibility that there are null pronouns that move as operators do, possibly at LF. In short, all of the displacements associated with pronominals can apply to anaphors, and it was precisely this range of displacements related to anaphors that enabled us to preserve the small domain for LAL as a universal as argued in chapter 5.

With respect to their categorial and phrasal status, pronouns have been characterized as determiners, nouns, and adjectives[6] in various contexts and grammatical descriptions, and they have been treated as both phrases and as heads in various studies. A priori, the range of structural possibilities for pronouns is a function of how they saturate the argument structure of a predicate within a given syntactic theory. If we assume that a nominal is required as the object of *devour* (which I choose because it is a very stubbornly transitive verb, e.g., *Don devoured *[it]*). then we must consider whether that requirement is met when nominals fill that position. In other words, if we ask what the pronoun *it* has in common with *the dog* and *Fido* in (2a, b) with respect to the complement selection properties of *devour*, there are three possible positions, stated in (3).

2a) The dragon devoured it/the dog/Fido.
b) It/Fido/The dog devoured the dragon.

3a) All three nominals are phrases of the same maximal syntactic category.
b) All three nominals are phrases that have, in some extended sense, the same kind of head.
c) There is no uniformity across the three cases, but there is some sort of lexical redundancy rule (permitting exceptions) that allows selection for one type of phrase to imply the selection of the others.

The last option looks the least attractive since it is the most stipulative. It also predicts that there are verbs that might take an open class of definite descriptions and proper names as potential complements, for example, but never a pronoun. If such cases exist, they are highly marked, and I will set that possibility aside, especially since there is no evidence at all that there are predicates that select for an open class of nonpronominal subjects but never permit a pronominal subject.[7]

Within a theory like that of Abney (1987), which allows determiners to head DPs that do not necessarily embed nominals, advocates of (3a) would have to assume that pronouns that act as arguments are phrasally DPs, either because they are Ds that project a DP or because they are Ns with null determiners that project a DP. The same reasoning applies for theories that assume that the topmost projection of a nominal is any other sort of functional projection. Alternatively, advocates of (3a) would argue that all of the proposed functional projections within nominals are illusory, determiners and other functional categories do not project, and instead nominals are always NPs. Given the modern range of work on determiners, I assume this last possibility is not viable without a host of other assumptions, and I set it aside.[8]

It is possible to be more precise about (3b) once we take into account extended projection theories of phrase structure, such as those advocated by Grimshaw (1989) and van Riemsdijk (1990, 1998). In these theories, it is possible that a projection headed by a noun is nominal even if the phrasal node that caps the argument is DP. Under an extended projection theory, only lexical categories head an XP that contains functional categories, even if the functional categories (sharing, in this case, some nominal feature) head projections embedding the NP headed by N. The absence of an overt determiner may mean that a direct object like *Fido* is merely an N, perhaps housed in NP, but that it is not a DP, while *the dog* is a DP, but both NP and DP are of the same lexical syntactic type, namely, nominal.

These assumptions permit a variety of possible structures, as illustrated in (4). The pronoun could be an N, perhaps contained in NP, or it could be an N heading an NP within a DP with a null determiner, or else it is a D, presumably with a null NP sister (necessary for the whole projection to be N-headed). If D has a sufficient nominal feature such that it can project nominalhood in the absence of NP, then the structures in (4e–g) are also possible for (4b). Those of the structures in (4) that are DPs are also possibilities under (4a) excluding the NPs, under the assumption that the "full-sized" maximal nominal is a DP.[9]

4a) [$_{NP}$ [$_{N}$ pronoun]]
 b) [$_{DP}$ [$_{D}$ e] [$_{NP}$ [$_{N}$ pronoun]]
 c) [$_{DP}$ [$_{D}$ pronoun] [$_{NP}$ e]]
 d) [$_{N}$ pronoun]
 e) [$_{D}$ pronoun]
 f) [$_{DP}$ [$_{D}$ pronoun]]
 g) [$_{DP}$ [e] [$_{D}$ pronoun]]

Almost all of these analyses, or variations on them,[10] have adherents, and though I will not explore most of them, it is notable that some of these distinctions have been employed to distinguish between types of pronouns, language internally and crosslinguistically, and between semantic interpretations of pronouns where the pronouns are taken to be of the same categorial type.[11]

For example, it is argued by Noguchi (1997) that English pronouns are D heads and that only D-headed pronouns allow bound (dependent) readings, while N-headed pronouns can only participate in coreference. Noguchi applies this distinction to Japanese *kare*, which generally does not participate in dependent readings (specifically those in which its antecedent is quantified) as has long been noted in the literature (see especially Saito and Hoji, 1983, and other references cited by Noguchi). He contrasts *kare*, for which he assigns an analysis like (4a), with *zibun* and with the neuter forms *sore/sono*, which do participate in bound readings, arguing that the latter forms are D-heads without null-NP complements as in (4f) (although relatively little turns on the claim that there is no null NP present as in [4c]; see Noguchi 1997, 771, fn. 9). Hirose (1997), taking a similar line, argues that pronouns used referentially are NPs structurally (like [4b]), while bound variable pronouns are DPs (like [4a]), although he assumes the null determiner has an anaphoric feature. Hestvik (1992) argues that a distinction between the phrasal character of pronominal types (heads vs. phrases, along the lines of Pica 1987) distinguishes those that move at LF from those that don't in order to derive antisubject orientation of LF-moved pronouns, but as demonstrated in chapter 3, this is unnecessary.[12]

Cardinaletti and Starke (1994), building on some observations of Kayne (1975), distinguish up to three classes of pronouns (in the most articulated systems) such that if a language has two classes, one is weak and the other is strong, and if there are three classes, there are two weak classes, where one of the weak classes is a clitic. These classes are distinguished by a variety of tests having to do with syntactic, prosodic, morphological, and semantic behavior that I will not review here, and their account involves some assumptions about categorial identity of the functional projections of nominals that appear to be undermotivated. They assume that, like sentences, nominals may have a CP projection and an IP projection, where these have different semantic force, and the typology of pronominals is one of relative structural deficiency, as in (5).

5a) Strong pronouns $[_{CP}$ $[_{IP}$ $[_{NP}$ pronoun]]]
b) Weak deficient pronouns $[_{IP}$ $[_{NP}$ pronoun]]
c) Clitic pronouns $[_{N}$ pronoun]

While strong pronouns and weak deficient ones are phrasal, clitic pronouns are $X^{o}$ heads. Only the strong pronouns have what they assume is a referential index and what they consider a range (some sort of restriction, for which +human is the default) that they identify as a property of the CP projection.[13] Their notion of referential index essentially corresponds to what I have called having deictic potential (see 3.2.3).

Two observations seem pertinent here. First, the claim that there is an IP–CP distinction in nominals is lightly defended at best, and semantically speaking, not naturally predictive of "referential" behavior. Moreover, the Cardinaletti and Starke account, based as it is on assuming the most articulated structure for the most deictic of pronouns would seem to be exactly contrary in spirit to the Noguchi and Hirose account, which identifies the lack of bound readings with structural deficiency, rather than the lack of deictic ones. One could imagine a tripartite distinction corresponding to that of Cardinaletti and Starke that might draw the two lines of thought together: Suppose that strong pronouns are DPs with an (empty) NP complement (4c) or else N-heads embedded in a DP (4b), weak deficient pronouns are DPs without an NP complement (4f), and clitics are just D heads without a maximal projection (4e); then the lack of the NP complement would notate the absence of a range. This possibility is illustrated in (6).[14]

6a) Strong pronouns [$_{DP}$ [$_{NP}$ pronoun]] or [$_{DP}$ pronoun [$_{NP}$ e]]
 b) Weak deficient pronouns [$_{DP}$ pronoun]
 c) Clitic pronouns [$_{D}$ pronoun]

Other possibilities are explored by Zribi-Hertz and Mbolatianavalona (1999), who argue on the basis of Malagasy pronominal paradigms that the criteria of deficiency for pronouns may not be uniquely structural, a point that will be reinforced below.

I do not see any reason in principle to rule out any of the structures in (4) on the basis of the central mechanisms of anaphora that I propose. The possibility that pronominal types could differ crosslinguistically beyond distinctions of feature content is consistent with the UH, as long as these differences follow from lexical properties not specific to anaphora, such as clitichood or an absence of overt determiners.[15]

### *6.1.1 The Weak Pronoun Competition*

Cardinaletti and Starke propose that their typology of pronouns in (5) is a set of forms in competition, such that one uses the most deficient form where it is available—a version of the economy of representation (Chomsky 1995b) in their account, since more deficient forms have less structure. The question then arises as to whether this competition, if it exists, is fully independent of the FTIP or if it should be folded into the FTIP competition, such that the hierarchy of deficiency articulates the pronoun portion of the most dependent scale.

One reason to suppose that the weak pronoun competition (WPC) is distinct from the FTIP competition is that the pronouns in question are not in c-commanded dependent environments with respect to their antecedents (as pointed out in 3.2.3); indeed these pronouns need not have a linguistic antecedent in many cases. Moreover, the WPC is a competition among pronominals, not among pronouns and all anaphors, since relational anaphors (see 6.2) do not participate.

If the competitions are distinct, then it is sufficient to assume that the FTIP competition rates all of these forms as tied on the most dependent scale, not choosing among them to represent the dependent reading. Where FTIP determines that a nonanaphoric pronoun is the most dependent form, the WPC will then select the weakest pronoun available in that class as the optimal pronominal to represent a backgrounded (old information) reading. The latter process could operate much as the FTIP algorithm does, substituting weaker forms for less weak ones within the same numeration to see if the derivation crashes. Thus the FTIP does not distinguish among (5a–c) or (6a–c) (if that is a better analysis of the range of distinctions), leaving such distinctions for the WPC algorithm (see 6.1.3 and 7.1 for further discussion of the WPC scale, reading, and algorithm).

From this perspective, the fact that there are nonanaphoric pronominals that lack deictic potential becomes important. Recall that the failure of deixis test only establishes a necessary condition for anaphoric status, not a sufficient one, since clitic pronouns can fail to establish independent deixis and yet may still fail to be anaphors[16] if they are not lexically marked as such. The line between an anaphoric clitic and a nonanaphoric clitic is nonexistent for the WPC (i.e., the property of being an anaphor does not figure in the scale), but it is crucial for the FTIP competition, since anaphors are always more dependent than pronouns. I postpone until 6.1.3 some of the interesting issues that arise with respect to null pronominals.

### *6.1.2 Anaphoric Pronominals*

If the only theoretical significance of pronominal status is that pronouns are more dependent than other nonanaphors for the FTIP, then it is neither contradictory nor unexpected for a pronoun to be marked as an anaphor, hence sensitive to LAL.[17] Presumably, the class of anaphoric pronominals is potentially as varied as the range of possible nonanaphoric pronominals. Thus all of the structures proposed as potential pronominal ones in (4) should be available in principle for anaphoric pronominals.

Thus a pronoun can be anaphoric or not, such that an anaphoric one will obviate nonanaphoric ones within the FTIP competition. For example, we have seen this sort of competition in chapters 3 and 4, where SIG forms, which seem the quintessential pronominal anaphors,[18] obviate potentially independent pronouns for inherent reflexives, local possessives, and, in MS and Western Germanic, for quantifier-bound readings in wider domains. I have pointed out that SIG forms and their Romance kin should be thought of as pronouns because they meet our criterion for pronounhood; that is, they consist solely of features and have no relational content (especially for German *sich*; see 3.3.1).[19] It is possible to argue further, however, that SIG forms are pronouns in Germanic and Romance because they participate in the same morphological paradigms and have the same internal structure.

The latter point is developed by Kayne (2000) in his study of Romance pronominals. For example, French clitic pronouns *me/te/se*, which appear as proclitics on verbs in declarative sentences have corresponding tonic, nonclitic forms *moi/toi/soi* (similarly, the possessive nonclitic forms *mon*, *ton*, *son*, "my, thy, his/hers," respectively, with *-a* in place of *-on* for feminine; and *mien*, *tien*, *sien*, "mine, thine, his/hers," respectively, the latter with gender agreement *-ne*). Kayne points out that an account of these parallels might exploit morphological decomposition of the relevant parts of these forms—in other words, all of these pronominals should either be seen as compounds or else inflected versions of base forms. Consider the contrast between tonic and accusative clitic forms.

7a) Jean me/te/se critique.
*Jean* me/you/*se* criticizes
"Jean criticizes me/you/himself"

b) Chacun parle de moi/toi/soi.
*each* speaks of me/you/*soi*
"Each one speaks of me/you/himself

Kayne proposes that the *m/t/s* series are first, second, and nonperson (following Benveniste, 1966, as discussed in 3.2.1)[20] and that these elements may each be composed with the singular morpheme *-oi* to create a tonic form, or else appear with an epenthetic schwa to form the clitic form. One advantage of looking at things this way is that the behavior of *se* as opposed to *soi* may be predicted, insofar as *se* is unspecified for plural, and hence can be anteceded by a plural or a singular, but if *-oi* is singular and never reciprocal then, like *moi* and *toi*, so is *soi* (although this is complicated by the generic character of *soi*). The *-oi* form does not occur with the plural for first or second person (instead there are the plural forms *nous* and *vous*, respectively, which Kayne also suggests are bimorphemic).

Kayne concludes that the "reflexive" *s-* of French and Italian is part of a natural class with *m-* and *t-* (and for many similar paradigms across the Romance languages). The same sorts of parallels in morphology would suggest a decompositional analysis for the *mig/dig/sig* pronouns of Swedish and Danish and similarly for corresponding forms in German[21] and Norwegian.[22] However, Kayne hesitates to call the *s*-forms pronouns, presumably because of the problems that would arise with respect to Principle B. Without Principle B in the way, we are free to characterize *s*-forms as pronouns that are also anaphoric.[23, 24]

We can conclude, at minimum, that forms sensitive to LAL can participate in pronominal paradigms. The only obstacle to assuming such forms are anaphoric pronominals has been Principle B, which suggests once again that Principle B should be rejected. Kayne's analysis also shows that the internal structure of pronominals and of pronominal anaphors can be structurally complex and, if he is right about French *-oi*, that semantic properties of the decomposable parts of pronominals can be active in limiting the availability of a given pronoun for specialized readings.

### *6.1.3 Null Pronominals*

Now that we have examined the status of overt pronominals, we can consider how the FTIP competition and the WPC should extend to null pronominals. As I remarked earlier, the fact that null pronominals, like clitics, cannot be used ostensively leaves undetermined whether or not they are anaphors subject to LAL. However, I have also maintained that designation as an anaphor is a marked property of lexical items, which is one reason I do not permit vehicle change to introduce anaphoricity (see 4.3.4). If empty categories are unmarked entities that are available in any language where syntactic conditions permit them to be licensed, then no null pronominal can be considered anaphoric. Recall that we no longer assume that the trace of A-movement is an anaphor subject to LAL (indeed it is often a null pronoun), though it is limited by whatever restricts chain formation by movement. Thus there are no universally omnipresent anaphoric elements, even null ones, with the consequence that the force of LAL may be vacuous in a language that lacks lexically marked anaphors.

Thus, the null pronominals that I do assume to exist, namely, PRO, pro, and null operators, are available in the lexicon of any language, though they have no language-specific lexical properties. As lexical options, I assume that they are selected from the lexicon for inclusion in a numeration. When they are not selected, derivations will crash or not, depending, as per usual, on whether all of the lexical properties of the numeration are appropriately checked and saturated by LF.

PRO is available, within the Chomsky and Lasnik (1995) MP Case theory, just in those environments where it can receive Null Case, which is the case assigned by infinitives to their subjects. Nominals marked with Null Case are required to be phonetically null. PRO is considered the unique nominal that is capable of bearing Null Case. If we accept these assumptions, then PRO is never in competition with any other form, and so there is no harm in considering it pronominal. This is also true for examples like (8) and (9), where an extra morpheme, that is, the complementizer *for* and the *'s* merged with genitive *his*, respectively, indicate that a case other than Null Case is being assigned.

8) *Cedric* said that (for *him*) to leave would be unfortunate.
9) *Cedric* said that (*his*) leaving would be unfortunate.

Thus PRO, lacking Null Case, cannot be a competitor in contexts like (8) and (9), so the overt pronominals that do appear are the most dependent forms available in this environment.[25] Theory internally, I cannot assume that PRO is anaphoric because PRO is introduced in a subordinate subject position, it gets Null Case in the subordinate clause (under MP assumptions), and there is thus no motivation to move it up into the domain of the matrix subject. In short, if PRO remains within the complement clause at LF, it cannot find its antecedent within the domain of LAL.[26]

Pro is presumed, in the standard literature, to be a pure pronominal licensed in the subject position of a tensed sentence (Chomsky 1982) for those "null subject parameter" languages that have the right licensing forms (for a variety of approaches, see Jaeggli and Safir 1989; for a more recent account with references, see Rohrbacher 1999). Pro has the ability to be interpreted as independent in reference within the sentence in which it appears and does not require arbitrary interpretation of the sort permitted by antecedentless PRO in English, for example. A variety of interpretive and distributional distinctions between pro and PRO are to be found in Jaeggli and Safir (1989), Safir (1996b), and Terzi (1992), and I will assume that they are distinct entities (for distinctions between PRO and pro with respect to the distribution of crossover effects and resumption, see Safir 2004). This leaves out of the account the susceptibility of PRO to control, on the one hand, and the ability of missing pro subjects to refer to already established topics in the discourse; both matters I set aside in the interest of brevity.

The reasoning about the nature of pro is similar to that concerning the nature of PRO: pro must be pronominal (a) because nulls are unmarked and anaphoric forms are marked and (b) because it can be independent in the domain of LAL. Since pro and PRO do not occur in the same syntactic context, PRO being restricted to null-case environments, pro and PRO are not in FTIP competition.[27]

Now we can consider whether pro can compete with overt forms. It is plausible that pro and overt pronominal forms occur in the same case environment, perhaps even in otherwise identical numerations, and if this is so, we must decide whether or not they compete only as other weak pronouns or as weaker pronouns. The question is not easily answerable, and it is interesting to consider why.

As noted earlier, the WPC is not conditioned by c-command or any other structural environment; hence the WPC overlaps with every environment where an FTIP competition would apply. Thus it would appear that in any environment where pro competes with an overt pronoun, the WPC will favor pro, if the most dependent and most structurally deficient scales line up. As Samek-Lodovici (1996, 68–74) notes, however, it is not obvious that pro is the most structurally deficient of the possible pronominal options. If pro is a maximal projection, whether NP or DP, then it is less structurally deficient than a clitic pronoun in the Cardinaletti and Starke (1994) account, where the clitic pronoun is just an N-head. If we adopt their scale but assume pro to sport a maximal projection, then clitics should win over pro wherever both are available. To ensure that pro is more structurally deficient than a clitic, Samek-Lodovici assumes that null pronouns are not represented in structure at all.[28] However, as mentioned earlier, it is not clear that structural deficiency is the right way to organize the scale, nor, even if it is, that pro could not be analyzed as a particular null form competitive with clitics (e.g., a null N or D without a maximal projection).

It seems clear that the desired result is that pro wins over overt pronouns for the WPC. Samek-Lodovici argues that the structural deficiency metric should predict not only where subjects of tensed sentences are permitted to be null, but also where such subjects are obligatorily null. Adapting observations from Calabrese (1986), Samek Lodovici shows that pro is only available when its antecedent is a topic in his sense (typically a subject in the previous discourse) as in these examples he cites from Italian.

10a) Mentre $\text{Sandro}_i$ ritraeva $\text{Carlo}_k$ Antonio $\text{lo}_{i/k}$ fotograva.
"While Sandro was painting a portrait of Carlo, Antonio was taking a picture of him."
b) Mentre $\text{Sandro}_i$ ritraeva $\text{Carlo}_k$ $\text{pro}_i$ /*$\text{pro}_k$ fotograva.
"While Sandro was painting Carlo, he was smoking."

Unlike pro, the clitic *lo* is not sensitive to the distinction and appears in an accusative position where pro cannot. It appears the WPC is a competition for the topic reading. Thus, null pronouns compete with overt pronouns on some sort of tonic scale for the WPC, where only the winner can represent the backgrounded topic reading.[29, 30]

Finally we must consider the status of null operators, which have been posited for parasitic gap constructions, complex adjectivals, and *that*-relatives (as well as for attitudinal operators; see Safir in preparation). When these entities land in or are generated in SPEC-CP, they cannot be anaphors by the reasoning concerning LAL in 5.2.3, since they are not in the domain that includes their antecedent. I have posited, however, the existence of operators that adjoin to TP and are bound in that position by subject antecedents. If all anaphors are lexically marked, then there can be no null operators that move to this position as anaphors. This position forces me to assume that overt forms, rather than empty categories, must move in syntax or at LF to the positions where they find their antecedents within LAL (I have remained non-committal up to now, but I will not pursue the matter).

### *6.1.4 Some Conclusions About Pronominal Forms*

The results of 6.1 are summarized in (11).

11a) Descriptively speaking, pronominals and the nodes that immediately dominate them consist exclusively of grammatical features and represent a radically reduced description.
b) There is no grammatical feature [+/-pronominal], nor any Principle B, but forms that are pronominal are more dependent than nonanaphors.
c) The internal structure of pronominals may be phrasal and/or morphologically complex.
d) Pronominals may be functional heads or lexical ones.
e) A pronoun can be anaphoric if it is lexically marked as such.[31]
f) It follows from (11e) that null pronominals (PRO, pro, and null operators) are never anaphoric since a null form cannot be lexically marked.
g) Since anaphors are more dependent than nonanaphors on the most dependent scale, it follows that anaphoric pronominals are more dependent than nonanaphoric pronominals.
h) The WPC is distinct from the FTIP competition. The former is not conditioned by c-command.

It is a potentially welcome result to discover that the FTIP competition is not the only regulated competition of its kind. I postpone discussion of the role of competitive principles and algorithms in the architecture of UG until 7.1.

## 6.2 Relational Anaphors

In contrast to the anaphoric pronominals, relational anaphors are not mere bundles of features (though they may evolve in that direction diachronically) but are also endowed with a relational argument structure. These elements may contain pronouns within them, but the head of the construction is, in these cases, a form that has not fully lost all of the semantic content of the term it is a conventionalized version of. Put another way, relational anaphors are morphologically complex or syntactically phrasal or both, just as pronouns are, but what is crucial about them is that they are complex in a way that often reflects argument structure (once) inherent in the meaning of the anaphor. Some of the forms in question include notions like *body part, same, own,* and *other*. From this perspective, the class of lexical "atoms" employed as reciprocal and reflexive marker anaphors, while not completely predictable, may nonetheless be selected from a semantically restricted class.

The influence that anaphors with relational content have over the interpretations they can represent has important consequences for the UH. I have stressed that virtually the only property of anaphors not shared by other sorts of lexical items is that anaphors are marked as such. Relational argument structure, however, is a property that an enormous range of lexical items share; hence allowing that some anaphors are relational costs nothing for our assumptions about the power of the lexicon. However, since chapter 4, I have also claimed that among anaphoric forms, some are identity specific and some are not, with consequences for whether or not the LRP applies to them (when their antecedent is a coargument). It is possible, however, that identity specificity is limited in a particularly striking way, namely, that it is strictly a property conferred upon relational anaphors (when reflexivity is not affixal; see 4.2.2).

In the next short sections, a brief sketch of some of the most typical relational atoms employed in the manufacture of anaphors is presented, drawing liberally from Safir (1996c), where the properties of all of these atoms are examined in greater detail and where further references are to be found.

### *6.2.1 Some Relational Atoms of Anaphora*

Many languages of the world establish anaphoric relationships by employing conventionalized forms based on body part predicates, often in construction with a pronoun. As is well known, body part terms, which in most instances involve an aspect of inalienable possession as a potential part of their meaning, frequently involve special syntactic properties that distinguish them from other sorts of possession. Whether or not such differences show up in every language, this is enough to show that inalienable possession is frequently targeted by syntactic processes, and so it is perhaps less surprising that syntactic relations that originate to express one relation, inalienable possession, can be conventionalized to express a slightly different relation, but one closely akin semantically, namely, the relation of identity.

More specifically, it appears that terms that designate body parts implicate the existence of an individual for whom the parts in question are integral, one who cannot be "alienated" from the part in question. One way of thinking of it is that body part implicates the existence of "the whole" of the part–whole relation. Insofar as this is true, we may express the semantic content of what I will call the BODYPART relation in the following way.

12) BODYPART($x$, $y$) holds if $x$ is animate and $y$ is a portion of the anatomy of $x$.

Thus if I say *Ralph raised his hand*, then BODYPART would appear to hold of the referent of *his* with respect to *hand*. It could be that Ralph has made a hand-raising gesture, in which case Ralph is $x$, but not if Ralph is displaying a hominid fossil he owns, in which case *his* does not refer to the hominid the hand came from. The existence of the BODYPART relation is not dependent on an overt pronoun, however.

In French, for example, (13a) both permits and pragmatically favors an interpretation where the hand in question is attached to the speaker and raised in a gesture, whereas no possession is implied in (13b) at all, though it appears superficially identical to (13a).[32]

13a) Il va lever la main.
he goes raise-INF the hand
"He is going to raise the/his hand."
b) Il va lever la pierre.
he goes raise-INF the rock
"He is going to lift the/*his rock."

Thus there is reason to believe that the relational force of BODYPART is not a property of anaphora per se, but a function of the way that implicit arguments of nominals can be bound to their antecedents, on the assumption that French *main* projects an argument structure (implying the inalienable possessor of the hand) in a manner that *pierre* ("rock") does not.

Now it would appear that when an anaphor is formed from a term that participates in a BODYPART relation, a particular form is grammaticalized to instantiate the part–whole relation as an identity relation, such that the part *stands for* the whole. I take this to be a form of metonymy, in much the way that reference to a well-known individual may be invoked by employing a variety of terms that characterize a portion of his or her anatomy (e.g., Jimmy Durante was known as "the nose" and "the schnoz," as it was his most prominent facial feature and a stock reference in his humor). Similarly, in English when a tour leader wants to make sure he or she hasn't lost anyone in the transition from one site to another, he or she may "count heads." Now simply imagine that a stock portion of the anatomy of all individuals is depersonalized such that that portion of anatomy stands for the identity of an individual without designating which individual that is. For conventionalized forms of this type, the interpretation in (14) substitutes for that in (12).

14) METONYMY for BODYPART(x, y) $\supset$ (x = y)

If so, then we have a grammaticalized relational anaphor, a body part anaphor, for which the (sometimes implicit) inalienable possessor must find an antecedent within the domain of LAL.[33]

Languages that employ body part anaphors differ somewhat as to which body part is conventionalized for this purpose. For example, Faltz (1977, 110, 138) reports that Fula (West Atlantic Niger-Congo), Hausa (Chadic), and Tamazight (Semitic) use morphemes meaning "head," as does Basque, while Hebrew uses a root meaning "bone." Hungarian employs a root meaning "body," and Faltz (1977, 120) adds that the Uto-Aztecan root in compound reflexives is also "body." Postma (1997, 295–296) points out that Sanskrit and Classical Arabic use roots that mean "soul/breath" (and according to Davison, 2000, Hindi *apne* has been traced etymologically to "soul," though I think the form is bleached to a pronoun now). Haitian Creole used the roots for "head," "body," and "face" in the early history of the creole, all in construction with a pronoun, but eventually the "head" root won out (observations on Haitian from Derek Bickerton, personal communication). Heine (2000, 9) lists a variety of African languages that variously employ "body," "head," "life," "soul," and "person," though the first two overwhelmingly predominate. Finally, Schladt (2000) provides an even more extensive list of reflexive forms, and once again, body parts predominate, particularly "head" and "body," but also "bone," "skin," and "face."[34]

I take SELF to be a body part in this sense. Postma (1997) claims that its etymology developed from a compound[35] consisting of a possessive pronoun related to the possessive pronominal anaphor SIN and the Germanic root for "body," which is related to German *leib*. Whether this is correct or not, it would appear that SELF behaves like a body part anaphor now. Like all body parts, SELF is a noun capable of filling an argument place without any associated pronoun. For example, body part anaphors permit thematic compounds (where languages employ such anaphors and permit thematic compounds) of the form SELF-N (in Germanic), where the N is typically a deverbal noun, as in *self-starter*, *self-feeding*, *self-hating*, *self-government*, and the like. SELF in particular also has, when it is used outside of anaphora, a reified substantive reading, such that it refers to an abstract, inalienably possessed quality of personal identity or the essence of personality, as in countless books exploring "the self" (or related concepts in a variety of Germanic languages).[36]

One property of body part anaphors that seems a natural extension of their body part meanings is that they are most typically distributive on plural antecedents for pragmatic reasons. For example, in (15a), the most natural interpretation is that every man painted his own elbow, not that some of the men painted some of the elbows while others painted their own elbows, though one could force such an interpretation with a rich context. Where a natural gesture is involved, as in (15b), the distributive interpretation is often inescapable.

15a) *The men* painted *their* elbows.
  b) *The men* flexed *their* muscles.

It is not the case that relational anaphors are always distributive rather than collective, although in many languages they favor or require distributive interpretations when they are in contrast with another anaphor. We have already seen such a function of contrast in the case of German (see 3.3.3), though we don't see the same contrast in English.

16a) Die männer sehen sich selbst.
  b) "*The men* saw *themselves*."

While (16a) favors an interpretation where each man sees only himself, (16b) is fully ambiguous in English between a collective and a distributive interpretation, where the collective interpretation might describe a showing of the team photo. However, we know independently that SELF forms in English differ morphologically from their German counterparts; *selbst* is a free morpheme disambiguator, specifying a reading for the underspecified *sich*, while pronoun-SELF in English, as argued in 6.2.3, has integrity as a compound, with contrasting consequences for the pattern of anaphora in these languages.

It is significant, however, that, there are some languages in which a metonymic BODYPART anaphor can be used to represent reciprocal readings, in spite of what our internalist account would lead us to believe. As in the case of pronouns adapted for uses that do not match their features (e.g., third person plural in English is used when speakers seek to suppress presumptions of gender for human singular referents), a metonymic BODYPART anaphor can be enlisted to represent reciprocity (with an appropriate meaning substitution) where there is no conventionalized reciprocal form, nor any anaphoric pronominal (e.g., like *se* in French and *sich* in German) to do the double duty. Yoruba, for example, has no "each other" type anaphor that is intrinsically reciprocal, so the relational BODYPART anaphor fills the functional void, and, in FTIP terms, is the only competitor for that reading, even though the term *ara* allows a compositional interpretation as well, which shows that it has an autonomous synchronic reading. (Third person singular honorific readings are possible with *wón*, in which case a singular reflexive reading and a compositional one, i.e., "his/her body," are also possible).[37]

17) Wón rí ara won.
    they see body them
    "*They* saw *themselves*."
    "*They* saw *each other*."
    "*They* saw *their* bodies."

Expansion of the distribution of a term that normally is restricted by its internal properties, which I will call *functional extension*, seems to arise only when there is no competitor for a reading. Heine (2000, 9–10) surveys a number of African languages that use metonymic anaphors (typically "head" and "body") for both reflexive and reciprocal readings. Moreover, as Frajzyngier (2000a, 187) points out, some languages in the Chadic family even use different body part terms for the reflexive and reciprocal readings, which seems a more radical adjustment of BODYPART interpretation to the purpose of expressing reciprocal readings.[38, 39] We can predict, however, though it seems obvious, that in any language where there is an intrinsically reciprocal anaphor, a BODYPART anaphor will not be ambiguous with a reciprocal reading (unless a verb is inherently reciprocal).

What cases like Yoruba show, however, is that we must evaluate the class of competing forms for each reading rather than rely exclusively on a radical internalist approach to the atoms of anaphora. In my critique of the Rooryck and vanden Wyngaerd (1997) approach in 4.3.3 and especially 5.2.3, it was pointed out that the extra semantic properties attributed to Dutch *zich* to account for its failure to support proxy readings are neither sufficient nor general enough crosslinguistically to account for the distribution of the readings SIG forms support. Rather I relied on a special property of SELF forms (inability to represent necessary indistinctness) and derived the distribution of Dutch *zich* in the context of competition with other forms: If a competing form with a more compatible meaning is not available, as in the case of a SELF form where it cannot satisfy LAL, then a SIG form can indeed support the proxy reading.[40]

A variety of languages employ a form that means "same" to indicate reference to an individual previously mentioned. We have seen, for example, that French employs pronominal anaphors to indicate dependent identity readings, but in certain syntactic contexts they also employ what I will refer to as *SAME forms* in construction with pronouns. These forms frequently serve to ensure cococonstrual where coconstrual might otherwise be optional (see Kayne 1975, 344–345). Other Romance languages also employ SAME morphemes in anaphora.

18a) *Jean* a parlé de *lui-même*. (French)
"Jean spoke of himself."
b) *Juan* habla de *si mismo*. (Spanish)
" Juan spoke of himself."
c) *Gianni* ama solo *se stesso*. (Italian)
"Gianni loves only himself."

In French, Spanish, and Italian, the morphemes in question are adjectives that independently (of anaphora) mean "same," and since they are not all cognate forms, it seems likely that some property of this meaning is being exploited to form anaphoric terms.

Let us suppose minimally that SAME is a relation of identity between some number of entities or events with respect to some standard or scale (for more explicit discussion, see Carlson 1987; Moltmann 1992). If we say *Orville arrives at the same time every day*, the standard is that time of day and each arrival by Orville are identical with respect to the time of day that it takes place. If a SAME anaphor is to achieve a reflexive reading in (18), however, the standard of sameness in this case must be sameness of referential value for the two arguments of *parler*, "to speak."[41]

Let us suppose then that when a SAME anaphor is in construction with a pronoun, the pronoun is modified in the way the standard of reference is (e.g., *stone* in *the same stone* is the standard of reference), which is to say that the anaphor is something akin to "the same him"; in other words, with respect to referents in discourse, this entity is the same as some other entity. It is this sort of relation that anaphora seems to exploit when it is grammaticalized, such that SAME in construction with a pronoun is marked as an anaphor and hence is subject to LAL.

What is abundantly clear, however, is that pronoun-SAME in Romance is never used to achieve a reciprocal interpretation, and this is no accident as long as we pay attention to what SAME means. SAME anaphors do not appear to allow even the limited flexibility we have seen for Yoruba with BODYPART anaphors. Those who treat both the pronoun-SAME construction and the pronoun-SELF construction as semantically unanalyzed markers of emphasis (e.g., Zribi-Hertz 1989, 1995) have no account of this fact.

A much less studied form of anaphor that supports dependent readings is the use of a morpheme meaning "own" attached to a possessive pronoun to pick up the reference of a discourse referent or to focus a possessor that may even be a name.

19a) *Andrea's own* husband would never get caught shopping for bikinis.
b) *Alice* met *her own* husband coming out of the store.
c) Barby said that would never happen to her.
d) Her own husband would never shop where she could see him.

Although Higginbotham (1985, 576–577) and Saxon (1991) have claimed that pronoun-*own* is locally restricted, Dowty (1980) argues that examples like (19a–d) argue against anaphoric status for pronoun-*own*, since it can appear without a c-commanding antecedent (19d) or as a contrastive intensifier on a name (19a). As pointed out in Safir (1996c), however, the locality restriction on pronoun-*own* is only visible where it does not have to be stressed.[42]

20a) *Eccles* expects the new boss to provide *his ówn* key.
b) **Eccles* expects the new boss to provide *his own* kéy.
c) *Rory* writes *his ówn* books.
d) *Rory* writes *his own* bóoks.

For a language that uses OWN anaphors as the primary anaphoric strategy, see the references cited in Safir (1996c) with respect to Amsterdaamse *zijn eigen*.

The use of OWN in a nominal to create an anaphoric relation is reminiscent of the inalienable possession function associated with body parts, but there is no part–whole relationship to transform into an identity relation—the head nouns in (20a–d) do not correspond to the identities of their antecedents. Rather *own* asserts a relation, one independently established by the genitive relation, which is one reason that *own* has been taken to be an intensifier (e.g., by Zribi-Hertz 1995). Perhaps this doubling effect is what creates an identity relation, such that the possessor in the genitive relation is in an identity relation with the possessor of the OWN relation. It would appear that anaphoric marking exploits this effect to fashion a conventional anaphoric relation, subject to LAL in those languages where it is so marked.

It appears that OWN anaphors are never used to represent reciprocal readings (see Heine 2000, 10), even when no specialized reciprocal form is available, which suggests that the semantic force of OWN is incompatible with reciprocity, but I will not pursue this idea further here.

In contrast to the SELF relation, the OTHER relation is a distinctness relation, such that for any $x$ and $y$ in an OTHER relation, $x$ is somehow distinct from $y$. Given the meaning of the atom, it is not surprising that it is never employed to represent a reflexive reading. Moreover, of all the anaphoric relational atoms compiled in Heine (2000, 9), which include BODYPART and OWN atoms, the two that seem most similar to OTHER, namely, "relative" (cited for Fulani) and "comrade" (cited for Gola and Karomfe), are also exclusively employed (as grammaticalized forms) for reciprocals. The construction of a reciprocal meaning from this relational atom requires more, such as a distributivity relation on each member of the set such that if A and B are in the set then A is to B what B is to A and so forth, but I leave discussion of these points for the appendix to this chapter. It seems clear, however, that the participation of an OTHER morpheme in reciprocals should not be treated as accidental.

On the other hand, the existence of reciprocal interpretations without specifically reciprocal forms shows that this interpretation must be available whether there is a form for it or not, just as coargument dependent-identity relations are available even in languages that lack anaphors. After all, the Romance *s-* series of pronouns can have reciprocal as well as dependent-identity readings, and we postulated that this is possible because pronouns of this sort lack any argument structure that distinguishes such readings.

This view of reciprocals compromises a claim made by Jayaseelan (1997) that is otherwise compatible with the analyses I have proposed here. Jayaseelan argues that all anaphors contain a pronoun, but the pronoun when embedded in (what I call) a relational anaphor structure is protected from Principle B. Since there is no Principle B in my account, the protection for the pronoun is from direct competition with an anaphor. However if the internal structure of *each other* is as in (21), where *other* is the relational head, and *each* binds a variable in SPEC-NP, it is not obvious that this anaphor contains any pronoun.

21) $[_{DP}$ each $[_{NP}$ x $[_{N'}$ other]]]

Although one could argue that the *x* in (21) is a pronoun on theory-internal grounds, the point to be made here is that *other* is not a pronoun by any obvious criterion. *Other* as an adjective can occur with *one*, which no nonpossessive English pronoun can; the noun *other* can appear with a definite determiner, which other English pronouns cannot; and *other* does not participate in a paradigm sensitive to person, such that there is no OTHER-form for "other one of us" or "other one of you." Heim, Lasnik and May (1991) only assume *other* is pronominal to account for the distinctness effect in the distribution of the reciprocal; that is to say, they attributed the latter effect to Principle B. Jayaseelan also endorses this view. Not only is Principle B no longer a good motivation, but treating *other* as a simple pronominal does not take into account its relational nature such that *each* binds an argument place of *other*, or why *other* should be used for reciprocity instead of *them/him*.[43]

The point here, one that harks back to the earliest generative work on reciprocals (e.g., *each* movement in Chomsky 1973), is that whether or not a given anaphor is employed as a reciprocal marker can often be derived from the internal semantics of the relational atom involved. It is curious that a result taken to be so obvious with respect to reciprocal relational anaphors did not catch on with respect to the analysis of other relational atoms within the mainstream literature.

### *6.2.2 On the Contribution of Relational Meanings to the Distribution of Anaphors*

We may now reach some conclusions about relational anaphors that appear to hold fairly generally.

22a) A limited number of synchronically extant lexical semantic relations may be adapted to form relational anaphors (e.g., SAME, OWN, BODYPART, and OTHER).

b) The roots on which relational anaphors are based specifically influences their interpretation as a dependent form with respect to distributivity, animacy, reciprocity, and identity-specific dependency (feeding LRP).[44]

c) A metonymic BODYPART anaphor is never ambiguous between reflexive and reciprocal readings unless there is no specifically reciprocal anaphor.

Notice that (22a) is consistent with the UH, in that all of the relational atoms cited have meanings outside the context of anaphora. The exploitation of relational atoms other than these is rare (but see note 41 to this chapter). I take (22c) to be a partial consequence of (22b) and a functional requirement that feeds the FTIP. Functionally speaking, reciprocity must be expressible. Where reciprocity is governed by LAL (rather than an affix), there will be a marked anaphoric form for the purpose, which, if it is not intrinsically reciprocal, will permit a reciprocal reading in the absence of a competitor (as in the case of Yoruba). However, when a given form supports both readings, regardless of its etymology, that form more typically turns out to be (synchronically) a pronoun, and if so, we expect it to have other pronominal properties (e.g., fitting into a pronominal paradigm), and we may expect it will be associated with a disambiguating adjunct anaphor. The conclusions (22a, b) have direct consequences for any given relational anaphor with respect to FTIP, in that interpretive possibilities a given relational atom permits determine which other potentially dependent forms it is in competition with for a given reading.

We have also posited (23a), which has (23b) as a natural consequence.

23a) Anaphors are a marked subset of forms that lack deictic potential.
 b) Fixing a given relational atom as anaphoric (subject to LAL) requires marking it as a conventionalized form for this purpose.[45]

Languages may or may not mark the relational atom in question with special overt morphology to signal its special role. In English, such marking is achieved by associating the SELF morpheme with an inconsistent paradigm of pronouns, some of which are possessive (*myself*, *yourself*, *herself*) and some of which are accusative (*themselves*, *himself*). This fact is related to the prosodically coherent behavior of the compound in English, as opposed to some languages where the pronominal case paradigm is regular.

As pointed out earlier with respect to Yoruba in (17), it is not necessarily the case that the form designated to act as an anaphor cannot have a literal meaning independent of anaphora where the pronominal paradigm is regular. Faltz (1977, 110) cites examples from Fula (Niger-Congo) and Hausa (Chadic) where the same inflected stem used for the dependent-identity interpretation has a literal interpretation wherever it cannot have an anaphoric one. In (24c), Fula *hooremum* is outside of its domain restriction, and so only pronominal inflection on the preposition, as in (24b), achieves dependent identity (indices illustrative).

24a) Demba yeewtini Yero hooremum.
 Demba talk-PAST Yero head+3sg
 "Demba$_i$ talked to Yero$_j$ about himself$_{i/j}$"
 b) Demba yiyi nooroondi seramum/sera hooremum.
 Demba see+PAST snake near+3sg/near head+3sg
 "Demba$_i$ saw a snake near himself$_i$/his head."

Just how a relational atom comes to find itself in a position that satisfies LAL at LF depends on how its nonanaphoric properties determine its potential to have a short-bounded, long-bounded, or unbounded domain.

### 6.2.3 *Relational Anaphors and Structural Complexity*

Since relational anaphors, unlike pronouns, retain semantic vestiges of argument structure, syntactic or morphologically expressed positions may be required to satisfy that argument structure. This suggests that relational anaphors will always be the heads of morphologically and/or phrasally complex constituents. What we need to know now is whether or not the internal structure of relational anaphors determines the domains in which they are available for FTIP competition. At least two important questions arise in this connection. First, can the parts of a complex relational anaphor participate autonomously in FTIP competitions? Second, does it matter whether or not the relational anaphoric atom is in a structural head position or a structural adjunct position within the morphological or phrasal form? Both of these distinctions appear to be underdetermined by what such forms mean. The answers to these questions are related, but I must build up to them with smaller steps.

Let us begin with the generalization in (25).[46]

25) Relational anaphors that head nominals have short-bounded domains.

The truth of this statement is not obvious, but most of the cases that seem to counterexemplify turn out to fall under the generalization in (26).

26) Relational anaphors that function as adjuncts on pronominal heads have the distributional profile of UD-forms.

Unlike the relational anaphor forms that serve as the lexical head of nominal arguments, the adjunct forms are typically optional, are anteceded by what they modify (e.g., a pronoun), and do not participate with their pronominal heads in FTIP competitions, though they may serve to disambiguate or emphasize. If pronouns with adjunct relational anaphors attached are treated as two forms in one phrase, then (27b) follows from (27a), the latter proposed in 3.2.2.

27a) Two forms cannot replace one in a test derivation within the FTIP competition.

b) Adjunct relational anaphors attached to pronominal heads do not compete with a simple pronominal head.

The result of (27b) is that the distribution of adjunct relational anaphors on pronouns will overlap with unmodified pronouns.[47] Since adjunct anaphors are predicates on what they modify, like other adjuncts, it follows that adjunct anaphors are anteceded quite locally, that is, by the heads they are adjoined to. Thus the pronominal head is evaluated separately from the adjunct as a pronoun for the purposes of FTIP. While

(26) does not immediately follow, it then becomes quite plausible, since if two forms tie on the most dependent scale, it is reasonable to suppose they must contrast in some other way. I shall argue that constructions like *John himself* are adjunct anaphor constructions, and I extend this reasoning to nonnominal adjunct relational anaphors like French *même*, among others, as well.

Returning now to (25), the question is why relational anaphors should contrast with pronominal anaphors in this way. Long-bounded domains arise where pronominal anaphors act as tense-sensitive operators, as in Hindi and MS. Suppose we derive (25) from (28a, b).

28a) Relational anaphor stems are lexical heads.
  b) Quantifiers are never N-heads.

If we take seriously the claim that relational anaphors preserve some of their lexical character, then (28a) is true by hypothesis. A consequence of (28a) is that relational anaphors are either N-heads or adjuncts. They are N-heads if they head arguments since they constitute the lexical head of the argument, and if they head projections that are adjoined to some other argument, then they are nonarguments predicated of what they attach to. Turning to (28b), quantifiers are most typically analyzed as determiners, functional Q heads, or perhaps adjectives (or adverbs) that bind a full nominal phrase or its head as a variable, but virtually no account I am aware of treats quantifiers as nouns themselves, since they can always occur with Ns (e.g., in English, *most/many/any/every/no/five men*). If the relational nominal is a nominal head, it follows from (28b) that it is not a quantifier. Moreover, we have examined a number of hypotheses about the structure of pronouns, most of which do not treat pronouns as nominal heads, but as determiners. If we assume at minimum that pronouns *can* be determiners (or specifiers) of nominals, then at least some pronouns may meet this necessary condition for operators, namely, that they not be N-heads. (Notice however, that I do not claim to be able to predict, on the basis of its form, that a pronominal anaphor will be an operator).[48] These assumptions are consistent with the UH, in that the properties we propose for anaphoric pronominals and most of the properties posited for relational anaphors are properties that hold of nonanaphors as well (i.e., being a D, an N, and/or an operator).[49]

If relational anaphors, when they are not adjuncts, have short-bounded domains, then it must be the case that the pronouns they are associated with are not their antecedents, but rather their antecedents must be outside of the complex anaphor as a whole. This effect is, in fact, derivable from (29).

29) A lexical head is never anteceded within its own extended projection.

Thus if SELF or pronoun-SELF is an N-head, then its antecedent is outside of the DP of which it is the lexical head. This general ban on internal antecedency is not a special fact about SELF anaphors but is just a restatement of Williams' (1982, 282) proposal based on the illformedness of sentences like (30a, b).

30a) *A picture* of *itself* is on the mantel.
  b) *Its picture* is on the mantel.

In these instances, where we can only fix the reference of the phrase headed by the noun *picture* after fixing the reference of its parts, reference fails. As Williams points out, however, predicative usages are possible; for example, *That is a picture of itself* presumably has a meaning that some (external) *x* has the property of being a picture of itself.

I am thus arguing that the emphatic usage[50] and the argument-head usage of relational anaphors are both anaphoric,[51] and both find antecedents outside of their extended projections. The relational anaphor adjunct is anteceded by what it is adjoined to, while relational anaphors that head nominals find an antecedent outside their extended projection but within the domain delimited by LAL.

I do not have space here to defend this system in detail, but for presentational purposes it is useful to illustrate how the system works with a sketch of the relevant relational forms in Germanic. To begin, consider some of the possible structures for pronoun-BODYPART, in this case pronoun-SELF in Germanic, where (31–33) are the likely candidates.

31a) $[_{N}$ pronoun-SELF$]$
b) $[_{NP}$ $[_{N}$ pronoun-SELF$]]$
c) $[_{DP}$ $[_{D}$ e$]$ $[_{NP}$ $[_{N}$ pronoun-SELF$]]]$

32a) $[_{DP}$ $[_{D}$ pronoun$]$ $[_{NP}$ SELF$]]$
b) $[_{DP}$ $[$pronoun$]$ $[_{D}$ e$]$ $[_{NP}$ SELF$]]$

33a) $[_{DP}$ $[_{DP}$ $[_{D}$ pronoun$]]$ SELF$]$
b) $[_{DP}$ $[_{DP}$ $[_{D}$ e$]$ $[_{NP}$ $[_{N}$ pronoun$]]]$ SELF$]$

Once again, the range of candidates could be expanded or contracted depending on the X'-theory assumptions one adopts, but in what follows, I shall rarely distinguish the subcases of (31) or (32) or (33) from one another. Rather I will focus on the three sorts of analyses in (31), (32), and (33) as analyses with notably different syntactic distributional consequences. The distinctions are as follows: In (31), I treat pronoun-SELF as a morphological compound rather than a phrase; in (32) I treat the pronoun as morphologically independent of SELF, though lexically required by SELF, where SELF is the head of the phrase (as in the selection of an idiom, which may be phrasal but must be selected with all of the associated forms in its lexical entry); and in (33) the relational anaphor is an adjunct, and the head of pronoun-SELF is the pronoun.

The analysis in (31), which I contend is appropriate for English, is one where pronoun-SELF competes with pronouns for the most dependent interpretation and the parts of the noun compound do not act autonomously in the determination of the anaphoric pattern. By contrast, the analysis in (32), appropriate for MS, is one wherein both constituents of pronoun-SELF play a role in the distribution of the form, but pronoun-SELF still competes with pronouns as a unit (since it enters the numeration by a single selection). Finally, the adjunct analysis in (33) is the correct analysis for German, where SELF only acts to disambiguate between dependent readings, but where SELF may be selected independently of the pronoun, and thus pronoun-SELF does not compete with pronouns to represent the dependent interpretation.

Consider first the contrast between English and the other Germanic languages. All of these languages can use a SELF form adverbially, and when they do, there is a locality effect, such that the adverbial SELF form must be bound by a clausemate (as is generally the case for adverbials).

34a) John went to fetch the fish *(him)self.
b) Jon er selv gået hen for at hente fisken. (Danish)
c) Lizzy Borden barbierte den Vater selbst. (German)
"Lizzy Borden shaved father herself." (Edmondson & Plank 1978, 374)
d) Jan kocht het boek zelf (Dutch) (Everaert 1986, 41, fn. 13)
"Jan bought the book himself."

35a) *Mary says John saw him herself yesterday.
b) **Maria* sier at Jon så Peter *selv* gar. (Norwegian)
c) **Maria* sagte, dass Hans Peter *selbst* gesehen hat. (German)

Only English, however, requires the adverbial–emphatic SELF form to be in construction with a pronoun, which I take to be evidence that the anaphor is a morphological compound in English that amounts to an X° form, even though the pronominal portion agrees in person and number with its antecedent (see also Hestvik 1990). As remarked earlier, in English, the choice of pronoun in the SELF compound spans different paradigms, including both genitive and accusative forms. For the same reason, even in emphatic usages that focus proper names, English must use a compound, but not Dutch (or Norwegian or German), illustrated below.

36a) John himself will cut the ribbon.
b) De man zelf wist van niks. (Everaert 1986, 36)
"The man himself knew nothing of it."

The SELF form is required for MS/Dutch in local contexts, but the SELF form of German is not required in such contexts for *sich*, where *sich* unambiguously corresponds to a full thematic argument (i.e., not a context of inherent reflexivization), as was pointed out earlier.[52, 53] Moreover, Faltz (1977, 122, 130) notes the contrast between Dutch and German in (37) where the Dutch sentence is in no way emphatic whereas the German sentence is.

37a) Hans sah sich selbst. (German)
b) Jan zag zichzelf. (Dutch)
"Hans/Jan saw himself."

Many theorists have pointed to the emphatic usage of SELF forms and SAME forms and argued that the reflexive usage is historically derivable, if not synchronically identical, to the emphatic usage (e.g., Moravcsik 1972; Edmondson and Plank 1978; Zribi-Hertz 1995; see notes 38 and 50 to this chapter). While the historical transition from disambiguator–emphatic to reflexive marker seems to be well supported (for English, see Keenan 1994), the view that the reflexive use is a function of the emphatic fails to explain why there is any locality effect for the "reflexive" usage and why these locally restricted forms are often stressless, or less stressed than emphatics, even in languages where the forms used in the two environments are identical (see note 54 to this chapter).

None of the languages in question permits reflexive readings where no pronoun appears on a thematic argument, as in **Celia saw self*, though the reasons for it differ. In English, the reason is that the form is a compound, while in German, it is because the form is an adjunct, as it is when it is used adverbially or emphatically on a name and hence cannot fill an argument position. In Norwegian, by contrast, the SELF-headed forms compete with simple pronominals for the dependent reading, as discussed in the next section, but it does not follow from anything I say that a pronoun *must* be present, or if present, must be overt. On the other hand, the presence of the pronoun in Norwegian may serve to signal the special function of SELF as a conventional anaphor (and hence an idiom for which the two parts are a single selection), since the pronoun follows an accusative paradigm (i.e., we get a SIG form instead of the possessive SIN form) as in (32c), which is the structure I will tentatively assume for MS.

For English, then, we only have to consider one form when we consider pronoun-SELF, but for MS, it is one form in a test derivation competing with a pronoun or name, but its internal parts are autonomous. I am proposing that the SIG portion of these anaphors behaves just as it does when it is not associated with SIG, moving at LF to a TP-adjoined position, but the SELF portion, since it is an N-head and thus not an operator, is not motivated to move. Thus the SELF head must be anteceded in the position where the nominal as a whole gets its case, as discussed in 5.1. The result is a nominal in which the SIG portion is anteceded by a subject and the SELF form must also be anteceded by a local antecedent, namely, the subject. I am also assuming that the metonymic identity relation that is used to construct the anaphor would not permit its internal parts to have distinct antecedents. Thus complex SIG SELF forms in MS are subject oriented, as required by SIG, and local, as required by SELF. The antisubject orientation of pronoun-SELF in MS as the next most dependent form then follows in the usual way.

Turning now to the adjunct analysis, the essence of the account of German *selbst* can be extended to French SAME anaphors. The latter have the force of adjuncts in construction with argument pronouns (as argued by Burzio 1991, 99; Zribi-Hertz 1995) and hence are often not necessary for identity-dependent readings, though they may reinforce such readings when they are not required.

Zribi-Hertz (1980, 1995), for example (but see also Faltz, 1977, 54; and Giorgi 1990, 131), arguing that *même* is an adjunct, points out that the use of *même* to achieve a dependent-identity reading (as opposed to an independent-pronoun reading) is optional in some cases but not in others, depending on the verb (see also Kayne 1975, 344–345). For example, the addition of the *-même* morpheme, which is independently a prenominal adjective (as in *la même chose* "the same thing"), is optional for the coreferent interpretation in (38a) but obligatory for the coreferent interpretation in (38b).

38a) Marie pense d'abord à elle(-même).
"Marie thinks first of her/herself"
b) Jean s'est attaqué à lui(-même).
Jean SE-is attack-PART to him(-SAME)
"Jean attacked him/himself."

Zribi-Hertz observes the contrasts in (39) and (40) and concludes, "The referential indexing of *lui* in neutral PPs is not constrained by [Principle B], but by the lexical choice of the predicate which occurs between the pronoun and the subject. Predicates which take a PP complement must be specified in the lexicon with respect to disjoint reference: thus, *être jaloux* is +DR [disjoint reference], while *avoir honte* is -DR" (1995, 347–349).

39a) *Pierre* est jaloux de *lui-*(même).*
"Pierre is jealous of himself."
b) *Pierre* bavarde avec *lui-*(même).*
"Pierre chats/is chatting with himself."
c) *Pierre* lutte contre *lui-*(même).*
"Pierre struggles/is struggling with himself."
d) *Pierre* a besoin de *lui-*(même).*
"Pierre has need of himself."

40a) *Pierre* a honte de *lui(-même).*
Pierre has shame of him(-SAME)
"Pierre is ashamed of himself."
b) *Pierre* parle souvent de *lui(-même).*
"Pierre often talks about himself."
c) *Pierre* travaille pour *lui(-même).*
"Pierre works for himself."
d) *Pierre* pense souvent à *lui(-même).*
"Pierre often thinks of himself."

The distinction between predicates that permit coreference without *-même* and those that don't does not appear accidental, which suggests that a semantic generalization rather than a feature is appropriate (Zribi-Hertz does show that it is not influenced by contrastive discourse factors). Moreover, it is not the case that obviation (her +DR) is canceled for such predicates, since *Mitterrand a lutté contre le mec*, "*Mitterrand* struggled against *the guy*," does not allow a reflexive interpretation either (just as FTIP predicts, since a pronoun is available for the dependent reading). Rather our sense of how many thematic actors are involved in a struggle (39c) would normally lead us to expect distinct actors, whereas being ashamed can frequently involve a single thematic actor. Thus, although I underpin it differently, I confirm Zribi-Hertz's generalization that *-même* merely disambiguates a potentially noncoreferent coargument interpretation (which is possible in all cases with simplex *lui*) by enforcing a coconstrued one.

From the point of view of the FTIP, the competition winner in all of the prepositional object cases in (38–40) is a tonic pronoun, since *lui-même* competes as a pronoun and ties, but lexical factors render the coreferent interpretation unexpected for (39) and hence in need of reinforcement. The reinforcement, in the form of *même* is possible but not necessary for (40). Thus pronoun-*même* is not in FTIP competition with the simplex pronoun, since the *-même* form is an adjunct, not an argument head, as illustrated by the structural possibilities in (41), from which I will not choose.

41a) $[_{DP}\ [_{D}$ pronoun$]\ [_{NP}\ [_{AP}$ SAME$]\ [_{NP}\ [$e$]]]\ ]$
b) $[_{DP}\ [_{DP}\ [$e$]\ [_{NP}\ [_{N}$ pronoun$]]]$ SAME$]$
c) $[_{DP}\ [_{DP}$ pro $[_{D}$ pronoun$]\ [_{NP}$ e$]]\ [_{AP}$ SAME$]\ ]$

In each structure, SAME heads its own extended projection within a DP that is an extended projection of the nominal head, and in each case SAME is anteceded by what its extended projection is adjoined to.

The predicates in (39) and (40) that show a contrast in French for the distribution of pronoun-*même* do not contrast in a similar way in English for principled reasons. In English, pronoun-SELF is an anaphor compound and an argument head and thus competes with simple pronouns in argument positions. Thus it is fully expected that all of the English translations of (39) and (40) should employ pronoun-SELF, which outcompetes a simple pronoun for the dependent reading in every case.

It is important to stress here that the status of pronouns with respect to FTIP does not differ in the two languages, only the nature of the competition. This is another reason to reject a rigid internalist position, which would assign different internal properties to French tonic pronouns from those found in English. For example, Zribi-Hertz treats pronoun-SELF as structurally identical to pronoun-*même*, so she must state that English pronouns obey Principle B and French pronouns don't (1995, 355). Like Bouchard (1984), I am arguing that there is no Principle B, hence no need to exempt pronouns from it. On the other hand, the competition is only predicted to be different in English if pronoun-SELF and pronoun-*même* are different in their morphological structure, as argued here.[54]

Since the adjunct *-meme* phrase is anteceded by what it is adjoined to, pronoun-*même* is not restricted by any of the conditions on short-bounded or long-bounded domains. For example, *lui-même* can appear in tensed subject positions as illustrated in (42a), and its presence can be optional in unbounded long-distance contexts like (42b, c, d). Moreover, under the right conversational conditions, pronoun-*même* does not even require a sentence-internal antecedent, as in the discourse (43) cited by Zribi-Hertz (1995, 343).

42a) *Jean* croyait que *lui-même* devait gagner. (Kayne 1975, 347)
Jean thought that him-SAME should win
"Jean thought he himself should win."
b) *Elle* veut que tu parle d'*elle*(?-*même*). (Kayne 1975, 347; compare Faltz, 1977, 153)
"She wants you to speak of her."
c) *Pierre* est consterné que la femme qu'il aime est incapable de voir au fond de *lui(-même)*. (Zribi-Hertz 1995, 350)
"*Pierre* is sorry to see that the woman he loves is incapable of seeing through *him*."

43) A: Le Roi m'a dit de faire des cendriers pour tout le monde.
"The king told me to make ashtrays for everyone."
Dois-j'en faire un pour la Princesse Kiki?
"Should I make one for Princess Kiki?"

B: Non, en faites un que pour lui(-même).[55]
"No. Only make one for himself."

Similar effects have been studied in detail for Spanish *mismo* by Sanchez (1993). Spanish differs from French insofar as the SIG-like element in Spanish (*sí*) is not semantically restricted in the manner of French impersonal *soi*. Thus in Spanish, anaphoric *sí* obviates pronouns in positions where French would use a tonic nonanaphoric pronoun, but apart from this difference, the structural relations between *mismo* and what it is adjoined to is the same. Faltz (1977, 143) observes that (44) is emphatic–contrastive when *mismo* (SAME) is employed but not when it is omitted. In (50), we see *mismo* modifying full nominals.

44) *Juan* halló una culebra cerca de *sí* (*mismo*).[56]
Juan find+PAST a snake near SIG SAME+Masc.
"Juan found a snake near him."

45a) La sociedad protege al hombre de la sociedad misma.
the society protects the-ACC man from the society SAME
"Society protects man from society itself." (Faltz 1977, 131)
b) María misma abrió la puerta.
María SAME+Fem opened the door
"María herself opened the door."
c) María vio a Juan mismo.
María saw Juan SAME+Masc.
"María saw Juan himself."

Sanchez (1993) argues that Spanish *mismo* is an adjunct modifier, noting that its nonemphatic usage is prenominal, a position that is consistent with the analysis developed here. She also argues that postnominal *mismo* is an operator that causes the nominal it attaches to to raise at LF, a matter I will not explore, but see her paper for interesting details.[57]

Thus, in the theory of anaphoric locality I propose, the generalizations in (46) should ideally follow (individually or collectively) from the principles in (47) if the theory is tight enough.

46a) Relational anaphors that head nominals have short-bounded domains. (=25)
b) Anaphoric pronouns can have long-bounded domains.
c) Pronouns with relational anaphors adjoined to them have the distributional profile of UD-forms. (=26)

47a) Relational anaphor stems are lexical heads. (=28a)
b) Quantifiers are never N-heads. (=28b)
c) Pronouns are usually (always?) functional categories.
d) A lexical head is never anteceded within its own extended projection. (=29)
f) Two forms cannot replace one in a test derivation within the FTIP competition. (=27a)

It is possible that (47a–d) might follow from deeper lexical–semantic principles and that (47e) may follow as a general property of the family of algorithms of which FTIP is a member, but for now, the statements in (47) appear to address the right level of abstraction. The principles in (47) are thus the core of my account of how the morphology of a form determines how it is available for FTIP competition.

Although the morphology-to-availability mapping relation is of interest in itself, recall that I have introduced it in order to show that no rigid internalist account, even one with as many advantages as the one presented here, can succeed in predicting the distribution of a given form without understanding how that form competes with others in a given syntactic context.

## 6.3 Case Studies of Competitive Narrowing

The insufficiency of an internalist account of pronoun distribution is perhaps quite obvious at this point, but the structure of the argument is the same as it is for the internalist account of anaphor distribution, and so it is worth reviewing here. I have been treating pronouns, apart from the WPC, as the default case for c-commanded coreferent readings whenever an anaphor is not available. This accounted for the antilocality of pronouns formerly characterized by Principle B and for the lack of antilocality where pronouns had no more dependent competitors.[58] Moreover, as argued in 6.2.3, where pronouns in French are not antilocal, it is because they lack competitors, but French tonic pronouns are not marked differently for antilocality than English ones. Thus antilocality is never an inherent property of pronouns to be derived from their internal properties, but merely a result of lost competition. Similarly, as argued in chapter 3, antisubject orientation of pronouns is not an internal property of pronouns either, but the result of lost competition.[59] Kayne's argument that the members of the *m-/t-/s-* series in Romance are all pronominal by their morphology gave us an internalist account of what constitutes pronounhood for those languages. I assume further that the *s-* series is marked anaphoric, but the fact that the *m-* and *t-* bases can be used to express reflexivity was derived from the lack of competitors, not any internal properties or syncretic stipulations about *me* or *te*. Recall also that the internal specification of SELF forms as being incapable of representing principled indistinctness (in Dutch, German, and MS) permitted us to avoid positing any internal specification for pronouns to permit that reading. Moreover, proxy readings, possible wherever indistinctness is not required, do not require any special property to be posited of pronouns either, since they can as easily represent proxies if no SELF form competes. Thus it has been possible to assume that pronouns are relatively unmarked for the readings they allow, are available in every position, and are empirically distributed in any position where they are not outcompeted. The internal structural properties of pronouns, apart from grammatical features affecting interpretation (e.g., gender, plurality), only appear to play a role in the WPC.

Extending this sort of reasoning to anaphors and UD-forms, we see the same sorts of explanation. The antilocality of pronominal anaphors in Germanic (excepting English and Frisian, which lack them) is just the same effect that we have observed for nonanaphoric pronouns that lose a competition in part of the domain where they are available, except that pronominal anaphors are only available in bounded domains. In MS, moreover, pronoun-SELF forms are not stipulated to be antisubject oriented, but they are by virtue of the subject-oriented form, SIG-SELF, which they compete with. In Yoruba there are no reciprocal forms, so BODYPART metonymy functionally extends to do double duty, representing both identity-specific and reciprocal readings. Thus it is not necessary, indeed it is wrongheaded, to derive a reciprocal reading for the BODYPART anaphor based on its internal properties.

Arguments such as these vindicate the mediated internalist approach over the rigid one, where the difference between the approaches is the FTIP. The following case studies, all from languages where coconstrual is marked on arguments (rather than affixes), serve to illustrate some of the ways in which competitive narrowing provides a more explanatory account than any rigid internalist theory can of a variety of restricted anaphoric patterns and interpretations.

### *6.3.1 Greek*

Iatridou (1986) argues that the Greek form *o idhios* is an anaphor that is locally free, but bound in sentence grammar. With examples like those below, Iatridou (1986, 767) illustrates that the near antecedent cannot be the antecedent of *o idhios*, but a more restricted local anaphor, *ton eafton tou* (the last morpheme marks person, number, and gender and varies accordingly), can be anteceded in just these environments.

48a) Egho idha ton eafton mou/*tis ston kathrefti.
I saw TON-EAFTON 1ps/3pfs in the mirror
"*I* saw *myself*/her in the mirror."
b) O Yanis aghapa ton eafton tou/*ton idhio.
John loves TON-EAFTON-3mps/*3pms IDHIO
"*John* loves *himself*."
c) O Yanis theli [i Maria na voithisi ton eafton tis/*tou].
John wants Mary helps TON-EAFTON-3pfs/*3pms
"*John* wants Mary to help herself/*him*."
d) O Yanis theli [i Maria na voithisi ton idhio].
John wants Mary helps 3pms-IDHIO
"*John* wants Mary to help *him*."

On the other hand, Iatridou points out that *ton idhio* does not have free reference in (48d), but must refer to *o Yanis*, while an independent pronoun in the same environment (49) can refer either to *Yanis* or some third party (but not to *Maria*, not only because of gender but also because the pronoun would lose an FTIP competition to *ton eafton tis*).

49) O Yanis theli [i Maria na ton voithisi].
John wants Mary him help
"*John* wants Mary to help *him*."

*O idhios* is not subject oriented, since it can refer to *Costa* or *Yanis* in (50a), and it can be the subject of a tensed sentence, as illustrated in (50b).

50a) O Yanis ipe ston Costa oti i Maria aghapa ton idhio.
John says to Costa that Mary loves IDHIO
"*John* told Costa that Mary loves *him*."
b) O Yanis pistevi oti o idhios tha kerdhisi.
John believes that IDHIOS will win
"*John* believes that *he* will win."

Dalrymple (1993, 75–76), citing evidence from Cleo Condoravdi, suggests that *o idhios* does not in fact have to be bound in sentence grammar, reinterpreting some overtly antecedentless cases that Iatridou treats as emphatic *o idhios* associated with pro-drop. If Dalrymple's description is more apt, *o idhios* is in fact a UD-form, but in either case, its ill-formedness in the more local environment is readily explicable as a case where an anaphor, *ton eaftou*, available only in the domain of LAL, has outcompeted it.

The case of Greek looks fairly regular from the point of view of the typology developed here. Pronouns are locally obviative because of the short domain of the anaphor, *ton eaton tou,* and the same form obviates the UD-form *o idhios* ("the same") in the local domain.[60, 61]

### *6.3.2 Malayalam*

A similar case arises in Malayalam, although a variety of potentially dependent forms complicates matters. We have already demonstrated the UD-form status of *taan*, but Jayaseelan (1997) points out further that *taan* cannot have a coargument antecedent, nor can the fully independent pronoun *awan*. We would only expect this gap if there is a competing coargument anaphor in this domain, and indeed there is, namely, one where the *taan* form (or the fully independent pronoun *awan*) is compounded with *tanne*.

51a) *raaman *t*an-ne/awan-e sneehik'k'u*nn*u.
Raman TAAN/him loves
"*Raman* loves *himself*."
b) raaman *t*an-ne *t*anne sneehik'k'u*nn*u.
Raman TAAN-TANNE loves
"*Raman* loves *himself*."
c) raaman awan-ne *t*anne sneehik'k'-u*nn*u.
Raman him-TANNE loves
"*Raman* loves *himself*."

However, the *tanne* compound is not restricted to the coargument domain, and so at first blush, it is not obvious that the appropriate complementarity effect should be expected—rather *tanne* compounds should outcompete *taan* wherever the antecedent c-commands, which is the wrong result.

52) raaman wicaariccu pen.kuṭṭikal. *t*an-ne *t*anne/awan-e *t*anne sneehik'k'u*nn*u ennə.
Raman thought girls TAAN-TANNE/him-TANNE love COMP
"*Raman* thought that the girls love *him*."

Jayaseelan notes, however, that all of the nonlocal cases of *tanne* compounds must be stressed, but local direct object *taan-taane* lacks this stress. Moreover, *tanne* permits adjunction to all sorts of nominals, including names, as Jayaseelan (1997, 194) points out. This suggests, within my system, that local *taan-tanne* is headed by the *tanne* part as in (53a), whereas in all the other *tanne* compounds, it is an adjunct, as in (53b), and as such, it attaches to both *taan* and independent pronouns without affecting their domains.

53a) $[_{DP}$ taan $[_{NP}$ tanne]]
b) $[_{DP} [_{DP} [_{NP}$ taan]] $[_{DP}$ tanne]]

Jayaseelan argues against the claim that stress distinguishes two separate distributions for *tanne* compounds, but the only case that appears to compromise this view is the fact that dative *tanne* compounds with local antecedents are also stressed, yet pronouns are also obviated in those domains. The need for stress in this coargument dative environment is unexplained by either account, however, whereas the absence of stress in the local domain for direct object cases is just the sort of distinction that would be expected if there is a difference between locally anteceded *tanne* compounds and those more distantly anteceded.[62]

Following a rigid internalist view, Jayaseelan assigns *taan* pronominal status in order to make it susceptible to Principle B, as well as discourse dependency. He then attributes the gap in the distribution of *taan* either to the saving effect of compounding with *tanne* (e.g., taan-tanne) or on the assumption that *tanne* is just *taan* with a focus particle. The plausibility of this account for Malayalam depends greatly on the decomposition of *tanne*, into *taan* + focus, which seems dubious in that there is no presumed focus on the anaphor in examples like (51b, c) (nor is *taan* + focus sufficient to ensure reflexivity, since it must be compounded). It is thus plausible to assume that the stressless form of *tanne* induces anaphoricity and hence susceptibility to LAL that outcompetes the simplex *taan* locally.[63]

At first, this might look like a standoff. Under a Principle B account, the fact that an anaphor with a distinct local pattern exists is then not related to or derived by the fact that *taan* is blocked in the local domain; instead we stipulate pronounhood for *taan*. Under the FTIP account, whether or not *taan* is a pronoun is not immediately relevant because there is no Principle B, but we have to stipulate anaphorhood for stressless *tanne*. However, the Greek case helps us decide. The morphological origin of the *o idhios* form is from the morpheme meaning SAME and is not plausibly pronominal. Following Jayaseelan's logic, however, we would have to assign pronominal status to *o idhios* in order to ensure that it would have the same distribution as *taan*. This seems artificial. The FTIP account treats the Greek and Malayalam cases as participating in a very natural pattern in which a more local anaphor outcompetes a UD-form. And of course we do not have to complicate linguistic theory with the existence of Principle B.

### *6.3.3 Japanese*

The most discussed dependent forms in Japanese[64] are "bare" *zibun* and compounds formed with *zisin*, either *zibun-zisin* or pronoun-*zisin*. According to Katada (1991, 289), the *zisin* compounds are local with the *zibun* compound subject oriented in contrast to subject-neutral pronoun-*zisin* case (were the pronoun is *kare* in these examples).

54) John-ga [Bill-ga Mike-ni zibun/zibun-zisin/kare-zisin-no koto-o hanasita to] itta.
John-SUB Bill-SUB Mike-IO ___-GEN matter-DO told that said
"John said that Bill told Mike about ___."
a) John = zibun/*zibun-zisin/*kare-zisin
b) Bill = zibun/zibun-zisin/kare-zisin
c) Mike = *zibun/*zibun-zisin/kare-zisin

If we take *zisin* to be a relational anaphor, an N-head associated with a pronoun (assuming *kare* and *zibun* to be pronominal) in its SPEC or D position (see Katada 1991, 294, although she does not consider the DP hypothesis), then the locality of these cases follows from the nonquantificational property of *zisin* as an N.

55) $[_{DP}$ zibun/kare $[_{D'}$[e] $[$zisin$]_{NP}]]$ or $[_{DP}$ (pro?) $[_{D'}$[zibun/kare] $[$zisin$]_{NP}]]$

The subject orientation of *zibun-zisin* is immediately understandable from my perspective. If simplex *zibun* is cross-classed (by stipulation) as an operator anaphor in its local distribution[65] or a UD-form in its broader distribution, then it will be restricted or in construction with *zisin* to be local, though it will contribute strict subject orientation locally, just as SIG does in the analysis of MS SIG-SELF. More puzzling, in this interpretation of the facts, is why *kare-zisin* is not antisubject oriented if it is in competition with *zibun-zisin*. Moreover, *zibun* and *zibun-zisin* would appear to be in competition, yet both are possible locally.

That *zibun* is a homonym for a local anaphor and a UD-form is defensible if it is sensitive to perspectival or contrastive effects as a UD-form but insensitive to these factors locally. A dual analysis of *zibun* along these lines has been proposed by Abe (1997), who argues that when *zibun* is anaphoric (local), it is not subject to Kuno's (1972) "awareness" effect, although *zibun* is sensitive to awareness restrictions in its wider distribution. Evidence that *zibun* behaves as a UD-form was presented in 5.3.[66]

However, it does not appear to be empirically accurate to treat the *-zisin* forms as necessarily local. Aikawa (1993) and Fuji (1994) demonstrate that both *kare-zisin* and *zibun-zisin* forms permit an emphatic contrastive usage in a variety of contexts where they are not bound locally, as in (56a, b) from Fuji (1994) and (57) from Aikawa (1993).

56a) [Kare-zisin-ga] boku-ni aini-kita.
he-ZISIN-Nom I-Dat meet-came
"*He himself* came to see me."
b) Titi-wa [musume-ga kare-zisin-o keratteieru] koto-o hazimete
father-Top daughter-Nom he-ZISIN-Acc hate that-ACC for-the-first-sitta.
time learned
"*The father* learned for the first time that (*his*) daughter hates *him*."

57) John-ga Bill-ni [[Mike-ga zibun-zisin-no rombun-o hihanisita]
John-Nom Bill-Dat Mike-Nom ZIBUN-ZISIN-Gen paper-Acc criticized
to] itta.
that said
"*John* told Bill that Mike criticized *his* paper."

These facts suggest an alternative DP-adjoined structure, such as those in (58a, b). If so, these complex forms are not in competition with each other (unless *kare* and *zibun* are in competition) for the emphatic readings these forms would require.[67]

58a) $[_{DP}[_{DP}$ zibun] $[_{NP}$ zisin]]
b) $[_{DP}[_{DP}$ pronoun] $[_{NP}$ zisin]]

The structure in (58) would lead us to expect that *zisin* could adjoin to nonpronominals as well, and this is indeed the case, as illustrated in (59) with examples from Fuji (1994; see also Jayaseelan 1997, 203). *Zibun* cannot appear where *zisin* can in (59), suggesting that unlike *zisin*, *zibun* is not an adjunct relational atom, but a pronoun.

59) [Taro/sensei/aitu-zisin]-ga Tokyo-ni itta.
Taro/teacher/guy-ZISIN-Nom Tokyo-Dat went
"Taro/the teacher/the guy himself went to Tokyo."

As an adjunct on a full DP, then, *zisin* is anteceded outside of the extended projection it heads by whatever it is adjoined to. In other words, *zisin* needs no other antecedent, when it is an adjunct on *zibun* or an independent pronoun, a proper name, or a description. Fuji (1994) shows, moreover, that whenever *zisin* combines with a nominal form that can be interpreted as the bound variable of a quantifier, it can be a bound variable (e.g., *sore-zisin, soitu-zisin,* as well as *zibun-zisin*), but it can never be a bound variable of a quantifier if it is combined with a form, like *kare* or *aitu* ("the guy") that cannot be quantifier bound.[68] This suggests that *kare-zisin* does not actually compete with *zibun-zisin* for any bound reading.[69]

The latter point brings us back to the apparent lack of complementarity between *zibun* and *zibun-zisin*. Some have attempted to argue that *zibun* is less than fully acceptable when anteceded locally (e.g., Katada 1991; see also Jayaseelan 1997). As Aikawa (1993, 1994) points out, however, there are interpretive differences between the two forms when they are coconstrued with local subjects. Consider (60a, b) versus the contrasts in (61).

60a) John-ga zibun-o nagutta/hagemasita/tunetta.
John-NOM ZIBUN-ACC hit/encouraged/pinched
"*John* blamed/encouraged/pinched *himself.*"
b) John-ga zibun-zisin-o nagutta/hagemasita/tunetta.
John-NOM ZIBUN-ZISIN-ACC hit/encouraged/pinched
"*John* blamed/encouraged/pinched *himself.*"

61a) Dareka-ga ?* zibun/zibun-zisin-o nagutta.
someone-NOM ZIBUN/ZIBUN-ZISIN-ACC hit
"*Someone* hit *himself.*"
b) Daremo-ga *?zibun/zibun-zisin-o hagemasita.
everyone-NOM ZIBUN/ZIBUN-ZISIN-ACC encouraged
"*Everyone* encouraged *himself.*"
c) Dare-ga ?*zibun/zibun-zisin-o taihosita no.
who-NOM ZIBUN/ZIBUN-ZISIN-ACC arrested Q
"*Who* arrested *himself?*"
d) John-to Mary-ga ? *zibun/zibun-zisin-o hagemasita/nagutta.
John and Mary-NOM ZIBUN/ZIBUN-ZISIN-ACC encouraged/hit
"*John* hit/encouraged *himself* and **Mary** hit/encouraged **herself**."

Aikawa remarks that in its local distribution, anteceded by a coargument, *zibun* can never be bound by a quantifier or be interpreted distributively, but *zibun-zisin* can.[70] Yet *zibun* can and must be interpreted distributively when its antecedent is not a coargument, as in (62) (I have adjusted the translations for clarity).

62a) John-to Mary-ga zibun-no uti-o tateta.
John and Mary-NOM ZIBUN-GEN house-ACC built
"*John and Mary* built *their* houses/*house."
b) John-to Mary-ga Bill-ga zibun-o semeta to itta.
John and Mary-NOM Bill-NOM ZIBUN-ACC blamed that said
"*John* said Bill blamed *him,* and *Mary* said Bill blamed *her.*"
*"*John and Mary* said Bill blamed *(both of) them.*"

Aikawa's analysis is that *zibun* is actually never a bound variable in its local distribution at all but is instead merely coreferent with its antecedent, the way *kare* is in its full distribution. Similarly, Jayaseelan (1997), citing unpublished work by Ueda (1984) and by Fukui (1984) that I have not seen, argues that *zibun* is a pronoun subject to Principle B. But Aikawa's view does not explain why *kare* and *zibun* should not then be interchangeable locally for a coreferent reading, as it is clear that *kare* is sharply out in these environments (e.g., in [60a] with *kare* in place of *zibun*), while Jayaseelan's view does not explain why *zibun* is so much better than a pronoun in these cases. Moreover, it is a stipulated mystery in Aikawa's account why the wider distribution of *zibun* lacks the restrictions it evidences in its local distribution.[71]

From the competition theory perspective, when the local domain of a form lacks an interpretation possible in its wider distribution, we immediately suspect a domain hole that results from competition with a more dependent form. If we assume that *zibun* competes with argument head *zibun-zisin* in the local domain (to which *zibun-zisin* with structure [55] is limited because it is headed by a relational N-anaphor) and that *zibun-zisin* wins this competition only with respect to antecedents that require a distributed interpretation, then the domain hole is derived from the competition without positing (radically) different distributivity properties for local *zibun*, as a rigid internalist account would be forced to conclude. Rather *zibun* has the same distributivity properties wherever it is available, but it is outcompeted for the distributed interpretation locally. Together, *zibun* and *zibun-zisin* obviate *kare* locally.[72]

One result emerging from the case studies of Greek, Malayalam, and Japanese is that UD-forms compete as pronouns and are obviated in their local domains by anaphoric forms with different interpretations and internal morphology, though the form in question may not be phonetically distinct in some languages (e.g., Japanese).

### *6.3.4 Hungarian*

In Hungarian,[73] pronouns with antecedents matching in person and number are excluded, and reflexive forms appear instead to represent dependent-identity readings. Although this part of the pattern of anaphora is unsurprising, den Dikken, Lipták, and Zvolenszky (2001) have pointed out that when the antecedent and its local dependent match in person, they do not always have to match in number to support a reflexive form. Thus in (63) a plural reflexive can be anteceded by singular first person antecedent, yet the reverse number relations are not possible.[74]

63a) *mi magamat képviseljük meg.
we myself-Acc represent-1pl.def PV
"We represent me."
b) én magunkat képviselem meg.
I ourselves-Acc represent-1sg.def PV
"I represent us."

It would appear that only the interpretations not permitted with reflexives are possible with pronouns.

64a) engem képviselünk/választunk meg.
me represent/elect-1pl.indef PV
"We represent/elect me."
b) *én minket/bennünket választok meg.
I us/ us elect-1s.indef PV
"I elect us."

Now there is a further interesting wrinkle that concerns the pattern of object agreement for what has been called *definiteness* in Hungarian. Verbs are marked to distinguish definite from indefinite objects, and reflexives of all persons are always definite (as [63b] shows), but there is an asymmetry between first and second person, on the one hand, and third person (nonperson, as remarked earlier), such that third person object pronouns are always marked definite, but first and second person object pronouns are almost always marked indefinite (which I illustrate with first person forms only).

65a) {szereti /szeret} {magát/ őt/ Jánost/a srácot}.
like-3sg-def/*like-3sg-indef REFL+3ps/ him/ János/the guy
b) {szereti /szeret}\ {engem/minket/bennünket/egy lányt}.
*like-3sg-def/like-3sg-indef me /us /us /a girl
"He/she likes me/us."

However, where first person pronouns, as opposed to reflexives, represent a reading similar to (63b), the agreement must be definite, as in (66a). Such cases are reported to be marginal, but with indefinite agreement they are thoroughly unacceptable.

66a) ?én minket/bennünket választom meg.
I us/us represent-1pl.def PV
b) *én minket/bennünket választok meg.
I us/us represent-1pl.indef PV
"I represent us."

Insofar as it is acceptable, (66a) would violate Principle B, interpreted as a disjoint reference prohibition (see 2.4.2).

Den Dikken, Lipták, and Zvolenszky argue that the first person object pronoun must avoid a Principle B violation caused by the inclusive anaphora, and the movement relation that they posit takes place is supposed to then "trigger" definite agreement rather than the indefinite agreement the first person object normally requires. They represent the first person plural pronoun as embedded in a larger small clause constituent (complement or adjunct), which serves as its local domain, protecting it from the locality of outside antecedence. The variables are third persons that could be associated with the speaker.

67a) [$_{NP}$ we/us [$_{SC}$ pro$_i$ [$_{PP}$ COMIT [ x(&y(&z . . . ))]]]]

Then the position of "we/us" is ignored, and binding theory is computed on the embedded pro. Additional structural assumptions are supposed to derive definite agreement in these cases, but I will not comment about the details, for which the interested reader is referred to the source. It seems to me, however, that a much simpler approach is available in a theory that derives Principle B from competition and does not require radical rigid internalist assumptions to defend Principle B.

From the point of view of competition theory, the only surprise in this data set, other than the permissibility of number mismatches, is that a first person plural pronominal object is possible in the same position where a reflexive form is also available. What we should expect is that either that the forms tie for this reading, or the interpretations for (63b) versus (66a) are different. It seems that the latter is the case. Den Dikken, Lipták, and Zvolenszky report the judgment of an informant as follows: "The pronoun will typically identify a group without individuating its members while the anaphor will be used if the speaker knows all the people who make up the group" (2001). If the competition in question is not for the same reading, then there is no reason to be surprised that a pronoun succeeds where the reflexive does not, and thus competition theory predicts this sort of exception to Principle B. No complex internal structure must be proposed to account for the failure of first person pronouns to be sensitive to Principle B in this environment under this interpretation.

Moreover, the pattern of agreement may also be explicable without appealing to syntactic structure that has the form, but not any meaning, consistent with the agreement. Suppose that the relevant meaning of this form of agreement is not so much definiteness–indefiniteness, but whether or not the reference of a nominal is determined by previous discourse.[75] "Definite" marking is used for reference that depends on previous discourse (linguistic or pragmatic), while "indefinite" marking is used for terms with novel referents, or terms that, by their nature, do not require a previous discourse for their reference to succeed. Building on a line of reasoning that begins with Kaplan (1989), I argue in Safir (in preparation) that first person pronouns can connect to their antecedents with every mention, not by reference to previous discourse, although such forms certainly can be dependent, as was illustrated in 2.4 and 4.2.2. When first person forms in Hungarian are reflexive, then they will trigger definite agreement, since they are dependent in those cases. Nonperson pronouns are always dependent on previous discourse and thus get definite agreement in Hungarian. What must be expected of definite agreement with a simple first person pronoun is that the reading in question must also be anaphoric but not representable by the reflexive.

In fact, what we see here looks like nothing more than a familiar group versus distributive dependent-identity contrast, where the reflexive form requires a form of distribution, as in other cases we have mentioned, and the pronoun permits the undifferentiated group to be a function of its antecedent,[76] inducing definite agreement for the first person object in just this case. The pronoun is the most dependent available form for the latter reading. Thus no special internal morphological structure is required for the first person pronoun in order for it to represent just this reading.

## 6.4 Prospects and Expectations

The brief case studies of the last section are intended to reveal the strengths of the competitive approach to anaphora and to put the theory's apparent weaknesses in perspective. What these case studies render obvious, however, is that there is a whole lot more work to be done before we can sufficiently master the level of morphological and interpretive detail it will take to feel confident that we have the right theory of anaphora.[77] I am, however, confident that the path we have led up to now is enough to show we are on the right track.

The essential results of this chapter are (a) that it is possible to construct an internalist theory, one consistent with the UH, which can determine, from the structural, featural, and semantic composition of a form, where that form is an available candidate to support a dependent reading. However, (b) no internalist account can determine the distribution of a form without considering the form in the context of the competitions it enters into, so (c) many of the internal properties that have been attributed to forms to predict their domains, such as antilocality or antisubject orientation, or to predict the range of dependent readings they support should instead follow from functional extension (as in the case of Yoruba) or more typically by competitive narrowing induced by the FTIP.

## Appendix to Chapter 6: Reciprocals and the Competitive Model

Up to this point, I have skirted issues concerning whether or not reciprocals should be regulated by the FTIP, which is limited to identity-dependent interpretations, or more broadly, whether or not the domain of reciprocals and/or the reciprocal interpretations a form can have are regulated by any competitive principle. Although the account I present here is quite flawed, it serves to demonstrate what sort of issues arise with respect to reciprocals within the logic of the competitive model.

There is clear evidence that the internal properties of forms interpreted as reciprocal cannot entirely follow from their internal properties. For example, Yoruba BODYPART anaphors can be interpreted as reciprocals by functional extension as shown in 6.2.1. Insofar as functional extension arises where there is no competition, one might argue that the case for some sort of competitive effect is made. However, we have also seen that forms that are pronominal, even independent pronominals, can have reciprocal interpretations in some languages (e.g., in Old English for third person plural and in German for first person plural). If we are not to attribute all such pronominal behavior to inherent reciprocal properties available to the pronouns in question (as a stipulated option), then we must try to derive the existence of reciprocal interpretations from some competitive process. In this we cannot do worse than any theory that simply stipulates the differences, as virtually all current theories do.

Before we address this issue, we must keep in mind that some languages mark reciprocals on arguments, and others mark reciprocity with an affix on a predicate. Languages that mark reciprocity on predicates tend to be limited to coargument relations in their effects, while those languages that mark arguments are not always so limited. Where the affix in question is a detransitivizer (as in Chichewa—see Sells, Zaenen, and Zecs, 1987, and Dalrymple, Mchombo, and Peters, 1994, who contrast the detransitivizing reciprocal with the transitive reflexive marker), whether it is lexically specific or productive, there is no obvious competitive issue to address (i.e., since a pronoun is not a possible competitor), and so I will set all affixal cases aside.[1]

Another class of cases to set aside may be exemplified by French pronominal reciprocal interpretation and its relation to the adjunct, *l'un l'autre*. Adjunct reciprocal markers do not necessarily contribute to obviation but do contribute to disambiguation. French permits TUT-reflexive interpretations as well as reflexive interpretations formed with first and second person pronouns or with *se*. In these cases, disambiguation in favor of the reciprocal interpretation is achieved by the addition of *l'un l'autre*.

1a) *Ils se* parlent *l'un l'autre*.
they SE speak the one the other
"They speak to each other."
b) *Ils se* parlent *l'un de l'autre*.
The speak the one of the other
"They speak of each other."

However, *l'un l'autre* has a variety of uses, more like English *one another* or *(the) one . . . the other* (both of which also deserve more study in English—see Dalrymple et. al. 1998) than *each other*. Unlike *autre*, the English cognate *other* in *each other* is not preceded by a definite article, though *each other* cannot be separated without introducing a definite article in front of *other*, (e.g., *Each man talked to *(the) other*), and when *each* and *the other* are used in a fashion parallel to French, they often have a disambiguating function, as in *The men talked each to the others* (often pronounced with a pause between *talked* and *each*) to indicate the distribution of the talking relationships within the group. Without entering into the details of reciprocal interpretation, what is relevant to our immediate concerns is that *l'un l'autre* is not a competitor with *se* as a most dependent form for the representation of the reciprocal relation, but a disambiguator (a similar point is made for French reflexive *-même* in 6.2.3).

Once the disambiguating reciprocal markers are put to one side, however, the open question remains as to the status of pronominals representing reciprocal interpretations and whether or not these compete with argument reciprocals for the reciprocal reading. German and English are languages where reciprocity is marked on arguments, and so the question can be posed as follows: Are idiomatic reciprocals (*each other*, *einander*) ever in competition with other forms, for example, independent pronouns, to represent reciprocal interpretations?

At first blush, the answer for English may not be interesting for a reason that undercuts a competitive account right away: Pronouns in English never permit reciprocal readings.

2a) *The men* praised *each other/*them*.
b) *The men* read *their/each other's* books.
c) *The men* expect *each other/*them* to win.

3a) *The men* said that Mary would defeat *them/*each other*.
b) *Each man* said that Mary would defeat *the other*.
c) *Each man* said that Mary would defeat *him/them*.

While (2a–c) could be taken to follow from a competitive account, it is not obvious why (3a) fails to mean what the compositional reciprocal in (3b) does, since the pronoun in (3a) is in a position where the reciprocal is not possible (it does not satisfy

LAL).[2, 3] Rather (3a) is at best vague, but it appears to heavily favor either of the readings in (3c), which are either "*x* said that Mary would defeat *x*" or "*x* said that Mary would defeat *y*," where *y* is a group that includes all the men in question (I set aside noncoconstrual readings). On the other hand, it is not obvious that any language permits a pronoun embedded as (3a) is to support a reciprocal reading, for whatever reason. Even if we abstract away from the last case, however, it has to be said for the Scandinavian languages as a whole that pronouns, including SIG forms, cannot be interpreted as reciprocal (see note 40 to chapter 6).

The issue that does not arise for English or the Scandinavian languages does arise, however, for German. German has an argument-marked reciprocal, *einander*, which is sensitive to LAL and appears to be possible in the same structural positions as plural first person pronouns and *sich*, both of which can be interpreted as reciprocal.

4a) John und Mary sehen sich/einander.
"*John and Mary* saw *each other*."
b) Wir Onkeln und wir Väter kritisieren uns/einander zu viel.
"*We uncles and we fathers* criticize *each other* too much."

The usual strategies in such cases (see chapter 3) are to argue for a tie on the most dependent scale, a difference in numerations, or a difference in meaning. Since I assume *einander* behaves as an anaphor, I cannot propose a tie on the scale unless I also treat German pronouns as optional reciprocal anaphors. While such a move is generally accepted for *sich*, it would also have to be extended to first person plural *ons*, which is just the sort of syncretism I have rejected for identity matching relations (such as reflexive readings). Rather I am assuming that pronouns support a variety of coconstrual relations unless they are stipulated not to support them, as in the case of English and Scandinavian. Moreover, since I assume that idioms are selected for the numeration as a unit, *einander* should be able to substitute into the same otherwise constant numerations that a pronoun does, with the result that pronouns like first person plural should always be outcompeted by *einander*, apparently contrary to fact. This leaves only the possibility that there could be an interpretive difference between the two that could permit an overlap that is only apparent. To explore this possibility, I must digress.

It is not uncommon in the world's languages for there to be more than one marker that permits a reciprocal interpretation, but a number of interesting generalizations have emerged that suggest a role for functional extension and a competitive algorithm.

It has been noted by Lichtenberk (1985) and Kemmer (1993) among others (see in particular the articles collected in Frajzyngier and Curl 2000a) that many languages have a "heavy" and a "light" reciprocal marker (which Kemmer treats in prosodic terms) and that the light marker seems to be more flexible in the range of interpretations it can support beyond the "prototypical" reciprocal relation. In many languages, the light marker is also used for reflexives, middles and passives as well as reciprocals (as *sich* and personal pronouns are used in German, except for passive), while some languages have specifically reciprocal light and heavy markers.

The prototypical reciprocal relation is exemplified in (5a), while a less prototypical relation is exemplified in (5b).

5a) *The men* criticized *each other.*
b) *The men* kissed (*each other*).

Examples like (5a) could describe situations where A criticizes B, and then B criticizes A such that distinct events (e) of criticizing could be involved for the relation R described by the predicate, as schematically described in (6a). The separately bound event arguments could turn out to be the same event (accidentally).

6a) AxAy (Ee(R(x, y, e)) & Ee(R(y, x, e)))
b) EeAxAy (R(x, y, e) & R(y, x, e))

The noted difference for English in (5b) (and similarly for *embrace* and *bump*) is that when *each other* is missing, then only the interpretation where a single mutual kissing event is involved is possible, as in (6b). For example, *the men kissed* cannot mean that man A kissed man B and then man B kissed man A. As Kemmer (1993, 113) points out, the adjective *simultaneously* added to (5b) without *each other* is particularly deviant because it presupposes the possibility of separate events of kissing. However, if *each other* is employed in (5b), then the prototypical reading is once again available, and *simultaneously* is again possible. If we assume, as Kemmer suggests, that the light marker in English is a null form (as it is for some inherent reflexives in English, as in *Darren dressed*; see 4.3.1), then it would appear that the light form, licensed by some predicates and not others, permits only the representation of indistinct events.[4]

The possibility that arises, then, is that the relation between the choice of forms and the distribution of readings is one of blocking, which I have modeled as competition throughout. Suppose that the heavy form, which in most languages is a form that appears to have more relational content, is a more specific, restricted form, in that, like SELF forms, it resists necessarily indistinct interpretations. Then necessarily indistinct interpretations it resists are typically those where there is less distinctness of events (rather than indistinctness of participants, as in the SELF/SIG contrasts discussed in chapter 4). In the context of the verb *kiss*, which licenses a competitor, the null reciprocal, the specific form in English, *each other*, outcompetes the null reciprocal for the distinct events interpretation. In other words, for *the men kissed each other*, *each other* outcompetes the null reciprocal only for the interpretation (6a), which *each other* can also represent, but not for the interpretation (6b), which *each other* cannot represent (except on the accident where both *e* variables happen to have their values coincide but are not necessarily indistinct).

Where there is no competing form licensed, that is, when in English a predicate does not license the null reciprocal, then the overt one functionally extends to cover interpretations that it would not support when faced with a competitor. For example, *each other* can support "chaining" interpretations, such as (7), which a specific reciprocal favoring (6a) should resist (it is not the case that if R(a, b), then R(b, a) for the predicate *follow*), but in this case there is no other competitor, given our stipulation about English pronouns.

7) *The men* followed *each other* onto the podium.

Returning now to the case of German, we can treat the pronominal reciprocal (e.g., *sich* and *uns*) as functional extension to cover cases where *einander* is not possible, while treating missing readings of the pronominal reciprocal as a loss in competition to *einander*. Kemmer reports (although not all my informants agree) that German speakers make the same distinction between *sich* and *einander* in German that is made in English for the null reciprocal (where it is licensed) and *each other*.

8a) Hans und Maria haben einander geküsst.
b) Hans und Maria haben sich geküsst. (Kemmer 1993, 112)
Both mean "*Hans and Maria* kissed *each other*."

If we identify the light marker as the one with less relational content, as we have for identity-specific anaphors like SELF versus pronominal anaphors like *sich*, then *sich* is expected to be the light marker and to support the readings that correspond to the English null reciprocal.

If such cases suggest that if we take heavy markers of reciprocity to be the more relationally specific ones, then these markers will have the narrowest range of interpretation when they are in competition with semantically underspecified light markers but the widest range of interpretation when they are not by functional extension. On this account, the fact that light markers cannot always compete is not taken to be a function of their interpretation, but rather of limitations on licensing imposed by lexical selection of light markers (as in the case of the English null marker).

There are many obstacles in the way of such an account, and it is possible that it is simply wrong. In some cases it is difficult to formulate a semantics for the specific form that extends to all the cases where it outcompetes a weaker form. For example, in Hungarian, there is a light–heavy contrast between two dedicated reciprocal forms, and the lighter one covers the indistinct events cases, which the heavy form does not. However, as Kemmer (1993, 126) reports, the heavy form supports chaining interpretations, hardly prototypical reciprocal situations. Moreover, in some contexts interpretations supported by the specific form can also be supported by the light form, in spite of my prediction that only the heavy form should triumph. The chaining interpretation in Hungarian is such a case, as in (9a, b) cited by Kemmer.

9a) egymást követ-i "follow/succeed one another"
b) követ-kez-ni "succeed, follow"

Other cases seem to show a contrast like that for *kiss* that my account will not capture.

10a) The hockey players collided for 15 minutes.
b) *The hockey players* collided with *each other* for 15 minutes.

While (10b) freely permits an interpretation where the hockey players collide over and over again, one can easily imagine a situationally odd interpretation for (10a) whereby a single collision between hockey players lasts 15 minutes. The use of *each other* correlates with the more distinguishable event interpretation, but since (10b) also includes the preposition *with*, a direct comparison of numerations is not straightforward (there are two differences between the numerations in (10a, b), both *with* and *each other* would have to be altered in the test numeration, which FTIP, for example, does not allow). On the other hand, the distinction between (10a) and (10b) for the individuated collisions reading is not as sharp to my ear as it is in the case of *kiss, embrace,* or *bump*.

Even if the competitive account of the relation between light and heavy forms fails, it is not obvious that there exist any competing explanations of why pronouns in some languages can support reciprocal readings, but not all such readings. For example, there is nothing in binding theory that addresses the difference between *sich* and *einander*, and the Reinhart and Reuland (1991, 1993) theory has nothing to say about reciprocals at all.[5] Instead of stipulating, as I do, that some pronouns cannot represent reciprocal readings, most opposing theories (tacitly) stipulate that otherwise independent pronouns count as reciprocals and anaphors in a given language, yet the latter accounts still do not predict how the semantic space of reciprocal event readings should be divided on principled grounds. Existing accounts suggest only tendencies. For example, Kemmer proposes that the prosodically light form tends to support interpretations where there is low elaboration of events, even though she acknowledges that prosody does not always distinguish heavy and light forms (1993, 120). My proposal ties the difference between light and heavy forms to the semantic residue inherent in relational anaphors as opposed to maximally reduced forms like pronouns—the more relational residue there is, the more adherence there is to reciprocal interpretations with distinguished events. Much empirical work must be done before the competitive approach can be refuted or affirmed, but hopefully the logic of the that approach is now clear.

7

# Principles of Anaphora in the Architecture of Syntactic Theory

While the patterns of anaphora are interesting in themselves, my account of why they should be the way they are is of little consequence if it is not understood as a clue to and a result of the organization of our innate linguistic faculty. I have made a case for a theory of anaphora that restricts dependent-identity interpretations within the syntactic configurations of sentence grammar, and in doing so I have proposed a number of principles that I take to be part of universal grammar. It is now time to consider how these principles should be integrated into the architecture of syntactic theory and whether our notion of that architecture must change to accommodate what I claim to have discovered.

Three contrasts will play an important role in what follows. One is between types of principles—those that are competitive and algorithmic and those that are unary. A second opposes principles that regulate convergence and that are blind to semantic interpretation versus those that regulate the interpretations that convergent derivations permit. A third key contrast is between totalistic as opposed to modular theories of competition, where the former permits of only one competitive principle (e.g., undifferentiated economy in minimalism, the central algorithm of optimality theory), while the latter permits a variety of competitive principles, perhaps generally limited in form (the view argued for here). I also touch on a fourth opposition, namely, certain tensions between reduction and explanation that have arisen in the practice of minimalist theorizing.

I have expressed the theoretical mechanisms I have proposed in this book within the framework of the MP. At this writing, minimalist architecture is largely centered around principles that construct structures and derivations and conditions of economy that limit the class of derivations and operations. Each derivation begins with a numeration, a selection of forms from the lexicon, and they are built into trees by the operations move and merge. When merge and move have exhausted the numeration and all uninterpretable features introduced into the derivation have been checked and erased, the derivation converges, which is to say the result is a well-formed representation. It would appear that the mechanisms that construct representations such as these do not necessarily speak to the question of how these representations are interpreted.

Except for LAL, the principles I have proposed do not contribute to the calculation of convergence; rather almost all of them serve to limit the class of interpretations that are possible for sentences that are otherwise convergent. As I shall demonstrate in 7.1, there are other principles, principles that are not directly principles of anaphora, that have the same key properties; that is, they apply only to convergent forms and serve only to determine and restrict the range of possible interpretations for convergent derivations. In other words, I will argue that most of the principles I propose are outside the calculation of convergence *because they are contingent on interpretive possibilities permitted by formal grammar*. From this perspective, the difference between principles that regulate convergence and those that regulate how convergent output is interpreted is one between components.

Like the derivation-building component, the interpretive component consists of both *unary* constraints and *competitive algorithmic* (*c-algorithmic*) constraints. C-algorithmic constraints always involve the comparison of operations or representations by some sort of algorithm that selects the best result. By *unary constraints,* I mean constraints that do not have to compare operations or representations to determine whether a given operation or structural representation is permitted, either with respect to convergence or with respect to a particular interpretation.

Minimality effects appear to be violations of a unary prohibition, since in some formulations, no intervener of the right type can be moved across, and in its strongest form, this means that no such operation could occur in a convergent derivation. Alternatively, one could allow operations to violate minimality, and the unary constraint could apply to the resulting representation, in which case more than one minimality violation might be predicted to be worse than just one, but each violation could be detected without comparison to other derivations or representations. In other words, the effects on acceptability may be flexible or variable, but the constraint is unary because it is not comparative. The Independence Principle, LAL, and the two coargument-related principles, the CDC and the LRP, are unary constraints in this sense, since their application does not require comparisons with other structures or operations.

The FTIP is clearly a c-algorithmic interpretive constraint, since it is executed by a competitive algorithm and chooses among convergent results. Typical formulations of minimalist economy constraints are c-algorithmic in this sense, as is the central algorithm of optimality theory (OT), but neither economy nor OT competition are interpretive in the sense I mean, since they contribute directly to convergence.

## 7.1 A Syntax-Sensitive Interpretive Module

Almost all the anaphora principles I have proposed are part of a syntax-sensitive semantic component that determines (and thereby limits) the class of possible interpretations for a structure that is well formed (converges) under the application of interpretation-blind derivation building. This section is devoted to fleshing out this interpretive component, highlighting its crucial properties, and explaining what alternatives to a modular approach would have to be committed to.

The claim that there are interpretive constraints that apply in a manner outside of those that determine the convergence of semantically uninterpreted forms is not unfamiliar historically, as it has generally been assumed that the LF component is a syntax-sensitive interpretive component. Even within minimalist theorizing, which has been preoccupied with the reduction of levels as a core motivation for theoretical design, interpretive principles applying to the output of convergent derivations have been proposed.[1] For example, Fox (1995, 2000) has proposed that LF-movement of quantifiers or quantified expressions only occurs if its effects are nonvacuous for interpretation, a principle he calls *scope economy*. For examples like (1), which is ambiguous depending on whether or not the existential or the universal has wide scope, LF-movement is only licensed to change the interpretation that would result if neither quantifier is moved by covert operations specific to quantifiers (indices below are illustrative only).

1a) $[_{IP}$ some student loves every professor]
b) *$[_{IP}$ [some student]$_i$ $[_{IP}$ $t_i$ loves every professor]]
c) $[_{IP}$ [every professor]$_i$ $[_{IP}$ someone loves $t_i$]]
d) *$[_{IP}$ [some student$_i$] $[_{IP}$ [every professor$_j$] $[_{IP}$ $t_i$ loves $t_j$]]]

Wide scope for the existential is achieved for this example if no LF-movement applies, as in (1a); hence raising *some student* by an LF operation would be vacuous with respect to relative scope and would be disallowed as in (1b). LF-movement of *every professor* is possible because the result would yield wide scope for the universal, as in (1c). LF-movement of the existential to a position higher than that of the raised universal expression would reverse scope again as in (1d), but it would not yield a result distinct in interpretation from the very first derivation, where no LF-movement is required at all and is thus disallowed.

As Fox observes, scope economy can only be measured with respect to a specified interpretation, in which case there must also be some sort of monitor that knows when two syntactically derived representations represent identical scope relations. He posits that this is measured in binary fashion; that is, for any two quantifiers, A and B, the QR of A must reverse its relative scope from B > A to A > B, and no other derivation would result in A > B with less effort. What is similar to the FTIP in this account is that (a) scope economy only regulates operations on representations that converge independently of scope determination, (b) scope economy is a c-algorithmic constraint that picks the optimal representation from a class of competitors, and (c) participation in the competition is conditioned by a specified interpretation.

Fox (1998, 2000) proposes another strictly interpretive constraint, Rule H, that must be understood as c-algorithmic. Rule H is part of what is responsible for the contrast between the covariant dependent reading possible for (2a) versus the absence of that reading for (3a).

2a) *Every woman* thought that *only she* voted for *her.*

b) *Every woman* thought that *only she* voted for *herself/*her.*

3a) **Every woman* thinks that *she* trusted *her.*

b) *Every woman* thinks that *she* trusts *herself/*her.*

Recall from the discussion in 4.1 that the difference in interpretation between (2a) and (2b) is that (2a) allows the inference that each woman believes that she only got one vote, while (2b) allows the inference that each woman believes that none of the other women voted for themselves, though each woman may have got a number of votes. Presumably, Pragmatic Obviation is overcome for the relation between *she* and *her* because *only* introduces an expectation that counters obviation. Recall that LRP will not permit *herself* to support the independent covariant interpretation. However, given that the reading in (2a) can be successfully represented, why isn't that representation available for (3a) on the basis of similar examples pointed out by Higginbotham (1985, 570) and as pointed out in note 6 of chapter 4? It seems there would be no difference in meaning between (3a) and (3b), since there is no distinction between *she* and *her* in (3a) as there is in (2a), but our system permits a dependency relation wherever one does not lead to some violation. For cases like (3a), it appears our system makes available a potentially large class of suspiciously superfluous representations.

Suppose, by contrast, we take the general tack that the pattern of dependencies in (3a) is generally excluded unless some factor intervenes, as in the case of (2a), to make it possible. The key factor, as both Heim (1993) and Reinhart (1997) assume, is that *only* introduces a separate operator on which the direct object can depend or not, while examples like (3a, b) have only a single operator on which the pronouns could depend. The key assumption that Fox introduces is that in the absence of such an intervening operator, the chained arrows of (2b) and (3b) are always the preferred pattern. Fox calls this preference *Rule H*, and it is presented in (4) as I reformulate it in the language of dependency rather than binding, which assumes coindexing (for discussion of the differences between Fox's interpretation of the rule and mine, see Safir (2004).[2]

4) Rule H: A variable, *x,* cannot be dependent on an antecedent, α, in case *x* could be dependent on a more local c-commanding antecedent, β, and yield the same semantic interpretation.

Rule H as formulated requires us to choose the representation in (3b) over that in (3a), unless we have a contrast in meaning, as we do between (2a) and (2b), thanks to the presence of a second operator. If (3b) is the only pattern of dependencies allowed for the sentence in (3), then the pronoun is obviated by the SELF form, in accordance with FTIP.

Now what is of particular interest to us is that Rule H is a crucial interpretive constraint choosing between two converging possibilities where a specific interpretation is held constant. In this way it is quite similar to FTIP, but FTIP compares numerations that lead to convergent derivations, while Rule H compares dependency patterns, as notated by arrows, that lead to convergent derivations. It is also a c-algorithmic constraint, in that two representations or more are compared and the best is chosen (the one with the most chaining under c-command). Thus Rule H rightfully belongs in the syntax-sensitive interpretive component.

It is not immediately obvious why a principle such as Rule H should exist, but it turns out to have a very interesting relationship to FTIP that is suggestive. As Geoffrey Pullum (personal communication) points out to me, the efficiency of the FTIP for an example like (5), where every form is ultimately dependent on *Shane*, might be questionable if every c-commanding potential antecedent for *him* could involve a separate FTIP competition with respect to the lowest *his*. The latter situation might obtain if the representation for (5) is one of the many possible ones illustrated under (5a), such as the one where the lowest *his* depends directly on *Shane*, or indirectly on *Shane* via the highest *he*, and so forth.

5a) *Shane* says *he* thinks *he* should have brought *his* picture of *his* mother.

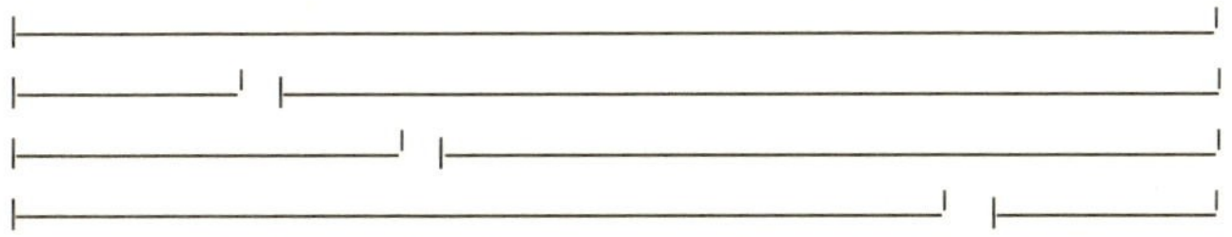

b) *Shane* says *he* thinks *he* should have brought *his* picture of *his* mother.

If Rule H did not exist, then the FTIP would have to run competitions for each potential antecedent that the lowest *his* might directly depend on to determine whether or not *his* is the most dependent form to represent that hypothetical relation, yet only the lowest c-commanding antecedent, as in (5b), matters for the choice of form. Fortunately, the efficiency of the FTIP is ensured by Rule H, which requires the lowest *his* to be directly dependent on the next lowest *his* as in (5b), unless some other factor, such as stress or quantification, intervenes to permit a distinct dependent interpretation on an antecedent other than the lowest potential c-commanding one. The fact that Rule H is a constraint that greatly facilitates the efficiency of the FTIP may not be an accidental factor in its origin.

Another likely c-algorithmic interpretive constraint is the WPC, as discussed in 6.1.1 and 6.1.3. Recall that this competition is between more and less tonic pronouns, if not also between names and these pronouns, in order to represent reference to old information in a discourse. Unlike the FTIP, c-command plays no role in the WPC, nor is the position of the antecedent in the discourse important, as long as reference is to a backgrounded, previously mentioned topic. In these circumstances, the weakest pronoun available must be employed if this reading is to be represented, the measure of strength usually being one of phonological weight, where the weakest pronoun is null in those languages that permit it (see Bresnan, 2001, where the scale in (6) is examined in some detail from an OT perspective).[3] At least this seems to be an accurate way to characterize where null subjects in tensed sentences are permitted in the Romance languages, as argued by Samek-Lodovici (1995). The WPC has much in common with the FTIP. It could proceed as follows:

6a) WPC: To determine whether a given form (or null pronoun) is permitted to represent the backgrounded topic, pick a weaker pronoun on the scale, substitute it in the numeration for the given form, and see if the derivation converges. If substitution with a weaker form converges, then the given form cannot represent the backgrounded topic reading. If no substituted form converges, then the given form can represent the backgrounded topic reading.

b) null pronoun >> clitic >> destressed pronoun >> tonic pronoun >> r-expression

Once again, the competition is between convergent derivations. Notice that it is not even necessary to refer to the antecedent in the algorithm, since all that is determined is whether or not the form *could* represent a previously mentioned topic, not whether or not it does. In this respect it differs from FTIP, which is determined with respect to a particular antecedent in a structural relation with the dependent. Notice also that the algorithm will quickly arrive at a result, since the scale, even for a language that permits the widest range of possibilities, is still very limited, as in (6b), and not every language will have a representative of every member of the scale.

Turning now to unary constraints, the Independence Principle clearly belongs in the syntax-sensitive interpretive component, since it never applies to rule out the derivational output D on the grounds that D has no interpretation. In other words, every sentence the Independence Principle applies to is convergent in the syntax and has a grammatical interpretation where no dependency relation is posited. Consider, for example, (7a), which is ruled out by the Independence Principle, a principle extended to weak crossover cases like (7b) in Safir (2004).

7a) Castro fell on himself.

b) His mother saw everyone.

Though *his* cannot depend on *everyone* in (7b), the sentence is thoroughly acceptable if *his* refers freely. Similarly, (7a) cannot refer to a statue of Castro falling on Castro, though it is perfectly acceptable if Castro, the man, falls on his statue (or if his torso were to fall on his disembodied legs; see 4.2.1). CDC likewise limits interpretations rather than convergence, such that *John and Mary saw him* is grammatical as long as *him* does not depend on *John*. (Although the matter is slightly more subtle, the same case can be made for LRP). In other words, if dependency arrows play no role in convergence, then any constraint that refers to them does not contribute to convergence.

By comparison, LAL, my version of the venerable Principle A, is a unary constraint that applies within syntax to limit the class of convergent derivations. An anaphor that does not respect LAL is not available to participate in the FTIP calculation precisely because it does not participate in a convergent derivation. Similarly, forms that don't have the right agreement or Case features to result in proper feature checking are also forms that are unavailable. These kinds of limitations on the available forms were discussed as scalar interventions in chapter 3, and LAL may be seen as a scalar intervention in this sense.

Notice, incidentally, that the c-antecede notion that is used to state LAL in 3.2.1 does not ensure that a syntactic anaphor must depend on its c-antecedent. Although we must ensure that the antecedent that licenses an anaphor is at least covariant with what that anaphor depends on, we can otherwise treat the c-antecedent as an interpretation-blind licensing element. Since we have assumed that anaphors are a subset of inherently dependent (deictically deficient) forms, it then follows from Rule H that an anaphor will have to depend on its most local c-commanding antecedent, except in cases like the O.J. ECM examples discussed in 4.1.1 and repeated in (8), and for English reciprocals in examples like (9).

8a) Everyone expects O.J. to be acquitted.
  b) Bill expects him to be acquitted.
     Sarah expects him to be acquitted . . .
  c) *Even O.J.* expects *him* to be acquitted.
  d) *Even O.J.* expects *himself* to be acquitted.
  9) *The men* think *they* are taller than *each other*.

As noted in the appendix to chapter 6 (note 2), (9) permits two interpretations, one nonsensical and local and the other scoping over the men's beliefs. Since there is no LRP-like constraint that requires local-dependency reciprocals, we predict the possibility that a distinct interpretation should permit *each other* to be locally c-anteceded by *they* but directly dependent on *the men*. This is not a superfluous reading since it corresponds to the wide scope one, and if c-antecedency required direct dependency, it would fail.[4] Since the wide scope reading is a distinct reading from the local one, it is permitted by Rule H.

Thus, in addition to the FTIP, there are at least three other competitions that compare convergent derivations in order to narrow interpretive possibilities. Each member of this family of c-algorithmic constraints addresses itself to a different interpretive limitation. Additional unary constraints, which regulate the distribution of dependency arrows, are also relevant to postconvergence interpretation, and it is possible that the arrows themselves, if they belong in representations at all, only enter derivations after convergence, where they then may be distributed, as part of formal representation, in any way that is not blocked by some constraint.[5] I have gathered these constraints, unary and c-algorithmic, into a postconvergence interpretive component, but it is worth considering whether some different models of the relation between syntactic derivation and interpretation might as easily accommodate the constraints I have discussed so far.

## 7.2 Totalist Versus Modular Competition

A totalist competition assumes that a single competitive principle finds the best representation or operation with respect to every aspect of representations or operations. For example, suppose there are five dimensions with respect to which the LF of a given numeration can be optimal, but no operation or representation can satisfy ultimate optimality on any dimension. Suppose that there are five points for each of the five dimensions, and the optimal result is one that scores perhaps as high as 18 of 25 possible points. In this way of measuring the optimal output, choosing the most dependent form to represent a dependency may turn out to be less important than high scores in some other dimensions. For example, if the most dependent form raises the score in one dimension by one but lowers the scores for two other dimensions, it is less optimal. In such a case, the highest score for any given dimension may be incompatible with the best choice to satisfy the dependency relation. Ranking the dimensions, such that satisfying one dimension is more important than satisfying another as in OT is just another way of dealing with the fact that for any given dimension other than the highest ranking one, the optimal choice is very likely not permitted by the totalist competitive algorithm. Thus it is often said from the OT perspective that constraints are violable, with a measurable cost, depending on how a constraint is ranked.

The c-algorithmic constraints discussed in the last section are not conceived of in a totalist system, be it one based on a general notion of economy or on the central OT algorithm. In effect, the constraints I have proposed are rigid and unviolable, such that the optimal form must be selected from each particular scale if a given interpretation is to be permissible. In this respect, the success of the FTIP as I have formulated it is evidence that it should not be part of the convergence calculation, since that success is predicated on abstracting away from the factors determining which forms are available. The same may be said of the WPC, but I have not really made that case here.

It is possible to imagine, however, that the FTIP and the other interpretive constraints could be integrated with the factors determining convergence if and only if the desired interpretation were part of the input. Then the fact that c-algorithmic constraints have commonalities could be reduced to the fact that they are part of the same calculation. The fact that the FTIP is inviolable would, for example, be a fact about the totalized competitive algorithm, which is inviolable in that it always picks the optimal representation or derivation.

There are, however, certain architectural limitations on how this can be expressed in totalist calculations. For both minimalist and OT calculations, the input is not normally assumed to include interpretations. In minimalism, interpretations are read off the result of the convergent derivation, whereas in most OT accounts, the issue is simply not clarified. If dependency relations are relations between phrases, then representing dependency relations as part of the input would be difficult for either theory, since phrases are not part of the input in either theory. For example, if the phrase *his brother* is the antecedent for *himself* in *his brother praised himself*, it would be necessary to ensure that the full phrase is the antecedent, not just *brother* or *his*. In short, it is not clear that every relevant aspect of interpretation is expressible in the input.

One way to express dependencies in the input would be to calculate dependency as relations between theta roles, as proposed in Williams (1994). Now let us suppose that theta assignment is part of the input, along with dependency arrows connecting theta roles, even before they enter the OT GEN operation, which generates the set of competitors, or minimalist derivation-building operations. This would mean first making a selection of forms bearing theta roles and then adding the asymmetric connections between theta roles in the otherwise unstructured input. The arrows, now conceived of as a crucial part of syntax, would end up relating syntactic positions on the basis of how the theta-bearing elements are built into structures.

There are several sorts of concerns that arise with respect to this way of totalizing the competition. The first is that not every form clearly represents a theta role, depending on what sort of analysis is accorded to forms like Dutch *zich* when it occurs in inherent reflexive constructions or middle formations. In other words, some exploration of what it is to represent a theta role for dependency relations would have to be examined. Second, theta assignment would have to be inherently asymmetric in a way that reflects c-command relations between arguments. These issues are explored in the appendix to chapter 4 where a structural account is favored, but the same generalizations could presumably be achieved by whatever needs to be said to generate the trees c-command is calculated on there (although one would have to scrutinize carefully how it is done).

Another difficulty that may be tricky to overcome in a natural way is that some thematic assignments are not based on selectional relations that could naturally be expressed in the lexicon. The possessor of *his rock* is not selected by *rock*, although some possessors do seem capable of bearing a lexically specific thematic role, as in *his attacker* or *their/*his dispersal*. If thematic roles such as the possessor in *his/the general's rock* only arise as a result of structural relations built by a derivation, then dependency relations cannot be part of an OT or minimalist input.

An even more difficult problem is posed by what it would mean to incorporate scope relations into the unstructured input, especially since scope is not always expressed on theta-role-bearing units but can also be expressed on adjuncts. For these cases, it is hard to see how scope economy could judge the best result on the basis of "the same interpretation" as input.[6]

From the perspective of minimalist economy, including a target proposition as part of the input would also be problematic for any theory of local economy. Local economy determines what the best operation to perform would be at any point in a derivation, the choices being to either merge or move, where each of these either diminishes the numeration or satisfies some feature-checking requirement. Such a process cannot be conditioned by a target proposition. For example, certain kinds of embedding are absolute barriers to scopal interaction, which could only be checked against the output; for instance, if the input has scope of *every* over *some* and the result is *Someone says Mary saw everyone*, some condition uniquely on output has to say that this sentence cannot support that meaning. This is probably one reason that Fox formulates scope economy as a competition that compares convergent derivations.

In fact, if one c-algorithmic constraint stands outside the totalized competition, the argument to derive competitive properties from totalization is immediately compromised. The issue can also be obscured by theoretical architecture, however. Suppose that it is true of Rule H that it is inviolable where no ambiguities are introduced by extra operators (I have not established this). It could be said of Rule H that it is always ranked very high, for example, in an OT system, such that no language ranks it low enough for it ever to be violated. However, this is much like setting it outside the central algorithm—the only reason for keeping it within the optimality calculation is that it is c-algorithmic. If even one c-algorithmic constraint can be outside of the totalized competition, then the parsimony argument against the existence of more is weaker, as it is parsimony based only on quantity rather than kind.

However, one practical argument against totalized competition is that it is an extremely difficult system in which to conduct an empirical investigation, since the calculations are so complex when so many ranked constraints must be evaluated for every aspect of a structure. No single constraint can be reliably investigated without taking into account every other, and hence an enormous number of possible constraint interactions. By presuming that the competitors are determined separately, the function of the WPC and the FTIP permit more transparent empirical investigation.

Indeed, this way of breaking down a problem into simple and transparent calculations may have a certain resonance with respect to computability. The algorithms that determine the winner are very simple and efficient, as they consider very few alternatives. Thus, unlike the totalized competition, *modular* competition requires many simple calculations for each sentence, as opposed to one very complex one. It is perhaps premature to judge the computability question, but the practical advantages for empirical study are clear.

There is, however, a more important reason to favor modular competitions. For a totalized competition, any derivation that is not relatively optimal in every respect is unacceptable. In a modular competition theory, a derivation can be optimal with respect to the principles of anaphora and nonoptimal with respect to other principles. This suggests that our judgments about the acceptability of sentences may permit degrees or qualities of acceptability to be distinguished, where the cause of these distinctions arises from the organization of formal grammar itself, rather than a homogenized strict binary prediction (grammatical vs. ungrammatical). In other words, a linguistic informant can say that a given sentence is optimal in every way but one, and some judgments of unacceptability for certain violations are known to be sharper than others. While I am not advocating that native speakers have intuitions about theory, in practice, every speaker is capable of modular and scalar judgments of acceptability, and some have insightful observations about what has gone wrong when a sentence is unacceptable in some specific way. Such an ability would be surprising from the perspective of a totalized competition theory.

The need for more than one competition has been acknowledged in the OT literature somewhat explicitly. For example, Burzio points out that his referential economy approach might be adapted to an OT model, but in so doing he remarks that "in some cases optimization involves choosing the best form consistent with a specific interpretation, while in others it involves choosing amongst interpretations consistent with a fixed form . . . . This means that constraints that need to interact with one another are in fact evaluating different sets of candidates, raising questions for the exact formalization of OT machinery" (1998, 105–106). These issues are taken up by Wilson (2001), who attempts to construct an OT formalization that explicitly develops Burzio's theory in terms of two competitions.[7]

Thus it appears that the c-algorithmic interpretive constraints proposed here must stand outside of the convergence calculation, and if so, c-algorithmic constraints do not reduce to any single competitive calculation. This conclusion reinforces that of the previous section, which argues that c-algorithmic interpretive constraints belong to an interpretive component operating outside the convergence calculation.

## 7.3 Design and Explanation

Since the focus of minimalist theorizing has been the determination and reduction of the principles that regulate convergent derivations, modular distinctions, while available in principle (in the form of distinctions between the sensory–motor interface vs. the interpretive interface, for example), have not been so frequently appealed to (with exceptions I will mention). Indeed one of the strategies of the MP has been to reduce the minimodular character of the LGB subtheories to the interaction of principles that structure derivations, such as move, merge, and the theory of features, and the principle(s) that choose one derivation over another as optimal, either by comparing possible subsequent operations at a given point in a derivation (local economy) or by choosing between complete derivations that could be formed on a given numeration (global economy). In the best case, it could be said that Case theory, agreement, and perhaps even theta theory are subsumed under feature theory and Chomsky's (1998) probe theory, where strategies of feature checking motivate movement to SPEC or incorporation to determine the distribution of case, theta roles, and agreement.

Yet, as a matter of theoretical design, it has not always been assumed that the best theory would be one in which very general but very flexible principles should determine the heart of the theoretical architecture of the theory. It is perhaps useful to recall that the modular character of the government-binding era of principles and parameters theorizing was seen at the time as one of its strengths. The development of the principles and parameters theory was a direct reaction to approaches of the late 1960s and 1970s where the flexibility of general rule formats permitted too many descriptions. For example, the two central rule formats of that era, phrase structure rules and transformations, were constrained by X'-theory and Boolean conditions on analyzability, respectively, in order to restrict their power, *but also to refine the division of labor*. Thus the subtheories of LGB served to compensate for some of the lost descriptive power, while at the same time breaking down that power into streamlined, relatively homogeneous minimodules.

The lesson of that era is that it is not necessarily more explanatory to reduce every sort of phenomenon to central principles if the price is a central principle or set of central principles that is too flexible, too permissive. For example, it has been suggested by Hornstein (1999, 2001) and Kayne (2001) that coconstrual itself can be reduced to movement, but in order to achieve the so-called reduction, movement for coconstrual turns out to have properties that are not permitted for any other sort of movement, such that the notion "movement" itself becomes so general as to be without explanatory force, as I argue in Safir (2003, 2004; with a preview in note 19 of chapter 2). Instead of reducing the central principles I have proposed to basic operations, a result to be welcomed if it is explanatory, I have confined them to a component where a more task-specific family of algorithms builds interpretations on the output of a minimalist syntax. It is still before us to consider whether or not deeper understanding can be achieved by reducing the anaphora principles studied here to more general principles underlying disparate phenomena, without either debasing the explanatory force of the general principles or cluttering the latter with relations external to their nature. Yet precisely where that enterprise can begin, this one must conclude.

# NOTES

## Chapter 1

1. This is largely taken for granted within the generativist literature on anaphora, although the point has been challenged from time to time. For discussion of one such challenge, see 3.1.2.1.

2. It is not my intention to present a history of theories of anaphora within generative grammar, but see chapter 1 of Lasnik (1989) for a very useful discussion of a portion of that history. Alternative theories of anaphoric phenomena are often modeled on the LGB discussion, including that of Pollard and Sag (1994) couched within HPSG, for example (see the appendix to chapter 4 for discussion).

3. As is standard, I do not assume that if X refers, then it refers to something that exists, since it is obviously possible for one nominal to depend on another for its reference and for that referent not to actually exist, as in the case of references to mythical creatures and the like, for example, *The unicorn injured itself.* I shall also restrict my discussion in this work to the relations between structurally represented nominals, and so I shall have nothing to say about anaphoric tenses and the like (see, e.g., Partee 1973).

4. Further adjustments to this domain, such as SUBJECT, I shall largely ignore. Those interested in some of the further adjustments in the LGB account of this domain should consult Lasnik's (1989) summary.

5. Issues arise as to whether or not anaphors contained in displaced constituents are evaluated on the basis of their predisplaced conditions (reconstruction) or on the basis of the position they are in after displacement. These issues are discussed in some detail in Safir (2004).

6. Not everyone regards (26) as fully acceptable. See the appendix to chapter 4.

7. For example, it might be assumed that *himself* moves to the SPEC Agr-O (of the higher clause, in the case of [28b]), voiding the barrierhood of the matrix VP, or else it might be assumed that the matrix is an L-marker (within the assumptions of the barriers framework). Similarly it is assumed that PP is not a barrier in (26), since the P is selected by *appear.*

8. This section draws heavily on my discussion in Safir (1997, 346–349).

9. It will be argued in 5.1 that the locality of chain-link relations is different than the locality imposed by restrictions on syntactic anaphors.

10. Indeed, Reinhart (1983a, 160) does not see indices as specifically necessary to represent the relations she posits. In a later version of this theory, Reinhart (1997) rejects the use of indices altogether (under the influence of Chomsky and Lasnik 1995), replacing them with the lambda notation conditioned by c-command. As discussed in 2.4, I will not employ indices either.

## Chapter 2

1. For example, it has been argued that the tense of a sentence can refer to events relative to the time of utterance in a manner that is anaphoric, both across discourse and with respect to sentence internal relations. For instance, a sentence like *Saul said Larry left three hours before then* can mean that Larry left three hours before some time prior to Saul's speech act (i.e., more than three hours before), or *then* could refer to three hours counting back from the moment of Saul's utterance, in which case *then* is anaphoric to a time expressed in the tense of the matrix clause. I will not be discussing any research on tense or sequence of tense here, but for recent work with references, see Bittner (1999), Schlenker (1999), and Kamp and Reyle (1993).

2. Dependent identity readings are a subset of covariant readings. See 4.1 for discussion of cases where covariant nominals do not depend either one on the other.

3. For example, imagine two strangers in a crowd witnessing the police involved in a violent arrest, and one stranger turns to the other and says, "They didn't have to hit him."

4. Evans (1980) distinguishes a class of pronouns that are coconstrued with a quantified nominal but are not bound pronouns dependent on their antecedents. He notes the following difference:

i. Socrates owns *a dog* and *it* bit Socrates
ii. Socrates owns *a dog* which bites *its* tail

In i., *it* is the unique dog that Socrates owns and that bit Socrates, whereas ii. is true if, out of any number of dogs that Socrates owns, one of them bites its tail. True bound variable dependence is regulated by c-command, according to Evans, whereas cases like i. are what he calls "E-type" pronouns. E-type pronouns are not in the scope of the quantified nominals to which they are related, or *it* in i. would not have the uniqueness interpretation that shows it is outside the scope of the existential (Evans 1980, 342–343). E-type pronouns are incompatible with a number of quantifiers, such as negation.

iii. *Many senators* admire Kennedy, but *they* are very junior.
iv. **No/every senator* admires Kennedy, but *he/they* is/are very junior.

Evans and just about every researcher since have treated E-type pronouns as ruled by scopal generalizations separate from those that determine the success or failure of quantified bound anaphora that is internal to the sentence, and with this division I concur, though my account of dependency will permit dependencies like that between *many senators* and *they* in iii. Ueyama (1998), for example, introduces a special indexing and dependency relationship in addition to formal dependency and distinct from coreference based on coindexing to account for a wide (and interesting) range of E-type cases in Japanese. I shall have very little to say about E-type pronouns.

5. This characterization of the facts about epithets needs to be reevaluated in light of some logophoric factors pointed out by Dubinsky and Hamilton (1998). See Safir (in preparation).

6. For some of the formative discussions, see Williams (1977) and Sag (1976).

7. For more on the interpretation of first person, see 6.3.4 and Safir (in preparation).

8. For one class of cases that must be distinguished from those in (23) and (24), see note 4 to this chapter on E-type anaphora.

9. In the appendix to Lasnik (1976) he cites quantifier judgments now considered nonstandard; for example, he stars *Noone's mother loves him* under the bound reading, though most speakers accept this.

10. Chomsky (1981) attributes strong crossover to the effects of Principle C under the assumption that wh-trace-variables are treated as names. This sort of approach is rejected for most A'-movements in Safir (2004).

11. Earlier formulations did not distinguish this principle from what became Principle C or else limited "X" to pronouns. See Keenan (1974), for example, who suggests that a pronoun cannot be the argument of a function that contains its antecedent, which if the subject is a function of VP, will have the effect of c-command in most cases. On the differences between the force of the Independence Principle in (39) and those effects that have been attributed to principle C, see 4.2.1 and Safir (2004) where the force of the Independence Principle is explored at length.

12. A different account of cases like those in (45a, b) is briefly presented in 7.1, where Rule H is discussed.

13. Indices have been employed for a wide variety of relations in generative grammar over the years, including to mark relations of agreement and syntactic chain relations that do not arise from movement (see, e.g., Safir, 1985, for discussion) as well as conditions on extraction such as ECP (see, e.g., Rizzi, 1990b, for distinctions between referential and nonreferential indices). In most instances, indices used for these purposes were based on the assumption that an indexing device is necessary for antecedent–trace relations in any case. I will not explore what the abandonment of indices would mean for these other relations.

14. In the system I develop in 2.5 and chapter 3, (64) does not permit *they* to depend on *Tom* or *Harry*, since *they* c-commands them, but coreference is not excluded.

15. Partitives of this sort are either not indefinite descriptions at all, or they are specific indefinites, since we can have *The men walked in. One of them sat down*, which would otherwise be expected to fail, as in *The men walked in. A man sat down*, where it is vague at best as to whether the man that sat down could be one of those that walked in or not. Judgments for existential sentences like *There is one of them in the room* appear to be very sensitive to context and have some of the flavor of list sentences, so I take it to be unclear, in this instance, as a test for indefiniteness.

16. Insofar as one accepts (52c), it does not support a sloppy reading in an ellipsis environment.

i. Every little boy thinks that little boy should be loved and every father does too.

If one allows F&M's vehicle change to reconstruct *that little boy* in this ellipsis environment as a pronoun, then one might expect that the pronoun could have a dependent reading with *every father*, which seems false. This suggests that there is something odd in the dependency relation between *that little boy* and its antecedent that is unlike that between quantifiers and pronouns. It could be that this usage of demonstratives involves a quantificational structure for *that little boy*, much like those cases discussed with respect to Rule H in 7.1 and Safir (2004), such that *only he* can break the chain of dependencies for "*Each boy* thinks that *only he* loves *his* mother," at least for one of the interpretations of sentences like this I discuss there. What is interesting for our immediate concerns is that a sloppy interpretation fails for "*Marcy* thinks *only she* is smart and Prunella does too." It appears that the anaphoric use of *that boy* has quantificational force in a similar way (and is marginal in that usage), but it does not have the exclusive meaning of *only*. In Safir (2004) it is argued to be a general condition on vehicle change that it cannot replace unpronounced quantified nominals (or the traces they would leave after LF-movement) with pronouns. If vehicle change is blocked for principled reasons here, then the absence of the bound interpretation for i. follows, since reconstructing *that little boy* will not match *every father*.

17. Farmer (1987) points out some interesting cases where disjoint reference is the wrong description of a noncoreference effect such as **John cramps his style* as opposed to *The men cramped each other's styles*.

18. For further arguments against c-command by the antecedent as a necessary condition on the dependency relation, see Safir (2004), where I also argue against Williams's (1994, 1997) contention that precedence is crucial for certain forms of dependency.

19. In recent work by Hornstein (1999, 2001) and Kayne (2001), it is proposed that all coconstrual relations should be derived from movement relations. What appears to be misunderstood in these proposals is that some pronouns do not have linguistic antecedents, and so not all pronouns can be derived as the spellout of movement to an antecedent position (e.g., A heavily perfumed woman exits a crowded elevator and one relieved occupant exclaims to no one in particular "Thank goodness she left."). If this is so, some additional principle must require a pronoun to have a linguistic antecedent *if possible*, or else the problem of accidental coreference, which Kayne (2001) in particular claims to resolve, still arises. Moreover, "movement" must then become highly unfamiliar, in that it must be permitted to non-c-commanding positions and across islands, across independent sentences and even across different speakers if movement to an antecedent is to be possible as required. Even in a theory that eschews covert movement, like Kayne's (2001), it is not obvious that anaphora should be reduced to overt movement. For a discussion and critique of these proposals, see Safir (2003, 2004).

20. This argument will have to be revised somewhat in light of the argumentation in Dubinsky and Hamilton (1998), where it is demonstrated that c-commanding coreferent A-position is possible for epithets outside of logophoric contexts. The issues surrounding this question are interesting and addressed in Safir (in preparation). The gist of it is that epithets are in competition with pronouns only in logophoric contexts; hence only in those contexts will the pronoun obviate the epithet. This move will seem more natural once it is demonstrated that pronouns of different sorts, sorts that normally do not compete, do compete in logophoric contexts in some languages, such that one obviates the other. I must then conclude, however, that epithets have the status of, or contain, pronouns in those environments (a possibility considered in Aoun and Choueiri 2000) where they can appear with a c-commanding antecedent.

21. There are languages where principle C does not appear to hold, as discussed, for example, by Demirdache (1997). She suggests that Lillooet Salish lacks presuppositional determiners, which under my set of assumptions, would mean that it is not dependent on any preceding nominal. If a Lillooet Salish r-expression is never dependent, then it is not available for that interpretation, so FTIP does not apply to it and Pragmatic Obviation is thus not triggered. Thus a Lillooet Salish r-expression should be allowed to corefer with a c-commanding antecedent. Coreference is not possible for r-expressions with coargument antecedents, however, which does not appear to be expected under my proposal.

22. For example, the Independence Principle rules out the possibility that in *He said Mary saw him* that *he* could depend on *him* (see also 4.1). Since dependency holds even where

quantification does not and since QR is limited by some class of islands, there will be domains where dependency is possible, but a quantifier does not have scope to bind a pronoun. These issues will be studied further in chapter 4, where aspects of dependency in reflexivity are discussed, and especially in Safir (2004), where the weak crossover phenomenon and other aspects of syntactically influenced bound variable readings will be examined.

## Chapter 3

1. The earliest statement of the competition idea with the explicit assumption that Principle B is derivable is embodied in this quote from Pica (1986), summarizing Pica (1984a): "Nous avons proposé . . . une théorie dans laquelle le principe (B) n'existe pas . . . . Un pronom α ne doit être libre dans sa catégorie gouvernante γ que si, et seulement si, il existe une anaphore β (de même sens) pouvant être employée à la place de α dans γ." [We have proposed a theory in which Principle B does not exist. A pronoun α must be free in its governing category γ if and only if there exists an anaphor β (having the same meaning) that could be employed in the place of α in γ] (196; my translation). In many ways, this is the essence of the approach adopted here, although the principle of complementarity stated this way is too specific, in that it does not also include competitions between anaphors or between pronouns and names. See Bouchard (1984, 58), who also proposes to derive Principle B, but does so by proposing a principle that says a local bound reading must be morphologically reflexive—which closely approaches R&R's later version of Principle B. Williams (2003) also offers a competition account based on the notion of "blocking" often appealed to in morphology (see also Williams 1997), although it is embedded in his theory of multiple representation levels, which does not permit easy comparison with the approach offered here. I refer the interested reader to his account and pass over it for reasons of space.

2. See Burzio (1991, 101–103) for the first discussion of the PRO theorem from the perspective of derived complementarity.

3. See, for example Dalrymple's discussion where she has to stipulate as a universal, "The domain of the negative constraint is not wider than the domain of the positive constraint" (1993, 167).

4. Readers less interested in the historical antecedents of the approach adopted here may choose to skip the rest of 3.1.2 and read the summary of it in 3.1.3, though some additional arguments for derived complementarity are embedded in 3.1.2.1 through 3.1.2.3.

5. Chierchia (1995, 168) mistakenly argues that *Which pictures that John took did he hang himself?* is predicted to be grammatical by Reinhart's rule of substitution, since *himself* cannot be substituted for either *he* or *John*. However, *him* is possible in place of *John*. Chierchia appears to assume that the substituting form interpreted as a variable must literally be *himself* in English.

6. This critique extends to Levinson's (1987) account insofar as he seeks to claim Dowty's (1980) approach as consistent with his own (see Levinson 1987, 413, fn. 40), and also to the account of Roberts (1987, 81) who attempts to extend an "avoid ambiguity" pragmatic version of Reinhart's (1983a) approach to pronouns.

7. Levinson (1991, 128, fn. 26) quotes Bite as follows: "It is typical of the functionalist perspective to be rather blasé about its radical innatist tendencies while taking more serious proposals to task." Levinson (1991) is gracious to quote his critic, but the criticism seems amply justified.

8. Huang (1991, 1994, 2000) also argues for a pragmatic reduction of the anaphora questions, but his account is mixed, treating some languages as having grammatically determined pattern of anaphora, and others, like Chinese, as having a pragmatically determined pattern (as these patterns are part of a general set of distinctions, between the different language types,

some not related to anaphora—see Huang 2000, ch. 4.4)). He is correct to point out that a hybrid account of this sort cannot be sustained in an LGB-like theory, since such a great difference is unlikely to arise from a parameter (and could not possibly be a parameter within the universalist theory proposed here—see 5.2 and chapter 6). However, I do not find his pragmatic account convincing, both for reasons already cited in rejecting Levinson's (1991) B-first account (Huang, 1991, 1994, also assumes a disjoint reference presumption), and because I reject Huang's contention that the distribution of anaphora in languages like Chinese has no distribution regulated by strictly syntactic principles. For discussion of Chinese that points to finer empirical distinctions to defend syntactic universals, see 5.5.2; 6.3.3; Huang and Liu (2001); and Cole, Hermon and Lee (2001) for Teochew. Abraham (2000) also proposes a functionally based theory that presumes noncoreference between coarguments (following unpublished work by Bernard Comrie that I have not seen), and it appears to be susceptible to the same sorts of objections as is Levinson's (1991) account.

9. Reuland (2001, 478–479) argues that Frisian and Dutch must have completely different dependency relations in these constructions even though the interpretations are the same. This seems both implausible and unnecessary.

10. Hellan also argues that the complementarity principle only regulates bound reference, not coreference (1988, 140), but he later introduces a third relation that is neither binding nor coreference; rather, it is an identity relation to which some portion of complementarity applies (1988, 278). The complication is motivated by the contrast between i. and ii.

i. Moren *hans* har *Ola* ofte snakket om
   mother his has Ola often talked about
ii. Moren *hans* håpet at *Ola* ville komme
   mother his hoped that Ola would come

While coreference is possible for ii. between *hans* and *Ola*, it is forbidden for i. Since *Ola* does not appear to bind *hans* in either case, it is necessary to account for how the application of fronting in i. (to first position, as indicated by the verb second effect) seems to treat *hans* as if it were still bound in its position of origin in i. (where it would be excluded, since a SIG form is available). Cases like these are discussed in Safir (2004) without recourse to a new form of coreference relation.

11. Besides the fact that the feature deficit idea does not work for SELF, the notion that the pronominal in the compound is anaphoric requires adjustment for all those Germanic languages, like Norwegian, in which SELF is compounded with both pronouns and SIG forms with differential results (see note 55 of chapter 6). There is a further problem with the mechanics of Burzio's account of pronoun-SELF forms. If SELF is an anaphor, it not only does not agree with its antecedent, it also does not agree with the pronoun associated with it, except in number.

12. The same may apparently be said of Danish *sig* and *sig selv,* which are also not acceptable for many speakers when they have plural antecedents. The SELF form permits plural antecedents, however, as long as it is not compounded with *sig*.

i. [Jon og Per]$_i$ fortalte Sofie om dem selv/*sig selv$_i$. (D)
   Jon and Per told Sofie about ___

For those speakers who avoid it with plural antecedents, we might say *sig* is specified for singular in Danish, but not in Norwegian or Swedish. I have encountered one Danish speaker (Line Mikkelsen, personal communication) who simply does not permit the possessive SIN at all, and she predictably permits only the otherwise independent possessive pronoun to express bound readings. This again suggests that a gap in the anaphoric paradigm is simply filled by the next most dependent form.

13. Actually, the *deres* is not excluded for all speakers in (22b), if distinctions concerning collectives are made. Arild Hestvik (personal communication) recalls that Tarald Taraldsen once pointed out to him that *deres* is only excluded in examples like (22b) under the distributive reading. Hestvik provides the following example:

i. Spillerne snakket om deres prestasjoner.
"*The players* talked about *their* achievements."

If the players are talking about their achievement as a team, it's acceptable, but if they are talking about their individual achievements as members of the team, it is necessary to use the anaphor, *sine*. To my way of thinking, *sine* outcompetes *deres* for the distributed reading that it requires, but if *sine* is not competing, then the next most dependent form is *deres*. In chapter 4 I consider competitions between anaphoric forms to represent particular readings, where the more specific form triumphs if it is available.

14. Franks and Schwartz (1994) also argue that Burzio's pseudoagreement should be abandoned in favor of a theory in which a bindee must agree with its antecedent and can do so if the bindee is nondistinct from its antecedent in phi features. They argue, for example, that French *soi* fails to agree with any antecedent specified for gender, suggesting that *soi* is specified as [-masculine, -feminine]. If it is specified, however, it is not featureless, hence not an anaphor in Burzio's system. Franks and Schwartz acknowledge (1994, 240) that they offer no account of morphologically complex forms, but their system, like the one proposed here, is scalar, in that what counts as an anaphor is the maximally underspecified form. Unfortunately, they do not say why some forms are only available to compete with other forms in certain local environments; that is, they dispense with principle A, and nothing in their theory does the work of it.

15. Underspecification is one of several possible approaches to a relative dependency ranking. See also Koster (1997, 244) who proposes a Principle of Maximum Specialization, also a derived complementarity approach, which requires that "in a grammatical dependency relation R, select the most specialized form." He continues, "A form A is more specialized than B if A can fulfill fewer functions than B." I have sympathy with this intuition, but Koster's proposal is insufficiently specific, since it would appear to predict that a pronoun would obviate an epithet in cases where the antecedent does not c-command, as in "*Everyone's* mother loves *the bastard*," but this is not the case. Part of the specialization that Koster has in mind concerns the variety of case environments in which a form can occur, such that the less generally available one is favored for a dependent interpretation. He shows that a direct object in Frisian can be represented by either of two pronouns if the pronoun is not dependent but must be represented by the one specific to object position (unlike the other, it cannot also be nominative) where a dependency relation holds (see his discussion of Frisian in Koster, 1997, 248–9)). This case is outside of the proposals I have in mind, but such contrasts appear to be uncommon, and so I set them aside.

16. Another recent approach based on a competitive principle is Richards (1997), which is rudimentary in theoretical form but sophisticated in its approach to complementarities based on distinctions of interpretation. Like Hellan and Burzio, he exploits the distribution of subject orientation to derive antisubject orientation. Richards relies on the notion (which I have rejected) that anaphors are maximally underspecified, a proposal detachable from the rest of his argumentation about the nature of what I call the most dependent scale. See 6.3.3, which benefits from his analysis. I postpone discussion of Wilson (2001), an optimality–theoretic approach based on Burzio's work, until 7.2.

17. The interpretation of adjunction could lead to questions in cases like i., where I shall assume that Y asymmetrically c-commands X.

i. $[_{ZP}$ Y $[_{ZP}$ X $[_{Z'}$ Z . . . ]]]

See the appendix to chapter 4 for a discussion of thematic considerations in the computation of c-command.

18. This exception to antecedent agreement suggests the intervention of another principle. See the discussion of "functional extension" in 6.2.1 and the appendix to chapter 6. See also the discussion of Hungarian in 6.2.4

19. A [-personal] pronoun must be dependent on a first person antecedent for examples like *Each of us thinks he is smart*. The unless-clause of antecedent agreement permits us to use *he* because first person singular *I* cannot yield the bound interpretation, given the proper interpretation of first person plural (see Safir in preparation).

20. Differences between anaphors that can represent distributed as opposed to collective plural readings are revisited in 6.3.3 with particular reference to Japanese and Chinese, where apparent overlaps in the domain of anaphors are distinguished for FTIP competition by their interpretation.

21. The assumption that control infinitives are CPs is one of convenience and could easily be abandoned in favor of the assumption that the minimal head c-commanding PRO is V, as in Bošković (1996). The case of PRO, called *Null Case* in Chomsky and Lasnik (1995), might as easily be assigned or checked by SPEC-head agreement with infinitival T. ECM cases are revisited in 5.1. See also 6.1.3.

22. If a boy is named Sue, then *Sue killed himself* is well-formed. I do not assume that proper names or indeed most definite descriptions are marked as grammatically gendered in English, so whatever gender feature the pronoun in pronoun-SELF has it will not conflict. Extragrammatical knowledge about the genders normally associated with particular names creates other expectations. However, pronoun antecedents that are explicitly gendered result in failure of agreement as a matter of grammar. This position is probably too strong, but I will assume it is correct.

23. In German, second person plural uses the SIG form *sich* for the dependent interpretation rather than the pronoun *sie*, the independent pronominal form for second person accusative for both second person plural and third person plural. If we were to say that there is no second person plural form marked as such in German, then we would expect that a plural that does not otherwise conflict in features with the second person would be employed, namely *sie* (rather than *uns*, which does conflict with second person, since it is explicitly first person). Like *sie*, *sich* is [-person] and so only conflicts with overt person marking, but *sich* is unmarked for number and is marked anaphoric, so *sich* will outcompete *sie* for the dependent interpretation. This result is consistent with the implicational relations in the text.

24. See Burzio (1996, 15) for some discussion of a complementarity breakdown with the nonanaphoric form *vas* ("you"), which is possible in place of *sebja* in (37b). This is in contrast to expected complementarity that holds between *sebja* and the nonanaphoric pronoun *ego* in (37a) and between *sebja* and the nonanaphoric pronoun *mne* in (37c). Burzio sees the breakdown in (37b) in terms of the "cost" of pseudoagreement when it is not completely (clausemate) local, in that it is somewhat disfavored in proportion to the specificity (in features) of the antecedent—personal pronouns being more specific than nonpersonal (= third person) pronouns. The interpretive nuances that distinguish the choice of *vas* and *sebja* in (37b) need more study, as do a range of other cases discussed by Timberlake (1979b), but distance from the antecedent appears to play a role in diminishing the contrasts.

25. Faltz (1977, 117–121) notes that in Pima, a Uto–Aztecan language spoken in Arizona, there is a pronominal form that is used for reflexive interpretations that can be employed for second and third persons, but not for first, that uses the first person pronoun. I do not know enough about this language to know if the second person accusative is in any way defective, but I would expect an unmarked anaphoric pronominal to fill a void in the accusative second person paradigm. I leave the matter unresolved, but see Faltz' discussion for some historical speculations.

26. There are cases that will test the limits of this proposal. See Hellan, page 105, example 15b, and page 67, example 19d, where the object in a PP can be the antecedent of *ham selv*, and also on page 160 with *sin* anteceded from a PP, but this may involve PRO subject of a nominal. Such cases raise issues for the relation between argument selection and c-command, some of which are touched on in the appendix to chapter 4.

27. Avrutin reports (38c) grammatical with *ego*, but Rappaport (1986, 104, fn. 8) reports variable acceptability across speakers where the pronoun is anteceded by the matrix subject. See the remark in note 47 of this chapter concerning the effect of distance on obviation for some bound variable readings. For some other interesting interpretive restrictions of varying strength in Russian, see Timberlake (1979a).

28. However, see Chomsky (1995b) and Bošković (2000) on late insertion.

29. This does not preclude a situation where otherwise independent pronominals can move covertly and compete with anaphors, but even in such a situation, the anaphor will win a competition with a pronoun to represent the dependent interpretation on a given antecedent. The point in the text is that covert movement of a pronoun should not be motivated by the competitions it loses.

30. There are cases that appear to challenge analyses based on movement to a position where only one antecedent is available. A few such cases are discussed in 5.2.4.

31. The claim that an anaphor is subject to LAL is stronger than it seems, insofar as the domain of LAL is not parameterized and so remains strictly local in universal grammar. As argued in 5.2, the empirical distribution of an anaphor will appear wider than the domain of LAL if nonanaphoric properties it has require it to move covertly in a way that is also characteristic of a corresponding overt movement. In other words, if an anaphor moves (covertly or overtly), it is not motivated by the search for an antecedent. Thus extended domains for forms treated as anaphors must receive independently motivated explanation. For a critique of what I take to be an overgeneralization of movement to achieve coconstrual, see Safir (2003, 2004).

32. For a similar view on what constitutes a pronoun, see, for example, Reuland (1996, 3). I return to the matter in 6.1 where pronouns are taken to be a reduced definite descriptions consisting only of grammatical features. It is not necessary to require special presuppositions for pronouns that other definites lack (e.g., as does Hans Kamp in lectures given at Rutgers University, fall 1999). Rather it seems that pronouns just need more presupposition for interpretation precisely because they are insufficiently descriptive definites, not because they are forms of a different sort. Otherwise the parallel between i. and iii. would have an accidental character.

i. Nine of the ten balls were on the table. #It was on the floor.
ii. Nine of the ten balls were on the table. The other ball was on the floor.
iii. Nine of the ten balls were on the table. #The ball was on the floor.

I will have nothing to say about the accessibility of antecedents for definites beyond those questions that pertain to FTIP (where c-command is crucial) and pragmatic obviation, but see 6.1.2 and Safir (in preparation) for relevant discussion.

33. Compare Koster's (1997) approach discussed in note 15 to this chapter.

34. Abraham (2000, 96) proposes a hierarchy of forms supporting "reference identifying function[s]" such that if a form higher on the hierarchy is "suspended" in some way, then the next lower element on the hierarchy is employed. Apart from the noncoreference assumption (see note 8 to this chapter), Abraham appears to be taking a heuristic tack, expressed in functional terms, similar to the one that is pursued in my formal syntactic treatment of the most dependent scale. However, his predictions are much less precise.

35. Third person clitics other than *se* in French are an instance of forms lacking deictic potential that are not anaphors. See my discussion of Cardinaletti and Starke (1994) in 6.1.

36. Conditions on clitics versus tonic forms are part of an independent competition (see 6.1.1), so clitic anaphors do not necessarily obviate nonclitic anaphors, at least not as a function of the most dependent scale. Thus French *soi* does not obviate *se* quite apart from the fact that the two are interpretively distinct (*soi* requires a generic antecedent, but see Safir in preparation).

37. G&R (1993, 83–84) correctly point out that bound readings for plurals do not have to be distributed, a view suggested by Williams (1986) that they reject. They point out cases like *Ben and Lucie consider themselves to be a perfect couple*, which requires a collective interpretation of Ben and Lucie as a pair (see 4.2.3). Not every language permits a relational anaphor (e.g., one like SELF) to support both collective and distributed interpretations. See the discussion of German *selbst* in 3.3.3 and the discussion of Chinese and Japanese in 6.3.3.

38. Cases like i, where the first subject is collective and the second singular, show the same sort of contrast.

i. At a press conference, the President and *his wife* present *her* differently than *she* would present *herself/?*her* if *she* were alone.

39. As further evidence for the existence of the relevant dependency relations, in (55–57), note that it is possible to get bound readings for the ellipsis, as in i. and ii., such that the elided pronouns correspond to "every Democrat's contributions to mankind" and "every convict's mother," respectively.

i. *Every Republican* and *his* wife overvalue *his* contributions to mankind and every Democrat and his wife do too.
ii. *Every bankrupt* and *his* wife blame *his* mother for wasting money, and every convict and his wife do too.

40. See 1.2.4 for an argument that the Chain Condition reduces to a restatement of LGB principle B, once the predictive force of the feature [+/-R] is understood. Reuland (2001, 464–465) acknowledges that syncretisms for first and second person are stipulative and attempts to argue that they are unnecessary if first and second person are in fact inherently singular or plural rather than singular or plural by virtue of an added grammatical feature. Then he takes the absence of a nonintrinsic number feature to permit first and second person forms to be subordinate members of A-chains within his system, the way forms like *zich* in Dutch can be (see 1.2.3). (See also van Gelderen's (2000) history of the English reflexive, which partially relies on this proposal, but she argues it is not sufficient).

Reuland also cites Benveniste (1966) concerning the difference between person and nonperson as opposed to third person, but even Benveniste does not claim first person lacks a number feature or that these persons have a distinct kind of number feature; rather he argues for a different interpretation of number on first and second person. A different interpretation for first person plural seems a better strategy, since agreement relations with first and second person plurals treat them as plurals (where adjective agreement, number concord, and subject–verb agreement are visible, and anywhere where a checking relation must hold). It is also difficult to see any motivation for treating the singularity of first person as any different from that of third person. The claim that "all occurrences of [the first person] have the same value in a given sentence" is of no help because it is not quite true, as in the guise cases discussed in 4.2.2. However, if the number features of first person are not independently motivated to be different than other number features, Reuland's explanation of why first and second person can violate the Chain Condition reduces to a stipulation about features, just as syncretism is.

41. The CDC only blocks a dependent interpretation; it does not specify that A and B are an obviative pair if A cannot depend on B in the relevant way. Even if this is necessary, which seems unclear (I leave the matter open), all that formal grammar contributes to the interpretation of coreference is the existence of an obviative pair, not whether the source of the obviation is from FTIP or CDC.

42. Berman and Hestvik (1997), developing observations by Seely (1993), also use examples like John wants Mary to represent them as evidence against principle B, but they do not observe that a different choice of verb yields a much less acceptable result, as in John wants Mary to despise them, which, if it is to be acceptable at all, might involve John's scheming to get Mary to hate the way they are together as a couple (suppose he wants to end the relationship). The individual-to-collective relationship will not be regulated by FTIP in that instance, which is why it is possible, however awkward. Hestvik and Berman also draw attention to the work of Seely, who conditions the noncoreference on "exhaustive binding," which involves assuming that every atom of the antecedent binds every atom of the dependent, such that an incomplete overlap allows the c-commandee to be free. The FTIP derives this as a consequence of either the competition between available forms to express the complete overlap or the discrimination that is possible where overlap is not complete (as discussed in 2.4.2).

43. For some interesting Hungarian cases where first person singular can unexpectedly antecede first person plural, see 6.3.4.

44. A similar point is made for French by Zribi-Hertz (1995, 347–349) where the choice of predicate influences whether or not *-même* is required to achieve coreference with a coargument (see also Zribi-Hertz 1980). In the cases where it is not required, principle B would fail. She also shows that disjoint reference for an individual with respect to a set in which s/he might be included holds for the predicates that require *même* for coreference, but not for those that do not require it for coreference. See 6.2.3. What she does not explain is why disjoint reference is not canceled in cases where a pronoun does not require *même* for coreference, for example, *Mitterrand a honte de lui/*Mitterrand/des Français*. "Mitterand is ashamed of him/Mitterrand/the French," where Mitterrand is one of the French. The unacceptability of the repeated name follows from the account in the text, since a name would compete with a pronoun in this environment for the dependent reading, with use of the name resulting in obviation.

45. There is no reason to believe that any discourse information is required to compute the FTIP competition. Thus we do not expect that it would be in any way natural to fold principle B (which, if we are right, does not exist) or FTIP into the theory of discourse, as Berman and Hestvik (1997, 17) suggest. The only evidence they present in favor of this conclusion that could bear on the issue involves cases like i.

i. John told Fred about them.

They consider i. ungrammatical under any interpretation of *them* coconstrued with *John* and *Fred,* and they argue that a discourse operation of summation of antecedents, one that syntax is insufficient to compute, creates the plural antecedent of *them,* which should be excluded by principle B. However, even the fact is far from clear. Suppose that John has learned from the oracle that Fred will one day be his homosexual lover, but since Fred still thinks he's straight, *John can't tell Fred about them yet* or Fred will freak out. Here it appears that summation, if that is what is involved, permits c-commanding antecedents to form a collective/tandem anteceded by the two referents introduced individually. Appeal to a principle-B effect appears empirically incorrect. This reading is permitted by FTIP since *them* is the most dependent form available to represent this reading. Moreover, as Berman and Hestvik acknowledge, F&M (1994, 40) point out the felicity of *John talked to Mary about them* under the same sort of interpretation, and they use it to argue against disjoint reference as the force of Principle B.

46. Borer (1984b) and McCloskey (1990) have appealed to Principle B to account for the exclusion of resumptive pronouns when they are too close to their A'-antecedents. Since I propose to eliminate principle B, I cannot very well extend it to A'-binding. Although I will not go into it here (see Safir 2004), I do not take traces to be empty category competitors with resumptive pronouns, and if so, the effect cannot be regulated by FTIP, or else our application of FTIP must be more nuanced.

47. Vikner (1985, 52–53) discusses cases where the acceptability of *sig* decreases with its distance from its antecedent (within an extended tenseless domain), and the acceptability of a nonanaphoric pronominal in the same position improves correspondingly, exactly as we would expect, if distance conditions the availability of *sig*. Arild Hestvik (personal communication) also informs me that in Norwegian, a pronoun in an embedded infinitive is acceptable for him with a reading bound to the matrix subject, even where a SIG form is also available. Presumably, this is evidence of a more robust attenuating effect than I would expect. See also note 27 to this chapter.

48. Another example of reasoning of this type is found in Richards (1997), who attempts to explain the absence of antisubject orientation for Japanese *kare-zisin* because it has different interpretive restrictions than its apparent competitor, *zibun-zisin*. See 6.3.3, note 67.

49. The account of overlap permitted by (67a) is that adopted to account for the apparent absence of principle-B effects in child language acquisition studies as discussed by Thornton and Wexler (1999; see references cited there). They argue that children accept a coreferent interpretation of sentences like *Mama bear is washing her* because the relation between *Mama bear* and *her* is not bound reference, but independent covaluation, to put it in my terms. They argue that the effects reemerge in ellipsis contexts, where the sloppy reading is unavailable for such cases, for example, *Mama bear kissed him, and then baby bear did*. This is also expected in my account, since SELF forms should outcompete the pronoun for the dependent reading, which should not be possible as a result for a pronoun, even an elided one, in either conjunct (see Safir 2004). Their results appear compatible with everything said so far, including their account of the difference between adults and children; children have less sense of what others should know on the basis of what they, the children, say, and so the force of obviation, expected noncoreference, is somewhat undermined. It is also possible, though less likely given Thornton and Wexler's arguments, that children do not immediately classify pronouns and SELF forms as competitors that do not tie. This is an area where the current approach could benefit from close comparison with results achieved in acquisition studies, but I have no space to pursue the matter here. See note 10 of chapter 4.

50. For further discussion of the relation between selection of PPs and the distribution of SELF forms in prepositional object positions, see Hestvik (1991) and a number of references cited there.

51. Hestvik (1991) actually takes his proposal to be evidence in favor of the accidental overlap of the domains for principles A and B of the BT under Chomsky's (1986b) BT compatibility theory and against an account like Burzio's. However, the FTIP algorithm, which makes more explicit predictions about compared derivations (a derivation with PRO and one without it are not compared), is immune to Hestvik's critique of derived complementarity accounts.

52. See Hellan (1988, 131–135) on a related overlap, where he argues that there are differences in whose perspective is reported in cases like i. and ii.

i. Vi fant *Jon* under sengen *sin/hans*.
we found Jon under bed SIN/his
ii. Vi jaget *Jon* tilbake til huset *sin/hans*.
we chased Jon back to house SIN/his

These cases may differ on the basis of whether or not the PP contains a PRO, as in the discussion in the text. I am assuming that in general, Norwegian *sin* is an anaphor that cannot be promoted to discourse dependent (see 5.4). However, for a few errant cases, see Holmberg and Platzack (1995, 88, fn. 26) and references cited there.

## Chapter 4

1. I postpone discussion here of coargument relations among complements that violate c-command, such as *We talked to Bill about himself*, until the appendix to this chapter, where some proposed alternatives to c-command are rejected in light of an account based on the lines of argument pursued here.

2. R&R also exclude (4a, c) by their chain condition, in that independent pronouns or names, which are [+R] in their account, cannot form a coindexing chain as a subordinate link. See 1.2.3 for a general outline of their system.

3. Clearly c-command working in these three principles overlaps forcefully here, which may account for the robust crosslinguistic generalization in i. (but see 6.3.1 for a potential counterexample).

i. No language signals a reflexive reading of a transitive predicate by marking the subject argument; that is to say, it is either the predicate itself or a complement argument that is marked.

The distinct influence of FTIP and the Independence Principle are examined in more detail in Safir (2004), and the c-antecedency condition is further defended in 4.1.

4. F&M (1994, 114–115) also reject the c-command account of (8), but they use such cases to argue for their alpha index (which represents covaluation, not dependency). Their reasoning rests on the acceptability of a reading for *Only Satan loves his mother and only Job does too* that is not contradictory. The relevant reading, the only acceptable one, according to F&M, is one where Satan is the only individual who loves his, Satan's, mother, while Job is the only one who loves his, Job's, mother, and the sentence would be false if anyone else loved either Job's mother or Satan's mother. I have had great difficulty finding any informants who agree with F&M that even the noncontradictory interpretation is acceptable.

5. Of course, this leaves us with (8), which I assume to be an instance where the interpretation of *Only Satan loves Satan* is not dependent and is in fact an instantiation context, like those discussed in 2.2, for example, as an answer to *Who loves Satan*?

6. There remains, however, a particular loose end that arises once antecedency and dependency are dissociated. Consider the contrast in i. versus ii.

i. **Every woman* thinks that *she* trusted *her.*

ii. *Every woman* thinks that *she* trusts *herself/*her.*

While ii. is straightforward (since *herself* is a coargument with *he*, the Locally Reflexive Principle [LRP] requires that *herself* should depend on *she*), examples like i., which are similar to examples pointed out by Higginbotham (1985, 570), do not appear to allow an interpretation where both *she* and *her* are dependent on *every woman*, but where *her* is not dependent on *she*, and it is not obvious that such an interpretation would be distinguishable from that of i. However, if i. is not permitted, it is not clear why (13a) is. The principle that makes the distinction is Rule H, which is discussed, along with its relationship to the FTIP, in 7.1.

7. There are relatively uncommon cases where a dependent-identity interpretation is thematically difficult to distinguish from a reciprocal one, for example, *The members of the team were so disorganized that they kept colliding among themselves.*

8. It is possible that this fact about SELF forms in coargument contexts is derivable from conditions on incorporation relations. If the SELF form, or the SELF portion of pronoun-SELF, is incorporated into the predicate that selects it at LF, then it might be that incorporation enforces the locally dependent reading and that general properties of argument incorporation limit the operation to coarguments. Such an account is proposed in Safir (1996c; see also Reinhart and Reuland 1991), and Anagnostopoulou and Everaert (1999) explore such an analysis for certain anaphors in Greek. If so, the incorporation in question may be triggered by lexical properties, so that LRP may not be expected to be a universal. Such an account must address the status of incorporation as an operation applying to SELF form coarguments embedded in PPs. See note 32 of chapter 6.

9. Since reciprocals are argument marked in English, we correctly predict they will permit proxy readings as well.

i. *Grisham and Le Carré* refuse to read *each other* in English.
ii. *Celeste and Margeaux* play croquet to damage, not to win, so *they* are always knocking *each other* out of play.
iii. *Marlene and Marilyn* were chagrined at seeing *each other* before *they* saw *themselves* at the costume ball.

This is further evidence that it is not a special property of SELF forms to permit proxy readings, and the same point holds of approaches to proxy readings like those of König and Siemund (2000, 48), which, though closer to this one in providing for pragmatic input, still hold that a crucial part of the meaning of SELF is implicated in licensing the proxy reading. The view taken here is that it is the absence of proxy readings with *zich* that requires explanation.

10. Lakoff (1968, 1996) uses the term *counterpart* for the cases I call *guises*, but his term is intended to be more general and has additional associations I do not endorse, so I employ *guise* for just those cases discussed. In choosing to use the word as I do, there is always the danger that various aspects of the Fregean world view will cling to this usage (e.g., where *The morning star is the evening star* has been described as identity asserting that the reference of these two descriptions, or guises, is the same). Consequently, please regard my

use of *guise* in this context as not only descriptive, but narrowly so. Also, my usage is not that of Thornton and Wexler (1999), who appear to use it for independent covaluation in a manner they adapt from Heim (1993).

11. See Roberts (1987, 58–59), who argues that the relevant notion of binding for Lakoff's cases is not one of coreference but whether or not two nominals "have the same or different discourse referents." However it seems necessary to establish that "I in the guise of you" and "I" pick out the speaker in both instances, though not always in the same shoes. For more on first person perspective as it relates to these case, see Safir (in preparation). The same comment applies to Chomsky's (1981:315) response to these cases, which treats the referents as different in the constructed hypothetical space of "if I were you." Semantic distinctions as to hypothetical spaces as a heuristic metaphor may be useful in exploring some of these interpretations, and the matter is explored in detail by Fauconnier (1994). Nonetheless, I restrict my interest to the semantic distinctions that are influenced by syntactic configurations. In the case in question, first person reference remains constant, but the question is really whether the reading has a component of dependency or not.

12. The use of the comparative improves the strict reading without damaging the prospect of a sloppy one, which is why I use it here; see Hestvik (1995).

13. Conduct the following thought experiment: Imagine two aliens consisting of pure energy without form. One telepaths to the other: *If were you I'd hate me*. Such examples show that whatever this distinction is, it is not about bodies.

14. For inherent reflexives, ter Meulen (1998) suggests that the identity formula should include an exhaustivity restriction understood in the sense that no other entity is in relation R to the subject. This is clearly not true for most reflexivity, since *John loves himself* does not commit us to any proposition concerning whether or not other people love John. Ter Meulen would have it that there is such an implication for *sich schamen*. However, I think this is a function of reduced adicity and resulting thematic indistinctness, so this inference may follow in the same way for *John cried*, in that it can't be that anyone else cried him, yet this is not normally thought of as transitive verb. Of course one can "cry (crocodile) tears," but the point is that the reduced adicity should derive the exclusivity implication (from indistinctness) and that the latter should not be encoded as essential to the interpretation of reflexivity.

15. Similar remarks apply to examples like i. discussed by G&R (1993, 83).

i. *Many students* expect *them* to leave.

I consider i. grammatical under the distributed interpretation for *many* and the collective interpretation for *them* such that each individual of the group encompassed by "many students" believes that the group will leave.

16. Everaert (1986, 52–53) notes the most similar class in Dutch is a lot like a middle, which in English is not marked with any overt morphology.

i. Hij verspreide het gerucht. "He spread the rumor."
ii. Het gerucht verspreidde zich. "The rumor spread."

17. Ter Meulen (1998) discusses a case she calls Russell's paradox, whereby *The barber shaves everyone that does not shave (himself)* is nonsensical without the overt reflexive, since people who don't grow beards have nothing to shave. In such cases, aspect and modality influence the force of the effect.

i. The barber will shave everyone who won't shave.
ii. The barber shaved everyone who didn't shave.

Only ii. has an interpretation that is susceptible to the paradox, where the people in question are too young to shave, but not in a scenario where the barber is rendering presentable those people who showed up at the reception having forgot to shave. In any case, it all plays on the idiomatic meaning of being inherently beardless, rather than a TUT-reflexive reading.

18. Everaert (1986) for Dutch, Hellan (1988) for Norwegian, and Cinque (1988) and Napoli (1979) for Italian discuss the semantic and syntactic classes involved more extensively, and insofar as morphological rules and lexical exceptions are frequently reported in comprehensive grammars, there is no dearth of information for a wide variety of languages. Geniušiene (1987) discusses the classes in English, including many fine-grained distinctions, and she compares these with the Baltic languages. She also provides a very useful survey of the range of inherent reflexives permitted in an even wider variety of languages. See also Faltz (1977) and especially Kemmer (1993), who also relates gestural reflexives to (body action) middles and the distinguishability of coarguments based on an initiator–endpoint distinction developed within the functionalist and cognitive grammar tradition (see her references).

19. Reuland (2001), which became available to me only at the last stage of revising this manuscript, proposes that reflexivity must overcome a violation of adicity by ensuring, with a SELF form, that the two arguments of the predicate are distinguishable in principle, an idea I find attractive, though I reject Reuland's appeal to branchingness as the key property of SELF (since many pronouns that permit adicity reduction are also complex; see 6.1.2). See also Kemmer (1993, 210–221) for an interesting discussion of the relation between distinguishability of participants and transitivity. Bouchard (1995, 282–283) discusses a range of distinctions pointed out by Ruwet (1991) concerning how an antecedent-dependent relation can be influenced by the nature of the predicates involved with regard to whether or not the antecedent is distinct from the dependent. I suspect that these cases, which have to do with the selection of control infinitives or subjunctives (anteceded by the matrix subject), should be thought of in light of the *de se*/non-*de se* distinction (see Landau 2000), though as pointed out in Safir (in preparation), the *de se* interpretation associated with control is insufficient to account for its semantic force of indistinctness. See also Williams (2003) for a blocking account of the *zich*/*zichzelf* relation, but one that will require interpretive assumptions to enhance distinctions between his notion of predicate structure and his notion of thematic structure.

20. See Everaert (1986, 49) for some apparent counterexamples in Dutch.

21. Concerning the analysis of *zich* and its relation to lexical operations, Everaert (1986, 66–67) points out that the *zich* form otherwise required for an inherent reflexive for *bewust* is missing in causative contexts, which he suggests is a result of the syntactic environment.

i. Jan makt hem (*zich) bewust van zijn falen.
   Jan makes *him ZICH* aware of his failure

On the basis of this evidence and because of the fact that *zich* elsewhere (e.g., in PPs) agrees with its antecedent in exactly the same way when it is not employed in an inherent reflexive context, he argues against treating *zich* as a simple (accidental) lexical marker of inherent reflexivity.

22. Vikner (1985, 51) points to a similar case in Danish (a subordinate clause is presented to abstract away from matrix verb movement, which is irrelevant here), where *sig* or *sig selv* can appear in a context where a full nominal is also possible (e.g., *Michael* could appear in the position filled by the anaphors below).

i. . . . at Peter satte sig/sig selv ned
   that Peter sat ___ down

ii. . . . at Peter brændte sig/sig selv
that Peter burned ___

Where the *sig* form is used, i. means "Peter sat down," but when *sig selv* is employed, i. means "Peter sat himself down," as if, Vikner remarks, "he had set himself down by means of e.g., a crane." In cases like ii., the devolitional reading requires *sig*, while the use of *sig selv* implies that Peter burned himself intentionally. The effect of *sig* as imposing the indistinct interpretation is independent of the argument structure distinctions between the two cases, in that the *sig* version of i. is not devolitional and can be modified by *med vilje*, "deliberately," while ii. with *sig* cannot be so modified.

23. There are other ways to diffuse this apparent violation of complementarity that may also account for it, though in a somewhat more roundabout way. For example, it could be argued that [*trok uit het moeras*] may be treated as a complex predicate or not, with one form favoring one analysis over the other, and presumably the different structures might be distinguished by constituency tests. However, it would still be necessary to say why it is that SELF forms favor one analysis over another in terms of how it functions as a proxy or as reflexive marker.

24. Lidz (1996), roughly following Reuland (1997), argues that SIG forms represent a form of reflexivity more economical than SELF forms, since SIG forms are markers of adicity reduction, and adicity reduction is more economical than chain formation, which is what he takes the coargument relation between SELF forms and their antecedents to be. If this is so, it is hard to understand why SELF forms are ever employed for coargument dependent identity in languages that permit some adicity reduction. In English and Dutch, a lexically select set of predicates may be thought of as having adicity reduction, but it is not obvious why the adicity reduction is not more generally available (but see Reuland, 2001, where SELF forms are argued to protect adicity distinctions). This is not a matter of which dependent forms are available, but rather a question of which predicates permit the reduced adicity. Under Lidz's view, it is possible that in languages that permit adicity reduction generally for all predicates (and thereby express reflexivity as indistinctness), there is no reflexive marking on arguments because such marking would always be obviated by lexical marking, which he and Reuland suggest is more economical. I am not aware of a good case, and as discussion in 4.4 will make clear, the case that Lidz presents to support such a position is not convincing.

25. Before leaving this topic, it is worth pointing out that the distinction between *zich* and *zichzelf* in Dutch may undermine an argument that R&R present as evidence for the RIP. They argue that if two internal arguments are coindexed with the subject, only one of them needs to be reflexive marked. R&R (1993, 668) present the following paradigm.

i. **Henk* wees mij aan *zich* toe.
"Henk assigned me to SIG."
ii. *Henk* wees *zichzelf* aan *zich* toe.
iii. **Henk* wees *zich* aan mij toe.
iv. *Henk* wees *zich* aan *zichzelf* toe.
v. ?*Henk* wees *zichzelf* aan *zichzelf* toe.

R&R argue that one SELF form is sufficient to mark the predicate as reflexive, so *zich* is licensed as long as it has a *zichzelf* coargument. On my assumptions, it would appear that only v. should be possible, since *zichzelf* is more dependent on the most dependent scale than *zich*. However, it is possible that the reason the double reflexive cases allow for *zich* and *zichzelf* but not *zich* and *zich* is that the action of assigning the relation *x to y* requires distinctness between *x* and *y*, and using *zich* for one of the two arguments and *zichzelf* for the other ensures this result. Cases i. and iii. are out for the usual reasons; *zichzelf* is a more dependent form, and there is no intervention from the distinctness requirement, since no anaphor is used for the parallel argument in the *x to y* relation. From this perspective v. is pragmatically odd for the same reason, which is that two *zelf* forms might appear to permit identical interpretations, depending on whether both *zichzelf*s are dependent on *Henk* directly or not, but just the same I predict they are well formed because they are both relations that permit distinctness under dependent identity. Thus v. competes with either ii. or iv., but not both at the same time, since they involve different test derivation substitutions. When ii. competes with v., the distinctness requirement enters in as an availability restriction (since the two argument positions are both dependent on the subject), mildly favoring results that require distinct identity dependent interpretations, namely ii. over v. The same applies for the competition between iv. and v. Since the availability restriction is weak, so is the resulting FTIP effect.

26. There are nuances in the interpretation of the notion of indistinctness that may involve culturally specific dimensions. Thus Rooryck and vanden Wyngaerd (1997) notice that *Freddy zah zichzelf/zich in de spiegel* ("Freddy saw himself in the mirror") can permit *zich* whereas *Freddy zah zichzelf/?*zich op de video-opnahme* ("Freddy saw himself on the videotape") does much less so. They suggest that there is greater spatiotemporal overlap in the mirror case as opposed to the video case, although they do not explore their notion of "spatial," since the mirror does not occupy the same space as the perceiver any more than the video image does. What seems to be crucial is the exact correspondence of the perceiver and the perceived, which holds for the mirror, up to the limit of two-dimensional versus three-dimensional representation, such that any movement (or stillness) of the perceived individual corresponds temporally to those of the perceiver, a description that is not true of the video image in the normal case. If this speculation or some other fine-grained notion of distinctness is correct, then there will be gray areas that may differ somewhat language to language, or even culture to culture speaking the same language, and the same goes for proxy interpretation. All that matters for our considerations, however, is that wherever the line distinguishing indistinctness and distinctness is drawn in a speech community, an anaphor may have the lexical property of being sensitive to this divide.

27. Lidz (2001b, 131) argues that Dutch *zich* is not "lexically specified for the near reflexive [i.e., proxy] function" because it does not support that reading in a PP, as in *Reagan zag de man op zich schieten* ("Reagan saw the man shoot at him"), which cannot mean that the man shot at a statue of Reagan. However, *zichzelf* is available here, outcompeting *zich*, so this fact does not reflect on whether or not *zich* could represent this reading when there is no competitor. Essentially the same point arises with respect to Kannada—see note 36 of this chapter.

28. Rooryck and vanden Wyngaerd are in effect pursuing a rigid internalist position (see chapter 6) insofar as they propose that dependent forms have more than feature content independent of their antecedents. They assume it is a property of *zich* that it requires a complete matching of the time slices of the individual with its antecedent with respect to the event described. The SELF portion, as described in the text, has a different relationship to the time slices but not to the identity of the individual (a position critiqued further in 5.2.3), and any deviations from these denotations require the intervention of some rule or thematic relation. The approach in the text is to take one of these interpretations to be unmarked and to derive the availability of the other from the nature of the competition, thus permitting shifts in how particular forms are interpreted depending on what they are in competition with.

29. In those rare cases where a missing argument of a transitive is interpreted as reflexive, the reflexive interpretation is necessarily indistinct and contrasts with the SELF form when a proxy reading is involved. Thus, once again in the wax museum, we can describe Marlene dressing her statue by *Marlene dressed herself* but not by *Marlene dressed*. For a related case, see note 17 of this chapter.

30. Zribi-Hertz (1980) remarks on distinctions between the interpretations of *lui* anteceded by a coargument versus *lui-même* and suggests that similar issues are at play, although the question arises as to whether there is competition between simplex and complex anaphors for a particular interpretation or disambiguation by means of an adjunct in favor of one interpretation. In the latter case, where the *-même* portion is an adjunct, it is not part of the FTIP competition. See 6.2.3.

31. My Norwegian informant for these examples, Arild Hestvik, also permits the pronoun *ham* in place of *seg* in (59b); this is a possibility he allows quite generally where *seg* can be anteceded outside of an infinitive. See note 47 of chapter 3.

32. See F&M (1994, 211–213) for the observation that the strict reading is available only for what I have called the *thematically unrestricted interpretation.* However, F&M consider this to be a matter of alpha versus beta indices, which I argue against in Safir (2004) and briefly in chapter 2.

33. This is not generally true if *zich* is a coargument embedded in a PP, but once again, this requires a more articulated analysis of how *zich* is licensed in PPs, as outlined in 3.3.4.

34. Faltz (1977, 14) suggests that the lexical reflexive might have the form $P(x, x) = Pr(x)$; that is to say, it is a semantic incorporation analysis. As mentioned in note 8 of this chapter, it is possible that some reflexive markers may require incorporation, and it is not clear, if one adopts such an analysis, how general it has to be. For example, this might lead us to distinguish morphological incorporation in syntax or LF from semantic incorporation for one case or another, or else it might lead us to interpret the syntactic incorporation as being necessarily a semantic incorporation, a matter I will not pursue.

35. The case of the Mohawk morpheme *atat*, examined in Baker (1996, 199–203, 219–20), seems potentially interesting from this perspective. Baker argues that *atat* is generated in the head of aspect-P (AspP), receives the external theta role of the verb (by various tests, Baker shows that verbs with *atat* are still transitive), and then must agree with the internal argument of that verb. The PRO corresponding to the internal argument moves to SPEC-AspP to achieve agreement. Thus the verb is still transitive, and it is not obvious that *atat* is an anaphor. However, if I do not treat it as an anaphor in competition with some affix that licenses PRO without argument absorption, then it is not clear why sentences of the form [pro-[V-pro]] without *atat* fail to have a reflexive interpretation. Baker (1996, 49) is attempting to predict the absence of NP-anaphors based on the assumption that pro-[V-pro] is a Principle B violation. However, it appears likely that *atat* is competitive with affixes licensing [pro-[V-pro]] structures. If Baker is right, almost every sentence in a polysynthetic language like Mohawk has a [pro-[V-pro]] form licensed by case or agreement morphemes and all contentful nominals are adjuncts related to this argument skeleton. For *atat* to triumph over competing affixes for the dependent identity interpretation, I must assume that it is more dependent, and since it must be anteceded, it is plausible to treat it as anaphoric. Baker only proposes that *atat* requires agreement, but treating *atat* as anaphoric is not incompatible with whatever it may require as an agreeing morpheme. The formation of reciprocals in Mohawk results from a disambiguating affix *te* that appears in addition to *atat*, but there does not appear to be any reason to assume that *te* is anaphoric.

36. Lidz (2001a) argues that the argument and nonargument distributions of the pronominal anaphor, as opposed to the complex anaphor, are the result of internal semantic properties of each, but the same sort of account given for Dutch *zich* versus *zichzelf* would appear to apply here. Suppose the verbal affix *koND* is an indistinctness marker, which would disqualify the complex reflexive, which both Lidz and I would treat as resistant to the indistinct interpretation. It then follows in my account, without stipulation about the nature of the pronominal anaphor, that only the latter could represent the indistinctness reading, without arguing that "pure anaphor" status, or indeed any special property, must be stipulated of it.

## Appendix to Chapter 4

1. Williams (1994, 213) introduces the notion *th-command* as a replacement for c-command.

i. For two theta roles X and Y, X *th-commands* Y if X is a coargument of Y; or, if X th-commands B, B is assigned to Z, and Z th-commands Y.

Williams sees it as an advantage that this notion will allow internal arguments of a verb to c-command constituents inside the subject (for cases like Pictures of himself please Harry, which I treat differently in 5.4), but this incorrectly predicts principle-C-like effects for cases like "The door of *Cal's* car crushed *him*," and even simple cases like *Rex excused himself* would be similar violations, since *himself* is a coargument of *Rex*; hence *Rex* is th-commanded by *himself.*

2. I assume that P-incorporation at LF is not blocked by intervening adverbs in examples like *Bill spoke angrily to John about himself*, any more than head movement is blocked at LF for verb raising. I also assume that the initial PP of the two PPs in (9a–d) is the only one that allows P-incorporation, so I am assuming that whatever structure one assigns to those two PPs in the VP, it must be one that does not allow the second of those two PPs to be structurally closer to the main verb, so as to permit incorporation. Notice that Pollard and Sag (1994, 264, fn. 17) cannot account for why examples like (9d) are not possible, since the *about*-object is more oblique than the *to*-object. In my account it is excluded because incorporation will yield c-command of *Castro* by *himself*, and *himself* has no c-commanding antecedent.

3. This A'-relationship has no effect on whatever induces raising in (11), since the A-trace, even if it is anteceded by an intervening operator with scope over IP, would still be the only form possible in that environment. See 5.1 for my theory of A-traces.

### Chapter 5

1. Notice that a weaker form of this is often appealed to, namely, that any movement possible in syntax is possible at LF (e.g., Reinhart and Reuland 1991, 302), but this allows that there are movements in LF that do not occur in syntax (see the discussion of [17]). Although I assume that movement is the device that accounts for thematic displacement, the contention that long-distance anaphors are constrained by the variety of movement types should extend to most other devices intended to capture the displacement relation in question. With respect to the more general question of whether or not coconstrual should reduce to movement relations, see note 19 of chapter 2 and Safir (2003, 2004) as well as note 16 to this chapter.

2. Accounts in frameworks without movement or traces obviously do not relate anaphora to movement in this sense. For an extended LFG account of anaphora, see Dalrymple (1993) and references cited there. For a critique of Dalrymple's typological approach, see 3.1.1.2. See also note 41 to this chapter. For an HPSG account, see Pollard and Sag (1994), which, except for its reliance on O-command (see the appendix to chapter 4) strongly resembles the LGB BT.

3. Chomsky (1995b, 261–271) suggests a version of A-movement in minimalism that only requires features to move at LF, not whole constituents (unless they are pied piped for some reason). In light of this proposal, a question arises as to whether the anaphoric feature of *themselves* moves at LF as a free rider on the case features. This seems plausible, given our assumption that anaphors bear an anaphoric feature, as argued in 3.2.3 and chapter 6. Lasnik (1999) argues, however, that case attraction motivates movement in overt syntax of the infinitive subject into the matrix SPEC-AgrO; he bases this argument on some evidence of bind-

ing and ellipsis (a view also developed by Johnson 1991). This will not affect our reasoning. However, Lasnik also claims that all LF-movement is feature movement and does not create new binding relationships, though the ones he discusses are relationships where there is a new position for a binder, not those where there is a new position for a bindee. It is new relations of the latter sort that my theory requires.

4. Van Riemsdijk, unlike Grimshaw, does not assume that C is a functional projection within the extended projection of V. I follow van Riemsdijk in this. Nothing in this section depends on whether or not I is lexical or a functional projection of V. Not all prepositions in these accounts count as lexical heads, a matter I have nothing much to say about beyond the following paragraph in the text.

5. Within the more specific assumptions of minimalism, there is another point of difference between chain links and anaphors. Subordinate chain links are strings with the same numeration indices as their antecedents, whereas antecedents to overt anaphors do not have the same numeration indices. See note 10 to this chapter.

6. Safir (1999) unaccountably fails to cite Brody's (1995, ch. 4) nearly identical proposal that both copies of the A'-chain must be retained. Moreover, some of Brody's earlier published arguments for this position anticipate arguments in Safir (1999) and should have been properly cited.

7. Examples like Lucy loves Bill, perhaps even more than Bill does are often judged acceptable with stress on the second *Bill*, which is just a version of the acceptability of *Even Bill loves Bill*; see 2.5 and 4.1. If *more* is stressed and the second *Bill* is not stressed, then clear unacceptability results, but the same is true of ii., unless parallelism is somehow reinforced by introducing stress on *himself* (and perhaps with the addition of stress on *Bill* as well).

i. *Lucy loves *him*, perhaps even MORE than *Bill* does.
ii. *Lucy loves *him*, perhaps even MORE than *Bill* loves *himself*.
iii. Lucy loves *him*, perhaps even MORE than *BILL* loves *HIMSELF*.

8. I will discuss the nature of pronouns more specifically in chapter 6, but I am assuming they consist of some subset of person, number, gender, and case features (and sometimes animacy or a few other sorts of features). Null pronouns do not require features to be bundled in the way overt forms do, such that in English, animate third person pronouns are always marked for gender, but it is not necessarily the case that a null pronoun would have to be, consisting as it does of only the specified grammatical features of what it replaces. Thus a noun unmarked for gender, like *senator*, will not have its gender determined by the insertion of a null pronoun in the place of its copy, since if it did, it would thereby be adding information and violating Inclusiveness, as I have interpreted that principle.

9. Vehicle change is not to be confused with "late insertion," which involves a form selected in the numeration but not inserted until the post-spell-out derivation; see note 28 in chapter 3.

10. While any anaphor must satisfy LAL, it may be that the copy set at the extraction site need not be evaluated by the FTIP with respect to its moved copy, since the tail of the chain is not dependent on its moved copy for its interpretation; rather it is indistinct from its antecedent. Notice also that nothing prevents vehicle change from applying when no clause boundary is crossed in examples like i., where the trace of *the turtle*, a copy, could be vehicle-changed to a null pronoun, as in ii.

i. The turtle was captured
ii. *The turtle* was captured the *turtle/pro*.

Once again, a null pronoun would satisfy the FTIP as the most dependent form available, given that vehicle change cannot introduce an anaphor, but since there is no anaphor that needs to be licensed or replaced, vehicle change is not crucial.

11. Chung (1989) argues that NP-trace is not an anaphor on the basis of the behavior of null anaphors in Chamorro. Null anaphors permit certain restrictions on plural subjects of transitives to be relaxed in Chamorro. For example, a sentence with a transitive verb cannot have a plural subject unless it is reflexive, or else its direct object contains a null possessor identified with the plural subject (the transitive reading requires a passivelike structure, such that the plural agents are oblique). Insofar as infinitives are marked as objective, raising the subject out of the complement of a raising verb should, under standard LGB assumptions, leave an anaphoric NP-trace. Thus for the raising verb in Chamorro that means "begin," one would expect traces, if they are anaphors, to license a plural subject for "begin" when that subject is raised out of the complement. However, such cases pattern with nonanaphoric null pronominals. On the basis of argumentation along these lines, Chung concludes that NP-traces are not anaphoric. This view is quite compatible with the argumentation in the text.

12. The ECP rules out empty categories that are not properly governed, as this is defined in LGB, where one of the paradigm cases is the subject position of a tensed clause. However, the ECP is not supposed to apply to empty pronominals, such as null subjects of tensed sentences, even though null-subject languages like Italian show ECP effects for LF-movement from subject position, as demonstrated by Rizzi (1982). Chomsky (1986b) argues that the failure of anaphors in tensed subject positions arises because these forms must move to be closer to their antecedents, but this motivation for movement is not accepted here. Even if we do accept it and at the same time permit the trace of movement to be treated as pronominal, then ECP should be neutralized for A-movement in any case.

13. There are alternative analyses of these constructions that render them orthogonal to the argumentation presented here. Déprez (1992) proposes a predication analysis, where the finite clause with a pro (or PRO) subject is predicated of a SPEC higher than SPEC IP that contains the element to be raised, as illustrated in i. and ii. If this analysis is correct, then the pronominal copy argument I have made is undone, but it is not an argument in favor of the view that the domain of LAL is that of chain links.

i. [e] seems [$_{SC}$ John [$_{PREDP}$ pro is eating fish]]
ii. [John] seems [$_{SC}$ t [$_{PREDP}$ pro is eating fish]]

The introduction of a special sort of predication employing finite clauses is potentially expensive in the range of constructions it allows, but this alternative seems plausible. For more on the typology of raising, see Massam (1985).

14. If, however, SIN anaphors in situ are introduced to the derivation in relation to a null operator they license and if it is the null operator that is anaphoric and that moves to a tense-related position (or being related to its antecedent by Chomsky's, 1998, probe-agreement theory), then it is perhaps possible to defend such an account. I will not explore this plausible alternative here, but I argue against anaphoric null operators in 6.1.3, mostly on theory-internal grounds.

15. The lexical categories in question are the open classes V, A, and N, and perhaps sometimes P. Notice that this notion of "subject" is not based on any notion of proposition or predication, although it is likely true that X' is generally predicated of its SPEC-XP, as a matter of semantic compositionality. Also, I do not assume that CP or SPEC-CP is an extended projection of V (see van Riemsdijk 1998); hence SPEC-CP is not a syntactic subject position. I also assume that direct objects are sisters to V, in which case they are not the specifier

of some lower V-like projection. Otherwise, objects are indistinguishable from subjects in the sense intended. If a composite V theory of objects is adopted, it will be necessary to build in some distinction that prevents direct objects from being classed as syntactic subjects.

16. In theories where all movement is taken to be overt, such as that of Kayne (2001) and others, what I am calling *overt* is just the tip of the iceberg. Even if one favors a theory without covert movement, the relations I describe as overt movement relations are the ones that the domain relations I am examining should then correspond to, however that is couched in such a theory. The further claim that all coconstrual relations are overt movement relations, explicit in Kayne (2001) and Hornstein (2001), I leave to Safir (2003, 2004).

17. A discussion of scrambling and anaphora in Hindi, originally part of this book, was moved to Safir (2004), where a richer range of background assumptions about copy theory permits a more precise presentation.

18. I will not explore the possibility that clitic movement is A-movement of a PRO associated with the clitic, as has been proposed by Roberts (1997), building on a theory of Sportiche (1996). The A-movement properties must then be able to move past intervening subjects in certain cases and out of PPs, and such a theory is defended by Roberts on the basis of the extension of A-movement possibilities by the merger of selecting heads with higher heads (via head movement). The proposal in the text relies essentially on the descriptive properties of clitic movement; thus if this proposal should turn out to be right, then the proposal in the text is not likely to be endangered by the reanalysis.

19. It is notable, however, that the clitic *en*, which corresponds to *de*-DP, and *y*, which is locative, move differently from the other argument clitics, though their interclausal movement is limited to the same structures that climbing of other clitics are, principally, causatives (see Kayne 1975, 428).

20. I am assuming here that even if the accusative is also cliticized, it is not in a position to c-command *se*, although the structural assumptions that ensure this are underdetermined. It may be assumed that a clitic is not a possible antecedent on its own, but that only its trace can count as one. The fact, however, is clear, as pointed out by Kayne (1975, 370, fn. 30), **Je se les présenterai*, "I presented *them* to *themselves*."

21. Pica (1987, 489) points out a derived subject problem that my account does not solve—passivized objects cannot be the antecedent of Italian *sé* as in i. versus ii.

i. Gianni ha reconciliato Mario con sé.
"*Gianni* has reconciled Mario with *himself*."

ii. Gianni estato reconciliato con sé.
"*Gianni* is reconciled with *himself*."

It is not at all obvious why this is so. The derived subject, if it passes through SPEC VP, is a syntactic subject and thus should be able to antecede *sé*, other things being equal. This brings to mind the restriction on Italian clitic *si*, which cannot be anteceded by a passivized subject (see Rizzi 1986, 70, who provides examples parallel to those for French in Kayne 1975). The view that the trace of the antecedent of *sé* intervenes between *sé* and its trace creating a chain problem is ultimately not more congenial in my approach, but if *sé* is moving covertly, we may hope for a generalization over the two cases, such that both may be argued to c-command the A-trace of their antecedent. In many recent analyses, however, it is not clear why this would be bad. I leave the matter open.

22. Other causative constructions in German where the complement subject is not overt may involve suppression of the specified subject, as in the French *faire-par* constructions, or the presence of a null subject that can be controlled and antecede the complement object lo-

cally, though the details of these cases are beyond our concerns, as they do not change our basic assumptions about domains. For a recent crosslinguistic classification of the differences between biclausal and monoclausal analyses of causatives partially motivated by the distribution of anaphoric domains, see Ackerman and Webelhuth (1998, ch. 9).

23. In this case it looks as though the intervening subject is skipped if it is not animate, as Reis (1976) points out. Similar considerations appear to apply even in English for Kayne's (1975, 323) examples with *let*. I have nothing to say about these cases.

i. Why are they letting honey drip on each other's feet?
ii. *Why are they letting the soldier photograph each other's feet?

24. When *sich* is in a PP, it does not have a reciprocal reading. It appears ad hoc to distinguish two *sich* forms, one having the properties of MS SIG, which cannot be reciprocal, and the direct object one, which allows both possibilities in German, but I have no proposal to derive the difference. On reciprocal interpretation of pronouns, see the appendix to chapter 6.

25. The question of whether or not prepositions may be stranded at LF received some attention in the 1980s (see, for example, Aoun, 1985, 62–65, who argues in favor of it), but there has been little attention to it in the 90s, probably because there is no principled reason to exclude P-stranding at LF, and empirical evidence that could unambiguously bear on the question is sparse. On the more general question of pied piping at LF, see Nishigauchi (1990) and Lasnik and Saito (1992), among others, and a short review of such work in Hornstein (1995, 28–34). Chomsky's (1995b, 263–264) minimalist position implies that such stranding should be possible, where principles that generally affect movement and PF considerations do not intervene.

26. In this context, some speakers would prefer to use *zichzelf* since *zich* is not tonic, and the conjunction appears to require focus. On this matter, see Sells, Zaenen, and Zecs (1987, 183), who also point out the contrast *Zij verdedigde zichzelf/*zich en haar vrienden*, "She defended *herself* and *her* friends." See Everaert (1986, 205) on the clitic status of German *sich*, which he suggests, unlike Dutch, can also be tonic.

27. There are a number of questions that arise for this analysis internal to Dutch. If Dutch is underlyingly SOV, sentential complements to the right of the verb are extraposed. Reinhart and Reuland argue that extraposed complements in Dutch will not permit verb-raising and hence will not permit long-distance domains. In their note 16 (1991, 319–320), they consider a case where there is no extraposition of the infinitival control complement, but there is still no extended domain for *zich*. They then propose an extraposition analyses that takes S-CP-V, derives S-t-V-CP, and then intraposes pieces of the extraposed CP (including a PP containing *zich*) to the left of the verb. Then it is suggested that these last movements do not improve the anaphoric possibilities for the *zich*, since *zich* is reconstructed—interpreted in the position from which it has moved. If this is true, however, what prevents the trace of the extraposed complement in simpler cases from being reconstructed in its pre-V position? In other words, it is possible that the extraposed *te*-infinitives are not structurally different at LF from the overt verb-raising cases, unless there is a principled reason to block reconstruction, which they appeal to independently in their note 16. The entire analysis is then called into question in light of work by Zwart (1997), who argues that Dutch is underlyingly SVO, just like Mainland Scandinavian. Though I am sympathetic to their attempt to derive the differences between French *se* and Dutch *zich* from the verbal morphology of Dutch infinitival complementation, the particular analysis for Dutch they propose seems problematic.

28. Pica begins by assuming that there is there is a systematic correlation between the morphological complexity of an anaphor and its locality restrictions such that complex anaphors are local, and simplex ones are long-distance anaphors. I reject this empirical generalization in note 46 of chapter 6, so I set the matter aside until then. Progovac (1992, 1993) proposes an account of Pica's simplex–complex correlation that is not based on movement. She suggests that the long-distance relationship between an agreement node and the simplex form is a function of the purported fact that the inflectional agreement head is the only head that strictly c-commands the simplex anaphor. The relation of simplex form to simplex form is what creates the affinity between the two, and the simplex anaphor is seeking an agreement node that counts as its SUBJECT. However, in most current theoretical frameworks, there are many kinds of inflectional heads, not to mention heads internal to VP that have been proposed, that would count as strictly c-commanding heads with respect to the purported simplex anaphor. Moreover, some of these intervening heads are potential landing sites that are not the highest tensed node. In other words, the anaphor is sometimes coconstrued with subjects nonmaximal in the domain (see 5.2.4), as in Progovacs's own example.

i. Profesor$_i$ poprosil assistenta$_j$ [PRO$_j$ čitat' svoj$_{i/j}$ doklad]
professor asked assistant-ACC PRO to-read SVOJ report-ACC

If the simplex anaphor is supposed to agree or form a relationship with anything but the highest inflectional agreement node, then it is not seeking agreement or finite tense, yet if it is not seeking agreement or finite tense, but some other relation satisfied by a lower head, then the long-distance relationship across such a head is a minimality violation. Cyclic movement through TP does not have this problem (see 5.2.3), although I agree with Progovacs that a posited head movement should not violate subjacency.

29. Roberts (1991) argues that such cases do exist, but the examples he uses to support his case support a different generalization, namely, that after a head A adjoins to a head B, B can be moved leaving A behind adjoined to the trace (or copy) of B, as in the case where a particle adjoins to a verb and then the verb moves without the particle to a higher position (as in the German separable prefix construction). See Baker and Hale (1990) for a refutation of true excorporation. Moreover, Li (1990) shows that head movement cannot adjoin to a functional projection and then subsequently to a lexical projection, which Pica's approach would require.

30. For example, Cole, Hermon, and Lee (2001), relying on earlier work of Cole and Sung (1994) and references cited there, argue that subcommanding arguments, arguments contained in potential subject antecedents, can count as syntactic antecedents for anaphors that they do not c-command, just in case they can percolate their referential index to the maximal projection of the subject argument that does c-command the anaphor. Thus in Chinese equivalent of "John's car harmed him," *John* is able to antecede *ziji* in the place of *him*. The percolation in question serves no other purpose but to achieve this effect. In Cole, Hermon, and Sung (1990), percolation is also supposed to account for the blocking effect, which is that if a first person antecedent appears between *ziji* and its intended antecedent, the relationship is blocked. However, Huang and Liu (2001), drawing from the literature (see references cited there), point out that even reference to first person in positions that cannot antecede *ziji* can also block, and so the blocking positions are not a subset of potential antecedent positions. As a result, the percolation device captures nothing more than subcommand, which it describes in syntactic terms. If subcommanding antecedents must be syntactically identified and conditioned, then the descriptive cost is high. See 6.3.3.

31. Everaert (1986) suggests anaphors are quantifiers bounded by domains of quantification; however, the analogy is underexplored. See note 35 in 6.2.1.

32. It does not follow that the existence of operators sensitive to the tense domain in a language L means that L will have anaphors that have the same domain. French wh-in-situ questions are possible out of infinitives, for example, *Tu crois avoir vu qui?* "You think you saw who?" (accepted by some French speakers according to Bošković 1997), but not tensed sentences, yet the domain in question is larger than clitic movement, which is not permitted in these cases. Dayal (1996) argues that the boundedness of wh-interrogative interpretation is not a result of tense but of the position of tensed complements in postverbal position. I will not evaluate this possibility, other than to note that it does not generalize to the French cases just mentioned.

33. It is arguable, moreover, that the wh-operators so restricted in Hindi are not merely heads, but full phrases, which, if so, is evidence that this domain restriction is also independent of the head–nonhead or simple–complex distinction; see note 46 of chapter 6. Incidentally, the orthography I use to represent Hindi varies with the sources from which it is drawn. I shall use *apne* as the citation form for the anaphor in question.

34. Focus movement in Hindi appears to target a position within the extended projection of VP rather than CP, but this movement is not tense restricted (and it requires a special intonation).

i. raam-ne SITAA-KO kahaa ki apu pasand kartaa hai
Ram-ERG Sita-ACC said that Apu like-do PR
"Ram said that it is Sita that Apu likes."

35. Davison's (2001) proposal that Hindi *apne* targets TP is couched in a version of the covert head-movement approach. She not only rejects Agr as the target of movement, however, but her discussion is also less wedded to cyclic excorporation than that of Cole, Hermon, and Sung (1990) and Cole and Sung (1994). She also has more subtle discussion of the relation of tense to aspect in Hindi, which may have structural consequences, if one assumes the presence of an aspect node. See also her useful discussion of the animacy conditions on antecedents in Hindi-Urdu, which remain at least partially without explanation.

36. Overt A'-movements typically license parasitic gaps, but so far as I know, there is no analog for SIG licensing based on pre-LF null-operator movement or pre-LF movement of an unpronounced copy.

37. Hellan (1988, 66) reports that SIG is possible in a conjunction as in *Jon fortalte om seg og sin nabo* "*John* told about *himself* and *his* neighbor." Such cases suggest that a parallelism reminiscent of across-the-board extraction is required (compare the clitic status of Dutch *zich* in [30] that does not coordinate in this way). One might hope that a similar approach would extend to a Russian example (with a dative subject) mentioned by Moore and Perlmutter (2000), *Borisu žal' sebja i svoju sem'ju*, "Boris is sorry for himself and his family." Similarly, the Italian SIG form *sé* can appear in conjuncts under similar circumstances; see Giorgi (1990, 60, fn. 30).

38. Maling (1986) notes that some speakers permit SIG forms to be anteceded by what appear to be direct objects. Reuland and Sigurjónsdóttir (1997) distinguish Icelandic SIG as being capable of perspective-sensitive antecedency outside of the domain of infinitives (i.e., where it appears in subjunctives—see Maling 1984; Thráinsson 1976). In this usage, largely confined to subjunctives, SIG is a UD-form sensitive to discourse role, rather than true strict subject antecedency, since as Sigurđsson (1990) points out, they can appear without a strict subject antecedent if discourse perspective is preserved, as in i. (here my approach is distinguished from Pica, 1991, 119, who has a more liberal notion of "strict subject-orientation).

i. Formaðurinn varð óskaplega reiður. Tillagan væri avívirðileg.
The-chairman became furiously angry The-proposal was-SUBJ outrageous
Væri henni beint gegn sér persónulega.
Was-SUBJ it aimed at SIG personally

The speakers Maling (1986, 56) cites who permit examples like ii. may be relying on this discourse-sensitive usage.

ii. Við töluð við *Jón* um vandamál *sin*.
We talked to Jon about problems SIN
"We talked to Jon about his problems."

A similar point is made for indirect objects anteceding possessive anaphors embedded in direct objects when the indirect object precedes, as noted in Herslund (1986, 135) for recent Danish speech and by Holmberg and Platzack (1995, 191) for Swedish. As Holmberg and Platzack note, a nonanaphoric pronominal possessive is in fact preferred in place of *sina* in such cases, just the opposite of what would normally be expected if these forms were in fact in competition.

iii. Kan du inte ge Johan sina kläder
can you not give Johan SIN clothes
"Can't you give *Johan his* clothes?"

On the other hand, Rögnvaldson (1986, 94), reports a malefactive case in Icelandic where *sin* is anteceded by a direct object, contrasting it with a benefactive dative example from Maling (1986) that favors the nonanaphoric pronominal. Rögnvaldson also discusses some antecedency effects that distinguish pronominal from nonpronominal antecedents. I don't know what to make of all these distinctions in terms of clausal versus nonclausal architecture, but at least the anaphoric and nonanaphoric pronominal possessives in these constructions remain in complementary distribution.

39. Franks would reserve subject status for the dative subject of the infinitive, which is possible in some Slavic languages but not others, while leaving the status of dative subjects of "impersonal" verbs less clear. (He also points out some rare instances where accusatives antecede reflexives in sentences with nominative arguments, although these may permit of small clause analyses. See his discussion as cited in the text.) Debates about the nature of dative subjects have a long history, and the issues have recently been raised again. For example, Moore and Perlmutter (2000) argue that impersonal dative subject constructions do not have surface dative subjects, although the arguments in question are assumed to have been underlying ones, given some primitive notion of "subject." The impersonal datives, which are predicate specific, Moore and Perlmutter treat as nonsurface subjects (as indirect objects), where their notion of "surface" rests almost entirely on the agreement relations that they stipulate to apply to surface subjects, but not underlying ones. Sigurðsson's (2000) reply to these arguments is to propose a biclausal analysis for most of the dative subject cases that Moore and Perlmutter treat as indirect objects, whereby the dative argument in question is the subject of a higher copular clause with a null copular (the present tense copular is null in Russian). What is at issue for me is whether or not there is a point in the derivation of these sentences where the dative argument in question passes through a main predicate specifier, either that of the impersonal verb or that of the higher copular. Then the only further question, in my account, is whether the SPEC-TP position is passed through or c-commanded by

the final landing site of the dative argument. Analyses wherein the dative of the impersonal raises higher than SPEC-TP position (but through SPEC-TP position) to a topiclike position would be consistent with my account (see Moore and Perlmutter, 2000, for reference to such a proposal by Schoorlemmer, 1995, which I have not seen). Beyond pointing out that there are plausible outcomes consistent with my theory, I leave this more specialized debate aside.

40. Marathi, as discussed by Dalrymple (1993), has two anaphoric forms, *swataah* and *aapan*, with different antecedency requirements. Dalrymple argues that short-distance *swataah* requires its antecedent to be a structural subject and short-distance *aapan* requires its antecedent to be a "logical subject," which is to say that a passivized object cannot antecede *aapan*, but the dethematized logical subject of passive can. The case or agreement relations of the syntactic subject do not matter, as Dalrymple shows. These forms are in complementary distribution in most cases, where *swataah* takes a coargument antecedent, except in certain cases that seem similar to the prepositional object cases in English and in other languages where complementarity breaks down (see 3.3.4). Even in these latter domains, however, *swataah* is preferred. For some speakers, *swataah* has a domain similar to Hindi *apne*, extending into tenseless complements. It would appear that *aapan* is a candidate for UD-form (see 5.3), since it can appear as the subject of a tensed sentence and be bound across finite clauses, but Dalrymple shows that it cannot be licensed by conversational roles, such as reported speaker or point of view, unless the antecedent is sentence internal and is a logical subject. There is also a pronoun that (a) is not possible where *swataah* is obligatory and (b) can occur with a coreferent interpretation wherever *aapan* can but (c) may also refer to any argument antecedent and have a sentence-external antecedent. From the point of view of FTIP, *aapan* and the independent pronoun are outcompeted by *swataah*, but from Dalrymple's description it would appear that *aapan* does not outcompete a pronoun, which is contrary to my expectation if it must have a clause-internal syntactic antecedent. The more likely case is that *aapan* must be in the scope of a syntactically realized attitudinal operator, a proposal developed for logophoricity in Safir (in preparation). Wali and Subbarao (1991, 1101) report that *aapan* does outcompete regular pronouns when its antecedent is quantified. I do not know, however, why *aapan* requires a logical subject antecedent, and my theory does not accommodate such cases. Dalrymple, employing an LFG framework, allows for this additional grammatical function to be active in syntax—a natural result in that theory. However, it is also the case that *aapan* can take split antecedents (see Wali and Subbarao 1991, 1096), one of which is not a logical or syntactic subject, while *swataah* cannot take split antecedents, as expected from its strict subject orientation derived by movement in my account.

41. In (53a) the use of indices is merely illustrative of coreference possibilities. I also translate the UD-form using the invariant root from the language, so as to avoid translations of UD-forms as "self," which prejudges properties that are distinguished in chapter 6. Glosses are as detailed as they were in the sources cited. Malayalam examples are from Jayaseelan (1997), except where noted, and Turkish examples are from Kornfilt (2001) or Kornfilt (personal communication), except where noted. Underlined segments in the Malayalam examples are dental, segments with overstrike commas are retroflex, and /R/ is an alveolar tap.

42. See Farmer, Hale, and Tsujimura (1986, 36 and fn. 3), who remark that the relation between Japanese *zibun* and its antecedent cannot be binding, since c-command is not observed. Sportiche (1986, 371) suggests that *zibun* acts as a bound variable and that where no c-commanding antecedent is available, it is bound by a null topic. There are certain affinities with this view explored in Safir (in preparation), but the null operator posited in that work, where one is posited at all, is a propositional attitude operator.

43. Jayaseelan (1997) makes a special point of arguing that split antecedency is not surprising in anaphors since they are really all pronouns or else contain pronouns, and pronouns take split antecedents (see Bouchard 1984; Lebeaux 1984). However, all of the cases where

he permits split antecedents are cases that fall under the UD-form characterization I have distinguished here (and so I have happily used his examples). What he does not explain, as I have tried to do in the last subsection, is why there are (pronominal) anaphors that cannot take split antecedents. I have argued that all the covert clitic and tense-sensitive operator-movement cases of anaphor movement could not have split antecedents in principle. On the other hand, it is possible, for some ancillary reason, that other dependent forms would not be able to take them. Insofar as I have been able to ascertain, Chinese *ziji* cannot take split antecedents (thanks to Rachel Yang, personal communication).

i. Zhangsan shuo Lisi zhidao Wangwu yuanliang-le ziji.
   Zhangsan say Lisi know Wangwu forgive-LE ZIJI
   "Zhangsan said that Lisi knew that Wangwu forgave himself."
ii. Zhangsan he Lisi zhidao Wangwu yuanliang-le ziji.
   Zhangsan and Lisi know Wangwu forgive-LE ZIJI
   "Zhangsan and Lisi knew that Wangwu forgave himself/themselves."

In i., *ziji* can only refer to any one of the three, but not to any pair, nor to all three. By contrast, *tamen-ziji* in the place of *ziji* can refer to any pair or all three. If the subject is a conjoined NP, then of course *ziji* can refer to the pair containing both conjuncts, as in ii.

In sum, unlike *tamenziji*, *ziji* cannot have split antecedents (see also Huang 2000, 98). I do not know why this is the case for *ziji* in its UD-form distribution (see 6.3.3).

44. For reasons of space, I have suppressed a wealth of detail in this section. There are actually interesting differences between contrastive predicate types (similarity predicates vs. exclusion predicates) with respect to the pattern of anaphora that a detailed defense of (61) should take account of. I have discussed these matters in Safir (1992, 1997). I also abandon here a defense of Principle B proposed in those two articles, which was based on exclusion predicates with clausemate antecedents, since the theory of opacity–transparency proposed in Safir (1997) does not make a clear prediction.

## Chapter 6

1. For presentational convenience, I am not assuming the existence of any parameters, which I take to be grammarwide principles not lexical distinctions, set differently for different languages. I do not preclude the existence of parameters outside the domain of anaphora, but otherwise I have nothing to say about them. See Baker (1996), who provides formidable evidence for at least one macroparameter.

2. See the surveys in Heine (2000), Schladt (2000), Lichtenberk (2000), and Frajzyngier (2000b) for recent discussion. These authors are particularly interested in the process of grammaticalization by which autonomous forms become conventionalized, slowly lose their independent meaning, and ultimately function strictly as grammatical markers. For example, they correlate increasing polysemy (e.g., representing reflexivity, middle, reciprocity and emphasis, and conceived functionally) with increasing grammaticalization, and they correlate loss of internal morphology and prosodic heft to increasing grammaticalization. Polysemy, however, seems to be also a function of the class of FTIP competitors (see 6.3) and the class of semantic atom on which a given anaphor is based (see 6.2.1). For a nice illustration of the stages of grammaticalization, see Schladt (2000, 114–116).

3. Van Gelderen argues that "the introduction of special reflexives cannot be for pragmatic reasons, i.e., to disambiguate a sentence, since first and second person reflexives do not create an ambiguous context and are still introduced" (2000, 248). However, Old English pronouns were also ambiguous between reciprocal readings and reflexive identity readings,

as discussed in 3.3.2 (and perhaps there is even a distributive effect, as in German; see 3.3.3). These disambiguating functions for first and second person SELF forms are useful even where coreference is clear.

4. I will not discuss indefinite pronouns at all because they are not syntactically anaphoric (subject to LAL), since indefinites typically introduce novel entities (e.g., Heim 1982). Indefinite pronouns like nongeneric *one* (for generic *one*, see Safir in preparation) do participate in dependent readings, for example, *John wouldn't name a favorite color, but every designer has one and every consumer does too*, but I will not discuss such cases.

5. Affixes that render coargument-dependent or indistinctness readings by adicity reduction are not anaphors under this view (see 4.2.2) since LAL is irrelevant to them, though diachronically speaking, it may very well be that such affixes evolve from weak anaphoric pronominals. Recall that the distribution of ellipsis and vehicle change is a key factor distinguishing affixes from pronominals, where the existence of strict readings always correlates with the availability of corresponding pronominal affixes with independent readings.

6. I won't examine the range of possibilities that need to be considered if some pronouns are adjectives, as Romance possessive pronouns have sometimes been supposed to be. The proposal that pronouns are determiners is originally due to Postal (1966).

7. Postal (1994) discusses some direct object positions where pronouns cannot occur under a dependent reading, such as "Katie attends *Yale*, but Amanda does not attend *it*," which he stars. I find this judgment highly dependent on habitual readings, since I accept *Katie attended the graduation, but Amanda did not attend it*. This difference suggests that the selectional properties of these verbs are having an effect on dependent readings, not necessarily pronouns, as one can see from epithet examples, such as "Katie attends *Yale*, but Amanda does not attend *the damn place*," which I find odd. However, *Yale* in place of *the damn place* is fine to my ear, perhaps because it is not dependent on the object in the first conjunct.

8. Much of the discussion in this section will have to be rethought if there are no syntactic category labels. Chomsky (1995a) proposes that projection is not expressed in terms of features of heads, and if so, there may be no theoretically defined property of being a D any more than there is a theoretically defined class of Ns, though empirical generalizations may pick out these classes. Since most of the discussion of the relevant issues is not couched in the bare phrase structure system and since it is not clear how the same sorts of generalizations would be captured in that system, I won't attempt such a reanalysis here. On the other hand, making distinctions in the lexicon with respect to category labels is potentially a very descriptive strategy, and so a less descriptive system, if feasible, would be attractive.

9. Longobardi (1994) argues that to be counted as an argument, a nominal projection must be introduced by D heading a DP. Under his account, (4a) and (4d), if they occur at all, do not saturate a theta role. He adopts a Russellian view of definite descriptions, where determiners introduce operators that range over the content-denoted NP. None of the theories reviewed in this section conforms to his requirement for argumenthood for all forms of argument-saturating pronouns.

10. For example, it has been proposed that pronouns are Ns that raise to D, perhaps through intermediate functional projections, such as one headed by number. See, for example, Bernstein (1993), and for early work extending nominal projections, see Szabolsci (1994). On head raising within nominals, see Longobardi (1994) and Giusti (1994) for discussion and references. For arguments regarding additional functional projections within pronominals, see Ritter (1995) on the role of number and person within pronouns.

11. Wiltschko (1998) also argues that some pronouns (i.e., relative pronouns) are associated with a null NP range, as in (4c), licensed by relation to a relative clause nucleus. However, she argues further that personal pronouns are the projection of an D-agreement morpheme

that fails to license a range-determining null NP (a structure more akin to [4f]). See also Ritter (1995), who introduces the D-agreement/D-pronoun distinction in her discussion of Hebrew.

12. Hestvik, like Hirose after him, appeals to restrictive modification of pronouns but argues in the opposite direction. Hestvik argues that apart from generic interpretations of the sort that Hirose points to, nongenerically interpreted personal pronouns in English do not permit restrictive modification as freely as is possible in Norwegian (Hestvik 1992, 570).

i. *he who she married
ii. han som hun gifted seg med
he who she married REFL with

He argues that pronouns corresponding to phrasal NPs do not have a place for these restrictions, but NPs merely headed by pronouns allow for sisters within NP. However, within the hypothesis space permitted by (4a–f) one can imagine a variety of compatible assumptions that do not require a phrasal–nonphrasal contrast.

13. Cardinaletti and Starke (1994) claim that pronouns that are not specified human–nonhuman cannot be coordinated, yet pronouns that are specified for +human can be coordinated. Homonymous pronouns that can be distinguished in this way, such that two pronouns that can be either human or nonhuman individually, must both be interpreted as human in coordination. The pronoun unspecified for human is the one they take to be deficient, and absence of the CP projection prevents it from conjoining with a CP. Although Zribi-Hertz and Mbolatianavalona (1999, 165) provide examples of English *it* that are unacceptable in a conjunction, I believe there are acceptable examples, such as *We don't want the coal-fired plant! It and its pollution will scar the town and the whole county!*

14. It is very likely that there are more functional projections above NP than just DP, in which case it may not be the nature of D that is crucial so much as its status as a functional projection in an extended projection that is somehow permitted to be nominal without containing an NP.

15. I have left variation in the class of possible r-expressions out of discussion here, but for an interesting attempt to derive the absence of most principle-C effects in Lillooet Salish from the internal properties of r-expressions (the absence of presuppositional determiners), see Demirdache (1997). Perhaps Demirdache's approach can shed light on some of the notably absent principle-C effects noted for Thai and Vietnamese by Lasnik (1989, 153–160), although these cases involve relative independence of putative antecedent and c-commanded r-expression. See note 21 of chapter 2.

16. Cardinaletti and Starke point to French examples such as *Mais, tu ne vois donc pas ce livre? Bien sûr que je le vois* "But don't you see *this book?* Of course I see *it,*" and remark that clitic pronouns of the sort they call *deficient elements* are permissible with contrastive stress or ostension only if they refer to an entity which is "already prominent in the discourse." This is not the exclamation-on-the-beach scenario of 3.2.3; hence I do not assume these elements have deictic potential, but neither are they subject to LAL, as anaphors are.

17. The exclusion of overt pronominal anaphors in LGB, which was designed to preserve the unique status of PRO, was a consequence of the accidental character of complementarity in that theory. See 3.1.1. Once we abandon Principle B, we return to the position favored by Faltz (1977, 46–47), in that Faltz regards locality-sensitive elements as anaphoric–reflexive, and some of these he regards as pronouns.

18. Only Everaert (1990) characterizes an element (Icelandic *sig*) as both pronominal and anaphoric, but even Everaert's treatment preserves the uniqueness of PRO by arguing that Icelandic *sig*, though a pronominal anaphor, is subject to a domain for Principle B that is much smaller than the domain in which it can be bound as an anaphor (for a more general

view of this sort, see also Everaert 1991). This permits *sig* to be bound in its anaphoric domain without violating Principle B, as long as it is bound outside the domain in which Principle B is enforced. While this achieves the effect that SIG is not normally bound locally, the fact that a SELF form is available in exactly those environments that Principle B is called upon to regulate is simply accidental.

19. Pica (1987, 491) claims that pronouns can't be reciprocal (a suggestion he attributes to Higginbotham) and *se* is not a pronoun therefore. However, first and second person plural pronouns in French and German permit reciprocal interpretations (for Italian, see Giorgi 1990, 142, fn. 22), and so only a claim of syncretism specifically designed to defend this generalization will make it so. It appears that tonic pronouns, as opposed to clitics, are never interpreted as reciprocal, a fact I do not explain. For some further discussion, see the appendix to this chapter.

20. Ritter (1995) argues that the internal structure of pronominals may differ depending on whether they are first or second person, on the one hand, or third person, on the other, such that the structure of third person pronouns is more complex. I will not explore this proposal, but it would appear to be worthwhile to examine it in the context of the person–nonperson distinction.

21. Faltz (1977, 46) classes *sich* as pronominal because it shows a propensity, as other German pronouns do, to be close to a fronted verb, while full nominals can appear on either side of the prepositional phrase in ii.

i. *Hans* sah ihn/*sich*/den Fritz im Spiegel.
Hans saw him/himself/the-ACC Fritz in+DAT mirror
"Hans saw him/himself/Fritz in the mirror."
ii. *Hans* say im Spiegel *ihn/**sich*/den Fritz.

Faltz also suggests that regularities of the Slavic paradigm *menja/tebja/sebja* would appear to treat *sebja* as a pronoun.

22. The fact that the MS SIG forms do not support reciprocal readings suggests we should appeal to Kayne's account of why French *soi* and Italian *sé* do not support reciprocal readings. However, these MS pronouns do not have clitic forms, so we must assume, in line with Kayne's analysis, that the *-ig* morpheme is inherently singular. This will effectively predict that *sig* cannot have a plural antecedent, and this seems to be true for many Danish speakers (Sten Vikner, personal communication), although not for Norwegian. As Vikner (1985, 53, fn. 13) points out, Danish also has possessive forms of the *m/d/s* series, *min/din/sin*, but for the plural, none of these stems is employed, and instead we find *vores/jeres/deres*. If the possessive *-in* morpheme is singular, as Kayne suggests for *-oi*, then this is unsurprising. From this perspective, German *sich* acts more like the French clitic *se* than the MS SIG forms in that *sich* can be reciprocal, but this is not so surprising in that second person plural is indistinct from the third (non-)person forms, including *sich* for dependent-identity readings where locality permits. This suggests that the *-ich* morpheme in German is not inherently singular.

23. Kayne does suggest that there is some reason to see the Italian *sé* as evidencing a principle-B effect when *sé* is not embedded in a PP. The effect of the PP is unexplained. Compare the following cases.

ia. Gianni si fotografo. "*Gianni* photographs *himself*."
b. Io mi fotografo. "*I* photograph *myself*."
c. Tu ti fotografo. "*You* photograph *yourself*."
iia. Gianni ha fotografato me/te. "Gianni has photographed me/you."
b. ??Gianni ha fotografato *sé*. "*Gianni* has photographed *himself*."
iii. Gianni ha parlato di *sé*. "*Gianni* has spoken of *himself*."

It is far from clear that iib. supports the conclusion that principle B is involved, since iib. is in FTIP competition with examples like ia., and the clitic is weaker. Kayne adds that iii. is not acceptable to all Italian speakers. One such speaker only accepts iii. in an "elegant stylistic register," preferring instead iv., unless the subject is quantified, as in v.

iv. *Gianni* ha parlato di *lui.*
v. *Ciascuno dei ragazzi* ha parlato di *sé.*

This could be the effect of requiring *sé* for the more specific bound reading but not permitting it where it is not dependent on its antecedent. It follows from FTIP that if *sé* is not available for this speaker for iv., then *lui* will be well formed where Principle B would otherwise rule it out. The fact that this speaker does not permit **Gianni ha fotografato lui* suggests that this is in FTIP competition with examples like ia., while there is no clitic competitor for iv. Thus the effect of the preposition purportedly blocking principle B is explained, not just stipulated, in our FTIP approach, which reduces Principle B to FTIP competition.

24. Kayne points out that underspecification with respect to number is not sufficient to achieve anaphoric status, since, if he is right, none of the members of the *m/t/s* series is marked for number but is singular only by virtue of combination with singular *-oi*. The possibility that underspecification for number is a necessary condition for anaphorhood, as Kayne suggests following the spirit of Burzio's (1996) approach, is also problematic for English SELF forms, which can be plural, as discussed in 3.1.2.3.

25. There are also distinctions between *de se* (conscious self reference; see Lewis 1979) and non-*de se* readings based on the use of PRO or a SELF form in environments where they could both linearly appear (e.g., *Wilson wants himself to win*), which further suggests, at least for obligatory control environments, that there is an additional reason not to put PRO in competition with overt forms.

26. Landau (2000) correctly argues that any theory in which PRO is bound as an anaphor under principle A is untenable, largely on the basis of the fact that contexts of obligatory control (OC) are not always exhaustive control (EC) but sometimes only partial control (PC), and he argues convincingly and at length that PC is typically OC. He points to examples like *Milton wants to go,* which allow for a PC reading where those who would go, consistent with Milton's desire, include not only Milton, but unspecified others, a reading not available with *Milton tried to go*, which is EC. If Landau is right that *want* is an OC verb, and anaphors are always exhaustively bound by their antecedents (see 3.3.1), then PRO must be not be an anaphor bound under principle A. Even though by this reasoning Landau eliminates the major motivation for assuming PRO is an anaphor, he assumes PRO is an anaphor anyway because it is sensitive to Chomsky's (1998) Agree mechanism that he employs to enforce OC. However, the same mechanism would appear to apply to any underspecified form under agreement, regardless of anaphoric status, and pronoun subjects must agree with the agreement features borne by their local tense (whether tense is anaphoric or not; see Landau). The only other reason Landau gives to treat PRO as anaphoric is that it appears sensitive to logophoric antecedency requirements, but as demonstrated in chapter 5 and Safir (in preparation), logophorically sensitive pronouns are not typically anaphors.

27. Presumably the same holds for implicit arguments, such as the missing agent of passive or implicit arguments in nominals like *Attacks on her character have helped Clarence*, where there is ambiguity as to whether it is Clarence who is responsible for the attacks or unnamed others. It is not obvious that any overt nominal as the subject of *attacks on her character* would represent a structure otherwise identical to the one that licenses the implicit argument interpretation. For criteria distinguishing implicit arguments from PRO and trace, as well as references, see Safir (1991). One of the leading proposals on control, that of Borer

(1989), treats PRO and pro as indistinct, but certain problems remain for that approach (see Borer 1989, 108, fn. 20; and Jaeggli and Safir 1989, 19–20). As Huang (1989) points out, many Chinese cases of pro seem to be subject to control, but once susceptibility to control and susceptibility to LAL are distinguished, there is no reason to treat pro or PRO as anaphoric. Note that Borer's anaphoric Agr proposal for certain cases of pro does not crucially require pro or PRO to be anaphoric so much as it requires the infinitive tense to be anaphoric (hence heading a projection that is within the domain of the higher verb and anaphoric to the antecedent of PRO–pro; for details, see Borer 1989). See also the previous note.

28. For the FTIP competition, it cannot be that pro is not structurally present at all, otherwise it would not compete with examples that have overt forms. The reason for this is that the FTIP is defined on substitutions in numerations, not additions to them, as pointed out in 3.3.3. I presume that the WPC has a substitution algorithm restricted in the same way (see 7.1).

29. Jaeggli (1986) points out that third person plural arbitrary interpretations, along the lines of English "they don't make cars like they used to," are only possible with pro, not with overt pronouns in Spanish, but they are possible in English, he argues, because there is no competition to represent the reading. It remains to be seen if this fact can be related to the tendency for pro to be favored for topics. See also van Steenbergen (1991, 234) for what looks like a competition between nulls and overt pronouns in Finnish.

30. It is unclear whether null objects are pro. At least some analyses treat them as variables bound by topic operators and subject to strong crossover, as argued by Huang (1984) for Chinese and Hasegawa (1985) for Japanese. Evidence for null objects that compete with pronouns will thus have to control these factors. I leave the matter open. I also set aside discussion of implicit arguments such as agents in cases like *discussion of the issue* (see Safir, 1991, and references cited there) and *wherever you live, you meet your friends at the local bar*, where *local* appears to harbor a bound variable, as discussed by Partee (1989) and Higginbotham (1997).

31. The property of being anaphoric need not be expressed by a binary feature, or else the minus value can be distinguished from the absence of anaphoric marking (e.g., where the +/– feature is not expressed at all). It does not seem to be necessary to have such added descriptive power.

32. I have argued in Safir (1996a, 1996c) that such examples involve covert syntactic incorporation, though I am not now certain that the evidence is robust enough to support that conclusion. On syntactic incorporation, see note 8 of chapter 4 and the discussion of Greek in 6.3.1.

33. Reinhart and Reuland (1991, 286) also propose that SELF is an identity relation imposed on a relational noun, but they do not relate the extra-anaphoric meaning of *self* to its meaning as an anaphor.

34. For speculations on why other inalienable relations are not used metonymically to form reflexives, see Safir (1996c, 558, fn. 8) and Schladt (2000, 112–113).

35. Postma (1997) argues that SELF forms induce upward entailment to the whole from the parts of an individual. Thus if Mary cut her foot, then Mary cut herself. There are problems with this form of entailment if it is supposed to be based on inclusion. If Tom bandages his fingernail, then one might say he bandaged his hand, but one would not say that if Tom trimmed his fingernail that Tom trimmed his hand. Yet there is a general sense in which Tom trimmed or bandaged himself if he did these things to his fingernail. The problem, however, is that metonymic anaphors, taken literally, include "head" and "face," in which case it is not upwardly entailed that damage to the hand is damage to the face or head. This would suggest that the upward entailment is from the part directly to the whole SELF, not necessarily to any other part of the SELF, as metonymic conventionalization as proposed in the text directly

implicates. Postma then predicts that if a given predicate does not allow the upward entailment, then it does not permit the reflexive. For example, if one amputates one's foot, one cuts off a body part, but eliminating a part crucially does not entail eliminating a whole, so **Amy amputated herself* contrasts with *Amy cut herself.* While this correlation appears to work, Postma also claims that nonagentive transitives with inalienable body part readings are always upward entailing, which is not always the case; for example, *Tawnee twisted her ankle/wrist/knee/hip* would lead us to expect **Tawnee twisted herself* (which has the wrong reading). It not clear to me how well the entailment strategy will work with the other relational anaphoric atoms, but if it does, it would appear that appeal to any specific relational anaphoric meaning, as opposed to the meaning of the predicate involved, may be superfluous.

36. See Safir (1996c, 564) and Di Sciullo (1996) for discussion of some of the ways that the root *self* still has some autonomous usage in English. The earliest structural analysis is that of Helke (1971), who assumes that the *self* morpheme is the same as the one that has autonomous usage and relates pronoun-*self* in English to idioms like "*He* held *his*/*her breath." Ingria (1982) argues that *self* in pronoun-*self* is not the same as the autonomous *self,* but I defuse the force of his objection in Safir (1996c, 557, fn. 7). I do not explore the restrictions on *self* within compounds, but see Sproat (1985, 289–306), Lieber (1992), Hendrick (1995, 324–325), and Di Sciullo (1996) for discussion.

37. Thanks to Olúsèye Adésolá (personal communication) for pointing out the reciprocal facts to me. Since Yoruba *ara* retains its BODYPART semantics in addition to its grammaticalized readings, it must be the case that there is no *necessary* connection between this form of polysemy and phonological reduction, although a weak correlation of this sort appears to exist, as pointed out by a number of scholars, such as Kemmer (1993), Heine (2000), and references cited there. Yoruba does have clitic pronouns, incidentally, but they are not anaphors, and hence not effective competitors with the conventionalized body part expression for a reciprocal interpretation. The mystery is why the reciprocal relation is always essentially local. See the appendix to this chapter.

38. It is perhaps worth pointing out that this reciprocal usage does not follow from any account that simply treats a metonymic BODYPART form as a semantically unanalyzed "intensive" or "emphatic," although such forms may serve that function in discourse (for discussion, see Safir in preparation). It is often claimed that an emphatic usage diachronically precedes a reflexive usage for a BODYPART, though what is described as emphatic is sometimes just disambiguation between possible dependent readings.

39. Some of the cases where two metonymic anaphors are used involve *body* as the reciprocal and *head* as the reflexive. It may be that *body* is closer to OTHER in some ethnosemantic systems, and hence is a better candidate for grammaticalization as a reciprocal. Frajzyngier (2000a) suggests that *body* is tied to a relation of exclusion, though the connection does not seem necessary or perspicuous to me.

40. Similarly, Pica and Snyder (1997) take what I am calling a *rigid internalist approach* to the available interpretations of *se.* They suggest that French *se* has an internal semantics flexible enough to represent both reflexive and reciprocal interpretations. The critique of Rooryck and vanden Wyngaerd (1997) in 4.3.3 extends to the Pica and Snyder account. Moreover, Pica and Snyder provide a semantic and syntactic analysis of *se* that makes it difficult to distinguish from their account of true relational anaphors. Such an approach also seems to underappreciate the evidence that *se* is pronominal and appears to require *me* and *te* to have the same relational analysis, which seems odd for their independent usage as pronominals.

41. It is not clear how to class the Finnish form *itse*, which, as Faltz (1977, 137) notes in passing, is originally related to a root meaning "reflection on water." Much depends on whether the form in question retains any relational meaning in comparison to other syn-

chronically extant usages. Schladt (2000, 106–107) notes that the Astronesian language Kwaio uses a form with a similar meaning to form reflexive readings, but this usage is "restricted to purely visual reflexivity." These meanings seem too particular to be classed as SAME atoms.

42. Zribi-Hertz (1995, 365) dismisses the claim that *own* is anaphoric but does so on the basis of examples that employ stressed *own*. If my interpretation of the data in Safir (1996c, 572) is correct, however, not every stressless case is anaphoric, since there I judged Mary might use his own picture against him acceptable with stress on *against* and an agentive reading for *his own*. This is a rare stressless case without a c-commanding antecedent. The acceptability judgment is not robust, but if it is correct to treat it as acceptable, I have no account of why it is not anaphoric.

43. Jayaseelan (1997, 225–228) discusses an interesting distributive pronoun–pronoun anaphoric form in Malayalam that has a distributional profile similar to the English reciprocal. However, even if some reciprocals or distributives are formed with pronominals, the point is that the nonpronominal roots that often occur in reciprocals have relational properties that are not accidental. Saxon (1984) describes a Dogrib form *ye-* that respects LAL, perhaps as clitic anaphor, but requires disjoint reference with the form it is dependent on. This would appear to be exactly what we would expect of an OTHER anaphor that was not associated with a quantifier that could partition it, but I have no information about the internal structure of *ye-*.

44. Recall from chapter 4 that the LRP requires a dependent-identity reading, as opposed to a codependent one, when an identity-specific anaphor is anteceded by a coargument. Reinhart and Reuland (1991, 292–294) suggest that SELF anaphors are local because they match the theta grid of what they (covertly) adjoin to. Thus the identity relation of the SELF form is imposed on the argument structure of the predicate they adjoin to. They are assuming, however, that predicates so adjoined are fully symmetric, which does not appear generally to be the case (see 4.2.1 on proxy readings).

45. In positing (23a, b), I must reject the proposal, defended in Safir (1996c), that relational anaphors are necessarily unsaturated terms (Pica 1987, 486–487) with a syntactically open argument place. One way of exploring this idea (loosely based on Pica 1987; Reinhart and Reuland 1991; and Safir 1996c) is to postulate that a body part anaphor saturates only its *part* argument and implies a *whole* that is related to it. The anaphoric relation results from the lack of a saturating nominal to fill the *whole* argument place; hence the whole projected nominal is deficient and dependent until an antecedent for the empty *whole* role is found. One problem with such a position is that body part anaphors most frequently occur in construction with pronouns, but they don't have to. Moreover, a relational noun like *husband* in English represents the predicate HUSBAND and saturates the *male spouse* part of its argument structure inherently. If *her* in *her husband* saturates the *female spouse* role of HUSBAND, then it would not be clear why *a/the/her husband* is not anaphoric. I now reject this line of reasoning, maintaining instead that conventional anaphors are marked as such.

46. Faltz (1977) was the first to distinguish compound reflexives on the basis of whether (what I am calling) the relational stem is (a) an adjunct on an argument headed by a pronoun, or (b) the head of an argument phrase. A loose correlation between the morphological complexity of an anaphor and its locality domain was first proposed by Faltz (1977, 153) who noted that complex anaphors tended to be more local. Pica (1987) is perhaps the first to attempt to explain how the phrasal properties of anaphors might predict the locality of their antecedence. He proposes that long-distance anaphors are morphologically simplex and subject oriented, while local anaphors are morphologically complex and have no subject orientation. A number of researchers have exploited versions of Pica's claim ever since (notably Battistella 1989; Cole, Hermon, and Sung 1990; Cole and Sung 1994). The basic idea is that complex forms are phrasal and therefore move, if they move, as XPs, whereas simplex forms

have the opportunity to move as X° forms. The difference between permissible landing sites was then supposed to explain why heads could move farther than phrasal categories.

However, in 6.1. it was established that most pronouns participate in phrases and are often themselves complex, or else a variety of successful generalizations that exploit distinctions in the phrasal or morphological complexity of pronouns must be abandoned. From the perspective of the UH, Pica's account is not an explanation in any case, since whether or not forms are complex or simplex has no relationship *outside of anaphora* to the domains in which forms can occur in, especially as it employs a form of head–phrasal movement contrast not otherwise attested, as pointed out in 5.2.2.1.

Both Jayaseelan (1997) and Kornfilt (2001) argue that Pica's morphological complexity proposal is counterexemplified by languages like Turkish, since they argue that a complex form is also employed as a long-distance anaphor. However, this is only a counterexample if there is any reason to see *kendi* + *Agr* as a long-distance anaphor. In fact the "long-distance" case does not evidence a long-bounded domain, but the domain of a UD-form. However, if the Faltz/Pica proposal were to take account of UD-forms, many of the examples that support it would be set aside as well. Many of the examples used to counterexemplify the Faltz/Pica generalization in Huang (2000, 96–97) might be addressed this way, but not the compositionality of simple pronominals. See also 6.3.

47. This does not mean that a pronoun could not replace a whole phrase in a test derivation, such that a pronoun could compete in a test derivation with a pronoun + adjunct form as a whole, but since a pronoun + adjunct form has the properties of its head, the result is a tie (pronoun and pronoun).

48. Notice further that Faltz (1977, 108) proposes that whenever an anaphor is pronominal, it is subject oriented. This seems to be thoroughly correct for the few languages where it has been investigated (and it is true for Germanic, Romance, Slavic, and Hindi), especially if we take the criterion for pronounhood to be that discussed in 6.1. This generalization is consistent with our analysis of covert tense-sensitive operator movement and clitic movement, but pronominal anaphors that are neither (covert) clitics nor (covert) operators could presumably have a short-bounded domain that does not show subject orientation. Thus I do not fully derive Faltz' generalization, if indeed it is a correct generalization. A counterexample to the general form of my analysis would be a pronominal anaphor with a long-bounded, tense-sensitive domain and no subject orientation. Such arguments may turn on whether or not a given form is pronominal or relational. See Faltz (1977, 116–117) on Wappo (Yukian—Northern California), Pima (Uto-Aztecan), and Hindi, which he treats as subject oriented and pronominal (but see 201, fn. 14, for some doubts). Keep in mind that perspective-sensitive pronouns bound by attitudinal operators (logophors, as in the West African Kwa languages) do not count as counterexamples, as their domains are not tense sensitive in the relevant sense; they are unbounded; and they do not respect the intervention of islands. See Safir (in preparation) for discussion.

49. Since OTHER is a relational anaphor, we correctly predict that complex reciprocals are local in the same way that SELF forms are. What does not follow, however, is that a reciprocal reading is not permitted where the anaphoric form is not permitted; for example, *The men think they like Mary* does not mean that each of the men thinks that at least one (or each one) of the other men likes Mary. This mystery remains open, but see the appendix to this chapter for discussion.

50. For a variety of early attempts to relate *self* as emphatic in its usage attached to full nominals, see Moravcsik (1972) and Edmondson and Plank (1978). Edmondson and Plank call the adverbial usage in (34) *intensive*, reserving *emphatic* for *John himself* and most of the long-distance cases, while König and Siemund (2000, 43) consider the latter *adnominal* and like me, use *adverbial* for cases like (34) (see their paper for a survey and recent refer-

ences), apparently to avoid mixing semantic distinctions with syntactic ones. I have chosen not to examine the semantic force of relational anaphors employed as intensives (with their scalar implications) or emphatics (normally contrastive) in this book, using these latter properties merely as diagnostics for usages that do not form reflexive readings. I do not agree that the use of intensives must be understood in order to understand reflexivity, although I believe there is reason to relate identity predicate adjuncts to intensification as a form of "greater than necessary" identity assertion, perhaps the source of the degree of expectation effects (Edmonson and Plank) or exclusion of alternatives (König and Siemund) that has been attributed to intensifiers. Responding to an early formulation of *self* as identity predicate, that of Browning (1993), König and Siemund go so far as to say, "A phrase like *President Clinton himself* would then simply mean *President Clinton/the same/and no one else*, a consequence that is clearly absurd" (2000, 57). Nothing in their essay convinces me it is absurd as a literal meaning that is then molded by pragmatic context. On the distribution of *he himself*, see McKay (1991; answering Bickerton 1987), who establishes that *he himself* is not a syntactic anaphor, but the absence of *him himself*, as opposed to *he himself*, remains an open question, as remarked in Safir (1996c, 553, fn. 4).

51. Fukuda's (1989) analysis anticipates my application of the adjunct–argument distinction to account for local versus nonlocal distribution of pronoun-SELF anaphors. Verheijen (1986) proposes a special syntactic category for intensive SELF forms, distinguishing readings by level of attachment of the SELF form, but this has no independent motivation.

52. This analysis differs in this respect from Everaert (1986, 38), for example, who treats *zelf* as an adjunct on the basis of the parallel with the emphatic usages, even though it is not emphatic when locally anteceded (and *zich* is not available). Everaert sets arguments and nonarguments in contrast to distinguish inherent reflexive and prepositional object uses of *zich*, (and Pica, 1984b, distinguishes argument and nonargument anaphors on a different basis), but among the distinctions I have made, only indistinctness interpretation and argument–adjunct contrasts are significant.

53. There are a few contexts where *selbst* is required in German. See, for example, references in Safir (1996c, 555, fn. 6).

54. Zribi-Hertz (1995) treats English pronoun-SELF and especially French pronoun-SAME as "unspecified bindable expressions" (UBEs), which are elements that are optionally bound, though they are always at least dependent on discourse (much like my description of a UD-form). However, Zribi-Hertz contends that these elements may be bound locally, so she must exempt them from principle B. If there is no principle B, then there is nothing to run afoul of. On the other hand, some of the same sorts of forms must be free locally but are dependent (whether c-commanded or not) outside the local domain, and these sorts of forms would require a separate classification for Zribi-Hertz. In my account, both varieties may arise naturally depending on whether or not they have competition in the local domain (see 6.3). Zribi-Hertz further proposes that stress on what I call an adjunct anaphor has the effect of destressing the pronominal associated with it, and destressing, she argues, renders a pronoun more discourse dependent. If this is so, then the deictic insufficiency of pronouns associated with relational anaphor adjuncts is derivable. While I believe this is true, the argument must be used with care. English pronoun-SELF has stress on the SELF portion, but no native speaker would fail to distinguish the degree of stress in i. as opposed to ii.

i. *Elam* loves *himself.*
ii. *Elam* believes that no one but *himself* is qualified.

While in both of these cases, stress falls on *-self,* the stress in ii. is unavoidably contrastive, whereas i. does not have to be contrastive at all and, unlike *-self* in ii., the *-self* portion in i. is necessarily present, not optional. Destressing of a pronoun in construction with a relational head may render the pronoun dependent, but it does not predict the difference between anaphoric and UD-form usages of the whole form, while the head–adjunct distinction does. Reuland (1997) suggests that UD-form pronoun-SELF may be structurally different from local pronoun-SELF, but unlike French pronoun-*même*, it is not the case that SELF forms promoted to UD-form elements can ever occur as the subject of a tensed sentence.

iii. ?*He* claims that Mary compares favorably with *himself* in this regard.
iv. *He* claims that **(he) himself* compares favorably with Mary in this regard.

The verb *compare* is as close as we can get to a verbal contrastive predicate, and not all speakers accept iii., but all speakers distinguish iii. from iv. This contrasts with French (57a). For these reasons I reject the view that SELF of pronoun-SELF in English is always an adjunct (also contra Di Sciullo 1996).

55. Actually, this example is suspect for my purposes, since promotion of an anaphor to UD-form might be involved, as argued for English in Safir (1992, 1997) and 5.4. Most of the counterexamples to the locality of English pronoun-*self* in Zribi-Hertz (1995) occur in comparison contexts. It is notable, however, that promotion of an anaphor to UD-form is sensitive to the internal composition of the anaphor. In MS, wherein there is a SIG-SELF–pronoun-SELF contrast, only pronoun-SELF can be promoted to discourse dependent, as illustrated in i. for Norwegian.

i. Carl sa at Marie hadde snakket med alle andre enn ham/ham selv/*?seg/*seg selv.
Carl said that Marie had talked to all others than him/himself/SIG/SIG-SELF
"Carl said that Marie had talked to everyone but him/herself."

Perhaps because SIG has no argument structure it cannot be exempted from LAL in the way that relational anaphors can, as discussed in 5.4. Notice, that pronoun-SELF is not antisubject oriented in these environments, as predicted, since it has no subject-oriented competitor. For further discussion, see Safir (1997:353, 358) and references cited there.

56. Faltz (1977, 144–145) points out that (44) is also possible with the nonanaphoric pronoun *el* (with or without *mismo*) in a more colloquial style of speech.

57. The issues in Italian for the SAME anaphor, *se stess+Agr*, are more complicated, as it appears that the SAME portion is part of a complex idiom, such that the *stess+Agr* part does not have the status of an adjunct in the local domain, in part because it appears to compete with *sé* in some local prepositional object environments. In this respect, it acts more like English, especially since *se stess+Agr* is not subject oriented. I will not explore the matter for reasons of space, but see Giorgi (1990) for discussion.

58. It has been suggested that the surface domains for forms supporting anaphora have the property of corresponding to subsets. Yang (1983) first proposed the idea that each larger domain contains all the positions that any smaller one does and Manzini and Wexler (1987) and Wexler and Manzini (1987) later exploited it as the subset relation in their learning schema (for a critique, see Safir 1987). They argue that universally fixed domains in the subset relation guide learning, such that the child's unmarked assumption is that anaphors are local, since this is consistent with the smallest possible language (the fewer places an anaphor can be, the fewer sentences in the language that have anaphors in them). However, the subset effect, where it holds, is an artifact of lost competitions, such that pronouns are obviated only where an anaphor is available. Because they assume Principle B, Wexler and Manzini have to argue that there is an expectation that pronouns are obviated in the widest possible domain, but pronouns are suspiciously available where anaphors are not. Moreover, there is a reason to

suppose that anaphors, once introduced (perhaps for functional reasons, to avoid ambiguity with noncoconstrued interpretations), are computationally more efficient, since their position on the most dependent scale means that there are no test derivations to run with pronouns or r-expressions. Apart from the fact that some domain properties derive from the inherent properties of anaphors, the assumption that children presume an anaphor to have a highly local domain unless there is evidence to the contrary remains plausible, but choosing the smallest language does not appear to play any role, as there are just as many sentences no matter which form wins the competition.

59. Lidz (2001a) argues that antilocality should be captured by a rigid internalist analysis and that any apparent complementarity effects are accidental. The issue concerns a Kannada pronominal anaphor *tann*+Case as opposed to the complex anaphor *tann*+Case-*taane*, which are argued to have different internal semantics, such that one is a "pure reflexive" and the other is "near reflexive." As pointed out in note 36 of chapter 4, however, there is no need to stipulate properties for both anaphors, once one of them, the complex one, is endowed with interpretive specificity.

60. For *o idhios* to be a UD-form would be unsurprising, as most SAME-based dependent forms are. It is plausible, however, that there is a null pronominal head that *o idhios* is an adjunct on, and if so, such elements do not compete with pronouns, unless they are perspective-sensitive A'-dependents. Enc (1989) treats Greek *o idhios* as necessarily locally A'-bound by a (null) logophoric operator (though she permits a message receiver to be a logophoric antecedent), supposedly ruling out any local A-binder. A'-binding by a logophoric operator would be consistent with the approach to logophoricity proposed in Safir (in preparation), but in contrast to my latter proposal, Enc assumes that A'-binding of *o idhios* must be local.

61. The distribution of *ton eafton tou* raises a variety of interesting issues that I set aside because they do not directly bear on the FTIP. The analysis of the internal morphology of *ton eafton tou* proposed by Anagnostopolou and Everaert (1999) (A&E) is broadly consistent with the view that it is a relational anaphor heading an argument position, and thus its distribution is predicted to be short bounded within my approach. Their account, however, is couched in the R&R framework and addresses tensions in that theory that don't arise in this one (such as the status of the +/-R feature that induces dependency and the +/-SELF feature that induces reflexivity). By classifying *ton eafton tou* as [+R, +SELF], they render it incapable of either dependent or nonreflexive interpretation, an apparent contradiction they resolve by forcing the relational portion of the anaphor to incorporate, along the lines of Safir (1996c). They then argue that examples like i. support the Reinhart and Reuland view that reflexivity is a thoroughly symmetric relation (the clitic doubles the dative *Petru*, where *Petru* is the antecedent of *o eaftos tu*).

i. O eaftos tu tu aresi tu Petru
the self his CL-DAT likes the Petros-DAT
"*Himself* pleases/appeals to *Petros*."

However, i. raises difficulties for A&E as well since incorporation is almost never permitted out-of-surface subjects for Baker's (1988) principled reasons, which they accept. Thus they must argue that there is a covert form of incorporation that occurs when *ton eafton tou* is not a subject, but an underlying internal argument of the psych predicate. If the dependency properties of *ton eafton tou* are determined on the basis of its underlying position, then it can as easily be argued that LAL is satisfied if the surface position of *ton eafton tou* is PF movement, an assumption just as necessary in the A&E account. If so, the view that reflexivity is asymmetric is not refuted. Once again, this does not preclude an analysis whereby *eafton* incorporates, but the assumption is not necessary in my account, at least not on the basis of these examples.

62. Jayaseelan (1997, 195, fn. 13) also claims that nonlocal *taan-tanne* is not subject to logophoric effects, but he seems to take a very narrow notion of these, presumably limiting them to verbs of saying, since the example he gives with the verb meaning "see" suggests a perceiver–experiencer as antecedent. In the wider sense of discourse sensitivity (e.g., in Kuno 1987; or Sells 1987), this case qualifies. It is clear, however, that *awan-tanne* is not sensitive in this way.

63. Jayaseelan (1997, 193, fn. 10) remarks that *taan* is also excluded in the ECM construction, so it does not appear to be a reflexive marker. I do not know if *taan-tanne* requires stress in this environment, but I would not expect it to.

64. The generativist literature on Japanese anaphora begins very early in the evolution of modern generative grammar (Kuroda 1965; Kuno 1972; and Inoue 1976) and has been very influential on the progress of our understanding of these issues. See Abe (1997), Aikawa (1993) and Katada (1991) for further references.

65. There is also the issue of whether or not the immediately subjacent subjects of complement clauses (near subjects) are anaphors with respect to their antecedents. Aikawa (1994) argues the *zibun-zisin* forms anteceded in these positions are emphatic. Huang and Liu (2001), however, argue that Chinese *ziji* when anteceded in the near-subject position behaves as a local anaphor, not restricted by discourse factors (see note 66 to this chapter). If so, I must argue that *ziji* (or a null form associated with it) must act as an operator anaphor moving it into the domain of LAL. This may be possible in Japanese and Chinese, languages without agreement, if a consequence of agreement between SPEC-IP and I is to extend the scope of tense (perhaps IP = TP), which would otherwise only obtain in I' by strict c-command. Semantically, this would be hard to detect since the subject originates in SPEC-VP, and that position would be in the domain of tense anyway. It is clear, however, that languages that have agreement do not permit the anaphoric domain to extend down to the near subject of a tensed clause complement.

66. There is also a difference in Chinese between local *ziji* and long-distance *ziji* (also argued in 5.3 to be a UD-form), which is detectable from the range of interpretational restrictions they are sensitive to. As Huang and Liu (2001) demonstrate, long-distance *ziji* is sensitive to discourse-perspective effects associated with its antecedents (e.g., the blocking effect induced by intervening first person forms), whereas local *ziji* is not sensitive to such effects. See also Cole, Hermon, and Lee (2001) for a similar distinction in Teochew, a Chinese dialect as it is spoken in Malaysia, and Reuland and Sigurjónsdóttir (1997), for a similar account distinguishing bounded versus logophoric distribution of Icelandic *sig*. Huang and Liu argue that locally subcommanded *ziji* also acts as an anaphor. Subcommand holds where the possessor of an inanimate subject serves as the antecedent for *ziji* (for details, see Tang 1989). Although there are accounts of antecedents percolating their antecedency (e.g., Cole, Hermon, and Sung 1990), no theory I am aware of gives an independently motivated account of why subcommand should license true anaphors. For Teochew, Cole, Hermon, and Lee argue that such cases have the properties of discourse-sensitive forms. See also note 69 of this chapter.

67. Richards (1997) also argues that *kare-zisin* and *zibun-zisin* are not in competition on the grounds that only *zibun-zisin* can support a bound-variable reading, and he claims that *kare-zisin* cannot support such a reading. Since they are not in competition, no antisubject orientation arises for *kare-zisin*. I have a different analysis of what counts as subject orientation (see 5.2.4), so it is not clear that I need to make this case. I also do not share Richards's view, a rather standard one, that strict readings are coreferent rather than dependent readings, yet he uses such distinctions to distinguish anaphoric relations as coreferent as opposed to truly anaphoric. I would not cut the pie the same way.

68. Fuji (1994) treats *zisin* as a determiner and *zibun* as a noun, but he assumes that *zisin* has relational argument structure, an assumption that seems odd for a functional category, though he notes that *zisin* contrasts with *zibun* in that *zibun* can be modified by a possessive, as in *kinoo-no zibun*, "yesterday's self." This appears to be a reified substantive usage—not what I would expect of a pronoun. Fuji also criticizes Aikawa (1993) for proposing a difference between local and long-distance *zibun-zisin/kare-zisin* that does not rely on a compositional analysis of its parts. Fuji, however, stipulates a difference between long-distance and local *zisin*, which then composes with *zibun*, *kare*, nominals, and so on. The internalist strategy I have chosen to express the difference is in terms of head versus adjunct.

69. This analysis of Japanese begs a comparison with Chinese, where compounds formed with a pronoun and *ziji* have also been characterized as local (e.g., by Huang and Tang 1991), although there is no form corresponding to Japanese *zibun-zisin*. Rather, Chinese *ziji* appears to more closely parallel *zisin* than it does *zibun*, as Jayaseelan (1997) has pointed out, in part because it appears in construction with a pronoun. If so, perhaps the form corresponding to long-distance *zibun* is null in Chinese. The analysis of *ziji* as being in association with a null pronominal form shielded from Principle B is first suggested by Tang (1989, 97–98), though she treats the form as a prefix; this position is adapted as structural embedding by Jayaseelan (1997, 210). If so, the distribution of *ziji* is only predicted if it is an adjunct on a null pronoun in its long-distance distribution but the argument head of a phrasal anaphor in its local distribution, where either a null form or *ta* functions as its determiner or specifier. The fact that *ta-ziji* is not subject oriented follows from the assumption that *ta* is an independent pronoun, not an operator, and acts the same way within the phrasal anaphor. The analyses of *ziji* as a relational anaphor that is the head of an argument and as an adjunct on a UD-form are presented in i. and ii., respectively, and *ta-ziji* as an argument-relational anaphor associated with a pronoun is presented in iii.

i. local anaphor $[_{DP}\ \text{pro?}\ [_{D'}[\text{D}]\ [\text{ziji}]_{NP}]]$
ii. UD-form $[_{DP}[_{DP}\ \text{pro?}]\ [_{NP}\ \text{ziji}]]$
iii. local anaphor $[_{DP}\ \text{ta}\ [_{D'}[\text{D}]\ [\text{ziji}]_{NP}]]$
iv. UD-form $[_{DP}[_{DP}\ \text{ta}]\ [_{NP}\ \text{ziji}]]$

If the parallel with Japanese is to be pursued, we also expect iv., a UD-form that should have an emphatic or contrastive force, much like pronoun-*zisin* and *lui-même* in French. Pan (1998) has demonstrated that the distribution of *ta-ziji* is in fact quite a bit wider than LAL would permit, and in almost every case where it is licensed, it functions contrastively. In most of those environments (but not all, as Pan emphasizes), the *ziji* portion of *ta-ziji* is emphatically stressed. Although Pan argues specifically against treating pronoun-*ziji* as a local anaphor and a contrastive UD-form, claiming the neutrally stressed usage is not always local and still sensitive to a [+human] restriction, the cases he presents to argue that neutrally stressed pronoun-*ziji* is not contrastive are always instances where pronoun-*ziji* modifies a contrastively stressed head. I take this to indicate that contrast still licenses long-distance pronoun-*ziji* and that contrastive stress is merely the occasional consequence of contrast as the licensing property. He does not present any case where long-distance neutrally stressed pronoun-*ziji* embedded in a contrastive constituent is blocked by a local [+human] subject, although this is crucial to his claim that there exists a stressless long-distance *ziji* that is not contrastive. I am not arguing that the stress pattern derives from adjunct status, though I assume that adjunct status favors such stress where some other contrastive form does not override it. From this perspective, the morphological picture for Chinese becomes symmetric, in that there are both local anaphors formed with *ziji* and UD-forms formed with *ziji*. The structural difference between head versus adjunct determines short- or long-distance distribution, respectively. Such an account requires a broader defense, but I have no space for it here. For an excellent overview discussion of Chinese anaphora, see Huang and Liu (2001). For a detailed pragmatic account of *ziji*, see Huang (1994) and further references and literature review in Huang (2000, 120–121), but also see the critique of Gricean approaches in 3.1.2.1.

70. Aikawa also points out that *zibun-zisin* cannot represent the reading available with *zibun* in i.

i. John-wa (kagami-ni) 3–nin-no zibun/*zibun-zisin -o mita.
John-Top mirror in 3–Cl-Gen ZIBUN/ZIBUN-ZISIN ACC saw
"John saw three selves (i.e., images of himself) in the mirror."

She takes the fact that *zibun* can fail to be distributive in this environment as evidence that it is not bound by *John-wa* but is rather independently coreferent with it. The inference is false, however, since it is based on the premise that collective readings can never be bound readings, a position rejected in 4.2.3 (and by Grozinsky and Reinhart 1993, 83–84). Aikawa claims to be able to derive the ill-formedness of *zibun-zisin* in i. under her assumption that bound-variable readings must be distributive. When it is bound nonlocally, she assumes *zibun* is a variable, hence distributively interpreted. Although I reject her reasoning, I fail to predict that ii. is ill-formed, except by the stipulation that *zibun* always prefers a distributed interpretation.

ii. *John-wa minna-ni [[Mary-ga kagami-ni 3–nin-no zibun -o mita] to]
John-TOP everyone-DAT Mary-NOM mirror-in 3–Cl-GEN ZIBUN -ACC saw that
itta
said
"John said to everyone that Mary saw three selves in the mirror."

See note 68, where differences in how the two forms can be modified may be relevant.

71. As in the case with Japanese *zibun* and *zibun-zisin*, Chinese has a distributional overlap in the local domain between *ziji* and *ta-ziji* and once again, contrasts emerge if distributed interpretations are considered. In Chinese, *ziji* is parallel to *zibun-zisin* locally, and as such, we may expect *ziji* to win the competition for the distributed interpretation. As Huang (2001, 64) observes, while i. and ii. must be interpreted distributively when *ziji* is employed, where *ta-ziji* is the local anaphor, the interpretation is readily collective.

i. Zhangsan he Lisi zai piping ziji/tamen-ziji.
Zhangsan and Lisi at criticize ZIJI
"Zhangsan and Lisi are criticizing themselves."

ii. Tamen you zai kuajiang ziji/tamen-ziji le.
they again at praise ZIJI/them-ZIJI ASP
"They are praising themselves again."

Thus it appears that *ta-ziji* and *ziji* are not in FTIP competition for the distributed readings. For interesting details and a discussion of the origins of distributivity in Chinese, see further discussion in Huang (1998).

72. Mysteries remain, such as why it is that *zibun-zisin* cannot anteceded by the nonlocal subject *John-ga* in (54). Given what I have said so far, the structure in (58b) ought to permit this reading, just as it does in (56b), and I leave the matter open

73. The data in this section are entirely based on den Dikken, Lipták, and Zvolenszky (2001). Some informants do not agree with their data. Even if there is a better interpretation

of the data than theirs, this discussion will serve to illustrate the logic of the system in what appears to be a theoretically and empirically interesting case. My thinking in this section is guided in part by a term paper written for one of my courses by James Thompson, as well as several discussions with him.

74. It may be significant that the verbs used to illustrate the failure of disjoint reference and the surprising success of singulars anteceding plural reflexives are of the class discussed in 3.3.1 for English (e.g., *represent*).

75. Den Dikken, Lipták, and Zvolenszky refer in their note 7 to a suggestion by Fiengo that the definite–indefinite distinction is really one of familiarity. My proposal shares something of Fiengo's, but it has more to do with whether or not a reading is dependent in the relevant sense, particularly given my analysis of person. Note also that universal quantifiers like *mindenkit* in the object position require indefinite agreement.

76. For examples like *mi engem képviselek meg*, "We represent me," which requires indefinite agreement, the relation between subject and object is probably not dependent, along the lines of the discussion of guises in 4.2.2. Since a plurality including the speaker is not plural speakers, as Benveniste (1966) has pointed out, it is not obvious that the speaker is being picked out of a set (denoted by the subject first person plural) such that anyone but the speaker could have been selected, so no dependent interpretation is likely or necessary.

77. For example, a case study of Turkish, as discussed in Kornfilt (2001), would be of particular interest, as there appear to be distributional overlaps of up to three forms locally, yet the interpretive differences between them, if there are any, have not been explored. I have also omitted discussion of morphologically logophoric pronouns, such as those found in many West African languages, though I believe a principled account of these forms has important consequences for the distribution of UD-forms in the more extensively studied languages. For discussion of these issues, see Safir (in preparation). For discussion of reciprocals, see the appendix to this chapter.

## Appendix to Chapter 6

1. This skirts an interesting and relevant issue, namely, whether or not affixal cases compete with full transitive cases from sentence to sentence. This is not permitted by the FTIP algorithm for dependent-matching identity, which only compares numerations distinct by only one form. I shall not explore the issue for reasons of space.

2. It has been pointed out by Lebeaux (1983) that sentences like *the men believe they are taller than each other* permit a reading where each man believes that he is taller than the others, as well as a nonsensical local reading whereby the men are taller than each other. This is expected under our approach to c-antecedency, where the anaphor *each other* is licensed by the c-antecedent *they*, but *they* and *each other* are codependent, such that both are directly dependent on *the men*. This approach depends on the local licensor for the anaphor, such that *The men thought that Alice was taller than each other* would not be licensed. Unlike Heim, Lasnik, and May's (1991) account, no appeal to scopal interaction is necessary. For a discussion of this case with respect to Rule H, see 7.1. Notice that the possibility of direct dependence on the higher antecedent distinguishes English reciprocals from SELF forms, which require local dependency as discussed in 4.1. In other words, there is nothing corresponding to the LRP for reciprocals. For other differences between reciprocals and reflexives in English, see Lebeaux (1983) and Everaert (2000).

3. As Pollard and Sag (1992) point out, there are cases where *each other* can appear without an antecedent in the same manner as SELF forms, though perhaps not quite so freely. The contexts where this is possible are typically contexts of promotion to UD-form (discussed in 5.4), as in i., which some do not accept, and ii., which most do.

i. *The men* told Selma to say that pictures of *each other* would be on sale.
ii. *The men* expected Paula to praise everyone but *each other.*

See Everaert (2000, 78), who suggests that the interpretation of *each other* is not truly reciprocal in these cases.

4. I am grossly oversimplifying here to make a point. The issues are far more complex as the literature shows. Much of this literature is reviewed in Dalrymple et al. (1998), though discussion there mostly addresses cases like *the men followed each other to the podium* (chaining), *the logs were piled on top of each other, people looked at each other in surprise,* and many other such cases which they do not bring to bear on the simultaneity or distinction of events so much as relations between participants in the predicated relations. For further discussion, see, Dmitriadis (2000), Sternefeld (1998), and several of the articles in Frajzyngier and Curl (2000a). There are also complexities involving cases that are closer to the issues raised by predicates like *kiss* as well. Consider *The men fought (each other).* When *each other* is missing, one possible interpretation is that there is a generic episodic quality to the relationship between the men such that no particular event of fighting is described, but a pattern. When *each other* is present, the pattern of fighting interpretation appears to be lost in favor of an interpretation where there were individuated events of fighting (perhaps only one such event), a reading that *the men fought* also allows. In these cases, however, *the men fought* also permits an interpretation where the fight is against third parties, so it is not clear what is licensing the null form here. By contrast, *the men kissed* does not permit a third party reading.

5. R&R and G&R do not remark on whether or not they believe there is any predicate-based principle enforcing reciprocal interpretation, but without it, it is not clear why *they saw them* could not have a reciprocal interpretation, short of relying on the assumption, as I do, that English *them* cannot represent the reciprocal relation. Their theory thus does not address the questions that arise concerning the reciprocal interpretations available with French *se* and German *sich.*

## Chapter 7

1. For example, remarks by Chomsky (1995b) suggest that convergent derivations are seeded with distinctions that are exploited by postconvergence interpretation. As Chomsky discusses N-features and D-features as they relate to the definiteness and specificity imposed on object-raised nominals, he remarks that the definiteness effect "does not rule out any derivations but rather describes how legitimate outputs are to be interpreted" (1995b, 350).

2. I will not defend Rule H at length here, but it is perhaps useful to point out that Rule H does not follow in my theory from the claim that direct dependency is the preferred form of coconstrual, as Reinhart (1997) suggests within a c-command licensing theory. Recall that I have argued in 2.2 and 2.3 that dependency should not require c-command, and so preference for a locally c-commanding dependent interpretation does not follow without stipulation. However, c-command is crucial for the very interesting and convincing argument that Fox (1998, 2000) provides for Rule H based on Dahl's puzzle (Dahl 1974), and that account does not follow from any preference for local dependency, as my critique of the strict reading under ellipsis in 2.2 shows. I will not repeat Fox's argument here or elaborate on Rule H for reasons of space, especially since the matter is addressed in Safir (2004).

3. Bresnan (2001) includes "bound pronouns" on this scale, but the issue that arises from my perspective is whether or not these are true competitors with the other forms. See the discussion of ellipsis and reflexive affixes in 4.4. The WPC as I conceive it is not part of the optimality computation that determines which forms compete, and this is a difference in the

way it is conceived of here from the way that Bresnan analyzes it, since she includes as part of the same competition some of the factors that determine which forms are available.

4. For example, (9d) should be excluded in Reinhart and Reuland's account, because *himself* must be part of a syntactic predicate and must be interpreted as reflexive.

5. I do not assume that the relation between a moved constituent and its copy is a dependency arrow, but I do assume that if the moved constituent is a quantifier, then it leaves a variable that depends on its antecedent when copies are interpreted at LF. I assume that vehicle change that introduces a pronoun for a complete copy of a displaced constituent is dependent on that constituent, but this too seems to be of no consequence before LF. Thus it is not clear that the arrows need to be introduced at any point or for any relations during the course of preconvergence derivations, though at LF it may be necessary that the arrows or their equivalent are part of the formal syntactic representation. See Safir (2004) for a detailed discussion of these relations.

6. It is possible that a similar issue could arise for the WPC. Suppose that backgrounded topic status is not an inherent property of any given phrase or form but simply the elsewhere case of not being focalized or emphasized. If so, then backgrounded topic feature must be assigned to every form in the input after the stressed or focalized forms are selected. Then the position that must be represented by the weakest available one to represent that reading will bear the relevant mark as part of the input. The assignment of this feature would constitute a new category of input-preparing rules. If a relativized account of backgrounded topic is empirically wrong, then of course this argument has no force.

7. I do not feel I can do justice to the proposals of Wilson (2001), who appears to have developed a very similar approach to the one proposed here within the OT framework. Wilson also argues that there must be two separate competitions, one "interpretive" that satisfies a syntactic optimization that results in a representation associated with an interpretation, and a subsequent "expressive" optimization that holds the interpretation constant and then applies a version of Burzio's referential economy. Many unfortunate choices of language and presentation render Wilson's proposal obscure (e.g., the model is called "bidirectional," but in fact one competition follows the other), and in particular it is never clear what counts as a semantic representation in the input to either of these competitions. The input to the interpretive competition does not require faithfulness to the lexical input, but it does seem to assume that some semantic target also plays a role. Wilson speculates that the inputs to the expressive competition could be LFs, but it is unclear what constitutes an LF in the OT model. Readers interested in an OT alternative to the approach I have proposed here are urged to consult Wilson's article. See Huang (2000, 126–130) for an independent critique of these OT approaches.

# BIBLIOGRAPHY


Abe, Jun. 1997. The locality of *zibun* and logophoricity. In *Report 1: Researching and verifying an advanced theory of human language,* 595–626. Tokyo: Kanda University of International Studies.

Abney, Steven. 1987. The English noun phrase in its sentential aspect. Ph.D. diss., MIT.

Abraham, Werner. 2000. The structural and lexical space between reflexive binding and logophorics: Sundry paradigms of reflexives and anaphora. In *Reflexives: Forms and functions*, edited by Zygmunt Frajzyngier and Traci Curl, 75–101. Amsterdam and Philadelphia: Benjamins.

Abusch, Dorit. 1989. Reflexives, reference shifters and attitudes. In *WCCFL* 8:1–13. Stanford Linguistics Association.

Ackerman, Farrell, and Webelhuth, Gert. 1998. *A theory of predicates*. Stanford, Calif.: CSLI.

Aikawa, Takako. 1993. *Reflexivity in Japanese and LF analysis of* zibun *binding.* MIT Occasional Papers in Linguistics, no. 4. Cambridge: MIT Department of Linguistics and Philosophy.

Aikawa, Takako. 1994. Reflexivity in Japanese: *zibun* and *zibun-zisin*. Unpublished manuscript, MIT.

Anagnostopoulou, Elena, and Martin Everaert. 1999. Toward a more complete typology of anaphoric expressions. *Linguistic Inquiry* 30:97–119.

Anderson, Steve. 1986. The typology of anaphoric dependencies: Icelandic (and other) reflexives. In *Topics in Scandinavian syntax*, edited by Lars Hellan and Kirsti Koch Christensen, 65–88. Dordrecht: Reidel.

Aoun, Joseph. 1985. *A grammar of anaphora*. Cambridge: MIT Press.

Aoun, Joseph, and Lina Choueiri. 2000. Epithets. *Natural Language and Linguistic Theory* 18:1–39.

Aoun, Joseph, and Dominique Sportiche. 1983. On the formal theory of government. *Linguistic Review* 2:211–236.

Avrutin, Sergey. 1994. *Psycholinguistic investigations in the theory of reference.* MIT Working Papers in Linguistics. Cambridge: MIT Department of Linguistics.

Bach, Emmon, and Barbara Partee. 1980. Anaphora and semantic structure. In *Papers from the parasession on pronouns and anaphora*, edited by K. J. Kreiman and A. Ojeda, 1–28. Chicago: Chicago Linguistic Society.

Baker, C. L. 1994. Contrast, discourse prominence and intensification, with special reference to locally-free reflexives in British English. *Language* 71:63–101.

Baker, Mark. 1988. *Incorporation.* Chicago: University of Chicago Press.

Baker, Mark. 1996. *The polysynthesis parameter.* Oxford: Oxford University Press.

Baker, Mark, and Ken Hale. 1990. Relativized minimality and pronoun incorporation. *Linguistic Inquiry* 21:289–297.

Battistella, Ed. 1989. Chinese reflexivization: A movement to INFL approach. *Linguistics* 27:987–1012.

Benveniste, E. 1966. La nature des pronoms. *Problèmes de linguistique générale.* Vol. 1. Paris: Gallimard.

Berman, Steve, and Arild Hestvik. 1997. Split antecedents, noncoreference and DRT. In *Atomism and binding*, edited by Hans Bennis, Pierre Pica, and Johan Rooryck, 1–29. Dordrecht: Foris.

Bernstein, Judy B. 1993. Topics in the syntax of nominals structure across Romance. Ph.D. diss., City University of New York.

Bickerton, Derek. 1987. *He himself*: Anaphor, pronoun or . . . ? *Linguistic Inquiry* 18: 345–348.

Bittner, Maria. 1999. Tense and aspect in cross-linguistic semantics. *Report #143: Working papers of SFB 340: Linguistic Foundations for Computational Linguistics.* Stuttgart: University of Stuttgart.

Borer, Hagit. 1984. *Parametric syntax.* Dordrecht: Foris.

Borer, Hagit. 1989. Anaphoric Agr. In *The null subject parameter*, edited by Osvaldo Jaeggli and Ken Safir, 69–109. Dordrecht: Kluwer.

Borer, Hagit. 1989. Restrictive relatives in Modern Hebrew. *Natural Language and Linguistic Theory* 2:219–260.

Bošković, Željko. 1996. Selection and the categorial status of infinitival complements. *Natural Language and Linguistic Theory* 14:269–304.

Bošković, Željko. 1997. LF-movement and the minimalist program. In *NELS 28*, edited by Kiyomi Kusumoto and Pius Tamanji, 43–57. Amherst, Mass.: GLSA.

Bošković, Željko. 2000. Sometimes in [Spec, CP], sometimes in situ. In *Step by step: Essays on minimalist syntax in honor of Howard Lasnik*, edited by Roger Martin, David Michaels, and Juan Uriagereka, 53–87. Cambridge: MIT Press.

Bouchard, Denis. 1984. *On the content of empty categories.* Dordrecht: Foris.

Bouchard, Denis. 1995. *The semantics of syntax.* Chicago: University of Chicago Press.

Bresnan, Joan. 2001. The emergence of the unmarked pronoun. In *Optimality-theoretic syntax*, edited by Géraldine Legendre, Jane Grimshaw, and Sten Vikner, 113–142. Cambridge: MIP Press.

Brody, Michael. 1995. *Lexico–logical form: A radically minimalist theory.* Cambridge: MIT Press.

Browning, Marguerite. 1993. Adverbial reflexives. In *NELS 23*, edited by Amy Schafer, 83–94. Amherst, Mass.: GLSA.

Burzio, Luigi. 1989. On the non-existence of disjoint reference principles. *Rivista di Grammatica Generativa*, 14:3–27.

Burzio, Luigi. 1991. The morphological basis of anaphora. *Journal of Linguistics* 27:81–105.

Burzio, Luigi. 1996. The role of the antecedent in anaphoric relations. In *Current issues in comparative grammar*, edited by Robert Freidin, 1–45. Dordrecht: Kluwer.

Burzio, Luigi. 1998. Anaphora and soft constraints. In *Is the best good enough?* edited by Pilar Barbosa, Danny Fox, Paul Hagstrom, Martha McGinnis, and David Pesetsky, 93–113. Cambridge: MIT Press.

Calabrese, Andrea. 1986. PRONOMINA: Some properties of the Italian pronominial system. In *MIT Working Papers in Linguistics, Vol. 8*, edited by Naoki Fukui, Tova R. Rapoport, and Elizabeth Sagey, 1–46. Cambridge: MIT Department of Linguistics and Philosophy.

Campbell, Lyle. 1997. *American Indian languages: The historical linguistics of native America*. Oxford: Oxford University Press.

Cardinaletti, Anna, and Michal Starke. 1994. The typology of structural deficiency: On the three grammatical classes. *University of Venice Working Papers in Linguistics* 4:41–109.

Carlson, Greg. 1987. *Same* and *different*: Some consequences for syntax and semantics. *Linguistics and Philosophy* 10:531–565.

Chierchia, Gennaro. 1995. *Dynamics of meaning*. Chicago: University of Chicago Press.

Chomsky, Noam. 1965. *Aspects of the theory of syntax*. Cambridge: MIT Press.

Chomsky, Noam. 1973. Conditions on transformations. In *A festschrift for Morris Halle*, edited by Stephen Anderson and Morris Halle, 232–286. New York: Holt, Rinehart and Winston.

Chomsky, Noam. 1976. Conditions on rules of grammar. *Linguistic Analysis* 2:303–351.

Chomsky, Noam. 1980. On binding. *Linguistic Inquiry* 11:1–46.

Chomsky, Noam. 1981. *Lectures on government and binding*. Dordrecht: Foris.

Chomsky, Noam. 1982. *Some concepts and consequences of the theory of government and binding*. Cambridge: MIT Press.

Chomsky, Noam. 1986a. *Barriers*. Cambridge: MIT Press.

Chomsky, Noam. 1986b. *Knowledge of language: Its nature, origins, and use*. New York: Praeger.

Chomsky, Noam, 1995a. Bare phrase structure. In *Government and binding theory and the minimalist program: Principles and parameters in syntactic theory*, edited by Gert Webelhuth, 383–439. Oxford, England: Blackwell.

Chomsky, Noam. 1995b. *The minimalist program*. Cambridge: MIT Press.

Chomsky, Noam. 2000. Minimalist inquiries. In *Step by step: Essays in minimalist syntax in honor of Howard Lasnik*, edited by Roger Martin, David Michaels, and Juan Uriagereka, 89–155. Cambridge: MIT Press.

Chomsky, Noam. 2001. Derivation by phase. In *Ken Hale: A life in language,* edited by Michael Kenstowicz, 1–52. Cambridge: MIT Press.

Chomsky, Noam, and Howard Lasnik. 1995. The theory of principles and parameters. In *The minimalist program*, edited by Noam Chomsky, 129–166. Cambridge: MIT Press.

Chung, Sandra. 1989. On the notion "null anaphor" in Chamorro. In *The null subject parameter*, edited by Osvaldo Jaeggli and Ken Safir, 143–184. Dordrecht: Kluwer.

Cinque, Guglielmo. 1988. On *si* constructions and the theory of *arb*. *Linguistic Inquiry* 19:521–582.

Cole, Peter, Gabriella Hermon, and Cher Leng Lee. 2001. Grammatical and discourse conditions on long distance reflexives in two Chinese dialects. In *Syntax and semantics 33: Long distance reflexives*, edited by Peter Cole, Gabriella Hermon, and C.-T. James Huang, 1–46. New York: Academic Press.

Cole, Peter, Gabriella Hermon, and Li-May Sung. 1990. Principles and parameters of long distance reflexives. *Linguistic Inquiry* 21:1–22.

Cole, Peter, and Li-May Sung. 1994. Head movement and long-distance reflexives. *Linguistic Inquiry* 25:355–406.

Cresswell, M. J. 1985. *Structured meanings*. Cambridge: MIT Press.

Cresti, Diana. 1996. Economy and the scope of amount phrases. In *WCCFL* 14:79–93. Stanford, Calif.: CSLI (distributed by Cambridge University Press).

Dahl, Östen. 1974. *How to open a sentence: Abstraction in natural language*. Logical Grammar Reports, no. 12. University of Götenberg.

Dalrymple, Mary. 1993. *The syntax of anaphoric binding*. Stanford, Calif.: CSLI.

Dalrymple, Mary, Makoto Kanazawa, Yookyung Kang, Sam Mchombo, and Stanley Peters. 1998. Reciprocal expressions and the concept of reciprocity. *Linguistics and Philosophy* 21:159–210.

Dalrymple, Mary, Sam Mchombo, and Stanle Peters. 1994. Semantic similarities and syntactic contrasts between Chichewa and English reciprocals. *Linguistic Inquiry* 25:145–163.

Davison, Alice. 2001. Long distance anaphors in Hindi/Urdu: Issues. In *Syntax and semantics 33: Long distance reflexives*, edited by Peter Cole, Gabriella Hermon, and C.-T. James Huang, 47–82. New York: Academic Press.

Dayal, Veneeta. 1993. Binding facts in Hindi and the scrambling phenomenon. In *Theoretical perspectives on word order in South Asian languages*, edited by Tracy Holloway King and G. Ramchand, 237–261. Stanford, Calif.: CSLI.

Dayal, Veneeta. 1996. *Locality in wh-quantification*. Dordrecht: Kluwer.

Demirdache, Hamida. 1991. Resumptive chains in restrictive relatives, appositives and dislocation structures. Ph.D. diss., MIT.

Demirdache, Hamida. 1997. Condition C. In *Atomism and binding*, edited by Hans Bennis, Pierre Pica, and Johan Rooryck, 51–87. Dordrecht: Foris.

den Dikken, Marcel, Anikó Lipták, and Zsófia Zvolenszky. 2001. On inclusive reference anaphora: New perspectives from Hungarian. Unpublished manuscript, City University of New York, Leiden University, and New York University.

Déprez, Viviane. 1992. Raising constructions in Haitian Creole. *Natural Language and Linguistic Theory* 10:191–231.

Di Sciullo, Anna-Maria. 1996. Word-internal pronouns and reflexives. In *Coherence and anaphora*, edited by Walter de Mulder and Liliane Tasmowski, 103–121. Amsterdam and Philadelphia: Benjamins.

Dmitriadis, Alexis. 2000. Beyond identity: Problems in pronominal and reciprocal anaphora. Ph.D. diss., University of Pennsylvania.

Dowty, David. 1980. Comments on the paper by Bach and Partee. In *Papers from the parasession on pronouns and anaphora*, edited by Jody Kreiman and Almerindo Ojeda, 29–40. Chicago: Chicago Linguistic Society.

Dubinsky, Stanley, and Robert Hamilton. 1998. Epithets as antilogophoric pronouns. *Linguistic Inquiry* 29:685–693.

Edmondson, Jerold, and Frans Plank. 1978. Great expectations: An intensive self analysis, *Linguistics and Philosophy* 2:373–413.

Enç, Murvet. 1989. Pronouns, licensing, and binding. *Natural Language and Linguistic Theory* 7:51–92.

Epstein, Samuel David. 1999. Unprincipled syntax: The derivation of syntactic relations. In *Working minimalism*, edited by Samuel Epstein and Norbert Hornstein, 317–345. Cambridge: MIT Press.

Evans, Gareth. 1980. Pronouns. *Linguistic Inquiry* 11:337–362.

Everaert, Martin. 1986. *The syntax of reflexivization*. Dordrecht: Foris.

Everaert, Martin. 1990. Nominative anaphors in Icelandic: Morphology or syntax? In *Issues in Germanic syntax*, edited by Werner Abraham, Wim Kosmeijer, and Eric Reuland, 277–307. Berlin: Mouton De Gruyter.

Everaert, Martin. 1991. Contextual determination of the anaphor/pronominal distinction. In *Long-distance anaphora*, edited by Jan Koster and Eric Reuland, 77–118. Cambridge: Cambridge University Press.

Everaert, Martin. 2000. Types of anaphoric expressions: Reflexives and reciprocals. In *Reciprocals: Forms and functions*. Typological Studies in Language, no. 41, edited by Zygmunt Frajzyngier and Tracy S. Curl, 63–83. Amsterdam and Philadelphia: Benjamins.

Faltz, Leonard. 1977. Reflexivization: A study in universal syntax. Ph.D. diss., University of California, Berkeley. Reprint, New York: Garland, 1985.

Farmer, Anne. 1987. *They held each other's breath* and other puzzles for the binding theory. *Linguistic Inquiry* 18:157–163

Farmer, Anne, Ken Hale, and Natsuko Tsujimura. 1986. A note on weak crossover in Japanese. *Natural Language and Linguistic Theory* 4:33–42.

Farmer, Ann, and A.K. Harnish. 1987. Communicative reference with pronouns. In *The pragmatic perspective*, edited by J. Verschueren and M. Beruccelli-Papi, 547–565. Amsterdam: Benjamins.

Fauconnier, Gilles. 1994. *Mental spaces*. Cambridge: Cambridge University Press. Original publication, Cambridge: MIT Press, 1984.

Fiengo, Robert, and Robert May. 1994. *Indices and identity*. Cambridge: MIT Press.

Fox, Danny. 1995. Economy and scope. *Natural Language Semantics* 3:283–341.

Fox, Danny. 1998. Locality in variable binding. In *Is the best good enough?* edited by Pilar Barbosa, Danny Fox, Paul Hagstrom, Martha McGinnis, and David Pesetsky, 129–155. Cambridge: MIT Press.

Fox, Danny. 1999. Reconstruction, binding theory and the interpretation of chains. *Linguistic Inquiry* 30:157–196.

Fox, Danny. 2000. *Economy and semantic interpretation*. Cambridge: MIT Press.

Frajzyngier, Zygmunt. 2000a. Coding the reciprocal function. In *Reciprocals: Forms and functions*. Typological Studies in Language, no. 41, edited by Zygmunt Frajzyngier and Tracy S. Curl, 179–194. Amsterdam and Philadelphia: Benjamins.

Frajzyngier, Zygmunt. 2000b. Domains of point of view and coreferentiality. In *Reflexives: Forms and functions*. Typological Studies in Language, no. 40, edited by Zygmunt Frajzyngier and Tracy S. Curl, 125–152. Amsterdam and Philadelphia: Benjamins.

Frajzyngier, Zygmunt and Tracy S. Curl, eds. 2000a. *Reciprocals: Forms and functions*. Typological Studies in Language, no. 41. Amsterdam and Philadelphia: Benjamins.

Frajzyngier, Zygmunt and Tracy S. Curl, eds. 2000b. *Reflexives: Forms and functions*. Typological Studies in Language, no. 40. Amsterdam and Philadelphia: Benjamins.

Franks, Steven. 1995. *Parameters of Slavic morphosyntax*. Oxford: Oxford University Press.

Franks, Steven, and Linda Schwartz. 1994. Binding and non-distinctness: A reply to Burzio. *Journal of Linguistics* 30:227–243.

Fuji, Masaaki. 1994. A compositional approach to Japanese anaphora. Unpublished manuscript, Rutgers University.

Fukuda, Kaoru. 1989. On emphatic reflexives. *English Linguistics* 6:36–51.

Fukui, Naoki. 1984. Studies in Japanese anaphora. Unpublished manuscript, MIT.

Geach, P. 1962. *Reference and generality*. Ithaca, N.Y.: Cornell University Press.

Gelderen, Elly van. 2000. *A history of English reflexive pronouns*. Linguistik Aktuell, no. 39. Amsterdam and Philadelphia: Benjamins.

Geniušiene, Emma. 1987. *The typology of reflexives*. Berlin: Mouton de Gruyter.

Giorgi, Allesandra. 1990. *On the Italian anaphoric/pronominal system*. Padua: Unipress.

Giusti, Giuliana. 1994. Enclitic articles and double definiteness: A comparative analysis of nominal structure in Romance and Germanic. *The Linguistic Review* 11:241–255.

Grewendorf, Günther. 1992. *German: A grammatical sketch.* Sprachwissenschaft in Frankfurt—Arbeitspapier, #8. Frankfurt am Main: Johann Wolfgang Goethe-Universität.

Grice, Paul. 1989. *Studies in the way of words*. Cambridge, Mass.: Harvard University Press.

Grimshaw, Jane. 1989. Extended Projection. Unpublished manuscript, Brandeis University and Rutgers University.

Grodzinsky, Yosef, and Tanya Reinhart. 1993. The innateness of binding and coreference. *Linguistic Inquiry* 24:69–102.

Hasegawa, Nobuko. 1985. On the so-called "zero pronouns" in Japanese. *The Linguistic Review* 4:289–342.

Heim, Irene. 1982. The semantics of definite and indefinite noun phrases. Ph.D. diss., University of Massachusetts at Amherst.

Heim, Irene. 1993. Anaphora and semantic interpretation: A reinterpretation of Reinhart's approach. SfS-Report-07–93. University of Tübingen.

Heim, Irene, Howard Lasnik, and Robert May. 1991. Reciprocity and plurality. *Linguistic Inquiry* 22:63–101.

Heine, Bernd. 2000. Polysemy involving reflexive and reciprocal markers in African languages. In *Reciprocals: Forms and functions.* Typological Studies in Language, no. 41, edited by Zygmunt Frajzyngier and Tracy S. Curl, 1–31. Amsterdam and Philadelphia: Benjamins.

Helke, M. 1971. The grammar of English reflexives. Ph.D. diss., MIT. Reprint, London: Garland, 1979.

Hellan, Lars. 1988. *Anaphora in Norwegian and the theory of grammar*. Dordrecht: Foris.

Hendrick, Randall. 1995. Morphosyntax. In *Government and binding theory and the minimalist program: Principles and parameters in syntactic theory*, edited by Gert Webelhuth, 297–348. Oxford, England.: Blackwell.

Hermon, Gabriella. 1992. Binding theory and parameter setting. *The Linguistic Review* 9:145–181.

Herslund, Michael. 1986. The double object construction in Danish. In *Topics in Scandinavian Syntax*, edited by Lars Hellan and Kirsti Koch Christensen, 125–147. Dordrecht: Reidel.

Hestvik, Arild. 1990. LF-movement of pronouns and the computation of binding domains. Ph.D. diss., Brandeis University.

Hestvik, Arild. 1991. Subjectless binding domains. *Natural Language and Linguistic Theory* 9:455–496.

Hestvik, Arild. 1992. LF-movement of pronouns and antisubject orientation. *Linguistic Inquiry* 23:557–594.

Hestvik, Arild. 1995. Reflexives and ellipsis. *Natural Language Semantics* 2:1–27.

Higginbotham, James. 1980a. Anaphora and GB: Some preliminary remarks. *NELS X*, edited by John Jensen, 223–236. Ottawa: Cahiers Linguistique d'Ottawa, University of Ottawa.

Higginbotham, James. 1980b. Pronouns and bound variables. *Linguistic Inquiry* 11:679–708.

Higginbotham, James. 1983. Logical form, binding and nominals. *Linguistic Inquiry* 14:395–420.

Higginbotham, James. 1985. On semantics. *Linguistic Inquiry* 16:547–593.

Higginbotham, James. 1992. Anaphoric reference and common reference. Unpublished manuscript, MIT.

Higginbotham, James. 1997. A plea for implicit anaphora. In *Atomism and binding*, edited by Hans Bennis, Pierre Pica, and Johan Rooryck, 183–203. Dordrecht: Foris.

Hirose, Yukio. 1997. Bound pronouns as N-bar proforms. *Lingua* 102:169–186.

Holmberg, Anders, and Christer Platzack. 1995. *The role of inflection in Scandinavian syntax.* Oxford: Oxford University Press.

Horn, Larry. 1988. Pragmatic theory. In *Linguistics: The Cambridge survey.* Vol.1, edited by F. Newmeyer, 113–145. Cambridge: Cambridge University Press.

Hornstein, Norbert. 1995. *Logical form.* Oxford, England: Blackwell.

Hornstein, Norbert. 1999. Movement and control. *Linguistic Inquiry* 30:69–96.

Hornstein, Norbert. 2001. *Move! A minimalist theory of construal.* Oxford, England: Blackwell.

Hornstein, Norbert, and Amy Weinberg. 1981. Case theory and preposition stranding. *Linguistic Inquiry* 12:55–91.

Huang, C.-T. James. 1982. Logical relations in Chinese and the theory of grammar. Ph.D. diss., MIT.

Huang, C.-T. James. 1983. A note on the binding theory. *Linguistic Inquiry* 14:554–561.

Huang, C.-T. James. 1984. On the distribution and reference of empty pronouns. *Linguistic Inquiry* 15:531–574.

Huang, C.-T. James. 1989. Pro-drop in Chinese: A generalized control theory. In *The null subject parameter*, edited by Osvaldo Jaeggli and Ken Safir, 185–214. Dordrecht: Kluwer.

Huang, C.-T. James. 1998. Blocking effects and agreement. Unpublished manuscript, University of California, Irvine.

Huang, C.-T. James. 2001. Distributivity and reflexivity. In *Linguistics and interdisciplinary research: Proceedings of the COE international symposium*, edited by Kazuko Inoue and Nobuko Hasegawa, 59–77. Tokyo: Kanda University of International Studies.

Huang, C.-T. James, and C.-S. Luther Liu. 2001. Logophoricity, attitudes and *ziji* at the interface. In *Syntax and semantics 33: Long distance reflexives*, edited by Peter Cole, Gabriella Hermon, and C.-T. James Huang, 141–195. New York: Academic Press.

Huang, C.-T. James, and C.-C. Jane Tang. 1991. On the local nature of the long distance reflexive in Chinese. In *Long-distance anaphora*, edited by Jan Koster and Eric Reuland, 263–282. Cambridge: Cambridge University Press.

Huang, Yan. 1991. A neo-Gricean pragmatic theory of anaphora. *Journal of Linguistics* 27:301–335.

Huang, Yan. 1994. *The syntax and pragmatics of anaphora: A study with special reference to Chinese.* Cambridge: Cambridge University Press.

Huang, Yan. 2000. *Anaphora: A crosslinguistic study.* Oxford: Oxford University Press.

Iatridou, Sabine. 1986. An anaphor not bound in its governing category. *Linguistic Inquiry* 17:766–772.

Ingria, Robert. 1982. Why English reflexives are pronouns, or Ingria Contra Helke. *MITWPL, no. 4*, edited by Alec Marantz and Tim Stowell, 55–79. Cambridge: MIT Department of Linguistics and Philosophy.

Inoue, K. 1976. Reflexivization: An interpretive approach. In *Syntax and semantics: Japanese generative grammar*, edited by M. Shibitani, 117–191. New York: Academic Press.

Jackendoff, Ray. 1972. *Semantic interpretation in generative grammar.* Cambridge: MIT Press.

Jackendoff, Ray. 1992. Madame Tussaud meets the binding theory. *Natural Language and Linguistic Theory* 10:1–31.

Jackendoff, Ray. 1997. *The architecture of the language faculty.* Cambridge: MIT Press.

Jaeggli, Osvaldo. 1986. Arbitrary plural pronominals. *Natural Language and Linguistic Theory* 4:43–76.

Jaeggli, Osvaldo, and Ken Safir. 1989. The null subject parameter and parametric theory. In *The null subject parameter*, edited by Osvaldo Jaeggli and Ken Safir, 1–44. Dordrecht: Kluwer.

Jayaseelan, K. A. 1997. Anaphors and pronouns. *Studia Linguistica* 51:186–234.

Johnson, David. 1977. On relational constraints on grammars. In *Syntax and semantics 8:*

*Grammatical relations*, edited by Peter Cole and Jerold Sadock. New York: Academic Press.

Johnson, Kyle. 1991. Object positions. *Natural Language and Linguistic Theory* 9:577–636.

Joseph, Brian. 1976. Raising in Modern Greek: A copy process? In *Harvard studies in syntax and semantics, no. 2*, edited by J. Hankamer and Judith Aissen. Cambridge: Harvard Department of Linguistics.

Kamp, Hans, and U. Reyle. 1993. *From discourse to logic*. Dordrecht: Kluwer.

Kaplan, David. 1989. Demonstratives. In *Themes from Kaplan*, edited by J. Almog, H. Wettstein, and J. Perry, 581–563. New York: Oxford University Press.

Katada, Fusa. 1991. The LF representation of anaphors. *Linguistic Inquiry* 22:287–313.

Kayne, Richard S. 1975. *French syntax: The transformational cycle*. Cambridge: MIT Press.

Kayne, Richard S. 2000. Person morphemes and reflexives in Italian, French, and related languages. In *Parameters and universals*, edited by Richard Kayne, 131–162. Oxford: Oxford University Press.

Kayne, Richard S. 2001. Pronouns and their antecedents. Unpublished manuscript, New York University.

Keenan, Edward. 1994. Creating anaphors: An historical study of the English reflexive pronouns.Unpublished manuscript, University of California, Los Angeles.

Kemmer, Suzanne. 1993. *The middle voice: A typological and diachronic study*. Amsterdam and Philadelphia: Benjamins.

Kidwai, Ayesha. 2000. *XP-adjunction in universal grammar: Scrambling and binding in Hindi-Urdu*. Oxford: Oxford University Press.

Kitagawa, Yoshihisa. 1986. Subjects in English and Japanese. Ph.D. diss., University of Massachusetts at Amherst.

König, Ekkehard, and Peter Siemund. 2000. Intensifiers and reflexives: A typological perspective. In *Reflexives: Forms and functions*. Typological Studies in Language, no. 40, edited by Zygmunt Frajzyngier and Tracy S. Curl, 41–74. Amsterdam and Philadelphia: Benjamins.

Koopman, Hilda, and Dominique Sportiche. 1989. Pronouns, logical variables and logophoricity in Abe. *Linguistic Inquiry* 20:555–588.

Kornfilt, Jaklin. 2001. Local and long distance reflexives in Turkish. In *Syntax and semantics 33: Long distance reflexives*, edited by Peter Cole, Gabriella Hermon, and C.-T. James Huang, 197–226. New York: Academic Press.

Koster, Jan. 1986. *Domains and dynasties*. Dordrecht: Foris.

Koster, Jan. 1997. Anaphora and uniformity of grammar. In *Atomism and binding*, edited by Hans Bennis, Pierre Pica, and Johan Rooryck, 235–250. Dordrecht: Foris.

Kuno, Susumu. 1972. Pronominalization, reflexivization, and direct discourse. *Linguistic Inquiry* 3:161–195.

Kuno, Susumu. 1987. *Functional syntax*. Chicago: University of Chicago Press.

Kuroda, S.-Y. 1965. Generative grammatical studies in the Japanese language. Ph.D. diss., MIT.

Lakoff, George. 1968. Counterparts, or the problem of reference in transformation grammar. Unpublished manuscript, Harvard University (distributed by the Indiana University Linguistics Club).

Lakoff, George. 1972. Linguistics and natural logic. In *Semantics of natural language*, edited by Donald Davidson and Gilbert Harmon, 545–665. Dordrecht: Reidel.

Lakoff, George. 1996. Sorry, I'm not myself today: The metaphor system for conceptualizing the self. In *Spaces, worlds, and grammar*, edited by Gilles Fauconnier and Eve Sweetser, 91–123. Chicago: University of Chicago Press.

Landau, Idan. 2000. *Elements of control*. Dordrecht: Kluwer.

Langacker, R. 1969. On pronominalization and the chain of command. In *Modern studies in English*, edited by W. Reibel and S. Schane, 160–186. Englewood Cliffs, N.J.: Prentice Hall.

Lasnik, Howard. 1976. Remarks on coreference. *Linguistic Analysis* 2:1–22. Reprinted in Lasnik 1989.

Lasnik, Howard. 1981. On two recent treatments of disjoint reference. *Journal of Linguistic Research* 1:39–53. Reprinted in Lasnik 1989.

Lasnik, Howard, ed. 1989. *Essays on anaphora*. Dordrecht: Kluwer.

Lasnik, Howard. 1999. *Minimalist analysis*. Oxford, England: Blackwell.

Lasnik, Howard, and Mamoru Saito. 1992. *Move a: Conditions on its applications and output*. Cambridge: MIT Press.

Lebeaux, David. 1983. A distributional difference between reciprocals and reflexives. *Linguistic Inquiry* 14:723–730.

Lebeaux, David. 1984. Locality and anaphoric binding. *The Linguistic Review* 4:343–363.

Lebeaux, David. 1998. Where does binding theory apply? Technical report of the NEC Research Institute. Princeton, NJ: Princeton University.

Lee, Seng Sheh Ruby. 1996. Redefining the binding properties of Mandarin reflexives. Unpublished honors thesis, University of Singapore.

Lees, R. B., and Edward S. Klima. 1963. Rules for English pronominalization. *Language* 39:17–28.

Levinson, Stephen. 1987. Pragmatics and the grammar of anaphora: A partial pragmatic reduction of binding and control phenomena. *Journal of Linguistics* 23:379–434.

Levinson, Stephen. 1991. Pragmatic reduction of the binding conditions revisited. *Journal of Linguistics* 27:107–162.

Lewis, David. 1979. Attitudes *de dicto* and *de se*. *Philosophical Review* 88:513–543.

Li, Yafei. 1990. $X^{o}$-binding and verb incorporation. *Linguistic Inquiry* 21:399–426.

Lichtenberk, Frantisek. 1985. Multiple uses of the reciprocal construction. *Australian Journal of Linguistics* 5:19–41.

Lichtenberk, Frantisek. 2000. Reciprocals without reflexives. In *Reciprocals: Forms and functions*. Typological Studies in Language, no. 41, edited by Zygmunt Frajzyngier and Tracy S. Curl, 31–62. Amsterdam and Philadelphia: Benjamins.

Lidz, Jeffrey. 1996. Dimensions of reflexivity. Ph.D. diss., University of Delaware.

Lidz, Jeffrey. 2001a. Anti-antilocality. In *Syntax and semantics 33: Long distance reflexives*, edited by Peter Cole, Gabriella Hermon, and C.-T. James Huang, 226–254. New York: Academic Press.

Lidz, Jeffrey. 2001b. Condition R. *Linguistic Inquiry* 32:123–140.

Lieber, Rochelle. 1992. *Deconstructing morphology: Word formation in syntactic theory*. Chicago: University of Chicago Press.

Longobardi, Giuseppe. 1994. Reference and proper names: A theory of N-movement in syntax and logical form. *Linguistic Inquiry* 25:609–665.

Maling, Joan. 1984. Non-clause bounded reflexives in Modern Icelandic. *Linguistics and Philosophy* 7:211–241.

Maling, Joan. 1986. Clause-bounded reflexives in Modern Icelandic. In *Topics in Scandinavian syntax*, edited by Lars Hellan and Kirsti Koch Christensen, 33–63. Dordrecht: Reidel.

Manzini, Maria-Rita, and Ken Wexler. 1987. Parameters, binding theory, and learnability. *Linguistic Inquiry* 17:413–444.

Marantz, Alec. 1981. *On the nature of grammatical relations*. Cambridge: MIT Press.

Massam, Diana. 1985. Case theory and the projection principle. Ph.D. diss., MIT.

May, Robert. 1977. The grammar of quantification. Ph.D. diss., MIT.

May, Robert. 1985. *Logical form*. Cambridge: MIT Press.

McCloskey, James. 1990. Resumptive pronouns, A'-binding and levels of representation in Irish. In *The syntax and semantics of modern Celtic languages*, edited by Randall Hendrick, 199–248. San Diego: Academic Press.

McKay, Terence. 1985. *Infinitival complements in German*. Cambridge: Cambridge University Press.

McKay, Thomas. 1991. *He himself*: Undiscovering an anaphor. *Linguistic Inquiry* 22:368–373.

Merchant, Jason. 2001. *The syntax of silence: Sluicing, islands, and the theory of ellipsis*. Oxford: Oxford University Press.

Moltmann, Friederike. 1992. Reciprocals and *same/different*: Toward a semantic analysis. *Linguistics and Philosophy* 15:411–462.

Moore, John. 1998. Turkish copy-raising and A-chain locality. *Natural Language and Linguistic Theory* 16:149–189.

Moore, John, and David Perlmutter. 2000. What does it take to be a dative subject? *Natural Language and Linguistic Theory* 18:373–416.

Moravcsik, Edith. 1972. Some crosslinguistic generalizations about intensifier constructions. In *Papers from the 8th regional meeting of the Chicago Linguistic Society*, edited by P. Peranteau et al., 271–277. Chicago: Chicago Linguistic Society.

Napoli, Donna Jo. 1979. Reflexivization across clause boundaries in Italian. *Journal of Linguistics* 15:1–27.

Nishigauchi, Taisuke. 1990. *Quantification in the theory of grammar*. Dordrecht: Kluwer.

Noguchi, Tohru. 1997. Two types of pronouns and variable binding. *Language* 71:770–797.

Nunberg, Geoffrey. 1979. The non-uniqueness of semantic solutions: Polysemy. *Linguistics and Philosophy* 3.143–186.

Nunberg, Geoffrey. 1993. Indexicality and deixis. *Linguistics and Philosophy* 16:1–43.

Nunes, Jairo. 1999. Linearization of chains and the phonetic realization of chain links. In *Working minimalism*, edited by Samuel David Epstein and Norbert Hornstein, 217–249. Cambridge: MIT Press.

Pan, Haihua. 1998. Closeness, prominence and binding theory. *Natural Language and Linguistic Theory* 16:771–815.

Partee, Barbara. 1973. Some structural analogies between tenses and pronouns in English. *Journal of Philosophy* 70:601–609.

Partee, Barbara. 1989. Binding implicit variables in quantified contexts. In *Papers from the 25th Regional Meeting, Chicago Linguistics Society: Parasession on Language in Context*, 342–365. Chicago: Chicago Linguistics Society.

Pica, Pierre. 1984a. Liage et contiguité. In *Actes de la table ronde sur l'anaphore*. Cahiers de l'ERA, no. 642, edited by J. C. Milner. Paris: Université de Paris VII.

Pica, Pierre. 1984b. On the distinction between argumental and non-argumental anaphors. In *Sentential complementation*, edited by W. de Geest and Y. Putseys, 185–193. Dordrecht: Foris.

Pica, Pierre. 1986. De Quelques implications théoriques de l'étude des relations à longue distance. In *La grammaire modulaire*, edited by Mitsou Ronat and Daniel Couquaux, 187–209. Paris: Minuit.

Pica, Pierre. 1987. On the nature of the reflexivization cycle. In *The proceedings of NELS 17*, edited by Joyce Mcdonough and Bernadette Plunkett, 483–499. Amherst, Mass.: GLSA.

Pica, Pierre. 1991. Antecedent government and binding: The case of long distance reflexivization. In *Long-distance anaphora*, edited by Jan Koster and Eric Reuland, 119–135. Cambridge: Cambridge University Press.

Pica, Pierre, and William Snyder. 1997. On the syntax and semantics of local anaphors in

French and English. In *Projections and interface conditions*, edited by Ann-Maria di Sciullo, 235–250. Oxford: Oxford University Press.

Pollard, Carl, and Ivan Sag. 1992. Anaphors in English and the scope of binding theory. *Linguistic Inquiry* 23:261–303.

Pollard, Carl, and Ivan Sag. 1994. *Head-driven phrase structure grammar*. Chicago: University of Chicago Press.

Postal, Paul. 1966. On so-called "pronouns" in English. In *Monograph series on language and linguistics, no. 19*, edited by F. P. Dineen. Washington D.C.: Georgetown University Press. Reprinted in *Modern studies in English: Readings in transformational grammar*, edited by D. Reibel and S. Schane, 201–234. Englewood Cliffs, N.J.: Prentice Hall, 1969.

Postal, Paul. 1971. *Crossover phenomena*. New York: Holt, Rinehart and Winston.

Postal, Paul. 1994. Contrasting extraction types. *Journal of Linguistics* 30:159–186.

Postma, Gertjan. 1997. The possessive nature of reflexive pronouns. In *Atomism and binding*, edited by Hans Bennis, Pierre Pica, and Johan Rooryck, 285–322. Dordrecht: Foris.

Progovac, Ljiljana. 1992. Relativized SUBJECT: Long-distance reflexives without movement. *Linguistic Inquiry* 23:671–680.

Progovac, Ljiljana. 1993. Long-distance reflexives: Movement-to-INFL versus relativized SUBJECT. *Linguistic Inquiry* 24:755–772.

Rappaport, Gilbert. 1986. On anaphor binding in Russian. *Natural Language and Linguistic Theory* 4:97–120.

Reinhart, Tanya. 1976. The syntactic domain of anaphora. Ph.D. diss., MIT.

Reinhart, Tanya. 1983a. *Anaphora and semantic interpretation*. Chicago: University of Chicago Press.

Reinhart, Tanya. 1983b. Coreference and bound anaphora: A restatement of the anaphora questions. *Linguistics and Philosophy* 6:47–88.

Reinhart, Tanya. 1986. Center and periphery in the grammar of anaphora. In *Studies in the acquisition of anaphora*. Vol. 1, edited by Barbara Lust, 123–150. Dordrecht: Reidel.

Reinhart, Tanya. 1997. Strategies of anaphora resolution. OTS working paper, Utrecht Institute of Lingusitics.

Reinhart, Tanya, and Eric Reuland. 1991. Anaphors and logophors: An argument structure perspective. In *Long-distance anaphora*, edited by Jan Koster and Eric Reuland, 283–321. Cambridge: Cambridge University Press.

Reinhart, Tanya, and Eric Reuland. 1993. Reflexivity. *Linguistic Inquiry* 24:657–720.

Reis, Marga. 1976. Reflexivierung in deutschen AcI-Konstruktionen: Ein transformationsgrammatisches dilemma. *Papiere zur linguistik* 9:5–82.

Reuland, Eric. 1996. Pronouns and features. Unpublished manuscript, Utrecht Institute of Linguistics OTS.

Reuland, Eric. 1997. Primitives of binding. Unpublished manuscript, Utrecht Institute of Linguistics.

Reuland, Eric. 2001. Primitives of binding. *Linguistic Inquiry* 32:439–492.

Reuland, Eric, and Tanya Reinhart. 1995. Pronouns, anaphors and case. In *Studies in comparative Germanic syntax*, edited by Hubert Haider, Susan Olsen, and Sten Vikner, 241–268. Dordrecht: Kluwer.

Reuland, Eric, and Sigri<lowercase eth>ur Sigurjónsdóttir. 1997. Long distance "binding" in Icelandic. In *Atomism and binding*, edited by Hans Bennis, Pierre Pica, and Johan Rooryck, 323–340. Dordrecht: Foris.

Richards, Norvin. YEAR? Competition and disjoint reference. *Linguistic Inquiry* 28:178–186.

Riemsdijk, Henk van. 1990. Functional prepositions. In *Unity in diversity: Papers presented to Simon C. Dik on his 50th birthday*, edited by H. Pinkster and I. Genée. Dordrecht: Foris.

Riemsdijk, Henk van. 1998. Categorial feature magnetism: The endocentricity and distribution of projections. *Journal of Comparative Germanic Syntax* 2:1–48.

Ritter, Elizabeth. 1995. On the syntactic category of pronouns and agreement. *Natural Language and Linguistic Theory* 13:405–443.

Rizzi, Luigi. 1982. *Issues in Italian syntax*. Dordrecht: Foris.

Rizzi, Luigi. 1986. On chain formation. In *Syntax and semantics 19: The syntax of pronominal clitics*, edited by Hagit Borer, 65–95. New York: Academic Press.

Rizzi, Luigi. 1990a. On the anaphor-agreement effect. *Rivista di Linguistica* 2:27–42.

Rizzi, Luigi. 1990b. *Relativized minimality*. Cambridge: MIT Press.

Roberts, Craige. 1987. Modal subordination, anaphora and distributivity. Ph.D. diss., University of Massachusetts, Amherst.

Roberts, Ian. 1991. Excorporation and minimality. *Linguistic Inquiry* 22:209–218.

Roberts, Ian. 1997. Restructuring, head movement and locality. *Linguistic Inquiry* 28:423–460.

Rögnvaldsson, Eiríkur. 1986. Some comments on reflexivization in Icelandic. In *Topics in Scandinavian syntax*, edited by Lars Hellan and Kirsti Koch Christensen, 89–102. Dordrecht: Reidel.

Rohrbacher, Bernhard. 1999. *Morphology-driven syntax*. Linguistik Aktuell, no. 15, Amsterdam and Philadelphia: Benjamins.

Rooryck, Johan, and Guido vanden Wyngaerd. 1997. The self as other: A minimalist approach to *zich* and *zichzelf* in Dutch. *Proceedings of NELS 28*. Amherst, Mass.: GLSA.

Rooryck, Johan, and Guido vanden Wyngaerd. 1998. Puzzles of identity: Binding at the interface. *Proceedings of NELS 29*, 307–323. Amherst, Mass.: GLSA.

Ruwet, Nicolas. 1991. *Syntas and human experience*. Chicago: University of Chicago Press.

Safir, Ken. 1984. Multiple variable binding. *Linguistic Inquiry* 15:603–638.

Safir, Ken. 1985. *Syntactic chains*. Cambridge: Cambridge University Press.

Safir, Ken. 1987. Comments on Wexler and Manzini. In *Parameter setting*, edited by Thomas Roeper and Edwin Williams, 77–89. Dordrecht: Reidel.

Safir, Ken. 1991. Evaluative predicates and the representation of implicit arguments. In *Principles and parameters in comparative grammar*, edited by Robert Freidin, 99–131. Cambridge: MIT Press.

Safir, Ken. 1992. Implied noncoreference and the pattern of anaphora. *Linguistics and Philosophy* 15:1–52.

Safir, Ken. 1993. A universalist approach to anaphora. Unpublished manuscript, Rutgers University.

Safir, Ken. 1996a. Abstract incorporation vs. abstract cliticization. In *CLS 31–II: Papers from the parasession on clitics*, edited by Audra Dianora, Rachel Hemphill, Barbara Luka, Barbara Need, and Sheri Pargman, 280–299. Chicago: Chicago Linguistic Society.

Safir, Ken. 1996b. *PRO* and *pro*: comments on Quicoli. In *Current issues in comparative grammar*, edited by Robert Freidin, 81–90. Dordrecht: Kluwer

Safir, Ken. 1996c. Semantic atoms of anaphora. *Natural Language and Linguistic Theory* 14:545–589.

Safir, Ken. 1997. Symmetry and unity in the theory of anaphora. In *Atomism and binding*, edited by Hans Bennis, Pierre Pica, and Johan Rooryck, 340–377. Dordrecht: Foris.

Safir, Ken. 1999. Vehicle change and reconstruction in A'-chains. *Linguistic Inquiry* 30:587–620.

Safir, Ken. 2003. Anaphors, movement and coconstrual. In *Grammatik i fokus: Grammar in focus: A Festschrift for Christer Platazack*, edited by Lars-Olof Delsing, Cecilia Falk, Gunlög Josefsson, and Halldór Sigurđsson. Lund, Sweden.

Safir, Ken. 2004. *The syntax of (in)dependence*. Cambridge: MIT Press.
Safir, Ken. In preparation. *Person, perspective and anaphora*. Unpublished manuscript, Rutgers University.
Sag, Ivan. 1976. Deletion and logical form. Ph.D. diss., MIT.
Sag, Ivan. 1981. Formal semantics and extralinguistic context. In *Radical pragmatics*, edited by Peter Cole, 273–294. New York: Academic Press.
Saito, Mamoru, and Hajime Hoji. 1983. Weak crossover and move ± in Japanese. *Natural Language and Linguistic Theory* 1:245–259.
Salmon, Nathan. 1992. Reflections on reflexivity. *Linguistics and Philosophy* 15:53–63.
Samek-Lodovici, Vieri. 1995. Constraints on subjects: An optimality-theoretic analysis. Ph.D. diss., Rutgers University.
Sanchez, Liliana. 1993. Non-determiner quantifiers in Spanish and sub-eventual structure. Unpublished manuscript, University of Southern California.
Saxon, Leslie. 1984. Disjoint anaphora and the binding theory. In *WCCFL 3*, edited by Mark Cobler, Susannah MacKaye, and Michael Westcoat, 242–251. Stanford, Calif.: CSLI.
Saxon, Leslie. 1991. On one's own: The semantics and pragmatics of reflexives. In *Interdisciplinary approaches to language: Essays in honor of S.-Y. Kuroda*, edited by R. Ishihara and C. Georgopolis, 501–517. Dordrecht: Kluwer.
Schladt, Mathias. 2000. The typology and grammaticalization of reflexives. In *Reflexives: Forms and functions*. Typological Studies in Language, no. 40, edited by Zygmunt Frajzyngier and Tracy S. Curl, 103–124. Amsterdam and Philadelphia: Benjamins.
Schlenker, Phillipe. 1999. Propositional attitudes and indexicality: A cross-categorical approach. Ph.D. diss., MIT.
Schoorlemmer, Maria Lucia. 1995. Participial passive and aspect in Russian. Ph.D. diss., Universiteit Utrecht. OTS Dissertation Series., LEd. Utrecht.
Seely, Daniel. 1993. Binding plural pronominals. In *CLS 29*, edited by Katherine Beals et al., 305–317. Chicago: Chicago Linguistic Society.
Sells, Peter. 1987. Aspects of logophoricity. *Linguistic Inquiry* 18:445–479.
Sells, Peter, Annie Zaenen, and Draga Zecs. 1987. Reflexivization variation: Relations between syntax, semantics and lexical structure. In *Working papers in grammatical theory and discourse structure*, edited by Masayo Iida et al., 169–238. Stanford, Calif.: CSLI.
Sigurđsson, Halldór. 1989. *Verbal syntax and case in Icelandic*. Lund, Sweden: University of Lund.
Sigurđsson, Halldór. 1990. Long distance reflexives and moods in Icelandic. In *Syntax and semantics 24: Modern Icelandic syntax*, edited by Joan Maling and Annie Zaenen, 309–346. New York: Academic Press.
Sigurđsson, Halldór. 2000. To be an oblique subject: Russian vs. Icelandic. *Working Papers in Scandinavian Syntax* 66:1–32.
Soames, Scott, and David Perlmutter. 1979. *Syntactic argumentation and the structure of English*. Berkeley: University of California Press.
Sportiche, Dominique. 1983. Structural invariance and symmetry. Ph.D. diss., MIT.
Sportiche, Dominique. 1986. *Zibun*. *Linguistic Inquiry* 17:369–374.
Sportiche, Dominique. 1996. Clitic constructions. *Phrase structure in the lexicon*, edited by Johan Rooryck and Laurie Zaring, 213–276. Dordrecht: Kluwer.
Sproat, Robert. 1985. On deriving the lexicon. Ph.D. diss., MIT.
van Steenbergen, Marlies. 1991. Long-distance binding in Finnish. In *Long-distance anaphora*, edited by Jan Koster and Eric Reuland, 231–244. Cambridge: Cambridge University Press.
Sternefeld, Wolfgang. 1998. Reciprocity and cumulative predication. *Natural Language Semantics* 6:303–337.

Stowell, Timothy. 1986. Null antecedents and proper government. In *NELS 16*, edited by Stephen Berman, Jae Woong Coe, and Joyce McDonough, 476–493. Amherst, Mass.: GLSA.

Szabolsci, Anna. 1994. The noun phrase. In *Syntax and semantics 27: The syntactic structure of Hungarian*, edited by E. Kiss, 179–274. New York: Academic Press.

Tang, Chih-Chen Jane. 1989. Chinese reflexives. *Natural Language and Linguistic Theory* 7:93–121.

ter Meulen, Alice G. B. 1998. On the economy of interpretation: Semantic constraints on SE-reflexives in Dutch. Utrecht Institute of Linguistics OTS.

Terzi, Arhonto. 1992. PRO in finite clauses: A study of the inflectional heads of the Balkan languages. Ph.D. diss., Graduate Center of the City University of New York.

Thornton, Rosalind, and Kenneth Wexler. 1999. *Principle B, VP ellipsis, and interpretation in child grammar*. Cambridge: MIT Press.

Thráinsson, Höskuldur. 1976. A semantic reflexive in Icelandic. Harvard University. Reprinted in *Syntax and semantics 24: Modern Icelandic syntax*, edited by Joan Maling and Annie Zaenen, 289–307. New York: Academic Press, 1990.

Thráinsson, Höskuldur. 1991. Long-distance reflexives and the typology of NPs. In *Long-distance anaphora*, edited by Jan Koster and Eric Reuland, 49–75. Cambridge: Cambridge University Press.

Timberlake, Alan. 1979a. Reference conditions on Russian reflexivization. *Language* 56:777–796.

Timberlake, Alan. 1979b. Reflexivization and the cycle in Russian. *Linguistic Inquiry* 10:109–141.

Toman, Jindřich. 1991. Anaphors in binary trees: An analysis of Czech reflexives. In *Long-distance anaphora*, edited by Jan Koster and Eric Reuland, 151–170. Cambridge: Cambridge University Press.

Travis, Lisa. 1984. Parameters and effects of word order variation. Ph.D. diss., MIT.

Ueda, Masanobu. 1984. On a Japanese reflexive *zibun*: A non-parameterization approach. Unpublished ms., University of Massachusetts at Amherst.

Ueyama, Ayumi. 1998. Two types of dependency. Ph.D. diss., University of Southern California.

Verheijen, Ron. 1986. A phrase structure for emphatic *self*-forms. *Linguistics* 24:681–695.

Vikner, Sten. 1985. Parameters of binder and of binding category in Danish. *Working Papers in Scandinavian Syntax* 23.

Visser, F. T. 1963. *An historical syntax of the English language*. Part 1. Leiden, The Netherlands: Brill.

Voskuil, Jan. 1991. Comments on "Reflexivity." Unpublished ms., University of Leiden.

Wali, Kashi, and K. V. Subbarao. 1991. On pronominal classification: Evidence from Marathi and Telugu. *Linguistics* 29:1093–1110.

Watanabe, Akira. 1991. Wh-in-situ, subjacency and chain formation. Unpublished manuscript, MIT.

Wettstein, Howard. 1991. How to bridge the gap between meaning and reference. In *Pragmatics*, edited by Steven Davis, 160–173. Oxford: Oxford University Press.

Wexler, Kenneth, and Maria Rita Manzini. 1987. Parameters and learnability in binding theory. In *Parameter setting*, edited by Thomas Roeper and Edwin Williams, 41–76. Dordrecht: Reidel.

Wilkins, Wendy. 1988. Thematic structure and reflexivization. In *Syntax and semantics: Thematic relations*, edited by Wendy Wilkins, 191–214. New York: Academic Press.

Williams, Edwin. 1977. Discourse and logical form. *Linguistic Inquiry* 8:103–139.

Williams, Edwin. 1982. The NP cycle. *Linguistic Inquiry* 13:277–295.

Williams, Edwin. 1986. A reassignment of the functions of LF. *Linguistic Inquiry* 17:265–299.

Williams, Edwin. 1994. *Thematic structure in syntax*. Cambridge: MIT Press.

Williams, Edwin. 1997. Blocking and anaphora. *Linguistic Inquiry* 28:577–628.

Williams, Edwin. 2003. *Representation theory*. Cambridge: MIT Press.

Wilson, Colin. 2001. Bidirectional optimization and the theory of anaphora. In *Optimality-theoretic syntax*, edited by Geraldine Legendre, Jane Grimshaw, and Sten Vikner, 465–507. Cambridge: MIT Press.

Wiltschko, Martina. 1998. On the syntax and semantics of (relative) pronouns and determiners. *Journal of Comparative Germanic Linguistics* 2:143–181.

Woolford, Ellen. 1999. More on the anaphor agreement effect. *Linguistic Inquiry* 30:257–287.

Yang, Dong-Whee. 1983. The extended binding theory of anaphora. *Language Research* 19:169–192.

Zaenen, Annie, Joan Maling, and Thráinsson, Höskuldur. 1985. Case and grammatical relations: The Icelandic passive. *Natural Language and Linguistic Theory* 3:441–483. Reprinted in 1990, *Syntax and semantics 24: Modern Icelandic syntax*, edited by Joan Maling and Annie Zaenen, 95–136. New York: Academic Press.

Zribi-Hertz, Anne. 1980. Coréférence et pronoms réfléchis: Notes sur le contraste *lui/lui-même* en français. *Linguisticae Investigationes* 4:131–179.

Zribi-Hertz, Anne. 1989. Anaphor binding and narrative point of view. *Language* 65:695–727.

Zribi-Hertz, Anne. 1995. Emphatic or reflexive? On the endophoric character of French *lui-même* and similar complex pronouns. *Journal of Linguistics* 31–32:333–374.

Zribi-Hertz, Anne, and Liliane Mbolatianavalona.1999. Towards a modular theory of linguistic deficiency: Evidence from Malagasy personal pronouns. *Natural Language and Linguistic Theory* 17:161–218.

Zwart, Jan-Wouter. 1997. *Morphosyntax of verb movement: A minimalist approach to the syntax of Dutch*. Dordrecht: Kluwer.

# INDEX OF LANGUAGES

Abe, 109, 120
Amsterdaamse, 200. *See also* Dutch
Arabic, 196
Austronesian, 96

Balkan, 154
Baltic, 254
Basque, 196

Chadic, 196, 198
Chamorro, 260
Chichewa, 137, 139, 221
Chinese, viii, xii, 13, 157, 165, 173–174, 243–244, 248, 263, 267, 272, 279–281
Czech, 171

Danish. *See* Scandinavian, Mainland
Dogrib, 274
Dravidian, 176
Dutch, xii, 17, 20, 68, 87, 98–99, 120, 123, 127–132, 134, 136, 139, 162–165, 169, 173, 198, 206, 211, 235, 244, 248, 253–257, 262. *See also* Amsterdaamse

English, 9, 13, 50, 65, 68, 71, 75–76, 82–83, 85–86, 90, 98–100, 105, 107, 109, 120–122, 124, 126–127, 130–133, 137, 141, 146, 150, 154, 159, 162, 167–168, 170, 172–173, 185, 188, 192, 196–198, 201–202, 204–207, 209, 211, 222–225, 233, 246, 248, 252–255, 259, 262, 266, 269, 271–274, 276–277, 282–283

Finnish, viii, 135–137, 272–273
French, xii, 69–71, 87–88, 128, 159–164, 185, 190–191, 195–196, 198–199, 204, 207–211, 221–222, 248–249, 261–262, 264, 269–270, 273, 276–277, 280, 283
Frisian, 19–20, 68, 76, 131, 211, 244
Fula, 196, 202
Fulani, 200

German, xii, 6, 17, 20, 76, 92, 96, 99–100, 104, 109, 120, 131, 161–165, 171, 173, 185–186, 190–191, 197–198, 205–207, 211, 221–223, 225, 246, 248, 261–263, 268, 270, 276, 283
Germanic, viii, 17, 71–72, 76, 79, 87, 96–97, 127, 129, 131–132, 135, 139, 190, 197, 205, 211, 244, 275
Gola, 200
Greek, viii, 154–155, 212–214, 218, 252, 272, 277

Haitian Creole, 196
Hausa, 196, 202
Hebrew, 186, 196, 269
Hindi, viii, xii, 78, 156, 164, 166, 168, 170, 172–173, 196, 204, 261, 264, 266, 275

Hindi/Urdu. *See* Hindi
Hungarian, viii, 196, 218–220, 225, 246, 249

Icelandic, xii, 98–98, 170, 172, 264–265, 279
Italian, xii, 71, 191, 199, 254, 260–261, 270–271

Japanese, viii, xii, 165, 173–174, 188, 215–218, 240, 246, 248, 250, 266, 272, 279–281

Kannada, 138–139, 176, 256, 277
Karomfe, 200
Kwa, 275
Kwaio, 274

Lillooet Salish, 242, 269

Malagasy, 189
Malayalam, viii, 174–176, 213–214, 218, 266, 274
Marathi, 266
Mohawk, 257
MS. *See* Scandinavian, Mainland

Niger-Congo, 196
Norwegian. *See* Scandinavian, Mainland

Old English, 96, 221, 267

Pima, 247, 275

Romance, viii, 6, 69, 87, 91–92, 162–163, 190–191, 199–200, 211, 268, 275

Russian, xii, 78–80, 87, 164, 166, 170–171, 173, 247, 264

Sanskrit, 196
Scandinavian, Mainland, xii, 13, 67, 76, 78–79, 99, 157, 164–165, 169–170, 173, 177, 181, 183, 190, 204–207, 211–212, 223, 262
  Danish, 67, 72, 78–79, 97, 191, 244, 254, 265, 270
  Norwegian, 13, 60–61, 67–68, 70, 72, 78, 99, 109, 123, 127, 132, 134–135, 139, 166, 169, 179, 191, 206–207, 244, 250–251, 254, 257, 269–270, 277
  Swedish, 67, 72, 191, 244, 265
Slavic, viii, 265, 270, 275
Spanish, xii, 199, 210, 272
Swedish. *See* Scandinavian, Mainland

Tamazight, 196
Tamil, 176
Telugu, 176
Teochew, 279
Thai, 269
Turkish, xii, 154–155, 174, 176, 266, 275, 282

Uto-Aztecan, 196, 247, 275

Vietnamese, 269

Waapo, 78, 275

Yoruba, xii, 198–199, 202, 221, 273
Yukian, 275

# INDEX OF NAMES

Abe, Jun, 215, 279
Abusch, Dorit, 117–118
Ackerman, Farrell, 262
Adésolá, Olúsèye, xii, 273
Aikawa, Takako, 215–218, 279–281
Akinlabi, Akin, xii
Anagnostopoulou, Elena, 252
Anderson, Steve, 97
Aoun, Joseph, 140, 242, 262
Avrutin, Sergey, 60, 80, 247

Bach, Emmon, 105
Baker, C. L., 98, 157
Baker, Mark, xi, 160, 257, 263, 267, 278
Bakovic, Eric, xii
Battistella, Ed, 165, 274
Bauer, Judy, xii
Benveniste, Emile, 78, 191, 248, 282
Berman, Steve, 95, 249–250
Bernstein, Judy B., 268
Bickerton, Derek, 196, 276
Bittner, Maria, 240
Borer, Hagit, 184, 250, 271–272
Bošković, Željko, 246–247, 264
Bouchard, Denis, 209, 243, 254, 266
Brody, Michael, 152, 259
Browning, Marguerite, 276
Burzio, Luigi, 57, 59, 61, 69–73, 78, 86, 178, 207, 236–237, 243–246, 251, 271, 284

Calabrese, Andrea, 193
Cardinaletti, Anna, 87, 188, 248, 269
Carlson, Greg, 199
Chierchia, Gennaro, 243
Chomsky, Noam, xi, 3, 8, 10, 14, 16, 25–6, 37–39, 43, 45, 58–60, 69, 84, 141, 147–151, 153, 156–157, 168, 189, 192, 201, 237, 240–241, 246–247, 251, 253, 258, 260, 262, 268, 271, 283
Choueiri, Lina, 242
Chung, Sandra, 260
Cinque, Guglielmo, 128, 254
Cole, Peter, 165, 244, 263–264, 274, 279
Cresswell, M. J., 27
Cresti, Diana, 152
Curl, Tracy S., 223, 283

Dahl, Östen, 283
D'Allant, Thiery, xii
Dalrymple, Mary, 60, 67, 183, 213, 221–222, 258, 266, 283
Davison, Alice, 169, 196, 264
Dayal, Veneeta, xi, xii, 166–167, 264
Demirdache, Hamida, 186, 242, 269
den Dikken, Marcel, xi, xii, 123, 171, 218–220, 281–282
Déprez, Viviane, xii, 260
Di Sciullo, Anna-Maria, 273, 277
Dmitriadis, Alexis, 283

Dowty, David, 62, 199, 243
Dubinsky, Stanley, 241–242

Edmondson, Jerold, 206, 275
Enç, Murvet, 176, 183, 278
Epstein, Samuel David, 140
Evans, Gareth, 25, 27–28, 30, 39–40, 42, 29, 110, 240
Everaert, Martin, xii

Faltz, Leonard, 66, 78, 96, 182, 185, 196, 202, 206–207, 209–210, 247, 254, 257, 269–270, 273–275, 277
Farmer, Anne, 65, 242, 266
Fauconnier, Gilles, 112, 117, 253
Fiengo, Robert, 27, 28, 36, 133, 257, 282
Fox, Danny, 106, 152, 229–230, 235, 283
Frajzyngier, Zygmunt, 198, 223, 267, 273, 283
Franks, Steven, 171, 245, 265
Fuji, Masaaki, xii, 215–216, 280
Fukuda, Kaoru, 276
Fukui, Naoki, 217
Futagi, Yoko, xii

Geach, P., 106
Gelderen, Elly van, 96, 248, 267
Geniušiene, Emma, 121–123, 175, 254
Giorgi, Allesandra, 207, 264, 270, 277
Giusti, Giuliana, 268
Grewendorf, Günther, 171
Grice, Paul, 62–66, 281
Grimshaw, Jane, 150, 187, 259
Grodzinsky, Yosef, 17, 21–22, 31, 37, 48, 50–51, 53, 55, 62, 84, 89, 92, 105, 119, 248, 253, 283

Hale, Ken, xi, 263, 266
Halle, Morris, xi
Hamilton, Robert, 241–242
Harnish, A. K., 65
Hasegawa, Nobuko, 272
Heim, Irene, 27, 29, 105–106, 201, 230, 253, 268, 282
Heine, Bernd, 196, 198, 200, 267, 273
Helke, M., 273
Hellan, Lars, xii, 57, 61, 67–69, 72–73, 87, 135, 244–245, 247, 251, 254, 264
Heller, Markus, xii
Hendrick, Randall, 273
Hermon, Gabriella, 165, 183, 244, 263, 274, 279
Herslund, Michael, 265
Hestvik, Arild, xi, xii, 60, 95, 101, 135, 188, 206, 245, 249–251, 253, 257, 269
Heycock, Caroline, xii

Higginbotham, James, xi, 25, 28, 39–40, 42–43, 45–48, 54–54, 61, 105–106, 199, 230, 252, 270, 272
Hirose, Yukio, 188, 269
Holler, Madeline, xii
Holmberg, Anders, 251, 265
Horn, Larry, 63
Hornstein, Norbert, 8, 35, 44, 144, 151, 237, 242, 261–262
Horwood, Graham, xii
Huang, C.-T. James, 18, 57–58, 165, 175–178, 263, 272, 279–281
Huang, Yan, 166, 178, 243–244, 267, 275, 281, 284

Iatridou, Sabine, 212–213
Ingria, Robert, 273
Inoue, K., 279

Jackendoff, Ray, 12, 112–114, 141–142
Jaeggli, Osvaldo, 192, 272
Jayaseelan, K. A., 175, 177, 201, 213–214, 216–217, 266, 274–275, 279–280
Johnson, David, 141
Johnson, Kyle, 259
Jónsson, Jóhaness Gisli, xii
Joseph, Brian, 154

Kamp, Hans, 240, 247
Kaplan, David, 220
Karaieva, Natalia, xii
Katada, Fusa, 175, 215, 217, 279
Kayne, Richard S., xi, xii, 8, 160, 162, 188, 190–191, 207, 209, 211, 237, 242, 261–262, 270–271
Keenan, Edward, 96, 185, 206, 241
Kemmer, Suzanne, 223–226, 254, 273
Kidwai, Ayesha, 169
Kitagawa, Yoshihisa, 177
Klima, Edward, 25–26, 140
König, Ekkehard, 252, 275–276
Koopman, Hilda, 109
Kornfilt, Jaklin, xii, 176–177, 266, 275, 282
Koster, Jan, 147, 162–163, 245, 248
Kuno, Susumu, 146, 157, 175, 177, 215, 279
Kuroda, S.-Y., 279

Lakoff, George, 41, 114, 117, 252–253
Lal, Roli, xii
Landau, Idan, 254, 271
Langacker, R., 25, 26, 140
Lasnik, Howard, 8–9, 25–6, 28–30, 34–9, 42, 45, 48–49, 53, 55, 58–59, 65, 73, 89, 91–92, 94–95, 144, 192, 201, 239–241, 246, 258–259, 262, 269, 282

Lebeaux, David, xi, 60, 84, 148, 151, 157, 266, 282
Lee, Cher Leng, 165, 176, 244, 263, 279
Lees, R. B., 25–26, 140
Levinson, Stephen, 57, 61–66, 69, 73, 96, 243–243
Lewis, David, 271
Li, Yafei, 160, 164, 176, 263
Lichtenberk, Frantisek, 223, 267
Lidz, Jeffrey, 112, 129, 135, 138–139, 255–258
Lieber, Rochelle, 273
Liu, C.-S. Luther, 165, 175, 177, 244, 263, 279, 281
Longobardi, Giuseppe, 268

Maling, Joan, 171–172, 264–265
Manzini, Maria-Rita, 59, 69, 183–184, 277
Marantz, Alec, 128
Massam, Diana, 260
May, Robert, 27–28, 34, 36, 133, 151, 201, 257, 282
Mbolatianavalona, Liliane, 189, 269
McCloskey, James, 250
McKay, Terence, 161
McKay, Thomas, 276
Merchant, Jason, 41
Moltmann, Friederike, 199
Moore, John, 155, 173, 264–266
Moravcsik, Edith, 206, 275

Naess, Alma, xii
Nagy, Szusza, xii
Napoli, Donna, 254
Neeleman, Ad, xii
Nichols, Lynn, xii
Nishigauchi, Taisuke, 262
Noguchi, Tohru, 188
Nuendel, Andre, xii
Nunberg, Geoffrey, 113, 117–118
Nunes, Jairo, 152

Pan, Haihua, 280
Partee, Barbara, 105, 239, 272
Perlmutter, David, 154–155, 173, 264–266
Pica, Pierre, 57, 60, 71, 84, 129, 157, 164–165, 182, 188, 243, 261, 163–164, 270, 273–276
Plank, Frans, 206, 275–276
Platzack, Christer, xii, 251, 165
Pollard, Carl, 6, 141–143, 146, 179, 239, 258, 282
Postal, Paul, 25–26, 28, 58, 141, 143, 268
Postma, Gertjan, 196–197, 272–273
Preuss, Suzanne, xii
Progovac, Ljiljana, 263
Pullum, Geoffrey, 231

Rappaport, Gilbert, 247
Reinhart, Tanya, 5–6, 8, 15–22, 25, 27, 30–36, 39, 42–43, 48, 55, 57, 61–62, 64, 72–73, 89–95, 97–98, 100–101, 104–106, 109, 111, 114, 127, 129, 132, 140, 146–147, 155, 163, 171, 179, 182, 226, 230, 240, 243, 251–252, 255, 258, 262–263, 272, 274, 278, 281, 283–284
Reis, Marga, 161, 262
Reuland, Eric, xii, 5–6, 8, 15–22, 55, 62, 89–95, 97–98, 100–101, 104–105, 109, 111–114, 127, 129, 132, 139, 146–147, 155, 163, 171, 179, 182, 226, 243–244, 247–249, 251–252, 254–255, 258, 262–264, 272, 274, 277–279, 284
Reyle, U., 240
Richards, Norvin, 245, 250, 279
Riemsdijk, Henk van, 150, 187, 259–260
Ritter, Elizabeth, 268–270
Rizzi, Luigi, 175, 241, 260–261
Roberts, Craige, 243, 253
Roberts, Ian, 261, 263
Rögnvaldson, Eiríkur, 265
Rohrbacher, Bernhard, 192
Rooryck, Johan, 112, 129–131, 169, 198, 256, 273
Ruwet, Nicolas, 254

Safir, Ken, vii, viii, xi, 8, 10, 24, 36–7, 40–42, 44–45, 48, 51, 55, 61–62, 75, 88, 92–93, 97–98, 101, 116, 133, 142, 145–146, 152–154, 156–157, 167, 174, 179–180, 182–185, 192–193, 195, 200, 220, 230, 232, 238–244, 246–248, 250–254, 257–259, 261, 266–268, 271–278, 282–284
Sag, Ivan, 6, 25, 46, 65, 69, 75, 117–118, 126, 141–143, 146, 178–179, 185, 205–206, 210, 215, 239, 241–242, 252–253, 258, 264–265, 273–278, 280, 282
Salmon, Nathan, 140
Samek-Lodovici, Vieri, xii, 193, 232
Sanchez, Liliana, 210
Saxon, Leslie, 199, 274
Schein, Barry, xi
Schladt, Mathias, 196, 267, 272, 274
Schoorlemmer, Maria Lucia, 266
Schwartz, Linda, 245
Schwarzschild, Roger, xi
Seely, T. Daniel, 249
Sells, Peter, 97, 134–137, 176–177, 221, 262, 279
Sidlauskas, Susan, xii
Siemund, Peter, 252, 275–276
Sigurðsson, Halldór, 59, 173, 264–265
Sigurjónsdóttir, Sigriður, xii, 264, 279
Snyder, William, 129, 273

Soames, Scott, 154–155
Sportiche, Dominique, 109–110, 140, 183–184, 261, 266
Sproat, Robert, 273
Starke, Michal, 87, 188, 248, 269
van Steenbergen, Marlies, 137, 272
Sternefeld, Wolfgang, 283
Stowell, Timothy, 167, 170
Subbarao, K. V., 266
Sung, Li-May, 165, 263–264, 274, 279
Szabolsci, Anna, 268

Tang, Chih-Chen Jane, 165, 175–177, 279–280
Taraldsen, Knut Tarald, xii, 245
ter Meulen, Alice G. B., 128–129, 140, 253
Terzi, Arhonto, 192
Thornton, Rosalind, 250, 253
Thráinsson, Höskuldur, xii, 97, 157, 172–173, 183–184, 264
Timberlake, Alan, 78, 246–247
Toman, Jindřich, 171
Travis, Lisa, 160
Truckenbrodt, Hubert, xii
Tsujimura, Natsuko, 266

Ueda, Masanobu, 217
Ueyama, Ayumi, 240

Verheijen, Ron, 276
Vikner, Sten, xii, 72, 97, 250, 254–255, 270
Visser, F. T., 96
Voskuil, Jan, 98, 129

Wali, Kashi, 266
Warner, Tom, xii
Watanabe, Akira, 170
Webelhuth, Gert, 262
Weinberg, Amy, 144
Wettstein, Howard, 32
Wexler, Kenneth, 59, 69, 183–184, 250, 253, 277
Wilkins, Wendy, 142
Williams, Edwin, xi, 25, 40, 48, 141, 143, 204–205, 235, 241–243, 248, 254, 258
Wilson, Colin, 237, 245, 271, 284
Wiltschko, Martina, 186, 268
Woolford, Ellen, 175
vanden Wyngaerd, Guido, 112, 129–131, 169, 198, 256, 273

Yang, Dong-Whee, 183, 267, 277
Yang, Rachel, xii

Zaenen, Annie, 134–137, 172, 262
Zecs, Draga, 134–137, 262
Zepter, Alexandra, xii
Zola, Scot, xii
Zribi-Hertz, Anne, 98, 146, 189, 199–200, 206–209, 249, 257, 269, 274, 276–277
Zwart, Jan-Wouter, xii, 262

# GENERAL INDEX


adicity reduction, 136, 140, 254–255, 268
agreement, 16, 60, 70–72, 79–80, 89–90, 92, 94, 118–120, 154, 156, 165, 171, 175–176, 186, 190, 219–220, 233, 237, 241, 245–246, 248–249, 257, 260, 263, 265–266, 268, 271, 279, 282
  pseudoagreement, 70–72, 245–246
  SPEC-head, 156, 246–247, 279
  verb agreement, 154, 175–176, 249, 257
  *See also* Antecedent Agreement
AgrO, 156, 171, 239, 258, 264, 272, 275, 277
anaphor, 6–9, 11, 13–14, 21, 38–39, 42–44, 48, 53, 55–58, 60–61, 63, 66–67, 69–72, 77–80, 84–89, 91, 93, 95–96, 98–99, 104–105, 107–110, 112, 117–120, 125–128, 130–132, 135–138, 141–142, 146–161, 163–165, 167, 169–186, 189–191, 193–207, 209, 211–218, 220, 223, 226, 233, 239, 243, 248, 251–252, 254, 256–260, 263–264, 266–269, 271–280, 282
  adjunct, 88, 202–204, 254, 276
  anaphoric atom, 203, 273
animacy, 143, 186, 201, 259, 264
  body part, 96, 196–199, 201, 212, 221, 274
  complex, 130–131, 164–165, 204, 257, 263, 274. 278
  definition of, 9, 15, 21, 42, 72, 77, 86, 107–108, 147–148, 179
  identity specific, 108–110, 115, 120–121, 124, 140, 184, 225
  local, 147–148, 184, 212, 214–215, 279–281, 274
  long-distance, 60, 146–148, 150, 158, 258, 263, 274–275
  metonymic, 198, 272–273
  null, 147, 260
  operators, 168–169, 215, 279.. *See also* operator anaphors
  possessive, 156, 265
  pronominal, 59, 120, 140, 153, 185, 190–191, 197–198, 204, 211–212, 225, 257, 267, 269, 275, 278
  reciprocal, 198, 201, 223
  reflexive, 6, 15, 146, 194
  relational, 96, 156, 185, 189, 194–197, 201–205, 210, 215, 218, 226, 273–278, 280;. *See also* OTHER, OWN, SAME, SELF, SIG
  simplex, 164, 263
  syntactic, 7, 9, 13, 43, 147, 157–158, 233, 240, 276
Antecedent Agreement, 16, 70–72, 75–78, 94, 119–120, 246
aspect, 253, 257, 264
  AspP, 257
availability, 7, 22, 31, 33, 69, 74, 76–77, 84, 89, 91, 108, 124, 130, 134–135, 153, 158, 180–184, 191, 211, 250, 256, 268
  and distribution, 31, 33, 69, 158, 180–181, 183
  *See also* scalar intervention

bare phrase structure, 268
binding, 8–13, 18, 21–22, 26, 30–31, 35, 37–40, 42–43, 49–50, 54, 57, 60, 62, 65, 68, 77, 86–87, 138–139, 146–148, 153, 157, 159, 161, 165, 173, 176, 178, 188, 193, 196, 206, 212–213, 216–217, 224, 230, 237, 240, 244, 253, 258–259, 263–264, 266, 269–272, 275–276, 279, 281, 283
  A-binding, 21
  A'-binding, 21, 250, 278
  definition of, 8–9
binding theory, 3, 5–6, 8–10, 12–16, 20, 22, 26, 39, 42–43, 45, 48, 50–51, 56–57, 59–60, 62, 65–67, 69–71, 129, 146–147, 183, 219, 226, 251, 258
BT, 3, 5–6, 8–10, 12–16, 20, 22, 26, 39, 43, 48, 50–51, 56–57, 59, 62, 66, 69–71, 147, 251, 258
BT-compatibility, 251
blocking, 14, 109, 168, 224, 243, 254, 263, 279
  and competition, 224, 243, 279
BODYPART. *See* anaphor, body part
bound anaphora, 30–32, 62, 240, 271
bound reading(s), 15–16, 21–22, 24–25, 30–32, 34, 38, 48–49, 51, 53–54, 62, 64–65, 70–71, 97–98, 142, 188–190, 216, 241–243, 245–248, 250, 271, 279, 281
bound reference, 25, 31, 33, 39, 64, 84, 244, 250

c-algorithmic constraints, 233–234, 237
c-antecedent, 77, 105, 107–110, 233, 282
  definition of, 107
c-command, 3, 4, 6, 9–10, 13–15, 17, 21–22, 25–40, 42–54, 57, 62, 66, 68–69, 73–75, 77, 81–82, 84, 86–88, 105–107, 109–111, 114–116, 140–141, 143–145, 148, 158–159, 161, 164–165, 167, 172, 174, 176–179, 189, 193–194, 200, 211, 213, 230–231, 233, 235, 240–242, 245–247, 249–251, 258, 261, 263, 265–266, 269, 274, 276, 279, 283. *See also* subcommand, o-command
  almost, 34–36, 53
  definition of, 9
Case, 10–12, 15, 19–20, 29, 59, 89, 138, 149, 153, 156, 159–160, 170, 172–173, 180, 186, 192, 202, 207, 233, 237, 245, 257–259, 266, 278
  accusative, 10, 18, 20, 61, 70, 121, 141, 149, 154, 159–160, 170–171, 190, 193, 202, 206–207, 246–247, 261, 265. *See also* ECM
  assignment, 10–12, 15, 19–20, 160, 172
  attraction, 149, 258
  checking, 233
  dative, 156, 160–161, 171–173, 214, 264–266, 278
  genitive, 75, 171, 179, 192, 200, 206
  inherent, 20
  nominative, 141, 155, 160, 170, 172, 245, 265
  null, 192, 246
causative, 136, 160–163, 171, 254, 261–262
CDC. *See* Coargument Dependency Constraint
chain, 16–18, 22, 90–92, 95, 139, 144, 146–148, 150–155, 158–159, 161, 170, 191, 240–241, 248–249, 251, 255, 259–261
  A-chain, 7, 16–18, 147–148, 151, 153–155, 158, 170
  A'-chain, 259
  Condition on A-chains, 16–18, 20, 90–92, 95, 155, 248–249, 251
  chain theory, 5–6, 8, 19, 21
clausemate, 13, 65, 67, 92, 101, 140, 206, 246, 267
clitic, 87, 148, 159–165, 170, 172–173, 177, 180, 186, 188–191, 193, 232, 248, 261–262, 264, 267, 269–271, 273–275, 278. *See also* pronoun, clitic
coargument, 15–16, 20, 47, 65–68, 70, 79, 90–95, 99, 101–114, 116, 118–121, 124–125, 127, 129, 132, 134, 137–140, 142, 145, 152, 158, 172, 179, 195, 200, 208, 213–214, 217, 221, 228, 242, 244, 249, 251–252, 254–255, 257–258, 266, 268, 274
  semantic, 20, 91
  syntactic, 16, 90
Coargument Dependency Constraint, 93, 95, 102–104, 118–120, 132, 140, 184, 228, 232, 249
coconstrual, 4–6, 8, 13, 22, 24, 27, 29, 33, 36–41, 48, 52–53, 61, 101–104, 109, 112, 114, 116, 121, 125–126, 132, 139, 185, 198–199, 212, 223, 237, 242, 247, 258, 261, 283
codependent, 7, 107–109, 111, 274, 282
collective interpretation, 16, 94, 119, 197, 248, 253
Complementarity Principle, 67–69, 71, 244
contrastive predicate, 14, 178–179, 267, 277
contrastive stress, 49, 119, 269, 280
control, 37–38, 77, 101, 132, 140, 145, 192, 246, 254, 261–262, 271–272. *See also* PRO
  exhaustive, 271
  obligatory, 271
  partial obligatory, 271
copy theory, 151, 154, 261
coreference, 5, 9, 12, 21, 23–34, 36–40, 42–45, 47–48, 50–54, 62–66, 73, 91, 94–95, 103, 106, 112, 114, 116, 188, 208, 240–242, 244, 248–250, 253, 266, 268
  accidental, 26, 38, 242
covaluation, 7, 9, 24, 42, 48, 117, 250–251, 253

crossover, 35–36, 142, 168, 192, 232, 241, 243, 292
strong, 168, 241, 272
weak, 35–36, 142, 232, 243

definite description, 6, 10, 26–30, 34, 37, 46–47, 53, 86, 186–187, 241, 246–247, 268
deictic, 7, 72, 86–88, 150, 153, 157, 173, 180, 184, 185–190, 202, 233, 248, 269, 276
deficiency, 233
potential, 86–88, 153, 157, 173, 180, 184, 188, 190, 202, 248, 269
dependency arrows, 25, 41–42, 44, 50, 108, 152, 232–233, 235, 284
dependency definition, 24–25. *See also* identity dependent
disambiguation, 96–97, 99–100, 106, 123, 185, 197, 202–203, 205–206, 208, 221–222, 257, 267–268, 273
discourse, 4, 7–8, 23–25, 27–29, 50, 63, 86, 97–98, 101, 106, 111, 170, 174, 176, 178–180, 192–193, 199, 208–209, 214, 220, 231, 240, 249, 251, 253, 264–265, 269, 273, 276–277, 279
discrimination, 46–47, 51–53, 89, 95, 249 (discriminating interpretation)
disjoint reference, 25–28, 38–39, 45, 47–48, 52, 58, 60, 63–67, 69–70, 85, 95, 147, 168, 208, 219–220, 242, 244, 249–250, 274, 282
distinctness, 116, 126–127, 129, 131–132, 136, 200–201, 224, 255–256. *See also* indistinctness
distributed/distributive interpretation, 7, 16, 74, 76, 80, 89–90, 92–94, 99–100, 104, 128, 197, 211, 217–218, 233, 245–246, 248, 253, 268, 281
domain, 7, 9–15, 18, 20, 22, 34, 36, 56–61, 67, 69, 77, 79–80, 85, 88–89, 92, 98, 101, 107–108, 120, 129, 132, 144, 146–151, 153, 155–167, 169–170, 172–175, 177–184, 186, 190, 192–193, 196, 202–205, 209–210, 212–214, 218–219, 221, 239, 243, 246–247, 250–251, 260–264, 266–267, 269–270, 272, 274–279, 281
bounded, 156, 158–159, 166, 169, 173–174, 178, 180–181, 183, 203–204, 209–210, 212, 275
Domain D (Domain of LAL), 9–10, 11 (definition), 13–14, 60, 77, 107, 148–151, 156, 159, 172
long-bounded, 158–159, 169, 173, 180, 203–204, 209–210, 275
of movement, 11, 146–147
short-bounded, 158–159, 174, 178, 180–181, 203–204, 210, 275

economy, 4, 8, 17, 69–73, 81–82, 85–86, 102, 189, 227–228, 234–237, 284
global, 237
local, 235, 237
morphological, 70, 72
scope. *See* Scope Economy
ellipsis, vii, 25, 33, 35, 40–41, 51, 84, 115–116, 133–134, 136–137, 152, 241, 248, 250, 259, 268, 283
parallelism, 36, 40–42, 48, 60, 134, 259, 264
strict/sloppy readings, 24–25, 30, 33–36, 41, 52, 84, 115–116, 133–138, 152, 241–242, 250, 253, 257, 268, 279, 283
*See also* vehicle change
Empty Category Principle (ECP), 11, 155, 166, 241, 260
epithet, 29, 49–50, 53, 74, 118, 241–242, 245, 268
Exceptional Case Marking (ECM), 10–11, 16–18, 20, 66, 77, 83, 91–92, 98, 108, 149, 154, 164, 171, 173, 233, 246, 279
excorporation, 165, 263–264
external argument, 15, 20, 141

features, 19, 41, 45, 69–72, 75–76, 78–79, 82, 86, 88–89, 92, 101, 118, 149, 153, 156, 163, 165, 179, 183–190, 194, 198, 208, 211, 228, 233, 235, 237, 244–249, 256, 258–259, 268, 271–272, 278, 283–284
feature-checking, 82, 101, 233, 235, 237
phi-features, 19–20, 41, 78–79, 185–187, 194, 211, 245–249, 259, 271, 278. *See also* agreement, gender, number, person, pronoun
focus, 30, 199, 206, 214, 262, 264
focused antecedents, 30
Form-To-Interpretation Principle, 5, 7–8, 50–55, 57, 61, 64–65, 68–69, 72–76, 78–79, 81–85, 89, 91, 94–97, 99–103, 105, 108–109, 111, 114–117, 124–125, 127–129, 133, 135–136, 138–140, 144–147, 152–153, 158, 169, 172, 174, 180, 182–185, 189–194, 198, 202–203, 208–212, 214, 221, 226, 228–229, 231–234, 236, 242, 246–247, 249–252, 256–257, 259–260, 266–267, 271–272, 278, 281–282
definition of, 50, 57, 74
FTIP Algorithm, 81–85, 99–101, 109, 189, 251, 282
role of c-command, 50, 68–69, 74, 111, 114, 140, 145, 231, 247
and Principle B, 54–55, 85, 89, 91, 95, 105, 174, 271

Form-To-Interpretation Principle (*continued*)
and Principle C, 54–55, 105, 114, 133, 144
test derivation, 82–84, 203, 210, 275, 278
FTIP. *See* Form-To-Interpretation Principle

gender, 19, 70, 72, 75–76, 89, 133, 156, 185–186, 190, 198, 211–212, 245–246, 259
generic, 191, 248, 268–269, 283
government, 3, 11, 16, 20, 59, 77, 197, 237
grammaticalization, 185, 267, 273
guise, 7, 74, 114–117, 120, 126, 249, 252–253

HPSG, 6, 239, 258

Identity, 4–7, 24–26, 28, 32–34, 37, 40, 54, 74–76, 84–85, 90, 93, 102–105, 108–121, 124–127, 132, 139–140, 144, 184, 188, 195–196, 198–202, 207, 212, 218, 220–221, 223, 225, 227, 240, 244, 252–253, 255–257, 267, 270, 272, 274, 276, 282
identity-dependent (dependent identity), 4–7, 24–25, 28, 32–34, 40, 54, 74–76, 84–85, 90, 93, 102–105, 110, 112, 114, 120–121, 124–125, 139–140, 198, 200–202, 207, 218, 220–221, 227, 240, 252, 255–257, 270, 274, 282
and reflexivity, 26, 108–120, 124–125, 139–140, 195, 201, 218, 230, 232–233, 252, 267, 274. *See also* reflexivity, LRP
and distributivity, 7, 220. *See also* distributive
and guise interpretation, 114–118, 120, 252. *See also* guise
and indistinctness, 120–121, 256. *See also* indistinctness
and proxy interpretation, 120, 144. *See also* proxy
Inclusiveness, 37, 43–44, 153, 259
incorporation, 144, 150, 184, 237, 252, 257–258, 272, 278
indefinite description, 29, 86, 241
Independence Principle, 40, 42, 44, 47–48, 54, 75, 105, 114–115, 140, 142–145, 184, 228, 232, 241–242, 251
index, 5, 8–9, 15–16, 21, 24–25, 34–35, 37–45, 50, 77, 82–83, 106, 144, 151–152, 161, 188, 202, 229, 240–241, 251, 257, 259, 263, 266
alpha, 251, 257
anaphoric, 38–39
cumulative, 40, 45, 48
referential, 38–39, 44, 188, 241, 263
and movement, 34–35, 37, 39–40, 42–44, 77, 161
numeration, 43–44, 83, 151–152, 259
indexical, 115
indistinctness (thematic), 7, 87, 116, 120–121, 125–134, 136–137, 139–140, 169, 185, 198, 200–201, 211, 224, 253–257, 268, 276
distinctness, 116, 120, 126–127, 129, 131–132, 200–201, 224, 255–256
infinitives, 10, 12, 37, 59, 66, 77, 132, 160, 163–164, 168–169, 192, 246, 250, 254, 257–258, 260, 262, 264–265, 272. *See also* ECM, control, PRO, domain
instantiation context, 27, 51, 111, 251

LAL. *See* Local Antecedent Licensing
late insertion, 247, 259
LF, 10, 34–35, 43, 51, 60, 77, 80–85, 89–90, 102, 133, 146–152, 159, 164–167, 170, 173, 177–178, 186, 188, 192–193, 203, 207, 210, 229, 234, 242, 252, 257–260, 262, 264, 284
LFG, 60, 101, 258, 266
Local Antecedent Licensing, 7, 77–79, 83, 86, 88–89, 102, 105, 107–108, 111, 119, 125, 144, 146–153, 156–161, 167, 169–170, 173–174, 178–180, 184–186, 190–194, 196, 198–200, 202–203, 205, 213–214, 223, 228, 233, 247, 259–260, 268–269, 272, 274, 277–280
Locally Reflexive Principle, 108–111, 115, 124–125, 140, 195, 201, 228, 230, 232–233, 252, 274
logophoric, 157, 165, 174, 178, 180, 241–242, 266, 271, 275, 278–279, 282
operator, 278
pronoun, 282
LRP. *See* Locally Reflexive Principle

maxim (conversational), 62–63
I-maxim, 63
M-maxim, 63
of quantity, 63
metonymy, 196, 212. *See also* SELF and BODYPART
middle, 139, 147, 223, 235, 253–254, 267
minimalist program (MP), 4, 10, 43–44, 57, 81–82, 85, 102, 151, 155, 159, 192, 227, 237
minimality, 228, 263
modularity
interpretive module, 228–233
modular competition, 234–237
most dependent scale, 78, 80, 86–89, 96–98, 102, 136, 174, 184–185, 189, 204, 223, 245, 248, 255, 278

movement
A-movement, 11, 77, 146–147, 150, 152, 154–156, 159–160, 164, 173, 191, 258-261
A'-movement, 147, 152–155, 159, 166–170, 173, 241, 264
covert, 7, 10, 34, 147, 157–158, 162–165, 169–170, 173, 177–178, 242, 247, 261
cyclic, 105, 168, 171, 263
domain of, 146–148, 180
head movement, 159–160, 163–166, 173, 258, 261, 263–264, 275
LF-movement, 35, 85, 146–147, 164–167, 170, 177–178, 229, 242, 258-260
overt, 147, 157–159, 163–167, 170, 242, 247, 261
wh-movement, 152, 168, 173, 175, 180
*See also* scrambling, copy theory

noncoreference condition, 5, 9, 12, 21, 25–31, 33–34, 37–39, 43, 45–48, 51–53, 63–65, 73, 91, 242, 244, 248–250. *See also* disjoint reference, Pragmatic Obviation, Principle B, Principle C
number, 19, 70–72, 75–76, 78, 89, 92, 154, 185–186, 206, 212, 218–219, 244, 246, 248–249, 259, 268, 271. *See also* plural
numeration, 10, 43–44, 81–85, 97, 99–102, 130, 135, 137, 141, 151–152, 189, 192–193, 205, 223, 226–228, 231-235, 237, 259, 272, 282. *See also* index

obviative, 31, 42, 59, 213. *See also* Pragmatic Obviation
obviative pair, 45, 48, 50–54, 64, 68, 74, 85, 97, 102, 249
o-command, 258
operators
null operator, 167, 170, 173, 192–194, 260, 264, 266
tense sensitive, 168, 172–173, 177, 180, 204, 267, 275
optimality theory, 4, 57, 86, 227–228, 232, 234–237, 284
OT. *See* optimality theory
OTHER, 200–201, 273–275
OWN, 200–201

parameter, 59, 183–184, 192, 244, 247, 267
partitive, 46–47, 241
passive, 11, 121, 143–144, 147, 170, 223, 266, 271
percolation, 165–263
person
first, 41, 61, 70–72, 78–79, 87–93, 115–117, 126, 131, 191, 219–223, 241, 246–249, 253, 263, 267–268, 270, 279
non-person, 191, 219–220, 246, 248, 270
second, 6, 70–71, 78–79, 87–88, 91, 131, 191, 219, 222, 246–249, 267–268, 270
third, 6, 60, 70–71, 78, 87–88, 106, 131, 198, 219, 221, 246–249, 270, 272
perspective (discourse), 174, 176, 180, 264, 279
plural, 48, 70–72, 76, 89, 92–94, 119–120, 172, 191, 197, 211, 244, 248–250, 260, 270, 282. *See also* number
possessive, 72, 156, 169, 171–172, 190, 197, 199, 202, 207, 244, 265, 268, 280. *See also* Case, genitive
pragmatic accounts of anaphora, 36, 244, 281
Pragmatic Obviation, 50–54, 64, 73–74, 83–85, 89, 97, 102, 117, 184, 230, 242, 247
preposition
anaphora in, 100–101, 270–271
stranding, 162, 262
Principle A, 6–7, 9, 13–15, 18–20, 22, 53, 57, 63–66, 69, 71, 76–77, 86, 92, 96, 109, 111, 146–149, 157, 178–179, 233, 245, 271
Principle B, 6, 9–12, 16–22, 26, 34, 42–43, 48–49, 55–58, 61–65, 69, 71, 73, 80, 85, 89–96, 105, 153, 155–156, 174, 185, 191, 194, 201, 208-209, 211, 214–215, 217, 219–220, 243, 248–250, 257, 267, 269–271, 276–277, 280
Principle C, 10, 12, 17–18, 21–22, 26–27, 29–30, 33, 36–37, 39, 42–43, 45, 51, 53, 55, 57–58, 61, 65, 68–69, 106, 114,133, 144, 184–185, 241–242, 258, 269
pro, 155, 192–194, 213, 219, 257, 260, 272
PRO, 12–14, 37, 59, 80, 101, 132, 192, 194, 243, 247, 251, 260–261, 269, 271–272
projections
extended, 74, 205
promotion to UD-form. *See* UD-form
pronoun (*or* pronominal)
affix, 20, 104, 112, 118, 120, 135, 140, 185, 221, 257, 268, 282–283
anaphoric, 72, 117. *See also* SIG
clitic, 87–88, 188–193, 269, 273
definition of, 6–9
E-type, 240
features of, 18–19, 69, 185–190, 194, 198, 208, 211, 246–247, 259
null pronoun, 154, 186, 191, 193, 232, 259–260, 280. *See also* PRO and pro
resumptive, 150, 154, 192, 250
tonic, 87–88, 190–191, 193, 208–211, 231–232, 248, 262, 270
structure of, 191, 194, 204, 270
*See also* Weak Pronoun Competition, Principle B

proper names, 26, 29, 47, 50, 53, 186–187, 206, 246
proxy, 7, 74, 112–114, 116–118, 120, 126, 129–136, 142–145, 169, 198, 211, 252, 255–256, 274
pseudoagreement, 70–72. *See also* agreement

quantifier
  and c-command, 30, 34–35
  as antecedent, 29
  *See also* scope

+/-R, 17–20, 22, 62, 92, 155, 248, 251, 278
r-expression, 6, 10, 17, 42, 45, 47, 52, 57–58, 61, 65, 68–69, 71, 74, 76, 87–88, 98, 232, 242, 269, 278
raising, 11, 20, 91, 143–145, 147, 149, 154, 163–164, 170, 229, 236, 258, 260, 262, 268
reciprocals
  reciprocal readings, 74, 99, 104, 109, 185, 197–201, 212, 221–223, 226, 252, 262, 267, 270, 273, 275, 283
  reciprocal morphology, 201, 212, 221–225, 194
  *See also* anaphor, OTHER
reconstruction, 145, 169, 239, 262
reflexive
  adverbial, 100, 123, 206–207, 275
  devolitional, 122, 125–126, 255
  emphatic, 65–66, 96, 99–100, 155, 185, 205–207, 210–213, 215–216, 273, 275–276, 279–280
  gestural, 49, 122, 125–126, 140, 254
  inherent, 13, 17, 60, 65, 67–68, 79, 99, 104, 121, 123–124, 127–129, 131–132, 190, 224, 235, 253–254, 276
  intensive, 273, 275–276
  long-distance, 60, 103, 109, 158, 165, 178, 275, 279–280
  near, 138, 256, 278
  reflexive marker, 15–17, 90–92, 105, 109, 112, 116, 120, 123, 127, 132, 135–140, 158, 172, 184, 194, 206, 221, 255, 257, 279
  reflexive predicate, 5–6, 8, 15, 22, 79, 90, 104–105, 109, 111, 121, 128–129, 139–140, 255
  reflexive reading, 15, 38, 66, 71, 79, 87, 91, 99, 109, 111–112, 118, 123, 126–127, 132–139, 152, 198–201, 207, 223, 251, 274, 276
  reflexivity, definition of, 15, 20, 105, 107, 110, 112, 114, 120, 125, 132–133, 139–140, 211, 255, 278
  TUT-reflexive, 121, 126–127, 135, 138, 221, 254
  *See also* anaphor, LRP, SELF, SIG
relative clause, 168, 174, 176, 179, 268
resumption. *See* pronoun, resumptive
Rule H, 229–231, 233, 236, 241, 252, 283
Rule I, 17, 21–22, 50–51, 53

SAME, 96, 199, 201, 206–207, 209
  meaning of, 199
  distribution of, 199, 277
scalar intervention, 79–81, 89
  agreement and, 79
  locality and, 89, 108–109
  morphological gap and, 79
  interpretive distinction and, 130–131
scope, 109, 140, 145, 151, 166, 174, 229, 233, 235, 240, 258, 266, 279
Scope Economy, 229, 235
scrambling, 259–261
SELF
  argument/adjunct distinction, 101–102, 123, 185, 201–211, 276–278
  meaning of, 117, 194, 252, 272
  distribution of, 57–58, 79, 96–100, 107, 127–132, 209, 215, 218, 250, 257, 276
  *See also* anaphor, metonymy, BODYPART
semantic argument, 20, 185. *See also* thematic role
SIG
  definition of , 67–72
  pronominal status, 185–189, 214. *See also* anaphoric pronominal
sloppy identity/readings, 25, 33, 35–36, 41, 52, 84, 115–116, 133–135, 137–138, 152, 241–242, 250–253. *See also* ellipsis
spell-out, 154, 162, 259
stress
  contrastive, 47, 49, 63, 119, 269, 276, 280
subcommand, 263, 279
subjacency, 166, 263
subject
  anti-subject orientation, 6, 13, 73, 79, 84–85, 102, 180, 188, 207, 211–212, 221, 245, 250, 277, 279
  strict subject orientation, 160, 170–173, 178, 215, 264, 266
  SUBJECT, 18, 60, 239, 263
  subject orientation, 7, 67, 79, 85, 157, 161, 167, 170, 177, 180, 215, 245, 279

tense, 157, 164–173, 177, 180, 204, 239–240, 260, 263, 265, 267, 271–272, 275, 279
thematic role
  assignment of, 97, 101, 125, 141, 154, 179, 235. *See also* Form-To-Interpretation Principle
  *See also* theta-role

theta-role, 17, 235, 257–258
topic, 192–193, 231–232, 266, 272, 284
  and pro-drop, 155, 213
  familiarity, 282
  old information, 189, 231
totalist, 227, 234–237

UD-form
  distribution of, 173–178, 183, 203, 210, 215
  promotion to, 178–180
UG (universal grammar), 4, 183, 194, 227, 247
UH. *See* Universalist Hypothesis
unary constraints, 228, 232–233
Universalist Hypothesis, 88–89, 96, 99, 157–159, 182, 184, 189, 194, 202, 204, 221, 275

vehicle change, 51, 116, 133–134, 137–138, 152, 154, 191, 241–242, 259–260, 268, 284
verb raising, 258
verb second, 163, 244

Weak Pronoun Competition, 189–191, 193–194, 211, 231–232, 234, 236, 272, 283–284
WPC. *See* Weak Pronoun Competition